THE FIFTH LIGHT HORSE REGIMENT

HISTORY

OF

THE FIFTH LIGHT HORSE REGIMENT

(AUSTRALIAN IMPERIAL FORCE)

FROM 1914 TO OCTOBER, 1917,

BY

BRIGADIER-GENERAL L. C. WILSON,

C.B., C.M.G., D.S.O., V.D., Croix de Guerre, A.D.C.

(Formerly Commanding Officer of the Regiment)

AND

FROM OCTOBER, 1917, TO JUNE, 1919.

BY

CAPTAIN H. WETHERELL

(an Officer of the Regiment)

The Naval & Military Press Ltd

Published by

The Naval & Military Press Ltd
Unit 10 Ridgewood Industrial Park,
Uckfield, East Sussex,
TN22 5QE England

Tel: +44 (0) 1825 749494
Fax: +44 (0) 1825 765701

www.naval-military-press.com
www.nmarchive.com

In reprinting in facsimile from the original, any imperfections are inevitably reproduced and the quality may fall short of modern type and cartographic standards.

LIEUTENANT-COLONEL DONALD C. CAMERON, C.M.G., D.S.O., V.D., Order of Nile.

Commanding Officer of Regiment from October, 1917, to Demobolization, 1919.

CONTENTS

	Page.
Introduction	7
Foreword by Field-Marshall Viscount Allenby, G.C.B., G.C.M.G., late Commanding the Egyptian Expeditionary Force	8
Foreword by General Sir H. Chauvel, K.C.B., K.C.M.G.	9
Chapter 1.—Formation	11
Chapter 2.—Voyage and First Stay in Egypt	14
Chapter 3.—Gallipoli, May and June, 1915	15
Chapter 4.—28th June Demonstration	19
Chapter 5.—July, 1915, Service Routine	21
Chapter 6.—Death of Colonel Harris	25
Chapter 7.—August Operations	27
Chapter 8.—Raid on Balkan Gun Pits	28
Chapter 9.—Lone Pine Reliefs	30
Chapter 10.—Sniping and Broomstick Bombs	32
Chapter 11.—Beach Raid	36
Chapter 12.—Wilson's Lookout	37
Chapter 13.—Ryrie's Post	42
Chapter 14.—Preparation for the Evacuation	44
Chapter 15.—The Evacuation	48
Chapter 16.—Conditions on Gallipoli	54
Chapter 17.—Egypt and Canal (December, 1915, to April, 1916)	58
Chapter 18.—Dueidar (April to July, 1916)	61
Chapter 19.—Romani Operations (July and August, 1916)	73
Chapter 20.—Mazar (September, 1916)	84
Chapter 21.—Dueidar (October and November, 1916)	86
Chapter 22.—Hassanyia and Masasid (November, 1916, to February, 1917)	87
Chapter 23.—Rafa (February and March, 1917)	92
Chapter 24.—Gaza (First), March, 1917	95
Chapter 25.—Gaza (Second), April, 1917	101
Chapter 26.—Wadi Ghuzze (April to July, 1917)	102
Chapter 27.—Wadi Ghuzze (July and August), Minor Enterprises	107
Chapter 28.—Asluj-Abda (October, 1917)	119
Chapter 29.—General Conditions: Sinai and Southern Palestine	121

PART II.

	Page.
Chapter 30.—Beersheba to Jerusalem (October to December, 1917)	127
Chapter 31.—Amman Raid (February, 1918)	132
Chapter 32.—Es Salt (April-May)	135
Chapter 33.—Jordan Valley (May-August)	137
Chapter 34.—Final Advance (September)	142
Chapter 35.—Ziza (September)	145
Chapter 36.—Wadi Hanein, Semakh and Rafa (October, 1918, to March, 1919)	149
Chapter 37.—Egyptian Rebellion (March to June, 1919)	150

APPENDICES.

	Page.
A.—Summary of Casualties of L.H. Regiments	152
B.—Roll of Officers	153
C.—Decorations Awarded	155
D.—Ration Scale (Gallipoli)	156
E.—Rations and Forage (Sinai and Palestine)	157
F.—Medical Organisation	158
G.—Appreciation	161
H.—List of Members of Regiment	162
I.—Maps	233

INTRODUCTION
BY
BRIGADIER-GENERAL L. C. WILSON,
C.B., C.M.G., D.S.O., V.D., Croix de Guerre, A.D.C.

Part I. of this narrative, which covers the period from the incorporation of the Regiment in September, 1914, until 27th October, 1917, has been written by me, who was with the Regiment continuously during that period, at first as Second-in-Command and subsequently as Commanding Officer. On that last mentioned day I handed over command of the Regiment to Lieutenant-Colonel D. C. Cameron, C.M.G., D.S.O., V.D., Order of Nile. My first draft was written in 1920.

Part II. has been written by Captain Wetherell, an officer of the Regiment.

This Narrative contains a record of what the Regiment did, and is an elaboration of the Regimental War Diary, less those details which would not be of interest to the general members of the Unit. Full advantage has been taken of the writer's private correspondence, written at the Front, and which has been available for reference purposes.

This publication has been printed at the expense of and is presented to the members of the Fifth Regiment by Lieutenant-Colonel D. C. Cameron as a souvenir of our participation in the Great War, and it is hoped that it will be the means of recalling to the minds of our comrades proud memories of the great events which occurred in those stirring times when on Gallipoli we had the honour to form part of the original Anzac Corps, when in Sinai we formed part of the Anzac Mounted Division, when finally we formed a unit—second to none—of the Desert Mounted Corps, the most efficient and most effective and, since the time of Darius the Great King, the largest mounted striking force that the world has seen.

L. C. WILSON,
Brigadier-General.

Brisbane, 30th September, 1925.

FOREWORD by Field-Marshal Viscount ALLENBY, G.C.B., G.C.M.G., late Commanding the Egyptian Expeditionary Force.

It is good that such notable achievement is not allowed to remain in the "whirlpool" of the Great War. I had the honour, & it has been my privilege in right hard and esteem, to have had the good fortune to see its work, at close quarter, when under & efficient leading of brilliant General Chaytor, ed by such a circle of devoted labour as I command, still this brilliant record of what a grand Regiment achieved in Palestine.

Allenby F.M.

New Zealand.
10. ii. 26.

LIEUTENANT-COLONEL HUBERT HARRIS, V.D.,
Commanding Officer of Regiment, 1914 to 31st July, 1915.
Killed in Action.

FOREWORD

BY

LIEUT..GEN. SIR HARRY CHAUVEL, G.C.M.G., K.C.B., late Commanding the Desert Mounted Corps.

In writing a few words of introduction to the History of the 5th Light Horse Regiment in the Great War of 1914-18, I am more or less introducing my own people, as this Regiment was raised from representatives of my original Regiment, the Upper Clarence Light Horse (later the Northern Rivers Lancers), and from the Queensland Mounted Infantry, a Regiment in which I served for many years.

The 5th Light Horse came under my command on Gallipoli in May, 1915, immediately after its arrival on the Peninsula, when it was attached to my section of the Anzac Defences as reinforcements during a Turkish Attack on the trenches held by the 1st Light Horse Brigade and the 4th Australian Infantry Brigade. It was then commanded by Lieutenant-Colonel Hubert Harris, an old friend and comrade of many years in the Queensland Mounted Infantry, who lost his life shortly afterwards. Again, in Novmeber, 1915, as a component part of the 2nd Light Horse Brigade, which was attached to the 1st Australian Division, the Regiment came under my command, and, with the exception of a short break during the re-organisation of the Australian and New Zealand Forces in Egypt after the evacuation of Gallipoli, continued to serve with me until the conclusion of the War.

Its service on Gallipoli is recorded on the maps of Anzac in "Harris' Ridge," "Wilson's Lookout," and "Chatham's Post."

Under the able leadership of Lieutenant-Colonel (now Brigadier-General) L. C. Wilson, the Regiment joined the Australian and New Zealand Mounted Division (commonly known as the Anzac Mounted Division) at Serapeum on the 16th March, 1916. It was the first Australian Regiment to cross the Suez Canal in the great advance which ended in the out-skirts of Asia Minor, and it took a prominent part in the triumphs and shared the hardships of the Anzac Mounted Division from the Battle of Romani, in August, 1916, to the dramatic collapse, at Ziza, in September, 1918, of the Turkish Forces which had been operating against the Arabs south of the Dead Sea, when, under the command of Lieutenant-Colonel Donald Cameron (who succeeded General Wilson on the 30th October, 1917) and led the Regiment with conspicuous success from the Battle of Beersheba onwards), it had the unique experience of joining hands with our late enemies in protecting the latter from our allies.

Commanded as it was, in succession, by three old comrades of the South African War, officered also largely by men with experience in South Africa, and composed of men from districts I know so well, I expected much of the 5th Light Horse, and I am very proud of its achievements. I wish its members every success in the future.

> HARRY CHAUVEL,
> Lieutenant-General,
> Late Commanding the Desert Mounted Corps.

Army Headquarters,
    Melbourne,
        February 24th, 1926.

HISTORY OF
THE FIFTH LIGHT HORSE REGIMENT
1914 TO 1919

PART I.

FROM SEPTEMBER, 1914, TO OCTOBER, 1917

CHAPTER I.

FORMATION OF REGIMENT.

After the departure of the First Light Horse Brigade, A.I.F., in September, 1914, it was decided to send another Light Horse Brigade overseas. The First Contingent included the First, Second, Third and Fourth Light Horse Regiments. The Second Brigade was to consist of the Fifth, Sixth and Seventh Regiments. The Seventh Regiment was to be a composite one—Headquarters, Machine Gun Section, and one Squadron from Queensland, the second from South Australia and the third from Western Australia.

When the Second Light Horse Regiment had left for overseas a camp was formed at the Exhibition Buildings, Brisbane. Lieutenant-Colonel Miell, of South Australia, was appointed to command the composite Regiment. He arrived in Brisbane and took over. After a few days at the Exhibition, the camp was shifted to Enoggera. Shortly afterwards it was decided by the authorities to despatch a third Brigade, and arrangements with regard to the Second Brigade were altered. The Second Light Horse Brigade, under the command of Brigadier-General Ryrie, was still to consist of the 5th, 6th and 7th Regiments, but the 5th Regiment was to be wholly formed in Queensland and the 6th and 7th Regiments in New South Wales. The 8th, 9th and 10th Regiments, forming the 3rd Light Horse Brigade, were formed in Victoria, South Australia and Western Australia respectively. Lieutenant-Colonel Miell accordingly gave over command of the original 7th and went to South Australia, where he took over command of the

9th Regiment. Lieutenant-Colonel Hubert Harris was appointed to command the 5th Light Horse Regiment, Major L. C. Wilson being second in command. Lieutenant-Colonel Harris took over on the 28th October, 1914.

Active recruiting was carried on and more than the necessary number of men volunteered. A selection was made after the men were tested in riding and shooting, equipment and horses were issued, musketry and training were carried on. While in camp at Enoggera the Regiment was presented with its first flag by the Governor-General, Sir Ronald Munro Ferguson, the flag having been made by four ladies interested in the Regiment, Mrs. L. C. Wilson, Mrs. Espie Dods, Miss Jean Darvall and Miss Forrest, the design being a brown kangaroo on maroon bunting.

On the 12th December, 1914, the Regiment, including the Machine Gun Section, entrained to the strength of 550 at Newmarket, for Liverpool, New South Wales, where it was intended that the 2nd Light Horse Brigade should concentrate and undergo further training. The fact that the Regiment was about to leave was not made public. The Regiment accordingly left Brisbane without any public demonstration or send-off.

The Regiment duly arrived at Liverpool on the 14th December, all horses having been dipped at Wallangarra en route. The other two Regiments of the Brigade, the 6th and 7th, were encamped at Holdsworthy, near Liverpool. On the 19th December the Regiment left Liverpool for Sydney by road, stopping at Flemington on the night of the 19th-20th.

On the morning of the 20th the Regiment embarked on the s.s. "Persic," Transport No. A 34. In the afternoon of that day, the transport moved into the harbour, and on the morning of the 21st December, 1914, left Port Jackson.

The names of the first Officers of the Regiment were as follows:

Head-Quarters.

*Commanding: Harris, Lieut.-Colonel H. J. I., V.D.
*Second in Command: Wilson, Major L. C.
Adjutant: Ridley, Captain J. C. T. E. C. (A. & I. Staff).

HISTORY OF THE 5th LIGHT HORSE REGIMENT. 13

Quartermaster: Brundrit, Hon. Lieutenant T. J.
*Medical Officer: Dods, Captain J. Espie.
Veterinary Officer: James, Captain, E. S.
Machine Gun Officer: Pike, Lieutenant E. R. B.

"A" Squadron.

*Midgley, Major S., D.S.O.
Donovan, Captain G. P.
Nimmo, Lieutenant R. H.
Fargher, 2nd Lieutenant T. B.
*Bolingbroke, 2nd Lieutenant A. G.
McLaughlin, 2nd Lieutenant H. F.

"B" Squadron.

*Johnston, Major H. H.
Robinson, Captain P. D.
*Wright, Lieutenant W. L. F.
Ryan, Lieutenant A. M.
McNeill, 2nd Lieutenant J. G. D.
Irving, 2nd Lieutenant H. K.

"C" Squadron.

*Righetti, Major E. E.
*Cameron, Captain D. C.
Kennedy, Lieutenant M. S
Chatham, Lieutenant W.
*Hanly, Lieutenant J. M.
*Lyons, 2nd Lieutenant W. M.

* Of these, eleven had served in the Boer War (1899-1902). Names marked with *.

CHAPTER 2.

VOYAGE AND FIRST STAY IN EGYPT.

The transport arrived at Albany on the 28th December. At this port the fleet, consisting of some sixteen steamers, assembled. The convoy left Albany on the 31st December, arrived at Aden on the 20th January, 1915, left that port on the 21st, and, passing through the Suez Canal, arrived at Alexandria on the 1st February.

The voyage lasted 42 days. One man died during the voyage and was buried at sea. Seven horses died from sickness. During the voyage intensive training was carried out. A certain part of the regiment was detailed to look after the horses, and the remainder underwent systematic instruction. Special attention was given to the training of non-commissioned officers. During the voyage the various examinations for N.C.O.'s were held, and shortly before the termination of the voyage those men who had shown greatest merit were appointed to non-commissioned rank. Regular courses of lectures were given to and by the officers. Musketry, including practices at landscape targets was given special attention to.

The same day that the regiment arrived at Alexandria, viz., the 1st February, the Regiment entrained for Cairo, where it arrived the same evening. The horses were then led from Cairo Railway Station to Maadi, a distance of 10 miles. It was not considered advisable that the horses should be ridden at once after six weeks on board ship.

At this time the Australian and New Zealand troops in Egypt were organised under General Birdwood as the Australian and New Zealand Army Corps (Anzac), the Second Light Horse Brigade (Ryrie) being Corps Troops.

As soon as the camp settled down, systematic training for mounted operations was commenced. Training from troop formation to brigade formation was carried out. Tactical schemes in the desert and round the foot-hills of Mokattams were practised. Special attention was given to rifle shooting. Route marches to Helouan were made. Swimming the horses across a branch of the Nile at the Barrage was engaged in to gain experience in crossing rivers.

HISTORY OF THE 5th LIGHT HORSE REGIMENT.

CHAPTER 3.

GALLIPOLI (MAY AND JUNE, 1915).

In April, 1915, all the available infantry in Egypt were sent to Gallipoli, where the first troops landed on the 25th April, 1915. Affairs were not, however, going as smoothly in Gallipoli as had been anticipated. Heavy casualties were reported, and large numbers of wounded men were returned to Egypt. It was soon apparent that the forces which had already landed were not sufficient to force the Dardenelles, and the matter of reinforcements came up for serious consideration. The question was mooted as to whether the Light Horse should go dismounted to Gallipoli.

Accordingly a meeting was held of the Commanding Officers of the Brigade, to ascertain the feeling of the units as to whether they should volunteer to go dismounted. At this meeting there were present Lieutenant-Colonels Cox, Arnott and Harris, together with the Brigadier-General, Ryrie. Lieut.-Colonel Harris was a strong advocate for that course, and the Brigadier decided to offer the services of the Brigade dismounted. The offer was accepted, and on the 9th May, 1915, the Machine Gun Section, under Lieutenant Kennedy, marched out for Gallipoli.

On the 15th May the Regiment marched out from Maadi, dismounted, with 23 officers and 431 other ranks, leaving three officers and 224 other ranks with the horses. Major Righetti was left in charge of all the Brigade details and horses. Father Bergin, of the Jesuit Fathers, accompanied us as Padre. He remained with us until October, when he was evacuated. In November his place was taken by Captain Mullins, who stopped with the Regiment until its disbandment in 1919.

The dismounted party left by train from Maadi at 7.40 p.m. for Bab el Louk, from where they marched to Cairo Railway Station, left the latter railway station at 11.30 p.m., arrived at Alexandria at daybreak on the 16th and embarked on the Transport A 25, late "Lutzow," together with the rest of the Brigade and part of the 3rd Light Horse Brigade

The Brigade arrived at Cape Helles on the evening of the 18th May, 1915, where brisk fighting was going on. We here had our first experience of seeing aeroplanes being shelled by the enemy.

On the morning of the 19th May we left Cape Helles and arrived at Anzac Cove at about 6.30 p.m. There was extremely heavy rifle and gun fire going on all that night. It turned out afterwards that a determined attack was being made by the Turks on the Australian lines. We on the ships, however, did not know that, and thought it was the usual performance that was being enacted, and, from the noise made by the guns, shells and rifles, the prospect did not look particularly healthy.

On the morning of the 20th May, 1915, the Regiment embarked on the trawler "Claxton." As the troops approached the shore on the trawler and later on in the boats, they were subjected to shell fire by the Turkish batteries. Fortunately, there were no casualties, although the shells were so close that they splashed water on the men. This silly practice of landing men in daylight within medium range of the Turkish batteries continued for some time, until one day a lighter had some fifty casualties, when it dawned on the person responsible for disembarkation of troops that they could be landed just as easily at night and without any such risk.

Immediately after the landing, the Regiment moved up Monash Gully to near the old Turkish Headquarters. At nightfall the Regiment received orders to report to Brigadier-General Chauvel, O.C., No. 3 Section of Defence. On moving out the Regiment was shelled, suffering four casualties.

Our march, or rather movement, along the road to General Chauvel's Headquarters was more exciting than dignified. These were the days before the sap that subsequently existed along the edge of this gully was built. The Turks had a post at the head of the gully, and had the road in full view and at short range. At short distances along each side of the road were built sand-bag traverses, and the safest way to negotiate the road was to run from one traverse to the next forward one on the opposite side, and so on along the road, thus regaining cover before the Turkish snipers could fire an aimed shot. One of our squadron leaders brought down on his head a

HISTORY OF THE 5th LIGHT HORSE REGIMENT.

shower of abuse from the local residents through his striking a match on this open road after dusk in order to light a cigarette.

On reporting to Brigadier-General Chauvel we were placed in reserve in the First Light Horse Brigade Lines for the night, and spent a very wakeful one, as another Turkish attack was expected, and our artillery was particularly energetic and the echoes were very marked. Owing to some peculiarity in the atmosphere, the course of the shells could be followed across the sky, as if the shells were red hot. This was the only occasion on which the writer noticed this effect.

The following day, the 21st May, 1915, the Regiment moved into bivouac in this valley. The day was taken up in digging in and digging communication trenches. In these lines were saw for the first time the "Japanese mortar," a very effective weapon, but unfortunately it only had a few rounds of ammunition. Its next appearance to us was at Ryrie's Post, about ten days before the Evacuation. It was again suffering from the said malady, shortness of ammunition, as by the time they had fired their ranging shots all the ammunition was expended. On the 23rd May, 1915, the Brigade was attached to the 1st Australian Infantry Division. On the 24th May an armistice was agreed upon between the Australian and Turkish Forces from 7.30 a.m. to 4.30 p.m., to bury the enormous number of Turkish dead which were lying between the two sets of trenches.

On the 25th May the Regiment viewed the submarining of the British battleship, H.M.S. "Triumph." Most of us saw the torpedo explode and the ship turn over and sink.

On the 26th May, Lieutenant Banff and the 4th Reinforcements arrived.

On the 30th May, Captain D. C. Cameron was wounded by rifle and four other ranks by shell fire.

On the morning of the 31st May the Regiment was attached to No. 1 Section, one Squadron going to each of the 9th, 10th and 11th Battalions. "C" Squadron, temporarily under the command of Major L. C. Wilson, was attached to the 9th Battalion and occupied the extreme right flank at Sapper's Post.

On the evening of the 6th June, 1915, Major Wilson received instructions to detail a party consisting of one officer and twelve other ranks to proceed at 11 p.m. to the "Twin Trenches," some 1,500 yards beyond our front line trenches toward Gaba Tepe, and ascertain if those trenches were occupied as strongly as usual and to rouse the enemy if they got an opportunity. Lieutenant Hanly, who had previously volunteered for this class of work, and twelve other ranks were accordingly detailed for this purpose, and proceeded to the Twin Trenches.

Lieutenant Hanly and party reconnoitred the Twin Trenches. In doing this the patrol mounted the enemy parapet and fired into their trench from that position. While doing this Lieutenant Hanly was shot. Two other men were wounded. Lieutenant Hanly was carried back a few hundred yards, when the sergeant in charge decided that life was extinct. As the patrol was still under heavy rifle fire, the body was left, and the rest of the party returned to our lines. A party was then sent out under Lieutenant Lyons to try and recover Lieutenant Hanly's body, but after a search, during which they were fired on by the Turks, had to return unsuccessful. Another party, under Lieutenant Chatham, also made an attempt the following night to find the body, but they also were unsuccessful. The officers of the Regiment arranged for a tablet to be erected in the Church at Dalby, Queensland, to the memory of this gallant officer.

On June 19th the Regiment took over the right portion of the 9th Infantry trenches in No. 1 Section. A covering party—Lieutenant Chatham and 34 other ranks—proceeded along "A" Ridge, while Major F. J. White and 200 other ranks of the 6th Light Horse Regiment constructed a communication trench 200 yards along from No. 1 Post to the Knoll 200 yards south-west of machine gun position on "A" Ridge, subsequently officially known as "Harris Ridge," in honour of our Regimental Commander. Lieutenant Chatham met a Turkish Patrol at 11.30 p.m., about 20 strong, near Balkan Gun Pits, and reported three Turks killed by rifle fire.

On 22nd June, 1915, the new post, which was subsequently called "Chatham Post," after Lieutenant Chatham, of the Regiment, was placed under command of the Regiment.

HISTORY OF THE 5th LIGHT HORSE REGIMENT.

CHAPTER 4.

28th JUNE DEMONSTRATION.

On the 28th June, information was received by Army Corps Headquarters at Anzac Cove from the Commander-in-Chief that an attack would be made by our troops at Cape Helles on a portion of the Achi Baba position, and he asked our Corps to help in any way they could, so as to ensure that the Turks facing our troops at Helles would not be reinforced by men opposite Anzac Cove. Accordingly, orders were issued for a demonstration at Anzac Cove, to prevent any reinforcements as above. The 5th Light Horse Regiment, two troops of the 7th Light Horse Regiment and two companies of the 9th Battalion, supported by the 11th Battalion of the 3rd Infantry Brigade, advanced on the right and attacked the Turkish trenches towards Gaba Tepe and towards the lower ridges of the Lone Pine position. The consequences of this advance were that the Turkish reinforcements at Eski Koui, between Anzac and Achi Baba, who in all probability would have gone to oppose our forces further south at Helles, were turned back and advanced to meet our attack. The 5th Regiment moved along Harris Ridge as far as the Balkan Gun Pits, where they were subjected to heavy machine gun and rifle fire from the Echelon trenches, and also from Gaba Tepe. They were also subjected to shell fire from one of our destroyers, the commander of which had not been informed that our men were operating outside our own lines. When the desired effect of holding the Turkish Reserves had been carried out, orders were given for withdrawal to our trenches. This operation was successfully carried out. The Regiment's casualties during the afternoon were heavy, amounting to 23 killed and 79 wounded.

The following is an extract from Army Corps Order of 29th June:

> "Our Light Horse and Infantry succeeded most excellently in doing what was intended, and were ably supported by all batteries of the Australian, New Zealand and Indian Artillery, and by the newly arrived Howitzer Battery of the Lowland Division. Between them the guns fired 1,400 rounds into the advancing Turks and into their reserves. On several occasions they caught

small bodies of Turks advancing in the open, killing and wounding many of them. The Turks were also seen to mass in large numbers in the deep valley behind Lonesome Pine and Johnston's Jolly. Our Howitzer Batteries got well into them there, and though it is impossible to say what the casualties were, we may take it that we probably inflicted very heavy losses upon them.

"The Army Corps Commander much regrets the casualties that took place in the 5th and 7th Regiments of Light Horse and the 9th and 11th Battalions, which were unavoidable, and which must always be expected when we undertake such operations. He is quite sure that the Commander-in-Chief will be more than satisfied with the way in which the Army Corps carried out his wishes, and General Birdwood wishes to convey his grateful thanks to the troops for their excellent work."

The following is an extract from Army Corps Routine Orders dated 2nd July, 1915:

"158 Complimentary.—The Army Corps Commander has much pleasure in publishing the names in the attached supplement of officers, N.C.O.'s and men which have been brought to his notice for good services performed during the operations on our Right Flank on June 28th, 1915. He wishes to thank them for the good services they rendered and to congratulate all ranks on the successful carrying out of the task allotted to them by the G.O.C.-in-Chief, which prevented the enemy reinforming the Krithia position from troops opposite our front:

"5th Light Horse Regiment:

"Major Midgley, S., D.S.O.—Led his Squadron throughout the action under heavy shell and rifle fire.

"582, Sergt. Waite, F. M.—Attended to and carried out a number of wounded from within fifty yards of the enemy's trenches under heavy fire.

"138, Pte. Silverlock, A. E. (M.O.'s Orderly).—Behaved gallantly throughout the day, tending wounded and bearing them back from the firing line.

"690, Pte. Urquhart, W. T. D.—Carried messages in firing line under heavy shell and rifle fire, also attended wounded men."

HISTORY OF THE 5th LIGHT HORSE REGIMENT.

CHAPTER 5.

JULY, 1915, SERVICE ROUTINE.

On the 29th June, 1915, the Regiment took over the line from the Beach to Machine Gun Corner on Harris Ridge, including Chatham's Post. This line, which formed the original front line on the right flank of Anzac, formed the base of the Regiment's position up to the end of November, when we shifted into Ryrie's Post. As previously stated, we moved along the Ridge to Chatham's Post on the 19th June. There was never any question of being satisfied with one's present position, it was a fixed principle to be always sapping or tunnelling to the front, with a view of occupying fresh ground, to give us more freedom in rear of our firing line and to wear down the enemy's morale. No one was allowed to be idle; all were worked to the limit of their endurance, and, when the numbers became reduced, some beyond it. Our only means of communication with Chatham's Post for some little time after its first occupation, was by means of the sap running some 30 yards parallel to the Beach to Wright's Gully and from that gully up to the Post. Accordingly, an alternate means was soon provided along the Ridge from the Machine Gun Post, the first part by tunnel and the second part by a deep sap. Later on a tunnel was made from near Regimental Headquarters to open into Wright's Gully. Rifle pits (the Gully Pits) were then made near the mouth of Wright's Gully on the edge of Blamey's Meadow, and a further batch called the "Centre Pits" half-way up the slope. These last mentioned pits were not sited by us, and were subsequently abandoned, as they had no field of fire. A continuous line of trench was then dug from Chatham's down to the edge of Blamey's Meadow, and thus became our front firing line towards Gaba Tepe. Another Beach Post, just forward of Wright's Gully, was erected, and a listening post formed further along the beach, where the wire between the forward trench and the Beach ended. As the firing line was now forward, it became necessary for the Garrison to move forward too, so as to be close to their fighting posts. A network of saps and communication trenches was brought into existence between Wright's Gully and the front line, and the men's dug-outs were built off them, "A" Squadron's around

Chatham's, "B" Squadron's near the mouth of Wright's Gully and "C" Squadron's in rear of Chatham's.

Chatham's Post was improved and strengthened by forming a second tier of firing and bombing trench on the top of the Post, with access thereto only from the rear. A good supply of bombs was always kept on the top tier, so that if the front and lower trenches had been rushed, the occupants would have found themselves in an unpleasant position. On the occupation of Wilson's Lookout very onerous works were taken in hand, but full particulars of these are described later in this narrative.

Normal life on the Peninsula embraced night post duty, night patrols, day observation, sniping, digging, wiring, ration and water carrying. Night patrolling is dealt with later, sniping in Chapter 10. Digging has been referred to above. If digging could be done with safety by day it was then done, but most of it had to be done by night, as the work was usually under enemy observation. Night post duty consisted of watching tactical points on the trench system, to stop a rush, give the alarm and observe and listen for enemy movement. The country right up to our trenches was covered by scrub, and but for our patrols an energetic and quickly moving enemy could mass within a few yards of our trenches. The enemy certainly had the capacity for moving quietly on the stony ridges in front of our position. A post usually consisted of an N.C.O. and three men, with an officer, assisted by a sergeant, in charge of a group of posts. The three men took it in turns to do sentry duty, two hours on and four off, while the N.C.O. was supposed to post every sentry and generally supervise his post. In some instances, double posts were constituted—two N.C.O.'s and six men—which made it easier and more comfortable for all, but unfortunately it was seldom that so many could be spared. In theory, a man should get at least two nights' sleep to one on night duty, but, owing to the shortage of men, it was often a night off to one on, and in the days of Wilson's Lookout it often worked out at two or three nights on duty to one resting. Night posts were posted just after dusk, so that the extra movement could not be observed by the enemy, and they remained on duty until "stand down" was given after daylight. The whole Regiment was roused every morning an hour before dawn and

HISTORY OF THE 5th LIGHT HORSE REGIMENT.   23

"stood to," fully equipped, in their fighting positions until "stand down." All ranks were ordered to sleep in their boots and clothes during the whole time we were on Gallipoli, and the order was rigorously enforced. Men could take their boots off in the daytime when things were seen to be quiet and so ease their feet. It must be remembered that from the end of May, when we first went into the trenches, until the morning of the 20th December, the last day of Evacuation, the Regiment was never for a day out of the front firing line, and that line was, in parts, only a matter of seconds from the enemy trenches. At Wilson's Lookout, at one time, the distance was 22 yards. In the event of an enemy raid, there would have been no time to put on boots or clothes.

In daylight there was no necessity to keep sentry posts on duty, so some two posts only for observations were detailed. Special members were selected for this purpose, and kept on the duty continuously, so as to become thoroughly acquainted with the country in front. They were supplied with telescopes and glasses, and it was their particular duty to watch for enemy movement, even though beyond artillery range, and all visible alteration in the enemy works. This information was sent daily to Brigade and on to higher formations, with the result that valuable deductions as to the enemy's movements and intentions were made by those whose duty it was to digest all these reports. Wiring was, of course, done at night. It was a particularly unpleasant occupation, owing to the proximity of the enemy trenches and the numerous rockets and flares sent up by them. When the work was impossible in the open, wooden frames with a mass of barbed wire wound round them, were made in the trenches and pushed up in front of the trench with poles. Later, when things were quiet, a man would crawl out and lash these frames into one long line. The transport of rations and water entailed a large amount of work. We were about a mile from the landing stages. The rations were usually brought from the Beach to Brigade Headquarters by mule pack, and carried by man pack from Brigade to the Regiment, a distance of about a quarter of a mile. Sometimes we had to bring the rations from the Beach. Water was always a serious question. There were no running streams in our jurisdiction. Wells had been dug in the gullies near the Landing Beaches, but the supply was small, and our water fatigues often had to wait hours before their turn came to fill their petrol tins. Two tins of two gallons each formed a load. A gallon a day per man was the normal issue (drinking, cooking and washing), but it was not always available. Later during our sojourn, water was brought by ship to the Peninsula. We made efforts to get water in our own area. Wells were sunk on the beach above high water mark and water—only slightly brackish— was got. The wells, however, only lasted a couple of days each, as the water in them very soon became too salt to drink, and the labour expended was not justified by the results. In our ranks we had alleged water diviners. One picked a site at the head of Wright's Gully. The enthusiasts dug down sixty feet, but without finding any water. Later on we lent one of our men to the British at Suvla Bay for water divining duty, and we understood that he was very successful in that locality. About this time the use of hydraulic sluicing as an offensive weapon was raised by Sergeant D. Fraser, of C Squadron, 5th Regiment. Several of the Turkish trenches were within a few yards of our front line. Fraser pointed out that if a powerful hydraulic sluicing plant was available, the parapet and head cover on these trenches could be washed away in the course of a few seconds. Salt water could be pumped up from the sea and brought by pipes to our frontline trenches and then thrown on to the enemy lines in the same way that mining by hydraulic sluicing is carried out in some parts of Australia and in British Columbia. It was pointed out that later on saps could be worked towards the other Turkish trenches to within sluicing range, when the nozzles of the hoses could be directed under cover. Sergeant Fraser first mentioned this to Major Wilson, to whom the scheme seemed an excellent one. Major Wilson passed the scheme on, and it went through the regular channels to the Corps Commander. The Corps made further investigations in the matter and arranged to send an officer to England to see about the necessary plant. Final arrangements, however, had not been made by the time of the Evacuation, so the scheme was not actually put into force.

On the 13th July, 1915, Lieutenant Mahoney and 62 reinforcements reported.

During the month of July, active patrolling took place

along Harris Ridge and along the beach towards Gaba Tepe and into Poppy Valley. These patrols were usually composed of an officer and about twenty other ranks. They would get out into the scrub on the ridge and wait for the Turkish patrols. It was impossible for our men to move about these stony, scrubby ridges without making a lot of noise, and the only satisfactory way was to get out early and wait for the enemy patrols.

On several occasions their patrols came into contact with ours. The Turkish patrols usually got the worst of it. Lieutenants Chatham and Bolingbroke and Sergeant Waite did very fine work on these patrols. On some occasions our people met enemy patrols of overwhelming numbers, and consequently had to retire. A certain number of casualties were suffered by our patrols on occasions such as these. This happened on the night of the 21st July when Lieutenant Bolingbroke and thirty men went out from Beach Post to patrol Harris Ridge. They found Harris Ridge, to within 100 yards of Chatham Post, strongly held by the enemy who opened heavy rifle and machine gun fire on our patrol. Owing to the darkness, their shooting was unaimed and our patrol got back with the loss of only one killed. Shortly after this, the same night, about 200 of the enemy attacked the Beach Post but were driven back.

CHAPTER 6.

DEATH OF LIEUTENANT-COLONEL HARRIS.

On the night of the 31st July, 1915, the 3rd Infantry Brigade made an attack on the Turkish trenches in front of Tasmania Post. The operations were to start shortly before moon rise. The 2nd Light Horse Brigade (Ryrie) were to man their trenches and open fire by way of demonstration to attract the attention of the enemy. Our C.O., Lieutenant-Colonel Harris, took up a position in the machine gun observation post. At 8 p.m. the 3rd Infantry Brigade attacked. This provoked heavy shell fire from the Turks. One shell exploded about our machine gun observation post. A bullet entered the loop-hole and struck Lieutenant-Colonel Harris on the neck. He died within two minutes. One man was wounded on the same evening on the beach post and another as he returned from ration fatigue. On the 1st August Colonel Harris was buried on Shell Green at 9.15 p.m., the ceremony being conducted by the Dean of Sydney and the Reverend Robertson. The officers of the Regiment arranged for the erection of a tablet in the Brisbane Grammar School to the memory of our late commanding officer. To Colonel Harris is due the credit of setting that standard of discipline and efficiency which marked the Regiment throughout its whole career.

The following is an extract from Brigade Routine Order, No. 163:—

"The Brigadier-General Commanding 2nd L.H. Brigade wishes to express his great regret at the death of Lieutenant-Colonel H. Harris, 5th L. H. Regiment, who was killed in action on the night of 31st July, 1915, and to convey his sympathy to the 5th Regiment, who have suffered such an irreparable loss. By the death of Lieut.-Colonel Harris the Brigade loses one of its best soldiers."

The following message was received from G.O.C., Anzac:

"To General Ryrie, Commanding 2nd L.H. Brigade.

"Please express to 2nd L.H. Brigade and especially to 5th L.H. Regiment, my deep regret at the death of Lieut.-Colonel Harris, which is such a loss to the whole force."

CHAPTER 7.

AUGUST OPERATIONS.

Major L. C. Wilson now took over command of the Regiment, and was promoted to the rank of Lieutenant-Colonel.

On 6th August our Third Reinforcements, under Lieutenant Newton, and details under Lieutenant Ryan, reported at Anzac for duty.

Arrangements were now taken in hand for the big offensive which the High Command decided to take with the object of breaking through to the Dardanelles and finishing the campaign on Gallipoli.

The Corps Commander, General Birdwood, called a meeting at Brown's Dip of all senior staff officers and officers of units down to regimental and battalion commanders, and explained the general scheme of operations. The primary operations consisted of a landing at Suvla Bay and an attack on the Turkish lines opposite the left flank on the Anzac position.

At the same time, a separate offensive was to be instituted along the whole of the Anzac position. German officers, trench and Lone Pine positions were to be attacked and held, and the 2nd Light Horse Brigade (Ryrie) was ordered to attack and destroy the enemy works on Green Knoll (Bird Trenches) and Balkan Gun Pits on Harris Ridge. The 5th Light Horse Regiment was entrusted with this duty, the remainder of the Brigade supplying covering fire on Pine Ridge and Turkish Despair Works. The operations were to start at 5.30 p.m. on the evening of the 6th August by the attack on Lone Pine. All ranks were supplied with white armlets and white badges to be sewn on the tunics between the shoulders. This was necessary to enable our people to distinguish one another in the dark. All bayonets were covered with sacking to prevent them glistening. The attack of the 5th Regiment was to commence at 8.30 p.m. It was not intended that the position seized by us should be retained, our operations being more in the nature of a raid.

All preparations were accordingly made, and at 8 p.m. the attacking troops filed out through our wire in front of our trenches. A few minutes before the order was given to attack, orders came from Brigade that the operations so far as our Regiment were concerned were cancelled. The troops withdrew to their lines.

CHAPTER 8.

RAID ON BALKAN GUN PITS.

Towards the end of August the Brigadier (Ryrie) asked the Regiment to undertake offensive operations against the enemy on our front, and accordingly a scheme was put to the Brigade for the Regiment to attack the Balkan Gun Pit Trenches and Bird Trenches, being practically the operations which we had prepared for on the night of the 6th August. The scheme was approved, and was carried out in the early morning of the 23rd August, 1915.

Those who were present at the Peninsula will remember that Harris Ridge, on which Chatham's Post was situated, ran towards Twin Trenches parallel to the seashore, and about 400 yards therefrom. The sea side of this ridge was covered with very thick, low scrub. The Bird Trenches were situated about three or four hundred yards along Harris Ridge from Chatham's Post. At 3.55 a.m. "A" Squadron (Major Midgley, D.S.O.) filed out through the wire at Chatham's Post and "B" Squadron (Major Wright) through the Beach Post. "B" Squadron moved along the beach about 400 yards to a position opposite Bird Trenches. "C" Squadron remained in Chatham's Post in support. One machine gun was removed temporarily to Ryrie's Post, and one remained on the rear line.

Arrangements had been made for co-operation with the torpedo-boat destroyer on picket duty. At 3.55 a.m. the destroyer was signalled that "A" Squadron was moving out. The destroyer immediately opened fire upon the Bird Trenches and continued firing rapidly for three minutes, then switched on to the Balkan Gun Pits, 500 yards down the ridge. In the meantime, "A" Squadron was advancing, all fire reserved. When within 100 yards of the Bird Trenches "A" Squadron was fired upon. They still reserved their fire. When still closer bombs were thrown at them, which passed over their heads without doing any damage. "A" Squadron then rushed the trenches, first throwing their bombs into them. Some of the Turks were killed, the others retired to the trenches on the east slope of the Ridge. These trenches were then bombed and fired into by our men with their rifles. The Turks kept low down in their trenches and fired in the air.

While this was going on, "B" Squadron, from the beach, opened fire on the Balkan Gun Pits and the trenches in that neighbourhood. Heavy reinforcements were now coming forward to the Balkan Gun Pits. "A" Squadron then retired to Chatham's Post by the seaward side of the ridge. As soon as "A" Squadron retired from the neighbourhood of the Bird Trenches, "B" Squadron fired on that place, and "C" Squadron opened along the Ridge as soon as "A" Squadron had retired from it, and covered the retirement of "A" and "B" Squadrons. As soon as "A" Squadron left the enemy trenches the machine guns opened along the ridge, and kept up a covering fire until both "A" and "B" Squadrons had returned to our line.

The operations were carried out in an extremely satisfactory manner, our casualties being three wounded only.

Prior to the operations, arrangements had been made by which the Squadrons could show their movements by the firing of green flares. These arrangements worked as anticipated, and enabled the covering fire to be put on to the ground which had been vacated by the attacking squadron as soon as it had vacated it.

The bombs used on this and other operations until shortly before the evacuation, when a few Mills bombs were issued, were of the "jam tin" type. These "jam tin" bombs consisted of a tin about the size of a 1 lb. jam tin, filled with shrapnel bullets with a central explosive charge. The firing apparatus consisted of a short length of fuse sufficient to burn about four or five seconds. The serious disadvantage about this type of bomb in comparison with the later semi-automatic Mills bomb, was that they had to be lighted with a special match or fusee. One result of this was that a lot of bombs were thrown before they had really been lighted, and so became duds. The lighting was also a serious objection when being used in the open or trench rails, as a man had to stop to light the match, and the lighted match gave away his position in the dark. Another objection was that the burning fuse emitted a trail of sparks, and it could be seen exactly from where it had come. In addition to this issue of these "jam tin" bombs, some members of the Regiment, particularly Major Midgley, became proficient in improvising similar bombs. Any old tin did for a container, while the explosive was got from the dud broom-stick bombs that were fired into our lines by the enemy, and the projectile in the bomb consisted of any bits of metal available. The fuse was obtained from the Engineers, and a very effective bomb was the result.

We also had a small issue of cricket ball bombs, which consisted of a round iron ball with an explosive charge inside. These were also lighted with an outside fuse, and in that respect were objectionable.

CHAPTER 9.

LONE PINE RELIEFS.

The Regiment was now called upon to supply reliefs for part of the Lone Pine position, which had been captured by our infantry on the evening of the 6th August. The whole of the Lone Pine positions had not been captured, and the situation was that our people held the western part of the position and the Turks held the eastern, there still being communication trenches between the two parts. The holding of Lone Pine had been a more expensive operation than the taking of it. On the 25th August we sent our first party of 130 men for duty for 48 hours. When we got there we found the position very unsatisfactory. The trenches themselves were most disagreeable; there were hundreds of dead bodies in the side saps and in the position, all, of course, in an advanced state of decomposition. A large number of these bodies were only partially buried. The sides of the trenches were oozing, and the whole of the trenches were covered with maggots which crawled over the men as they lay down to rest. The enemy were occupying their trenches within 20 to 30 yards from ours. If any movement were made, or a person spoke in ordinary tone, it immediately attracted bombs. It is satisfactory to state that this condition of affairs was soon changed. We at once brought a number of periscope rifles into use, and obtained a large supply of bombs, and started an offensive against the Turks, and in a very short time obtained superiority and kept down their periscopes and suppressed their observation.

Part of the work of the troops on duty in these trenches was to smother the live bombs thrown in by the Turks before they could explode, often a matter of a fraction of a second. The men detailed for this job were given blankets, which they folded into eight or more thicknesses. As soon as a bomb dropped in the trench, it was the duty of the blanket man to jump at it and cover it with the blanket. Owing to the looseness of the blanket, and yet to the thickness of the folds, the flying pieces of bomb were smothered and did no harm. This was the sort of work which once earned Victoria Crosses, but with us was treated as an ordinary part of the day's work, and obtained no special recognition.

On the 29th August "B" Squadron, of the 11th Light Horse Regiment, under Major C. Lee, reported to this Regiment for duty, and was taken on as "D" Squadron. The reason for this was that the 4th Light Horse Brigade, when it came to Gallipoli, was not retained as a Brigade, nor were the Regiments kept together. The various Squadrons were sent round to the other Light Horse Regiments as reinforcements. While these reinforcements were moving into their new lines, the unusual movement attracted the attention of the Turkish gunners, with the result that some twenty shells were dropped in our area. One of these wounded our gallant Medical Officer, Captain Espie Dods, while he was in the open attending to a wounded man. The M.O. was evacuated, but returned in time for the operations in November (Wilson's Lookout). During his absence his work was carried on first by Captain Pilcer, then by Captain MacDonnell and then Captain Cooke (themselves evacuated), and finally by Major Croll.

CHAPTER 10.

SNIPING AND "BROOMSTICK" BOMBS.

While this Regiment occupied the extreme right flank and on Harris Ridge, special attention was given to the matter of sniping and breaking in of the enemy's loop-holes. Special men were set off as snipers, and taken off other duties to enable them to give exclusive attention to their special job. As a sample of the work done, that of No. 355, W. E. Sing, can be referred to. Up to the end of September, this man was responsible for 150 casualties to the Turks by sniping. A special firing position was erected for him overlooking the Turkish lines at ranges from 150 to 400 yards. The modus operandi was as follows: Sing noticed a movement such as a glimpse of a face at a loop-hole. An observer then directed his telescope on the place indicated. Sing covered it with his rifle, and the moment the object again appeared the observer gave the word to fire. This Sing did, usually with success. The number of cases above reported was authentic. Sing often fired on other occasions, but where the result was doubtful or unobserved, no claim was made for a casualty. Sing's success was due, to a large extent, to his good eyesight and to his patience. He would remain for long periods with his eye along the sights of his rifle, whereas other men would not have the patience to do so. Sing's operations were far in excess of those of any other member of the Regiment, but many other men had casualties to their credit. General Birdwood, the Corps Commander, on the occasion of one of his numerous visits, commented on the effective sniping of this Regiment, as being far in excess of that of any other unit of the Anzac Corps. Sing was awarded the D.C.M. for his excellent work in this respect.

To prevent enemy sniping, special attention was given to the Turkish loop-holes. These loop-holes on our front were made of green bricks, that is, bricks unburned, but dried in the sun, about 12 in. x 8 in. x 4 in. As soon as these loop-holes were made or repaired within a distance of 400 yards, snipers were put on to them. The heads of the bullets were filed or rubbed off. Such a bullet hitting a brick would smash it to pieces. Five or six shots usually broke up the

BRIGADIER-GENERAL L. C. WILSON,
C.B., C.M.G., D.S.O., V.D., Croix de Guerre, A.D.C.,
Commanding Officer of Regiment 1st August, 1915, to
October 1917, and thereafter Commander of
Third Light Horse Brigade.

four bricks forming the loop-hole, which then collapsed and became useless. This procedure was carried on to such an extent that sometimes there was not a serviceable enemy loop-hole facing Chatham's Post within 400 yards of that place. Special attention was also given to the Turkish periscopes. The moment they appeared they were fired on, and smashed. This smashing of loop-holes and breaking of periscopes resulted in our people being almost free from enemy snipers. It might be mentioned that this sniping could not have been carried out without the aid of the telescopes which we had constantly in use. These were the telescopes that were originally issued to the regimental signallers. Without these telescopes the enemy movement would not in most cases be seen.

The following is a divisional memo. of 11th August, 1915:

> "From captured diaries and other sources of information it is apparent that the enemy has been suffering steady losses from the fire of our snipers. Commanding and other officers will explain to the men the value of thus establishing a fire superiority and encourage continual effort."

In September the Turks were first observed using periscope rifles. We had had them for some time, and found them very effective. During that month we also had our first experience of the so-called "broomstick" bombs. The first few did very little harm, but, towards the end, they became very deadly. They consisted usually of quick-firing gun brass cartridge cases. These cases were filled with dynamite, gelignite or other high explosive, together with iron slugs and pieces of metal of all descriptions. As many as 45 plugs of dynamite have been counted in one dud bomb. At the top of the case there was a percussion cap apparatus, and into the base of the cartridge case a wooden stick, 1½ inches through and about four feet long, was screwed. On the other end of this stick there was a leather washer to fit the barrel of the mortar from which it was fired. These things towards the time of the evacuation had a range of seven or eight hundred yards. The whole of our lines were in easy range of them. Our dug-outs consisted of niches cut in the reverse slopes of the hills. They had no head cover, as there was no wood or galvanized iron available for that purpose. Several feet of earth roofing would have been required to keep these bombs out. Head cover, which was proof against bullets, was no protection against them. Light head cover was smashed in without the least trouble. The only protection against them would have been proper shell-proof dug-outs. It was not possible to make such dug-outs in our lines. Some were attempted, but, owing to the absence of timber for holding up the walls and roofs, they collapsed. The men would not willingly go into them. In any case, the front line trenches had to be open to enable the defenders to resist attacks. These "broomstick" bombs during the next couple of months claimed many casualties from our Regiment, and were undoubtedly the worst things we had to face. Shells you could usually avoid by keeping well under cover, but these things came straight down from the sky, and we had no protection of any sort. As many as 200 a day dropped on the lines held by our Regiment prior to the Evacuation.

In addition to these cartridge case bombs, they sometimes screwed obsolete howitzer shells on to the end of the rods, and also iron cylinders like stove piping, 15 inches long and weighing about 20 lb., these last containing a treacle-like fluid. What they were we do not know. They did no harm; probably something that failed to explode.

On the 29th September our first trench mortar was erected at Chatham's. Its first visible effect was to keep down somewhat the enemy sniping. Apparently the Turks were afraid to fire as much as formerly, as by so doing they would attract a bomb from this mortar. About this time there was issued to us for use a contrivance named "Charley's Wallaby Rest," Major Charley, of the 6th Regiment, being the inventor. The apparatus consisted of a steel shield with loop-hole through which a rifle protruded. The butt of the rifle worked over a lateral graduated scale, and also a horizontal one. The idea was in the day time to register an enemy loop-hole and take notice of the lateral and horizontal graduations, then at night one could, with the aid of the register, fire at the same loop-hole, and possibly catch enemy snipers or observers. The principle was good, but there were serious defects in the apparatus itself. Instead of the fixed part of the rifle being

HISTORY OF THE 5th LIGHT HORSE REGIMENT. 35

near the muzzle, it was near the trigger; the result was that a slit about 6 inches x 3 inches had to be left to give the muzzle room to move to the right or left. The enemy's bullets soon found their way through this large hole. Moreover, the steel shield was made of soft metal, and the enemy's bullets perforated it like cheese. It was almost committing suicide to operate one of these machines, so not much benefit was derived from them.

On 2nd October 142 reinforcements, under Lieutenants Atkinson and Brown, reported.

During October we obtained a fishing net from Alexandria, with a view of catching some of the numerous fish that frequented the Aegean Sea. Major Croll, our Medical Officer, and Captain Wright took special interest in this matter. A raft (A.E. 606) was manufactured from some barrels and timber that had been washed up on the beach, from which to drop the net, but owing to the absence of proper oars it was rather cumbersome. Fishing had to be done at night, as daylight operations attracted bullets and shells. Unfortunately, this particular net would not hold the fish that were caught in it; the twine was perished. We sent for another and stronger net, but it had not arrived at the time of the Evacuation. We also arranged for a supply of eggs for the Regiment. Several large consignments came to hand, and were distributed at cost price among the members, but the entry of Bulgaria—from whence they came—into the War put an end to this welcome change of diet.

In October we were offered a couple of weeks change to the Islands. A vote of the Regiment turned the offer down. At the time the question of broomstick bombs had not become acute. A change meant that on our return we would probably have to dig a fresh set of dug-outs and collect a fresh lot of camp equipment. The opinion was almost unanimous that the short change was not worth subsequent inconvenience.

CHAPTER II.

BEACH RAID.

On 9th October, 1915, a successful minor operation took place. On that day a deserter from the Turkish lines was seen creeping along the beach from Gaba Tepe towards our lines. The enemy opened a brisk fire on him, and he finally, in a wounded condition, took cover under a bank on the beach about 600 yards south of our forward line. The enemy kept up a desultory fire on him all the rest of the afternoon. It was decided to bring this deserter in. Arrangements were made with the artillery at our call to put up a barrage, if required, beyond the deserter and on the scrubby part between Harris Ridge and the sea. Our machine gun also registered on this position. Lieutenant Brundrit (who had lately given up the position of Quartermaster and taken over a troop) and a party of 25 men moved out along the beach at dusk. This party moved under cover of the cliff for the first part of the journey, and when the cliff ended had to crawl for about 150 yards to keep from view of Harris Ridge, and the scrub thereon, which came to within 100 yards of the beach. A squadron of the Regiment was also sent out along the beach under cover of the cliffs as a support to Lieutenant Brundrit's party. The remainder of the Regiment occupied the trenches and prepared to give covering fire, if required, as the whole of the country in question was within easy rifle range. Stretcher bearers were taken with Lieutenant Brundrit's party. A "point" of four men, under Sergeant McDonald, reached the wounded man and proceeded twenty yards past him as cover to the patrol. It was now dark. Sergeant McDonald's party then saw advancing towards them, ten yards away, four Turks, followed by a supporting party of 15 or 20, apparently on a similar errand to our own. Our advance party immediately lay down and opened fire on them. Two of the Turks fell. The Turkish supporting party returned the fire. Lieutenant Brundrit brought up more men to the support of his advance party, the deserter was put on a stretcher and the Turks retired, some to the scrub and others along the beach. All our men then returned to our lines with the deserter and without any casualty. As stated above, arrangements had been made for a strong covering fire in case Lieutenant Brundrit and his party were attacked in force from the scrub. They ran great risk, however, as practically the whole of their advance was a flank march within 100 yards of the scrub, on the west slope of Harris Ridge, which could easily have been occupied in force by the enemy. As anticipated, it was a question of who could get there first after the light began to fail. Although Lieutenant Brundrit had over 600 yards to go to the enemy's 100, he, by commendable despatch, got there first by a few seconds and carried out his object. Both General Birdwood, the Corps Commander, and General Walker, the Divisional Commander, sent their congratulations to Lieutenant Brundrit on his exploit.

During the month of October catapults were introduced. These catapults consisted of a triangular frame with a sling which was made of india rubber bands. The sling fired a cricket ball bomb and had a range up to 120 yards. They were extremely effective, and the men became very efficient in their use. One great advantage of them was that they were practically silent in the throwing and therefore did not attract so many bombs in return.

CHAPTER 12.

WILSON'S LOOKOUT.

Towards the end of October it was observed that the Turks were building new works below the Bird Trenches, that is, between Chatham's Post and Bird Trenches, to the left of the Saddle. It was accordingly decided to push forward the forward tunnel in front of Chatham's and open a new firing line which would cover the dead ground. A tunnel to the right of the existing tunnel and on the right of Harris Ridge, to act as an alternative means of communication to this new firing line, was also started.

Further activity on the part of the Turks between Chatham's Post and Bird Trenches was now reported. It was suspected that they were intending to advance their line to high ground about 120 yards in front of Chatham's Post. It was imperative that they should not be allowed to do this, as, if they did, from this new position they could enfilade the rear of Ryrie's Post and Tasmania Post. Such a state of affairs would be most serious.

Accordingly on the afternoon of the 3rd November, 1915, instructions were received from Brigade to form a post 50 yards in advance of our forward tunnel, that is, 120 yards in front of Chatham's, with the object of preventing the enemy from occupying the ground which would enable them to bring direct rifle fire on the troops in rear of Ryrie's Post and Tasmania Post. A covering party, under Lieutenant Brundrit, was accordingly sent out after dark (night of 3rd-4th), followed by a working party, under command of Major Midgley, D.S.O. Possession was taken of the first old Turkish trench abutting on the right arm of the "T" of the forward tunnel and of the second old Turkish trench, which terminated 50 yards in front of the last mentioned trench. Substantial sandbag barricades were erected at the south end of the last mentioned trench, and to the left side, to block fire from Bird Trenches and Holly Spur. A couple of thousand sandbags had been filled during the afternoon, and these were passed along a chain of men to the required position. The two old Turkish trenches were deepened, barbed wire was laid in front of the new trench, the first old Turkish trench was connected with the second and a communication trench was cut back from the second old Turkish trench on the west slope of Harris Ridge to the mouth of the small branch tunnel which, eighteen yards from Chatham's Post, branches from the main tunnel to the right. The enemy did not interfere with our work on that night.

As a matter of fact, the enemy working parties could be heard a few yards away. Both sides had a definite job to complete, i.e., be dug in before daylight, and were quite happy to be left alone while they were doing it. It afterwards turned out that the enemy were digging a sap to the very ground that we had seized, and another 24 hours would have found them intrenched thereon. By dawn we had the ground sufficiently prepared to withstand rifle and gun fire during the day, and by the following evening we were ready to withstand any assault.

On the night of the 4th-5th the enemy made four attacks on the new post with bombs, machine guns and rifles, all of which attacks were repulsed. The expenditure of bombs by our people was very heavy—800. Some of the enemy reached the reverse side of our parapet, where they were killed with bombs, and pieces of Turks were to be picked up in our trenches. Sergeant Orr here did a brave act. One of our men threw a lighted bomb, but it struck the parapet and fell back into a tray of unlighted bombs. Sergeant Orr picked up the tray and threw the lot over the rear parapet. During this night the Turks erected two substantial barricades in front of our position, one at a distance of 22 yards, and the other at a distance of about 70 yards. These were connected by a communication trench with the lower part of Bird Trenches. On the night of 5th-6th we opened up five rifle pits off the left arm of the "T" of the main tunnel. These pits faced the east end of the Bird Trenches. Wire was laid in front of these pits. On the 7th instructions were received to advance the Post to the third old Turkish trench, a distance of 30 yards, which would enable us to enfilade the first Turkish barricade. A covering party, under Captain Brundrit, and working parties were accordingly moved out shortly after 8 p.m. on the 7th-8th. This third old trench was occupied and the enemy bombed out of their first barricade, which was levelled to the ground with slabs of guncotton—Lotbiniere bombs. Traverses and parapets were erected on the new ground. A communication trench back to the second old trench was opened up and wire was laid in front of the new position. This work was done under heavy bomb, rifle and machine gun fire from Turkish Despair Works, Bird Trenches and the second Turkish barricade. While commanding the covering party, Captain Brundrit was killed. This gallant officer, a splendid example to his men of contempt of danger, was emptying his revolver at a range of some fifteen yards into a group of Turkish riflemen, when he was shot through the head. The officers of the Regiment arranged for the erection of a memorial tablet to Captain Brundrit in the Grammar School, Brisbane.

On the 8th November the enemy subjected the new position to heavy artillery fire from a battery which they had planted near Twin Trenches, less than 2,000 yards, and demolished part of the forward parapet. The trenches were, however, being continually deepened, and so obviated the necessity of the original high parapets.

On the afternoon of the 8th November, the garrisoning of the advanced post for 24 hours was taken over by 100 men of the 6th Light Horse (Cox) and a similar number of the 7th Light Horse (Onslow) took over the position on the afternoon of the 9th for a similar period.

Since the 4th November, working parties of the 4th, 6th and 7th Light Horse Regiments were supplied for consolidating the work. On the night of the 5th-6th and for some days afterwards a reserve of 200 infantry from the 3rd Infantry Brigade were available by night in case of a serious attack being made. Their services were not, however, called upon for this purpose, but their presence was of great value in giving confidence to the garrison and working parties. The assistance of the artillery throughout these operations was invaluable, and same was promptly rendered on request. The presence of the destroyer on our right flank was also of great service.

The new ground seized through the above operations was officially designated "Wilson's Lookout," in honour of the C.O. of the Regiment.

The following Order was issued by the Corps Commander on the 8th November:

"The Army Corps Commander wishes to express his appreciation of the action of the 2nd Light Horse Brigade in successfully advancing their position to Wilson's Lookout, on Harris Ridge, between the 3rd to 8th November, 1915. The operation was skilfully planned and carried out with vigour and determination. General Godley congratulates the 5th Light Horse, to whom the operation was entrusted, and to whose resource and gallantry the excellent result achieved is largely due. The enemy casualties in this engagement had been stated by prisoners to have reached a total of 500 killed and wounded. The following officers and N.C.O.'s have been particularly brought to the Army Corps Commander's notice:

"Major Foster, W. J., Brigade Staff.

"Captain Straker, E. O., Brigade Staff.

"Captain Stanley, R. A., 2nd Signal Troop.

"Lieutenant-Colonel Wilson, L. C., 5th Light Horse Regiment.

"Major Midgley, S., D.S.O., 5th Light Horse Regiment.

HISTORY OF THE 5th LIGHT HORSE REGIMENT. 41

"Lieutenant Brundrit, T. J., 5th Light Horse Regiment (killed in action).

"Lieutenant Gee, H. J., 11th Light Horse Regiment.

"No. 164, Sergeant Orr, J. E., 5th Light Horse Regiment.

"No. 212, Sergeant Ryan, P. F., 6th Light Horse Regiment."

From the time the Regiment occupied "Wilson's Lookout," conditions of life there were very strenuous. "Broomstick" bombs rained upon us day and night. The guns which the enemy brought up and placed in the scrub near the Twin Trenches were less than 2,000 yards from our lines. They enfiladed the main trench of the Post. This trench was well traversed, but one was only safe from these guns if close under a traverse. Machine guns and artillery from Gaba Tepe fired into the new post on its right rear. The Bird Trenches overlooked us from the front, the Turkish Despair Works were some 150 yards on our left, the enemy artillery opposite Lone Pine shelled us from our left rear; in fact, our "front" faced an arc of more than 180 degrees. Casualties through battle and sickness had been very heavy, and the men were getting three out of four nights on duty. The working parties were heavy. For some time our only covered means of communication between Chatham's and the new post was a long, narrow tunnel, in which two men could pass with difficulty. A heavy shell exploding above this tunnel might wreck it at any moment. An alternate communication was necessary, which meant a lot of work. The whole of the new works had to be deepened and improved. Every night the results of the enemy artillery fire during the day had to be rectified. The effective strength of the Regiment was 320, all ranks.

The C.O. accordingly requested the Brigade to furnish parties from the 6th and 7th Regiments to assist in holding the Lookout. The C.O. of the 6th Regiment (Cox) demurred to this, and informed the Brigadier (Ryrie) that we should easily hold the position with the men at our disposal, to which the Brigadier replied: "Alright, you have more men than they have, if you think they have enough, you can easily hold their line with your regiment. The 5th Regiment will take over Ryrie's Post, and the 6th Chatham's and 'Wilsons.' "

The exchange was accordingly effected on the 26th November.

During the three weeks that the 5th had held Wilson's Lookout, we had 17 killed and 64 wounded, and 89 evacuated through sickness. The strain had been heavy. During the first five nights of Wilson's Lookout, there had practically been no sleep for anyone and after that the men had night duty three nights out of four. Add to this the strain caused by the "broomsticks," and the result was physical collapse of many and consequent evacuation.

During the last ten days we had the loan from the other three regiments of the Brigade, three out of every four nights, of three officers and sixty other ranks to help garrison the Lookout. It was the objection of the 6th Regiment to supply their quota that brought about our relief.

CHAPTER 13.

RYRIE'S POST.

On the 26th November, we shifted into our new line—Ryrie's Post. The 6th Regiment were not, however, pleased with their transfer. Three days afterwards they applied for and obtained the help of 100 Infantry per day to help them in holding the post, and also applied to the Brigade for assistance from the other regiments thereof. This regiment with the others supplied a quota.

It had now started to rain. On the 27th it snowed, and up to the end of the month the ground was still frozen. The cold caused the troops much suffering. Some two months previous to this we had been informed that wood and iron would be made available for huts and the dugouts. It never arrived, however. Consequently, at the time when the snow fell, no cover was available for the troops, except that of each man's oil-sheet. When a man went on night shift, he had to take his oil-sheet with him, so that his dugout in his absence got drenched with rain, even if it had been dry before.

The cold north wind and rain followed by the snow caused cases of frost-bitten feet, and one case of collapse. There were no means of artificial warmth available other than the very limited amount of firewood issued. Numerous cases of rheumatism were reported. Until the weather thawed again the water ration was cut down to one-fourth—two pints per man per day—owing to the freezing of the water pipes. This short issue of water meant that the vegetables, rice and dried fruit issued could not be used and the troops had to live on bully beef and biscuit. No fresh bread during this period was issued, as there was no water with which to make it. At the time that this shortage of cover was felt, there was much discontent, as it was then thought that we would be there for the whole of the winter. We afterwards understood why this timber had not been sent, as the question of evacuation had been decided. This, no doubt, accounted also for the fact that our reinforcements were not coming forward and that the regiments were down to about half strength. This reduction in numbers, of course, meant that the men who were there had to do double work, and this reacted on the sick rate, which naturally increased when men were on night duty night after night without relief.

Shortly after the snow storm in the end of November, there was an issue of rubber trench-boots (twelve per squadron) and an issue of 25 macintosh capes per squadron, just about enough to cause everybody to think that a full issue should have been made. Those issued were hardly enough for the actual sentries in the trenches, and it meant that every time a sentry was changed he had to take his top boots and cape off, the result being that he often got a chill.

CHAPTER 14.

PREPARATION FOR EVACUATION.

On the 14th December 1915, we first received advice that it was intended to evacuate the Anzac position, and we received instructions to get all our heavy baggage away. On the 17th December, definite instructions were received for the evacuation at a time and place to be communicated later. The next day we were informed that the times fixed were the nights of December 18th-19th and 19th-20th. The personnel of the Regiment were told off in the various parties as follows:

To Leave Night 18th-19th December, 1915.

No.	Rank Name
	Capt. Mullins, T.
	Lieut. Christie, R.
118	S.Q.M.S. Luxford, S.
447	Armr./Sergt. Armour, W.
231	Sergt. Towner, A. G.
201	A/Sergt. Hammond, H. A.
897	Pte. Davison, E. C.
468	Pte. Waldon, W.
657	Pte Ogden, H. E.
614	Pte. Fogarty, A. G.
9	Pte. Lyons, J. M.
	Capt. McLaughlin, H. F.
23	S.S.M. Warnes, H. W. S.
563	S.Q.M.S. Marshall, H. G.
478	Sergt. Smith, A. V.
247	Cpl. Dale, J.
71	Pte. Davis, W. E.
944	Pte. Hansen, V.
272	Pte. Hennegan, S.
708	Pte. Baldwin, R. J.
462	Pte. Byrne, G. W.
	Lieut. Richard, R. R.
127	Sergt. Munro, V. A. C.
712	Pte. Daly, G. D.
863	Pte. Drury, A. M.
13	Pte. McCormack, C.
1009	Pte. Burrell, T. F.
511	Pte. Cooper, W. J.
739	Pte. Rose, A. E.
1090	Pte. Hallet, W. B.
1082	Pte. Treloar, A. V.
1087	Pte. Gardner, J.
951	Pte. Kebblewhite, E. A.
975	Pte. Westhoven, E. C.
1089	Pte. Lenihan, M.
271	Pte. Hosie, H.
375	Pte. Day, S.
549	Pte. Currie, T.

No.	Rank Name
378	Pte. Guard, S. C.
161	Pte. Miller, E. R.
970	Pte. Shaw, H. H.
645	Pte. Morrison, F. A.
895	Pte. Stanley, G. W.
1001	Cpl. Anderson, J. F.
248	Cpl. Hanly, P.
1037	Pte. Parker, H.
1121	Pte. Weddell, W.
110	Pte. Giles, M. W.
19	Sergt. Stewart, R. J.
344	S.Q.M.S. Failhall, J. H.
648	Cpl. Williams, P. C.
225	Pte. Beazley, R. A.
39	Pte. Dawson, W. V.
125	Pte. Mitchell, A. A.
275	Pte. Richards, J. (A.V.C.).
1004	Pte. Austin, J.
1184	Pte. Markwell, J. T.
1152	Pte. Bonner, T.
586	Pte. Herbert, J. C.
1059	Pte. Handley, R.
194	Pte. Casey, E.
1034	Pte. McMahon, T. J.
986	Pte. Connell, J. T.
646	Pte. Walker, D. B.
1061	Pte. Hensley, S.
667	Pte. Ainsworth, F.
170	Sergt. Tooth, E. W.
772	S.Q.M.S. Hockings, E. R.
528	Cpl. Coffill, F.
11L.H./317	Pte. McMahon, S. M.
11L.H./387	Pte. O'Connor, W.
11L.H./257	Pte. Curel, J.
11L.H./303	Pte. Langston, F.
11L.H./345	Pte. Roach, T. T.
1067	Pte. Gilbey, W. H.

HISTORY OF THE 5th LIGHT HORSE REGIMENT.   45

No.	Rank	Name
554	Pte.	Sweet, J. T.
961	Pte.	Oldham, W.
735	Pte.	Norrie, A.
501	Pte.	Dwyer, W. E.
206	Pte.	Greene, W.
783	Pte.	McGee, M.
1122	Pte.	Waller, W. E.
1123	Pte.	Croft, S. F.
427	Pte.	Irvine, W. R.
1098	Pte.	Allen, G.
1175	Pte.	Hession, H.
1003	Pte.	Armstrong, G. W.
1125	Pte.	Childlow, R. J.
709	Pte.	Crutchfield, G. A.
1110	Pte.	Rowley, A. W.
1107	Pte.	Clarke, R.
1117	Pte.	Wallace, G. H.
641	Pte.	Higgins, J.
771	Pte.	Hinton, F. W.
258	Pte.	Jenns, S. C.
11L.H./20	Pte.	Cory, C. R.
11L.H./842	Pte.	McLean, A.
11L.H./242	Pte.	Reynolds, W.
11L.H./255	Pte.	Cooper, E. W. S.
11L.H./401	Pte.	Simpson, W. C.
11L.H.	Lieut.	Koch, W. J. F.
11L.H./227	Sergt.	Farlow, F. G.

No.	Rank	Name
11L.H./231	Sergt.	Wells, E.
No.	Rank	Name
11L.H./305	Sergt.	Laxton, F. P.
11L.H./388	Sgt.	Woodbine, N.
11L.H./362	Pte.	Watson, W. W.
11L.H./404	Pte.	Duffy, J.
11L.H./840	Pte.	Stevens, H. R.
11L.H./862	Pte.	Gunstan, J.
11L.H./320	Pte.	Nolan, W.
11L.H./341	Pte.	Reid, R. J.
11L.H./18	Pte.	Carr, E.
11L.H./777	Pte.	McGrath, J. P.
11L.H./670	Pte.	Smoothy, L.
11L.H./309	Pte.	Lingard, N. A.
11L.H./348	Pte.	Rouse, E. M.
11L.H./315	Pte.	McKay, L. P.
11L.H./841	Pte.	Patterson, A. L.
11L.H./861	Pte.	Hatfield, L.
11L.H./250	Pte.	Buckley, J. H.
11L.H./389	Pte.	Barnett, H. W.
11L.H./370	Pte.	Youngman, J. D.
11L.H./299	Pte.	King, J.

To Leave Night 19th-20th December, 1915.

A.1 PARTY.

No.	Rank	Name
	Capt.	Dods, J. E.
	Lieut.	Orr, J. E.
293	Sergt.	Ogg, E. C.
288	Sergt.	Edginton, J. P.
530	Cpl.	Chaille, W. M.
542	Pte.	Russell, A.
1104	Pte.	Neilson, C.
815	Pte.	Bauer, A.
1103	Pte.	Gilles, W. J.
1202	Pte.	Underhill, J. F.
696	Pte.	Bansgrove, W.
267	Pte.	Knight, P.
250	Sergt.	Radcliffe, B. H.
328	Cpl.	Webster, T.
557	Pte.	Mouritz, E. R.
958	Pte.	McLellan, A.
883	Pte.	Norman, T.
1113	Pte.	Lambert, N.
535	Pte.	Allen, A. G.
441	Pte.	Fuge, A. S.
532	Pte.	Player, A. E.
1188	Pte.	O'Dwyer, S.
1594a	Cpl.	Norcott, A. J.
719	Pte.	Evans, E. O.
2168a	Pte.	Hollow, E. C.

A.2 PARTY.

No.	Rank	Name
	Lieut.	Brown, H. S.
684	Sergt.	Jones, J. G.
509	Sergt.	Poynting, A. H.
321	Cpl.	McMullen, R. V.
610	Cpl.	Mullins, D.
932	Cpl.	Boyd, J.
866	Cpl.	Elliott, L. E.
508	Cpl.	Kirkland, H. K.
274	Pte.	McAllister, C.
873	Pte.	Joyce, F. J.
881	Pte.	Moore, J. C.
1014	Pte.	Drochman, F.
810	Pte.	Moss, F. A.
315	Pte.	McMullen, A. J.
820	Pte.	Jones, S. R.
890	Pte.	Rooks, J. H.
421	Pte.	Lockhart, W. E.
982	Pte.	Gauld, R. L.
346	Cpl.	McKinnon, L.
5561	Pte.	Cummings, R. L.
5562	Pte.	Shoobridhe, F. S. R. (A.A.M.C. Attached).
74	Sergt.	Foot, G.
51	Pte.	O'Hara, D.

HISTORY OF THE 5th LIGHT HORSE REGIMENT.

No.	Rank	Name
149	Pte.	Christensen, T.
487	Pte.	Sidney, R. V.

A.3 PARTY.
Major Lee, C. A.
Lieut. Munro, C. A.
2nd Lieut. Wetherill H.

No.	Rank	Name
11L.H./347	Cpl.	Rowe, T.
11L.H./276	Sergt.	Hoffman, G.
11L.H./380	Cpl.	Billington, W. H.
11L.H./10	Pte.	Baker, H. F.
11L.H./332	Pte.	Philp, E. G.
11L.H./17	Pte	Carr, C.R.
11L.H./357	Pte.	Schmid, J. F.
11L.H./756	Pte.	Butcher, A. C.
11L.H./281	Pte.	Graham, V.
11L.H./13	Pte.	Bruce, E. L.
11L.H./358	Pte.	Taylor, R.
11L.H./268	Pte.	Evans, G.
11L.H./853	Pte.	Rae, G. H.
11L.H./274	Pte.	Gaut, O.
11L.H./856	Pte.	Perry, N. J.
11L.H./31	Pte.	McElligot, J.
11L.H./294	Pte.	Jarman, H.
354	Pte.	Hall, R. L.
11L.H./775	Pte.	Middleton, J.
11L.H./293	Pte.	Irwin, R.
224	Pte.	Emmerson, H.
232	Pte.	Graham, J. A.

B.1 PARTY.
Capt. Newton, F. G.

No.	Rank	Name
503	Cpl.	Ross, B. J.
298	Cpl.	Kerr, L. A.
430	Cpl.	Tidmarsh, R. H. B.

No.	Rank	Name
722	Cpl.	Hughes, G.
707	Sergt.	Billington, R. S.
695	Pte.	Capper, V.
88	Pte.	Price, B. H. E.
791	Pte.	Simpson, H.
620	Pte.	Kennedy, J. A.
53	Pte.	Baker, L. J.
613	Pte.	Heaney, H. R.

B.2 PARTY.
Lieut. Mahoney, B.

No.	Rank	Name
6008	Pte.	Williams, A. E.
5472	Pte.	Nobes, M. C. (A.A.M.C. Attached).
75	Sergt.	Gahan, J.
740	Cpl.	Robertson, J.
477	Cpl.	Anderson, R.
294	Pte.	Carroll, W.
938	Pte.	Card, H.
42	Cpl.	Johnstone, W. G.
58	Pte.	Kessler, C. J.
465	Pte.	Johns, H. A.
11L.H./264	Pte.	Dreyer, W. C.

B.3 PARTY.
Major Johnstone, H. H.

No.	Rank	Name
11L.H.	Lieut.	Gee, H. J.
11L.H./299	Sergt.	Brierty, A. A.R.
11L.H./228	Sergt.	Kreig, S. P.
11L.H./313	Cpl.	McGregor, G.
11L.H./338	Pte.	Quinn, W.
11L.H./262	Pte.	Dougherty, C.
11L.H./285	Pte.	Healy, J.
11L.H./368	Pte.	Wilson, A.
11L.H./837	Pte.	Budd, R.
11L.H./24	Pte.	Edwards, E.

Left 20th December, 1915.

C.1 PARTY.
Lt.-Col. Wilson, L.C. (in charge of all Brigade "C" Parties).
Lieut. Stanfield, E. A. F.

No.	Rank	Name
292	Sergt.	Solling, R. A.
635	Cpl.	Wood, C. N.
482	Cpl.	Smith, G. J.
	Lieut.	Cain, J.
61	L./Cpl.	Taylor, C. E.
729	Pte.	Murphy, J. J.
180	Sergt.	James, R.
596	Pte.	Weiss, L. E.

C.2 PARTY.
Major Midgley, S., D.S.O. (In charge of all Regimental "C" Parties).
Capt. Wright, W. L. F.

No.	Rank	Name
133	Sergt.	Paul, W
283	Pte.	Cox, C. E.
284	Pte.	Clark, D. L.
326	Pte.	Corner, F. E.
422	Pte.	Howard, E. J.
504	Pte.	Anderson, C. A.
983	Pte.	Cannavan, P.
939	Pte.	Cannavan, T. P.

C.3 PARTY.
2nd Lieut. Waite, F. M.

No.	Rank	Name
941	Cpl.	Fraser, H. L.
516	Cpl.	Duke, A. D.
469	Pte.	Murray, E. J.
759	Pte.	Byers, L. R.
413	Pte.	Hardwick, R. C.
1015	Pte.	Felmington, B.
817	Pte.	Williamson, R. B.

HISTORY OF THE 5th LIGHT HORSE REGIMENT. 47

For some weeks prior to the Evacuation, and as we now know, in anticipation thereof, "silent ruses" were instituted. The first one, of three days and nights' duration, took place in the first week in December.

In ordinary course, there was a large amount of movement behind our lines, and this movement could be observed by the Turkish observation posts on Gaba Tepe. During the night, along the whole front line, desultory firing usually took place. Every sentry during each shift fired off a number of rounds at the enemy loopholes, and every now and again a machine gun would open fire towards the enemy trenches. Occasionally the artillery would fire a few rounds at night also. To carry out the "Silent Ruse," orders were issued that for the next three days movement in the rear of our line was to be reduced to a minimum, and that there was to be no firing from our lines by day or night, unless we were attacked. The result was that during these ruses there was an uncanny silence on our side. During the first two nights of the first silent ruse, the Turks did nothing, but on the third night they could stand it no longer, so they sent over a strong reconnaisance to investigate the cause of the silence. This reconnaisance came to within ten yards of the lines when the 7th Light Horse, who were on the alert, opened on them, with the result that the enemy left behind 20 bodies, which would mean probably another 50 wounded.

Three nights before we came away, we had another silent ruse for half an hour. The Turks stood it for fifteen minutes, then every man in their lines opened rapid fire. They apparently thought we had men out in front to attack them and that our reason for ceasing fire was so as not to hit our own men. Later on, the same night, we had another silent ruse for half an hour, but by this time the Turks had been educated and they would not open up. From this, it will be seen that we were getting them ready for the condition of things at and immediately after evacuation of our trenches Prior to Saturday, the 18th December, almost all the army stores, guns, mules, horses, etc., had been sent away by sea. Some of the troops, including the 4th Light Horse Regiment, which was attached to the 2nd Brigade, and some battalions complete, were sent away, while the numbers of the remainder were reduced.

CHAPTER 15.

THE EVACUATION.

The strength of this regiment on Friday, the 17th, was 263. Twenty-five men were sent away that day, leaving 238 on Saturday morning. On Saturday morning 100 were sent away, leaving 138. These 138 were divided into three parties, A, B and C, of 75, 35 and 28 men each. Each of these A, B and C parties were again divided into three sections, 1, 2 and 3.

On Sunday, the Brigade, originally of the strength of about 2,000 (4th, 5th, 6th and 7th Regiments) was now represented by about 450 men. As our Brigade held the extreme right of the line, we had about a mile to go to the place where embarkation was to take place.

On Sunday, the 19th, the Regimental A party, total 75, was to leave at 5.30 p.m., in three sections at intervals of fifteen minutes between sections, B party, total 35, was to start at 9.30 p.m., in three sections, and at similar intervals, and C party, total 28, was to start at 2.30 a.m. on the morning of the 20th in three sections, at intervals of fifteen minutes between sections. It will thus be seen that, from 10 p.m. to 2.30 a.m., an interval of 4½ hours, four regiments, which consisted of about 2,000 men, would be represented by 112 men. It was arranged that the Brigadier, General Ryrie, should leave with the B party at 10 p.m., and from then on Lieut-Colonel L. C. Wilson would have charge of the Brigade line with the C parties of the three regiments.

Major Midgley, D.S.O., was placed in charge of the Regimental C party of 28 all ranks; Lieutenant Stanfield, Major Wright and Lieutenant Waite in charge of C.1, C.2 and C.3 sections respectively, and Lieutenant Cain with the machine gun section with C party.

On 18th December an Army Corps Order, reading as follows, was issued:

"The Army Corps Commander wishes all ranks of the Division to be informed of the operations that are about to take place and a message conveyed to them from him to say that he deliberately takes them into his

HISTORY OF THE 5th LIGHT HORSE REGIMENT.   49

confidence, trusting to their discretion and high soldierly qualities to carry out a task, the success of which will largely depend on their own individual efforts.

"If every man makes up his mind that he will leave the trenches quietly, when his turn comes, and see that everybody else does the same, and that up till that time he will carry on as usual, there will be no difficulty of any kind, and the Army Corps Commander relies on the good sense and proved trustworthiness of every man of the Corps to ensure that this is done.

"In case by any chance we are attacked on either day, the Army Corps Commander is confident that the men who have to their credit such deeds as the original landing at Anzac, the repulse of the big Turkish attack on May 18th, the capture of Lone Pine, the Apex and Hill 60 will hold their ground with the same valour and steadfastness as heretofore, however small in numbers that may be, and he wishes all men to understand that it is impossible for the Turks to know or tell what our numbers are, even up to the last portion of C party on the last night, as long as we stand our ground."

As the first parties went away, ammunition which would have been used by them was thrown into the sea, and supplies were gradually reduced in this manner until there were just sufficient for the parties remaining on the Peninsula.

It was important that the departure of the last of the parties should not become known or suspected by the enemy. To prevent such suspicion arising, the following ruse was availed of. Rifles were lashed and sighted through loop-holes pointing to the Turkish trenches. An empty tin can was attached to the trigger of the rifle; above this trigger a tin filled with water was suspended, with a small plugged hole in the bottom. The last men to leave the trenches were to remove the plugs from the top tins and let the water trickle into the bottom tins. When a bottom tin was full, the weight would pull the trigger and the rifle would explode. The result of this was that rifles would go off in our lines half an hour after the last man had left. The same result was obtained in another way by tying a weight on to the trigger of the rifle, then by another string taking the load off the first string. A "bomb lighter," otherwise a tightly rolled piece of bagging which burned at the rate of a foot an hour, was then so placed that when the bomb lighter had burned down a certain distance, it would burn the string which kept the load off the trigger. When this happened, the weight would drop with a jerk and fire the rifle. Large numbers of rifles were fixed up in these ways with the result that rifles were exploding for a considerable time after the last man had got into the boats. Bombs were also thrown out in front with long fuses attached to them with the result that these bombs exploded after the last man had gone. During the last two days special movement went on behind our lines, so that the enemy observation on Gaba Tepe would not become suspicious. Bogus fatigue parties carried empty water cans backwards and forwards so as to be taken for the usual water fatigues—sort of theatrical armies, same men seen often.

Sunday night, 19th-20th, the night of the final evacuation, was calm with a bright moon. The boots of the men were covered with sacking to prevent the noise of marching being heard. Bayonets were covered in bagging to prevent them glistening in the moonlight.

Lieutenant Wetherell drew attention to the fact that it is not possible to see through a searchlight ray. It was the usual practice for a torpedo-boat destroyer to be stationed a few thousand yards off the right flank, from which she shelled the various Turkish positions during the night, and also kept her searchlight on the beach to see that there was no enemy movement thereon.

For some nights prior to the Evacuation, she was instructed to keep this light as a fixed ray for half an hour at a time at one spot. On the night of the Evacuation the destroyer put this ray on just prior to the time the parties were due to move, and kept it on until they had gained the boats. It was, therefore, not possible for the Turkish observation post at Gaba Tepe to notice any movement in rear of our lines.

As previously stated, most of the stores, etc., had been got away in good time. Some four worn-out guns were left. These fired up till late on Sunday evening, and were then destroyed. One 5 inch howitzer was left until the last, when, with the aid of one of the improvised bomb-lighter fuses, this gun was exploded after the parties had retired to the beach.

A premature explosion might have caused the Turks to suspect movement. It was the usual nightly practice of "Beachy Bill" to shell the beach. On the afternoon of the Sunday, it looked as if the Turks had gained some information of the intended departure, for on that afternoon they ranged on the exact spot on Brighton Beach that the pontoons on which we were to embark were to be erected after dark. This apparently was a coincidence, as while the Evacuation was on no unusual artillery firing took place.

Arrangements were made by the medical authorities that, if casualties occurred during the Evacuation, a medical party would remain behind to look after them. This party was to take its chance. There was no shortage of volunteers for the duty. Orders were issued that if men were wounded in the final parties and could not walk to the boats, they were to be left behind. Special instructions were also issued that once a party had left the trenches in accordance with the schedule, they were on no account to return to them to support the others still there in case of an attack.

The A and B parties moved off to time. Lieut.-Colonel Wilson then took over command of the C parties of the Brigade and handed over command of the Regimental C parties to Major Midgley, D.S.O. A and B parties had each one slight casualty from "overs" about a mile from the shore. They were the only casualties that the Regiment suffered during the Evacuation. Word came later that the C parties would commence to leave at 2 a.m. instead of 2.30 a.m., as the lighters of the B party had made a quicker trip than anticipated. C party moved in accordance with the amended timetable. C.1 left the trenches, and Lieutenant Cain and his machine gun took up a position on a ridge a few hundred yards the trench side of the embarkation pontoons. C.2 moved out and to the boats at 2.15 a.m. Lieutenant Waite (C.3) counted his party—8 all told, and moved at 2.30 up to the rear line, pulling into the communication trench behind him the barbed wire prepared for that purpose. While waiting on the rear line for the C.3 party of the 6th Regiment from Wilson's Lookout to pass, Lieutenant Waite's attention was drawn to the fact that Trooper Murray, of the C.3 party, was not present. An examination of those present disclosed the fact that one of the eight was a C.2 man and that Murray was still in the front line. The officer and a man at once went to the front line, which they reached with some difficulty owing to the wire in the communication trench, and found Murray still at his post, the end of the line. What had happened was that the O.C., C.2 party, had wrongly counted in Major Midgley, the commander of all the Regimental C parties, as one of his ten and left one of his own behind, and that when Lieutenant Waite collected seven men (one of whom in the dark was not noticed to be the C.2 man) he thought his party of eight was complete, and moved off accordingly. As it turned out, no evil resulted from the mistake and Murray joined his party, all of whom arrived in due course at the boats.

The Brigade C parties embarked on the boats at Brighton Beach as ordered. The last got aboard at 3.27 a.m. on the morning of 20th December, 1915. These parties transferred from the boats which were towed by a pinnace to a trawler, and proceeded to Mudros where they were transferred to the transport "Beltana" where the balance of the Regiment, less B parties, were awaiting. The same afternoon the transport sailed for Alexandria. B parties sailed to Alexandria per transport "Anchises." The "Beltana" arrived at Alexandria on the 25th. The troops proceeded the same night to Cairo, detrained at Helmieh about 3 a.m. on the morning of the 26th December. On the morning of the 27th December, the Regiment proceeded to Maadi and occupied the old camp, where we found eight officers and 418 other ranks—details and reinforcements—awaiting us. The number of all ranks who left Anzac on the 18th, 19th and 20th December amounted to 263.

STATE AS AT EVACUATION.

Landed at Anzac, May, 1915	477
Reinforcements	552
	1029
Effective Strength, 18th December	263
Embarked after notification of intended Evacuation, to reduce numbers	16
Prisoner of War	1
Dead	75
Wounded, to Hospital (and still absent)	121
Sick, to Hospital (and still absent)	540
Transferred, etc.	13
	1029

HISTORY OF THE 5th LIGHT HORSE REGIMENT.   53

Casualties, Anzac Campaign—
- Dead (including 3 officers) 75
- Wounded (including 16 officers) 266
- — 341

Total evacuation for sickness—
- Officers 25
- Other ranks 779
- — 804

Grand total sick, wounded or killed (some of whom sick or wounded more than once)   1145

Of these who landed with the Regiment in May, 1915, there were on the Peninsula at the Evacuation 105 all ranks. Of these who were on the Peninsula without a break there were 49. Lieut.-Colonel L. C. Wilson and Captain Stanley, of the Brigade Signalling Troop, were the only two original officers of the Brigade who survived the Campaign and never left the Peninsula between 20th May and 20th December, 1915.

When we arrived back at Cairo we found several officers and men who had been to England. It is here worthy of record that not a single officer or man who had been evacuated from the Peninsula to England returned to the Peninsula. From what could be learned from the men who went to England, every encouragement seemed to have been given to them to stop there, and no one ever appears to have been urged to go back to the Peninsula. The comfort of those who left the Peninsula was more considered than the interests of those at the Front who had to do extra work owing to the reduced strength of their units.

The following special Order was issued by Lieut.-General Sir Alexander Godley, K.C.M.G., C.B., Commanding Australian and New Zealand Army Corps:

"The Army Corps Commander has received for transmission to all ranks of the Army Corps congratulations from Sir Charles Munro, the Commander-in-Chief, and Sir William Birdwood, Commanding the Dardenelles Army, on the successful conduct of the difficult and delicate operation of withdrawing from the Gallipoli Peninsula. In forwarding these messages to the troops, Sir Alexander Godley wishes to express to all officers, N.S.O.'s and men his thanks for the loyal co-operation and his admiration of the steadiness and coolness with which they carried out the orders. Had it not been that everyone played his part thoroughly and efficiently this most difficult task could not have been carried to such a successful conclusion.

"Australians and New Zealanders have added yet another gallant feat of arms to the already notable record of achievements of which their Dominions are so justly proud."

Very few decorations of any description were given for services on the Peninsula. This Regiment cannot complain, however, with regard to the share which it got of these that were issued, as the C.O., Lieut.-Colonel L. C. Wilson, and Major Midgley, D.S.O., each got a C.M.G.; Captain Dods, the medical officer of the Regiment, a M.C.; and Trooper Sing, a D.C.M. The last-mentioned members of the Regiment, together with Captain Brundrit and Captain Mullins, were also mentioned in Despatches.

CHAPTER 16.

CONDITIONS ON GALLIPOLI.

Before completing the narrative of our experiences at Gallipoli, a few words on our domestic economy would not be out of place.

First, as to our housing accommodation, if such a term can be used where there was no house. We had no tents or huts. Tents would have been too noticeable from the Turkish lines and from their aeroplanes and would have attracted shell-fire. We had no huts, as there was no wood or galvanised iron available for that purpose. What little wood and iron there was, was used for erecting head cover over the machine gun positions. We had no large dug-outs of the sort used in France and Belgium—subterranean rooms safe from shell-fire. The soil was of a friable nature and the large excavations would have required timbering to make them safe, and there was no timber available for that purpose. A couple of experiments were made in that respect, one at Ryrie's Post and a similar one at Chatham's, but the excavations were so dangerous looking that men would not willingly go into them. Large lumps of earth were continually falling from the roof and the whole dug-out was liable to collapse at any moment, particularly if a shell exploded on the surface above. Our dugouts, accordingly, consisted of narrow slits on the edges of gulleys or off the sides of saps. In the former case, their height deepened on the steepness of the slope, and in the latter case, on the depth of the sap off which they were dug. This usually meant a depth of about six feet. In width, these dug-outs were about 2ft. 6 in., the width being governed by the breadth of the oil-sheet which commonly formed the roof. Each of these dug-outs usually provided a habitation for two men.

There was no local fuel. What we had, was brought from overseas and was barely sufficient for cooking. There was none available for warming dug-outs in the cold nights of November and December. Shortly prior to the Evacuation, there was a rumour that stoves were to be supplied, one to each forty men. They, however, did not come to hand. Even if they had, they would not have been of much use owing to the fact that there were seldom more than two persons living in the dug-out. They would, of course, have been of use if forty men had lived in the same dug-out, but for reasons stated this was not practicable.

The matter of water supply has been dealt with in Chapter 10 of this narrative.

As to rations, see Appendix D. There were no local supplies. All came overseas. The scale set out in the Appendix was the scale in the latter days of our stay on Gallipoli. For some time after arriving on the Peninsula, the principal ration was bully beef (Fra Bentos) and army biscuit with a moderate issue of apricot jam (Sir Joseph Paxton). The men did their own cooking, or small parties of three or four arranged for it amongst themselves. Cooking did not amount to much while there was a bully beef issue. Variety was very limited. Bully beef could be eaten cold, or used in the form of stews, curries or rissoles. The biscuits were sometimes ground up into powder and made into porridge.

We had no canteen—wet or dry—on the Peninsula. Rumours from time to time spread that one was intended to be installed, but it did not materialise. On one or two occasions, a small consignment of canteen stores came to Anzac but when distributed amongst the whole army, the amount was not of any practical value. On another occasion, each unit sent a small party across to Mudros for canteen stores, but, again, supplies were very limited in extent. During October, we obtained from Imbros eggs packed in cases of approximately sixty dozen each. These eggs were sold at cost price to the members of the Regiment at 2/6 per dozen. Our Regimental Fund purchased the first case and subsequently some fifteen more cases were received, costing between £120 and £130, No loss was incurred or profit made on these transactions. On Bulgaria coming into the War, this most acceptable variation came to an end, as the eggs came from Bulgaria. There was always a small amount of extra rations obtainable on the Beach from the crews of the trawlers. These people made a lucrative business of supplying, at exorbitant rates, groceries to the fatigue parties visiting the Beach. This source of supply was limited and was of no practical value to the men as a whole. Later on in the War, a few persons derived extra rations through the Parcel Mail, but in Gallipoli days this means of supply was very little used.

A few weeks after we occupied the line from the Beach several large casks of wine were washed ashore. They had probably broken away from some wreck. A little of this wine got into consumption in the Unit, but not much. As soon as it was known it was on the Beach, the Brigade authorities despatched a party to smash in the casks, fearing, no doubt, that misuse might be made of the wine.

There were no organised amusements on the Peninsula. Life was too strenuous and the general conditions forbade it. Even if the men had the energy, they could not be spared to train. Sports meant being in open spaces, and open spaces were particularly unhealthy. Occasionally, small parties were sent out to inspect other lines to see how the others lived, but casual wandering about was discouraged. The water and ration parties to the Beach continually suffered casualties from shell-fire, chiefly from "Beachy Bill," and men soon learnt that the safest place to be was in their own trench system.

There was no leave to Egypt or England. On one occasion, as previously mentioned, an offer was made to the Regiment for a short period of leave to Mudros, but for the reasons previously mentioned, it did not eventuate.

HISTORY OF THE 5th LIGHT HORSE REGIMENT.

There was no organised training in the way it was carried out in the latter parts of the War. Conditions were against it. From time to time, however, new weapons and apparatus were evolved, and the learning to handle this material evoked interest and gave variation to the monotony of trench warfare. Amongst such novel apparatus, there were periscopic rifles, jam-tin bombs, cricket ball bombs, Lotbiniere bombs, catapults, trench mortars, wallaby rests, Verey lights, rockets, and bomb lighters.

Mail at Gallipoli was rather erratic, as was also the matter of cables. One was supposed to be able to send cables by post to Egypt and have them despatched from there, but experience showed that in some cases a cable took six weeks to arrive in Australia.

The normal medical organisation is set out in Appendix F hereto. The sick rate is evidenced by the evacuations, which were much heavier than for any other similar period of the War. This was, no doubt, owing to the special circumstances of this campaign. The strain, both mental and physical, was heavy. The Regiment was in the front trenches continually from 30th May to 20 December—nearly seven months—without a single day in rest. There were no conveniences for giving a soldier a rest or a chance of recuperating otherwise than by evacuating him, and, as previously stated, there was no leave from the Peninsula. Although the Turks did not deliberately shell the ambulance camps, a man could not recuperate there as day and night there was a continuous scream of shells and hiss of bullets passing over the ambulance tents. Such conditions did not tend to peace of mind of patients and the only thing to do was to get them off to the hospital ship and away to Egypt or England as soon as possible. Apart from the noise of guns and projectiles, the supply of suitable food for men in a bad state of health was indifferent. As usual, there was a difference of opinion on the matter of evacuations. It was reported in the trenches that an appeal had come from headquarters of the Australian Division asking medical officers for the honour of Australia to go slow in the matter of evacuations, while on the other hand, most medical officers thought it their duty, notwithstanding such appeal, to evacuate the sick and wounded men as soon as possible so as to give them a chance of recovering.

CHAPTER 17.

CAIRO and CANAL (December, 1915, to April, 1916).

Upon our return to Maadi, action was at once taken to reorganise the Regiment and to train it as a mounted unit. The Regiment remained at Maadi until 23rd February, 1916. During this period heavy reinforcements arrived, reinforcements which had been ordered to make up the wastage which had taken place and which was expected to take place at Gallipoli.

Upon our return from Gallipoli, we found awaiting us the first instalment of comforts forwarded us by the 5th Light Horse Comforts Fund. This fund had been instituted in Brisbane in September, 1915, to send comforts to the Regiment in the field, as the Red Cross Society restricted their operations to the sick and wounded. The members of the original committee were Mesdames Hubert Harris, L. C. Wilson, Espie Dods, Frank Little, Macansh, McNeill, T. G. Miller, Ridley, W. F. Taylor, and Misses Macansh and Harris. Ladies who subsequently joined the committee were: Mesdames Leeds, Lockhart Gibson, John Sinclair, Andrew Scott, H. Love, Billington, D. Nelson and Pike, and Miss I. Sword. In the end of 1916, the Regimental Comforts Fund co-operated with certain other similar funds in opening the Coo-ee Cafe at Brisbane. From the Coo-ee Cafe the Regimental Fund drew, in the two years of the former's existence, £2,271 as its share of the profits. During the three years' operations of the Regimental Comforts Fund that fund remitted, either in money or in the form of purchased goods, £3,000 to the Regiment. In addition to this, they collected gifts, such as socks, etc., and forwarded them to the Regiment. The remittances of monies and goods were highly appreciated by the troops. They often came to hand when it was not practicable to obtain variations to army rations in any other manner. The army authorities would send them up to the front area when transport was not available for canteen stores. These comforts were valued at more than their intrinsic value—a sentimental value was placed upon them, as their arrival showed the recipients that their women-folk in Australia were working in their interest, and so tended to keep up the general morale.

HISTORY OF THE 5th LIGHT HORSE REGIMENT.   59

On the 7th January, 1916, Lieutenants Goymer and Dawson and 100 other ranks, being part of the 12th Reinforcements, reported. On the 10th January, reinforcements, 49 other ranks, being our 8th Reinforcements, reported from Mudros where they had been since the middle of November last. On the 18th January, Lieutenant Hannay and 2nd Lieutenant Land and 28 other ranks reported from the Western Front. These officers and men had been part of a composite regiment which had been formed in Egypt for action on the Western borders of Egypt against the Senussi. The operations against these tribesmen had been successful, their power had been broken, and those members of the Western Forces who were Light Horsemen were returned to their units. On the 19th February, 1916, Lieutenant Barwise and 102 other ranks of the 13th Reinforcements, reported for duty. At this date the Daily State was at its maximum, namely, thirty officers and 1052 other ranks. On the 22nd February, Major C. Lee with four officers and 121 other ranks, who, up to this time, had formed D Squadron of the 5th Light Horse Regiment, reported back to their original regiment, the 11th Light Horse, as that regiment was being re-formed.

About this time the 4th and 5th Australian Infantry Divisions were being formed in Egypt from surplus reinforcements and members of the 1st and 2nd Divisions. Artillery and Engineers were required, and as Light Horse units had a large surplus of reinforcements, volunteers from such surplus were called for the Artillery and Engineers. Some 390 of our reinforcements transferred to the Artillery, as did also a large number to the Engineers. We still had a surplus, and a considerable part of such surplus was shortly afterwards transferred to the Imperial Camel Corps, two and a half of the four battalions of which consisted of Australians. These troops were later on in 1918 formed into the 14th and 15th Light Horse Regiments. The Regiment itself was, in the meantime, organised up to its official War Establishment. Mounted drill was carried out in the Desert round Maadi, and musketry practice on miniature ranges was extensively carried out also.

On the 23rd February, the Regiment moved from Maadi to Serapeum on the Suez Canal, entraining at Abu-El-Ela Station, strength 550 all ranks, according to War Establishments, less those at the School of Instruction at Zeitoun. On the 9th March, Lieutenants Martyr and Nicholson and 102 others ranks, being our 14th Reinforcements, reported to our Details Camp at Maadi.

Upon the organisation of the Infantry for service in Europe, the 1st (Cox), 2nd (Ryrie), 3rd (Antill) Light Horse Brigades and the New Zealand Mounted Rifles Brigade (Chaytor) were formed into the Australian and New Zealand Mounted Division, commonly known as the Anzac Mounted Division. To this Division was attached four batteries of Horse Artillery—Territorials—viz., Inverness, Ayrshire, Somerset and Leicester. The whole Division was under the command of Major-General Chauvel.

On arriving at Serapeum, part of the Regiment was engaged in occupying the Suez Canal Defences. "B" Squadron (dismounted) occupied the inner line at Serapeum on the East Bank Defences, while "C" Squadron (mounted) occupied the post at Devorsoir on the Canal, some few miles to the South.

That part of the Regiment which was not engaged in the above duty was occupied in training, including out-post schemes and similar exercise. While at Serapeum, the Brigade was inspected by General Birdwood, accompanied by His Royal Highness the Prince of Wales.

While at Serapeum, numerous requests were made to this and other Light Horse regiments to supply officers for the new infantry battalions which were being formed to constitute the 4th and 5th Divisions. Several members of the Regiment transferred to the Infantry under this scheme, including Captain McLaughlin and Lieutenants Hannay, Christie and Orr, all getting increased rank. Several of our N.C.O.'s were granted commissions in the Infantry.

Upon our return to Egypt, our medical officer, Captain Dods, M.C., transferred to the 1st Australian Division, with increased rank as D.D.M.S. His place was taken by Major Maclean, who carried on until the end of 1916, when he returned to Australia on Transport Duty. Captain Fitzhardinge then took over the duties of M.O. and held that position until the end of the War.

HISTORY OF THE 5th LIGHT HORSE REGIMENT.

On the 4th April, the Regiment moved from Serapeum to Moascar en route to Salhia, at which place it arrived the following day—5th April. Salhia was the place where Napoleon started from on his invasion of Syria. On the 14th April, our 15th Reinforcements, including 2nd Lieutenants Archer and 2nd Lieutenant Trout, arrived at our Training Squadron, which was now situated at Tel-el-Kebir. The Regiment remained at Salhia from the 5th to the 22nd April, the time being occupied in training. On the 21st April, instructions were received that the Regiment should proceed to Katia, via Kantara and Dueidar.

CHAPTER 18.
SINAI-DUEIDAR (April to July, 1916).

At this time, the 5th Mounted Brigade (Yeomanry) consisting of the Warwicks, Worcesters and Gloucesters, were stationed in the Katia Oasis Area with posts at Romani, Katia, Oghratina and Hamisah. Reports had lately been received by the authorities that signs of movements on the part of the Turks had been noticed in the Abd and Bayoud Districts, and it was to act as supports and reinforcements to the 5th Mounted Brigade that the 5th Regiment was moving out to Katia.

The Regiment accordingly marched from Salhia on the 22nd April, 1916 and arrived at Kantara at 1 p.m. Our orders were to move next day to Dueidar, an oasis twelve miles out on the Darb Sultani, or the Royal Road to Syria. At 7 a.m. on the 23rd, instructions were received from the G.O.C. 52nd Division (General Lawrence) that Dueidar post was at that time being attacked by the enemy, and we were instructed to send out one squadron at once and to follow on with the balance of the Regiment. Section headquarters at Kantara did not seem to be very anxious about the matter and did not apparently treat the enemy's action as very seriour. At 8 a.m. "C" Squadron, under Major Cameron, moved out towards Dueidar and reported at Hill 40 to Lieut.-Colonel Leggett, commanding the 155th Infantry Brigade. Major Cameron was then instructed to proceed at once to Dueidar and pursue the enemy. "C" Squadron arrived at Dueidar at 12.15 a.m., where it found the Turkish rear-guard still firing into that post.

Dueidar was held by a small garrison of Royal Scots Fusiliers. The Post defences consisted of one redoubt on the south-eastern ridge overlooking the oasis. This redoubt was poorly wired and had no covered communication with the oasis. It subsequently appeared that a Turkish Force of some 5,000 men had, on the morning in question, attacked all the British posts in this advanced area. They attacked the post at Oghratina and destroyed or captured the garrison. They did the same to the Yeomanry at Katia.

At the same time as they were attacking Oghratina and Katia, a party, estimated at about 700 men on camels, moved against Dueidar and attacked it shortly after dawn. A heavy fog covered the whole landscape and the enemy were within fifteen yards of the redoubt before their presence was noticed. The garrison telephoned to Hill 70, and a further party of about 100 infantry was sent to their assistance. The garrison with these supports defended themselves against the attack. The Turks kept up the offensive until "C" Squadron arrived on the scene, when they retired. The garrison had some 23 killed, while we counted 75 bodies of the enemy lying on the sand near the oasis. "C" Squadron moved in a south-easterly direction for a distance of eight miles but did not get in touch with the enemy other than two armed men who were taken prisoners.

At 8.30 a.m., the remainder of the Regiment, less the Transport, moved to Hill 70 where they reported to Lieut.-Colonel Leggett. Here we left "B" Squadron and the Machine Gun Section, the remainder moved on to Dueidar with two companies of the 4th Royal Scots Fusiliers. While moving out our flank guards picked up several prisoners who were working dismounted wide on the flanks towards Hill 70. These men had been left by their comrades without camels and could not get away when the remainder retired.

On arrival at Dueidar, Colonel Leggett instructed the C.O.—Lieut.-Colonel Wilson—to pursue the enemy who at that time were supposed to be on foot. We accordingly moved east and south-east and picked up five prisoners, but otherwise did not get in touch with the enemy. Some eight miles out we got in touch with "C" Squadron. We saw tracks of a large number of camels moving towards Mageibra, estimated at at least 500. One of our aeroplanes dropped a message that the Turkish column were retiring towards that last-mentioned place.

When leaving Dueidar, Major Cameron's instructions had been that, after pursuing the enemy, he was either to come back to Dueidar or report at Katia, whichever was the more convenient. When these instructions were given, it was not known that the Yeomanry posts at Katia and Oghratine had already been destroyed. At 5 p.m. an urgent message was received from Colonel Leggett stating that the Turks had successfully attacked Katia and were moving on Romani and for the Regiment to return to Dueidar before dark. This was accordingly done, "B" Squadron and the Machine Gun Section rejoining the Regiment at Dueidar at 8 p.m. During the night a certain number of stragglers from the 5th Mounted Brigade passed through Dueidar. It was subsequently ascertained that that brigade has lost 600 men, either killed or taken prisoners.

When news of the disaster to the 5th Mounted Brigade had been reported at Kantara, urgent instructions were sent to the rest of the 2nd Light Horse Brigade (Ryrie) at Salhia to proceed at once to Romani. This they did by forced marches. They, being short of rations, availed themselves of the supplies in the deserted Yeomanry camp at Romani, much to the subsequent disgust of the Yeomanry. On the 24th April strong patrols from this Regiment were sent out communicating with others patrols at Railhead on the north, Romani patrols on the north-east, and Warwicks (Yeomanry) patrols on the south. By these patrols various stragglers from Katia were picked up but no touch was gained with the main enemy forces. Information from some Camel Transport natives—fugitives from Oghratina—was obtained to the effect that there were wounded British soldiers still lying at Oghratina. This information was telephoned across to Romani and a squadron was sent out from that place, by the 6th Light Horse Regiment, to Oghratina, where they picked up several wounded Yeomanry and brought them in.

On the 25th April, Lieut.-Colonel L. C. Wilson, the C.O. of this Regiment, took over formal command of Dueidar Post under the 155th Brigade which was now under the command of Brigadier-General Pollock McCall. Action was at once taken to improve the defences of the post. A large number of casualties suffered by the garrison on the attack of the 23rd had been inflicted while the men had been moving from the redoubt to and from the oasis across the open sand. Accordingly, a communication trench was dug from the oasis to No. 1 redoubt. Other posts were established around the oasis.

On the 30th April, 1916, Lieutenants Rutherford and Plant with 45 reinforcements marched into camp. The Regiment now engaged in a series of patrols. On the left we got into touch with the patrols from Romani, and on the right kept in touch with those from Ballybunion, to the front we patrolled out at this time a distance of about eight miles.

The country to the front of Dueidar was a fair sample of the Sinai Desert. The country is by no means flat. It is undulating with numerous gullies and ridges. The whole country is practically soft sand. In parts it is covered with a low scrub of two or three feet in height at intervals of five or ten yards apart. In other parts where the sand is shifting there is no vegetation of any kind. It is impossible to ordinary wheel traffic. To the tyres of some of the light vehicles we attached broad iron tyres. These prevented the wheels from sinking in the sand. Later on, contrivances known as "pedrails" were attached to the gun wheels. These were much more efficient than the sand tyres. They consisted of pieces of wood about a foot long and six inches wide attached to a couple of chains. This chain of boards was fixed on to the wheel. The particular piece of board under the wheel prevented the wheel from sinking in the sand while the short length of board did not clog up with sand like a broad iron tyre did.

Scattered over the strip of land from the Coast inland to a distance of ten to fifteen miles are numerous oases. These oases consist of from a few to several hundred date palm trees each. Wherever they are, water can be found at depths of from three to ten feet. In a few of these oases were native wells, the sides being rivetted with the ribs of palm trees, They were not of much use for obtaining large quantities of water as they usually choked up with sand when pumped from. The water to be found in these oases varies in quality.

It is all slightly brackish, some of it is fairly good for drinking purposes, and in others it is too salt for that purpose. Shortly after we came into this area, systematic well-sinking was carried on in the outlying oases, with a view to future requirements. The C.O. of this Regiment, shortly after our arrival at Dueidar, introduced what are known as "Spearpoint Pumps." They are known in Egypt as "Abyssinia Wells," or "Norton Tubes." The C.O. had seen them working in the Ayr District in North Queensland. They consisted of a tube 2½ inches in diameter with a solid point. Just above the point the sides of the tube were perforated and covered with a strong perforated gauze. Wherever there was water within ten feet of the surface, these tubes could be hammered into the sand and when they reached the water-bearing strata, an ordinary military pump could be attached to the tube and the water could be pumped therefrom without limitation. These "points" could be hammered into the sand in a quarter or half an hour, whereas, it would have taken half a day at least to dig a well to have reached the same water-bearing strata. Moreover, they never choked and the water was free from surface pollution. We had several of these tubes made in Cairo and each squadron subsequently carried a complete set on pack horses during our sojourn in the Sinai Desert. Their value was so apparent that other units subsequently adopted them and several hundred were made for the use of the troops in this area by our engineers.

During the campaign the medical authorities, whenever practicable, clorinated the water used for drinking purposes. This made the water rather unpalatable, but like all other unpleasant things one got used to it. There was an issue of tablets in small glass bottles which all ranks were supposed to carry for water purification. A tablet dissolved in a bottle of water was guaranteed to kill all germs therein. No doubt it did, as one of these tablets left in contact with leather burnt a hole in it. It was soon discovered that in solution they were an excellent preparation for removing rust from bits and stirrup irons. These leather-burning and rust-removing qualities of the tablets were sufficient to make men look askance at them. Apart from this, they made the water offensive to the taste, and accordingly they were never used for the purpose for which they were issued.

The Sinai Desert is very sparingly populated. On most of the oases there were traces of habitation which consisted merely of wind brakes made from palm leaves. Those inhabitants we had come across were very miserable specimens of humanity. Later on, all Bedouins seen by us were sent to the rear as we had good reason to believe that they were acting as intelligence personnel for the Turks. Our first stay at Dueidar—April to August—was not uninteresting. We were detached from our own Brigade and we had to look after ourselves. The military situation was such that it behoved us to keep on the alert. Dueidar had been attacked on the 23rd April without the slightest warning, and there was no reason why the same thing could not occur again. It was no use depending on aerial reconnaissance, for, although our 'planes made daily reconnaissances far to our front, they failed to discover prior to the 18th July the existence of a Turkish column of some 18,000 men who had been marching for some weeks across the Desert from Beersheba. The Turks had marched by night and camped by day in the oases. When our 'planes were overhead, all movement was suspended, with the result that the presence of the enemy was unsuspected. The German 'planes were equally at fault. They came over daily and reconnoitered at least as far as the Canal. These visits of enemy planes were a source of great inconvenience to us. A regiment of massed horses was a too inviting target. As soon, therefore, as an enemy plane was seen approaching every man moved his horse out into the desert, scattering as much as possible. Although it never happened to this Regiment, there were several instances on record where enemy planes dropped bombs amongst masses of our horses, with serious results to our people. Amongst documents captured from them after their defeat at Romani, on August 4th, was "an appreciation of the situation," from their point of view. This document set out the numbers and composition of the forces against which they believed they were operating and contained the statement that the British Forces in the Romani area consisted of one cavalry division and some guns. As a matter of fact, there was a British infantry division there also. So much for aerial observation. In view of the above possibilities, the greatest care was taken to avoid another surprise. Dueidar Post had its own dismounted garrison who were responsible for holding the redoubts. In the event of a threatened attack, this Regiment was at once to get out into the open and retain its mobility. An hour before dawn— varying from 3 a.m. to 3.30 a.m.—during the three months that the Regiment was there for the first period, the Regiment saddled up and stood to arms ready to move at the word of command with nosebags and water-bottles filled and a day's rations in the haversacks. Occasionally, to test the preparedness the Regiment was moved off on the Desert and check inspections were made.

The normal life at Dueidar during our first stay there, apart from special reconnaissances or special patrols, included horse pickets, observation posts, night patrols, stables, waterhorses and musketry. The local infantry garrison did the bulk of the garrisoning of the redoubts around the oases, but we from time to time supplied parties to assist them in this respect. As we always had our horses to attend to, it was only reasonable that the local garrison should do most of this night work. We supplied working parties to improve the defences of the Post. When we first arrived there, there was only the one redoubt partially built with no communication built back to the oasis. As time went on, a complete circle of redoubts were built around the Post. We helped in the making of a communication trench to the original No. 1 Redoubt. The whole work of these redoubts consisted of sand bags owing to the fact that the soil was pure loose sand. The garrison of the redoubts furnished their own communication patrols from redoubt to redoubt, but we supplied several cossack posts of about eight men, who rode out at dusk and camped out about a mile from the Post on the possible lines of approach of the enemy, and thus afforded protection against a surprise attack, as happened on the day we arrived at Dueidar.

During the whole of our sojourn at Dueidar we kept a day observation post on Hill 383—three miles away. The party moved out so as to get on to the hill as the sun appeared over the horizon, when helios could be used. Later, we ran a telephone line out to this post and did not have to depend on helio. signalling alone.

Stabling and watering the horses, as usual, took up a good deal of time.

Sinai Desert is hot by day and comparatively cold by night. In fact, in the winter or spring it is excessively cold at night. The men wore their clothes to suit the climate and during the day some of them went about without their singlets and shirts. If some of them, dressed as they were, had been captured by the Turks, the latter would have formed a very erroneous idea as to the equipment of our army, as they could have correctly stated that the prisoners were sadly deficient in clothing.

As a regiment, we became very efficient in the matter of moving from camp at night. The Regiment could, and did. saddle up and move from camp at all times of night without a match being struck or light shown and without any noise louder than an occasional whispered order. A large amount of our marching was done at night. Most of our marches in the Desert commenced in the evening so as to get to our objective just prior to dawn. We became proficient in the use of the prismatic compass and of the North Pole Star. No smoking or talking was allowed. Advance guard was well to the front. Flankers were well out on the flanks. At first the neighing of the horses of these detached parties was noticeable and might have caused our presence to be discovered. This was remedied by ordering that such a detached party should never consist of less than two men in number. This had the desired effect in stopping the horses from neighing.

While at Dueidar thorough training in musketry was carried out, taking the form of troop competitions in which every man of the troop had to be included. The bulk of the items of the competition were "rapid" practices, with the result that the shooting efficiency of the Regiment was markedly improved. Substantial prizes were awarded the winners from the profits of the Regimental Canteen.

Being detached Regiment, we had no Brigade Signal Troop from which to borrow signalling equipment. Even if there had been, it is highly improbable that any extra gear could have been got from them, and the usual answer to such requests would have been received, "It's not on your establishment." Accordingly, out of the Canteen Funds, we purchased extra telephones and had pack-horse carriers made for laying out and picking up wire. This trouble was well repaid during the fortnight after the 18th July, when we were enabled to keep in touch by phone with our distant nightposts at Hills 383 and 331. We were the only regiment so equipped. With the aid of our Canteen Fund, we improved on the machine gun equipment issued, with the result that we reduced very considerably the time that it took to get these guns into action.

Being a detached Regiment, we had no Brigade Signal Brigade Canteen. Arrangements were accordingly made to run a canteen of our own, and during our first three months at Dueidar the service was excellent. Our Quartermaster—Lieutenant Luxford—arranged for regular supplies from Port Said, both wet and dry. The dismounted garrison at the Post were only too anxious to deal at our Canteen, and as all goods were sold at a small advance on their cost, handsome profits were made which enabled us to purchase extra articles of equipment, such as telephones, spear pumps, water troughs, pack saddlery, etc., which were otherwise unobtainable, and give good prizes for musketry and sports. This extra gear certainly tended to the increased comfort and convenience of the men. Later on, when A.I.F. Headquarters took over the supervision of Regimental Funds, this sort of expenditure was stopped, and a very cramped interpretation was put on the words "comfort and convenience of the men." One was allowed to buy from Regimental Funds a tin of tobacco, or a tin of fruit, but not a pump to supply the men with clean water.

During this period a limited number of the men were allowed leave to Port Said. It was a tradition amongst the British Military Police that the Australian soldier was a wild and ferocious person when on leave, and had to be treated accordingly. The Military Police were therefore very prompt in arresting men on charges of alleged drunkenness or for being improperly dressed. Fortunately for our men, at this time the local commandant at Port Said had no jurisdiction to deal with these cases but had to remit them to the soldier's C.O. in the Field. So many glaring cases of unjust charges came before the C.O. of this Regiment, that in all cases of pleas of "not guilty," he insisted upon the prosecuting Military Police coming out to Dueidar to give their evidence in person.

The results, from a regimental point of view, were very satisfactory; most of the cases broke down; the Military Police got annoyed that any doubt should be cast on their testimony; they did not enjoy that ride across the Desert from Gilban to Dueidar, and accordingly desisted from worrying the 5th men for trivial irregularities.

From April, until we left Dueidar in August, 1916, extensive patrols and reconnoisances were carried out by the Light Horse. On May 6th, the 6th (Fuller) and 7th (Onslow) Regiments from Romani made a reconnoissance to El-Abd. This Regiment, less "A" Squadron, moved to Hamisah as a flank-guard to the main force, which proceeded to El-Abd. On the 10th May, "A" Squadron made a reconnoissance to Jeffeir, arriving at 4 a.m., three troops of "C" Squadron proceeding to Hill 331 in support. On the 16th May, the Brigade made a reconnoissance to Bayud and Mageibra. "B" Squadron of this Regiment proceeding to Jeffeir, as a flank-guard to the operation. "B" Squadron collected some thirty camels at Jeffeir. During these operations a Signal Station was erected on Hill 426. The weather on this occasion was exceptionally hot, numerous collapses occurring from sun-stroke in the other portions of the Brigade which proceeded to Bayud. The shade temperatures were very high, up to 120°. A temperature of 90° has been noted at 4 a.m.

On the 17th May, Colonel Royston, C.M.G., D.S.O., of the 12th Light Horse, took over command of the Dueidar Post, the 12th Regiment at that time occupying that Post as the dismounted garrison thereof. On the 18th May, a Brigade reconnoisance was made to Gedaidia, this Regiment furnishing two troop patrols from "A" Squadron to Hamisah and three troops to Hod-el-enna in support. On the 31st May, the Brigade made a reconnoisance to Salmana, this Regiment taking up a covering position at Hamisah. On June 2nd, the C.O. of this Regiment—Lieutenant-Colonel Wilson—again assumed command of the Dueidar Post from Colonel Royston, C.M.G., D.S.O. On the 5th June, 1916, the New Zealand Mounted Rifles (Chaytor) made a reconnoissance to El-Abd. "C" Squadron of this Regiment and one machine gun left Dueidar at 11 p.m. and proceeded to Hamisah as flank-guard. They left there at 9.45 a.m. and returned to Dueidar at

HISTORY OF THE 5th LIGHT HORSE REGIMENT. 71

4 p.m. On the 10th June, 1916, a general reconnoissance was made to Mageibra, Bayud and Jeffeir. "C" Squadron of this Regiment, under Major Cameron, with one troop of "A" Squadron, left at 10 p.m. on the 10th June, arriving at Jeffeir at 3.55 a.m. on the 11th, the last 5 miles in a very heavy fog. Two troops of "A" Squadron, under Captain Bolingbroke, left camp at 3 a.m., on the 11th June, and proceeded to Hill 331 in support of "C" Squadron. All troops returned to camp at 2.30 p.m., on the 11th, no enemy having been seen.

On the 12th June, the 12th Regiment returned to Dueidar dismounted, and Colonel Royston, C.M.G., D.S.O., reassumed command of the Post. On the 19th June, the C.O. of this Regiment again assumed command of the Post from Colonel Royston, C.M.G., D.S.O., who took over temporary command of the 2nd Light Horse Brigade. On the 22nd June, a composite squadron, two troops of "A" and two troops of "B," under Captain Wright, was sent to Jeffeir to surround that place at dawn with a view to capturing enemy patrols, who, it was thought, might be visiting there. The squadron did not arrive at Jeffeir until after dawn, 6.30 a.m., and no enemy were seen. The squadron returned to camp at 4.30 p.m. on the 23rd. On the 30th June, the C.O., Lieutenant-Colonel Wilson, and Major Cameron accompanied the divisional reconnoissance to El-Abd. Two patrols of the enemy were seen during these operations.

On 2nd July, 1916, information was received at Dueidar from an aeroplane report, that 50 Turks and 170 camels were seen at Jeffeir late in the afternoon. It was accordingly decided to capture this party. It was no use advancing straight on Jeffeir, and the only chance of capturing them would be to make a wide circuit and come in on Jeffeir from the East before dawn. The Regiment accordingly moved out from Dueidar at 9.50 p.m., marched to Dhaba, from there by compass bearings to a point east of Jeffeir, where we arrived at 3.15 a.m., just before dawn. The well was reconnoitered at 3.45 a.m., but there were no men or camels there. Numerous tracks of camels and a few men were observed, so Major Cameron with "C" Squadron was sent to follow them up. Whilst so doing, an aeroplane passed over and subsequently dropped a message to Major Cameron that the enemy were two miles further on in the sand ridges. Major

Cameron accordingly pressed on, the remainder of the Regiment following in support. The plane used smoke balls to show the position of the enemy. It also dropped bombs on them. The camels and men were scattered. "C" Squadron tracked them down and collected five Bedouins and 109 camels. The Regiment returned to camp, via Bada, arriving at Dueidar at 11.55 a.m., on the 3rd. The horses had thus done 40 miles without water and showed no ill-effects therefrom. This particular operation was a very satisfactory one. The country, after leaving Dhaba, was unknown to any member of the Regiment. It was rough. The march, after Dhaba, was regulated by three separate compass bearings, particular note being given to the distances marched. There is no prominent landmark at Jeffeir to mark its location. There are no palm trees there, and the name simply represents a well in the sand. Notwithstanding this, the Regiment arrived at the exact place and at the exact time required. This operation also showed the co-operation which could take place between the Air Service and the Mounted Troops. The aeroplane in this case, by dropping smoke bombs, showed us exactly where the enemy were and saved unnecessary time and exertion in looking for them. The Section Commander (General Lawrence) issued a complimentary Order on this operation, particularly referring to the co-operation above referred to.

The following is an extract from Divisional Routine Orders, of 10th July, 1916:

On the the 5th inst. at Romani, the Commander-in Chief, Sir A. J. Murray, K.C.B., K.C.M.G., C.V.D., D.S.O., made the following complimentary remarks to the G.O.C. Division which are communicated to all ranks.

> "Whatever I ask you people to do is done without the slightest hesitation and with promptness and efficiency. I have the greatest admiration for all your command.

> "My remarks apply equally to your other brigade at Serapeum."

On the 8th July, the Anzac Mounted Division (Chauvel) carried out a reconnoissance. "B" Squadron of this Regi-

HISTORY OF THE 5th LIGHT HORSE REGIMENT.

ment proceeding to Hamisah as a flank-guard. On the 14th July, notification was received that the C.O., Lieutenant-Colonel L. C. Wilson, and Major Midgley, D.S.O., had been awarded the C.M.G. for services on Gallipoli.

On the 17th July, 1916, the 3rd Scottish Horse relieved the 12th Light Horse Regiment (dismounted) at Dueidar, and Lieutenant-Colonel Moir-Byers took over command of Dueidar Post.

CHAPTER 19.

ROMANI OPERATIONS (July and August, 1916).

On the 18th July, 1918, Major-General Chaytor, the Commander of the Anzac Mounted Division, left Romani by aeroplane on a reconnaissance towards El-Abd. On the same afternoon, the 2nd Light Horse Brigade moved out from Romani, with the intention of carrying out a reconnaissance as far as El Abd. General Chaytor, from his aeroplane, observed large Turkish forces between El Abd and Oghratina; upon his return he informed the Brigade—which had then reached Katia—of his discovery. The Brigade accordingly halted at Katia for the night. Before dawn it moved eastward towards El Abd. This Regiment was not participating in the reconnaissance, but Captain McNeill, of "B" Squadron, was with the 6th Regiment to learn the local geography. It appears that the advance scouts of the Brigade shortly before dawn, near Oghratina, rode into the infanty advance guard of the Turkish force. Captain McNeill reported a few exciting moments as the Turkish infantry tried to surround the advanced horsemen, who, however, galloped over them in the first tinge of dawn back to their own supports. It appeared afterwards that this was a strong Turkish force of some 18,000 troops, under the German General, Von Kressentein, who had some weeks previously moved from Beersheba with the intention of taking possession of the Canal. The 1st and 2nd Light Horse Brigades, who were based at Romani, immediately got in contact with this Turkish force, each brigade doing a 24-hour tour of duty.

During the next fortnight, these brigades kept in close touch with the Turkish force and delayed their advance considerably. This delay enabled the Higher Command to make arrangements for a stand of the British troops at Romani.

On the 1st July, 1916, the Kantara Outpost Command had been formed under Brigadier-General the Marquis of Tullibardine. Its area included Dueidar, but special instructions were issued that the 5th Regiment was not to be embodied in the scheme of defence as the Regiment was to remain mobile.

On the Turkish invasion being reported, a Force, known as the Section Mounted Troops, under Brigadier-General Chaytor, was formed under the direct orders of the the Section Commander, General Lawrence, the command consisting of the Canterbury and Auckland Mounted Rifles, the 5th Light Horse, two squadrons of the Warwickshire Yeomanry, one squadron of the Worcestershire Yeomanry, one squadron of the Gloucester Yeomanry, and the Somerset and Leicestershire Batteries, R.H.A. In the meantime, our position in the 2nd Light Horse Brigade had been taken by the Wellington Mounted Rifles.

From the 18th July, when the Turkish force was reported until the subsequent advance after the defeat of the Turks at Romani, this Regiment was engaged in sending out strong patrols to Dhaba on the East and Aras on the South, by day. By night, posts were kept at Hill 383 (three miles) and 331 (six miles) and at a point three miles out to the east of Dueidar. Telephone wires were run out to these night posts and early warning would have been received of an attack on this particular front. Stand-to at 1.30 a.m.

On the 26th July, the Turks had a force at Mageibra. The High Command was very anxious to know where the Turkish attack was likely to eventuate: whether through Dueidar or more to the South, or whether it would be made through Romani. To keep in touch with the Turks at Mageibra, a patrol of two officers and thirty other ranks (Lieutenant Stanfield and Lieutenant Broughton) were sent to Nagid, from the 26th to the 30th. The headquarters of this patrol were at Nagid, and their duty was for one officer and four men to be day and night on the ridges overlooking Mageibra,

HISTORY OF THE 5th LIGHT HORSE REGIMENT   75

so as to keep close observation of movements there. This particular duty was well carried out by these officers. The work was exciting, as they were operating some twenty miles in front of our line of posts, and the Turks soon discovered their presence. They made numerous attempts to capture them. They were chased away temporarily on various occasions, but always came back to their posts when the Turks had retired. General Chaytor was very complimentary on the excellent way in which this work was carried out. After this four days' tour of duty officers from other units took over the duty.

On the 3rd August, the patrols watching the enemy at Mageibra reported that a large hostile force was advancing from the latter place towards Hamisah and Nagid. It was estimated that the enemy force in this vicinity towards evening was holding an outpost line on the high ridge, 2,000 yards east of Nagid, extending south-east towards Bir-Waset. Instructions were accordingly received from General Chaytor that this Regiment should reconnoitre Nagid at dawn, the object being to locate the enemy flank and to find out, if possible, his strength. Any serious engagement with the enemy was to be avoided. The Regiment accordingly left Dueidar at 12.30 a.m. on the night of the 3rd-4th. A halt was made at Nuss to consult Major Whitehorn, who was stationed there in charge of a squadron of the Auckland Mounted Rifles, which was supplying the officers' patrol watching Mageibra. This patrol was captured that night, being caught between two columns of Turkish infantry. The Regiment left Nuss at 2.45 a.m. in a south-east direction, in order to arrive at Nagid from the south. This was accomplished, and at dawn the advance guard reported Nagid "All clear." The advance guard moved on to the high ridges 2,000 yards north of Nagid. Upon reaching this position, the advance scouts detected a body of the enemy, apparently two battalions of a strength of about 1,500, marching in a north-west direction. The enemy had as protection a flank-guard and advance-guard of camel men. The enemy, seeing out advance scouts and patrols, immediately took up a position along a high ridge, between our position and the valley up which they were marching to Hod-el-enna. They opened fire with machine guns and mountain guns. We had two casualties, one being Lieutenant G. Hicks (wounded).

Having carried out our instructions of ascertaining the position of the enemy, their strength and movements, we reported by telephone to General Chaytor. In the meantime the main Turkish columns were attacking the British lines at Romani. Instructions were received from General Chaytor to proceed three miles back from Nuss on the road towards Dueidar and there await instructions from him. This movement was carried out. Touch was obtained with various signalling stations, but no instructions could be obtained or information gained as to the whereabouts of the New Zealand Brigade. After waiting there a couple of hours, the Regiment moved to the north-west of the Sand Hills. Similar efforts were here made and patrols sent out, but no information could be obtained. It afterwards appeared that a message was sent from that brigade to the Regiment to report at Canterbury Hills, but this message never arrived. Accordingly, at sun-down the Regiment returned to Dueidar to re-ration and get orders.

The presence of this Regiment at Nagid in the morning had undoubtedly a material effect on the Turkish Reserves. It subsequently appeared that they were stationed that night at Marieah, and two battalions seen by us were, no doubt, part of that Reserve marching to reinforce the attack at Et Maler. We were afterwards informed that, upon the fire opening at Nagid, there was a cessation for two hours of reinforcements to the Turkish firing-line.

At 7.30 p.m. Brigadier-General Antill with the 3rd Light Horse Brigade arrived at Dueidar from the south, and instructions were received that this Regiment should be attached to him for the time being. On the morning of the 5th, the 3rd Light Horse Brigade, plus this Regiment, marched from Dueidar to Nuss. On arrival there, we joined up with the New Zealand Brigade and again came under the command of the Brigadier of that unit.

At 10 a.m. the New Zealand Brigade (Chaytor), including this Regiment marched towards Katia along the telegraph line. The 3rd Brigade (Antill) marched towards Hamisah. The 1st Brigade (Meredith) and 2nd Brigade

(Royston) and 5th Mounted Brigade (Yeomanry) were marching towards Katia from Romani.

It should be here remarked that on the previous evening at sunset the Turkish attack at Romani had been repulsed with heavy losses, both in killed and prisoners, and that the remnants of the Turkish force had retired towards Katia.

When the New Zealand Brigade, to which we temporarily belonged, had arrived within a couple of miles of Katia Oasis, the Brigadier (Chaytor) sent for the C.O. and informed him that the five mounted brigades were going to charge Katia Oasis and rush the Turkish position mounted. The General pointed out the fronts to be attacked by the New Zealand Brigade and explained that a battery of heavy Austrian guns were supposed to be amongst certain palm trees to our front. The 5th Regiment was accordingly instructed to gallop the Turkish position and they would be supported by one of the New Zealand regiments, the idea being that the other four mounted brigades were to charge in on our flanks. The Regiment was accordingly formed in two lines, "A" and "B" Squadrons in the front line, and "C" Squadron in the second line, the squadrons being in line of troop columns; the ground to be covered was sand, over which was scattered small brush. Bayonets were drawn and fixed on the rifles, which were to be used as lances. Orders were issued that on approaching the Turkish position the troops would gallop up into line and the Regiment would sweep through the Turkish position. The Regiment accordingly moved off at a fast trot, with bayonets fixed, over a distance of about a mile and a half. Within half a mile of the objective the troops galloped into line, and the Regiment charged the oasis. A splendid line was kept, the Regiment moving with the precision of a peace manoeuvre. As a matter of fact, the guns had been removed from that part of the Oasis which we attacked, and when we arrived there, there were only some dozen Turks who were taken prisoners. As we approached our objective, machine guns, rifle fire, and artillery opened on us from the Turkish position further to the rear. We had now gained our objective, and it was apparent that the other brigades were not charging in (mounted) as anticipated. This being so, it was useless for this Regiment alone to charge across the open country to the main position of the Turks. The Regiment was accordingly dismounted, and we worked towards the right and went into action against the Turkish position. It was found that the main Katia Oasis was strongly held with machine guns and artillery. The ridges immediately to the south were also strongly held. We moved about a mile to the south-east edge of the Oasis, but by doing so, we found we were being enfiladed from the right. A small patrol from the 3rd Light Horse Brigade was noted on the ridges to the right, but that is all we saw of them. It subsequently appeared that the 3rd Brigade stopped at Hamisah and did not take up the position allotted to them in the general scheme. The three brigades on our left did not push in and accordingly, at dusk, the order was given to retire to Romani for water. It was well after dark before we had collected our wounded, buried our dead, and got the Regiment formed up. We afterwards learnt that the enemy retired at the same time that we did. During this afternoon we had 28 casualties, including the following officers:—Majors Wright and Bolingbroke, Captains Chatham, McNeill and Plant, and Lieutenant Waite, all wounded.

There was no water available for the horses in the neighbourhood, as the Turks held the water in the Katia Oasis. It was therefore necessary to proceed back to Romani. We arrived there shortly before dawn. There was a great demand for the limited amount of water available, and it was sunrise before our horses were watered. By the time that was complete, orders were received to move back to Katia again. Accordingly, at 6 a.m. on the 6th August, the Brigade again moved on to Katia. This we found evacuated by the enemy and held by our infantry. The weather was very hot, the sand was very soft, the "going" consequently bad. There was no water between Katia and Romani, and some of the infantry were in a lamentable condition from thirst and sunstroke.

We moved on to Um-Ugba, where we found that the enemy had occupied a strong position at Oghratina, which they had prepared prior to advancing on Romani. The Brigade was under shell fire, but we only suffered one casualty from this. On the night of the 6th-7th August, we bivouacked at El-Rabah. The following morning we again moved towards Oghratina, where we found the enemy still holding the same position. We were again subjected to shell fire, suffering one casualty. We camped at El-Rabah again on the night of the 7th-8th August.

On the morning of the 8th August, we again advanced towards Oghratina, this Regiment forming the advance guard. Oghratina was found to be "all clear." We now discovered how it was that the enemy had been able to bring guns—including some long-range 4.2's—across the Desert. In parts, we found long stretches of pine planking—ten inches wide by two thick—laid parallel, the width of the gun wheels apart. Apparently, these planks would be laid down, the guns drawn over them, then the planks picked up and carried to the front again, a tedious, but yet effective process. In other parts they had laid down two parallel narrow strips of brushwood, one strip for each set of wheels. This system was adopted where the brush was handy.

We moved on towards Dababis, picking up 25 stragglers, including a German ambulance conductor; large quantities of abandoned stores and ammunition were also collected. The Brigade camped that night at Dababis, this Regiment supplying the outposts. The enemy were found to be in strength at El-Abd. Several officers' patrols were sent out during the night, South, East, and North-east, and did very good work, one patrol (Lieutenant Graham's) riding over a Turkish outpost. The whole of his patrol, however, got back without casualties. On the 9th August it was decided to attack the Turkish position at El-Abd. The New Zealand Brigade (to which we were still attached) was ordered to make a frontal attack from the West, along the telegraph line, supported by the 3rd Brigade (Antill) on the right-flank, and 1st Brigade (Meredith) and 2nd Brigade (Royston) on the left, with the 5th Mounted (Yeomanry) Brigade in reserve. The Auckland Mounted Rifles and the Canterbury Mounted Rifles got into position and began the attack at 6.30 a.m.

At the beginning of the operations, this Regiment was in reserve and in support to the guns. Shortly after the attack commenced, the Machine Gun Section, under Lieutenant Cain, was sent forward into the firing-line with the Auckland Regiment, together with one troop of "C" Squadron, under Lieutenant Boyd. The balance of "C" Squadron, under Major Cameron, was sent to the extreme right of the Brigade line, covering the flank of the Auckland Rifles. Two troops of "B" Squadron were sent as escort to the guns and one troop as escort to the ammunition, two of these troops being subsequently brought up to the firing-line, one on the right with "C" Squadron, and the other on the left with the remainder of the Regiment. The remainder of the Regiment, consisting of "A" Squadron and portion of "B" Squadron, were sent up on the left of the brigade line to support the Canterburys and to keep in touch with the 1st and 2nd Brigades. It thus happened that during this day's fighting, part of the Regiment was on the extreme right of the Brigade and the balance on the extreme left. The 3rd Brigade did not come up on the right-flank of the line as anticipated. It appears they met strong opposition and were not able to take up their allotted place. The result of this was that the Turks started to out-flank the New Zealand Brigade line occupied by "C" Squadron, and some very brisk fighting at very close quarters ensued, there being a distance of yards only between the opposing men. On our left flank touch was obtained with the 2nd Brigade. Fighting continued throughout the day. The enemy's numbers were greatly in excess of ours and their artillery was very active. Late in the afternoon, a determined counter-attack was made by the enemy. They opened an extremely heavy artillery and machine gun fire on the 2nd Brigade, to our left. That brigade was forced back, which resulted in our left flank being open. As a gap was now occurring in the Division's line our left flank was thrown back to prevent the Turks getting in behind our left rear. Shortly after this, instructions were received from General Chaytor that the whole force would retire. The Division accordingly retired to Oghratina. During the day we collected 13 prisoners. Our casualties for the day amounted to 37, including Major Johnstone and Lieutenants Wood and Graham wounded. Sergeant Hector McLean was subsequently awarded the D.C.M. for his gallantry during these operations.

On the 10th August the Brigade again advanced to Dababis. The C.M.R. Regiment reconnoitered El-Abd and found the enemy still in possession.

On the 11th August this Regiment reconnoitered E-Abd and found the enemy still holding the same line in strength

HISTORY OF THE 5th LIGHT HORSE REGIMENT.

and displaying great activity with camel trains on the road towards Salmana. The Regiment was shelled during the day. We here observed a fight between two aeroplanes. The day was slightly cloudy, and one of our aeroplanes was circling over El-Abd reporting the enemy movements. Without any warning, a German aeroplane swooped like a hawk from the clouds and emptied his machine gun into our plane and disappeared again. Our plane turned round and volplaned towards the rear of our lines, one of the crew having been killed and the other seriously wounded.

On the 12th August the Brigade advanced through El-Abd, and it was found that the Turks had retired to Salmana. All our dead from the Battle of Abd were buried and crosses put over their graves.

Officers' patrols were sent out during the night, under Lieutenants Broughton, Billington and Boyd.

On the 13th August the Regiment reconnoitered Salmana. Lieutenant Broughton with a patrol of six, who had gone out at 2 a.m., entered Salmana at 5 a.m., taking three prisoners there. There was no other sign of the enemy. A phial was picked up at Geeila Oasis, and it was subsequently ascertained that same contained live cholera germs from a Berlin laboratory. Whether these germs were being carried about for medical experiments or whether they were for purposes of polluting the water, was a matter of doubt. On the evening of the 13th August, the Regiment was relieved at El-Abd by the Auckland Mounted Rifles and returned to Dababis, where the Brigade headquarters were stationed.

It was now decided by the Higher Command that it was impracticable for the mounted troops to follow the Turks any further at present. We were too far from our base and there was not sufficient camel transport available to supply a mobile column.

On the 14th August, 1916, the Brigade shifted camp to Amara, where General Chauvel addressed the Brigade and expressed great satisfaction with regard to the work of the Division throughout these operations. These operations had been very severe on the horses. The water supply was not as good as it might be, and accordingly 100 sick, wounded and knocked-up horses with the necessary complement of men were sent back to Dueidar. Parties were also sent there to bring back clothing for all ranks. When the Regiment left Dueidar on the morning of the 5th August, it was not anticipated that they would be out for more than a short reconnaissance, consequently they had only those clothes which they rode out in and most of them were without tunics and overcoats; the result was that by the end of the operations at Salmana, a large number of them were almost naked. The Regiment's casualties for these ten days operations had amounted to 8 other ranks killed, 10 officers and 49 other ranks wounded.

The following is a copy of a report in the diary of a Turkish officer captured during the Romani operations, of an encouraging speech made by Djemal Pasha at Beersheba on 1st July, on the eve of the departure of the Turkish Army to the Canal:

"Brave soldiers, you are going into the Desert. I ask you to have patience and perseverance. You will return bearing your arms in victory or you will leave your bones in the Desert. Everything is bad in the Desert, hunger, nakedness, dirt, every privation, therefore, I ask you to have courage and perseverance. O! my soldiers."

On the 19th August the Regiment moved out at 2 a.m. on reconnoissance to Ganadil and Geisi, aeroplanes having reported that there were small parties of hostile camel-men at these places the previous day. The Regiment marched direct to Salmana, then two miles due East, then swung round to come in on Ganadil from the rear. Ganadil was found all clear of the enemy. "C" Squadron, under Lieutenant Boyd, then proceeded to reconnoitre Geisi, which was also found to be clear. An observation post on the left flank—Trooper Axelson of "B" Squadron—having reported seeing two or three men moving on the edge of the Bardawill, five miles north-east of Salmana, "C" Squadron was sent out to investigate, it being thought that they were hostile Bedouin. The remainder of the Regiment, after watering at Ganadil, returned to Salmana to feed horses. At 1.30 p.m., a message was received from Lieutenant Boyd that his Squadron had captured 68 Turkish soldiers, who were in a very exhausted condition for want of water. These prisoners were brought to Salmana. It appears they were reinforcements discharged from hospital at El-Arish, that they had marched from that place with the intention of reporting to the 31st Regiment at Mazar. They had no guides, however, and missed that place and overmarched it by some 16 miles. They were in a very bad condition when our squadron met them, and showed no fight. Owing to their weak condition, the members of the Regiment dismounted from their own horses and gave them a lift for three miles, where we met ambulance waggons which, in the meantime, we had sent for.

On the 25th August, 1916, the New Zealand Mounted Rifle Brigade reconnoitered the ground north of Salmana to Mat-Eblis and the Island of Galss, with the object of capturing any hostile forces that might be there and of destroying enemy property. A composite squadron of the 5th Regiment, under Major Cameron, accompanied the column. The column moved across the salt pans of the Bardawil, and in due course arrived at Galss. The travelling was bad, owing to the existence of large salt crystals on the salt pans which were very severe on the horses' feet. The column returned to Amara at 8 p.m., having found the country reconnoitered clear of the enemy. The water available at Galss was very limited, and the column had to depend upon the spear pump carried by our squadron.

While at Amara on the 23rd August, our Machine Gun Section (two maxim guns) marched out to form part of the newly constituted 2nd Brigade Machine Gun Squadron of 12 guns, the Regiment having been supplied with three Lewis guns—one per squadron—on the 2nd August.

On the 27th August, 1916, the Regiment took over the front outpost line. "A" Squadron proceeded to Hod-El-Bada, "C" Squadron to Hod-El-Hisha, and the Regimental Headquarters with "B" Squadron took over the post near Abd. On the 27th August a Turkish patrol was picked up by Lieutenant Ryan at Salmana. The patrol stated they had received instructions to patrol from Mazar, but had decided to come in and give themselves up.

The squadrons at Hisha and Bada changed camp each night, with a view of misleading any possible raid thereon.

On the 30th August, 1916, 100 men with 109 horses reported from Dueidar. These horses took the place of those that had been knocked up during the late operations. Patrols were sent out daily from our three squadron posts and at various times picked up Turkish patrols and deserters.

On the 3rd September the Regiment was relieved on this front line and moved to Hod-El-Fatir, and became attached to the 3rd Light Horse Brigade (Brigadier-General Royston, C.M.G., D.S.O.).

On the 11th the Regiment took over an outpost line from the 9th Regiment and occupied same until the 16th idem. While holding the posts, the Squadron supplied the usual outposts with Cossack posts, etc., by day and night. On the 11th September, the 2nd Brigade (Ryrie) relieved the 3rd Brigade and took up its headquarters at Hassaniya. This Regiment now rejoined its own Brigade—the 2nd. Patrols were sent out from day to day.

CHAPTER 20.

MAZAR (September, 1916).

On the 16th September orders were received to operate against the Turkish advance garrison at Mazar. These operations were to be undertaken by the Anzac Mounted Division (Major-General Chauvel). Accordingly, on the 16th September, the Regiment, less one squadron then on outpost, left Fatir at 2.5 a.m. The outpost squadron joined the Regiment at Bada. The Brigade arrived at Geeila at dawn. It remained there during the day under cover of the palms. Our aeroplanes were active with a view of preventing Turkish reconnoissance, but overdid their work, as the unusual aerial activity on our part, we heard afterwards, caused the Turks to come to the conclusion that an offensive was in hand. The Brigade left Geeila at 4.45 p.m. This Regiment formed the advance-guard. At a point on the southern road, north of Hill 157, the 3rd Light Horse Brigade (Royston) moved south-east, with a view of attacking Mazar from the east. The 2nd Brigade moved on east, this Regiment forming the advance-guard as before. When within about two miles of Mazar instructions were received for this Regiment to reconnoitre the enemy. Arriving at a line running north and south through Hill 30, our advance scouts located two enemy outposts, one on the road and one half a mile to the north. Two troops then advanced dismounted on the south post and three troops were sent to outflank it on the right, the machine guns taking up position to cover the advance. One troop was sent north to Point 50. Before the attacking troops could reach the enemy outposts, the enemy retired on camels. It was now dawn. The Regiment then advanced to a ridge overlooking Mazar. Three troops of "A" Squadron advanced on the right and two troops of "C" Squadron to the front, 1000 yards further on. The left flank of the advance line was within 200 yards of the enemy trenches and the right flank was within 800 yards. Rifle fire and machine gun fire was opened on the enemy. A message was then received from the Brigade that Mazar was said to be to the south and for the Regiment not to advance any further east. It appears that this information was obtained from a native Egyptian guide, who alleged he knew the country. As a matter of fact, he was wrong. Mazar, which was a locality, not a village, was really in our immediate front. The instructions given to the 3rd Brigade was that their objective was to be reached at 6 a.m. The Camel Brigade was supposed to cooperate with the Division, but for some reason it did not put in an appearance until after the 3rd Brigade had withdrawn.

At 6.10 a.m. the C.O. intercepted a message from the 3rd Brigade that it had decided to withdraw. Shortly afterwards, we received a message to keep the 3rd Brigade in view and conform. The C.O. then intercepted a message from the 7th Regiment to the Brigade that the 3rd Brigade was retiring and that the 7th Regiment was withdrawing. Our advance squadrons were accordingly withdrawn to conform. General Chauvel and General Ryrie then arrived at R.H.Q., and gave instructions that we were not to retire beyond our then position until satisfied that the 3rd Brigade and the 7th Regiment had retired. On ascertaining that those two units had retired and that the batteries had done so also, the Regiment escorted the guns to the rendezvous. During the latter part of our stay at Mazar, the enemy anti-aircraft guns were converted into field pieces and shelled us.

The Regiment marched to a point north of Moseifig,

where it halted for water. Water, as a matter of fact, had been brought out by a large number of camels for the column, but owing to defective arrangements, the first units to the watering supply drank all the water and there was none left for the second half. One squadron only of this Unit watered, and the remainder being unable to obtain any moved on to Salmana, arriving at 7 p.m. Here we got water. We camped until 3.30 a.m. the following morning, and then moved on to Hassaniya with the Brigade. Our casualties during these operations were one man killed and three wounded.

On the 24th September a census of the Regiment was taken, which showed that 160 of the original members of the Regiment were then with the Unit in the field.

CHAPTER 21.

DUEIDAR (October-November, 1916).

On the 29th September, 1916, the Regiment moved from Fatir to Romani and then on to Dueidar, where it arrived on the 2nd October. During October and up to the 28th November, the Regiment was engaged in re-organising and recuperating and in clipping horses. We were liable for a few short patrols, but they were of no great severity. Training was entered upon, both for officers and men. A course of musketry, which took the form of competitions and which practically every man in the Regiment joined in, was carried out with excellent results as to accuracy and smartness in musketry.

Three rifle and one revolver match with the local infantry garrison were held, all of which were won by the Regiment. During October, 6 officers and 212 other ranks had leave to Sidi Bishar, the Change-of-Air Camp at Alexandria. Several officers were sent to the Cavalry School which had been instituted at Zeitoun, Cairo. About this time, the Regiment adopted a regimental badge, the design of S.Q.M.S. Maxwell of "A" Squadron—an emu within the letter "Q" with a wattle wreath and underneath a boomerang with the words "5th Light Horse Regiment, A.I.F." We also acquired another flag, the first one having been worn out. This second flag consisted of the regimental badge worked in the centre of the regimental colours, blue over red, and was presented to us by the ladies of the 5th L.H. Comfort Fund at Brisbane.

CHAPTER 22.

HASSANIYA-MASAID (November, 1916-February, 1917).

On the 28th November, 1916, the Regiment left Dueidar for Hassaniya, Dueidar Post being taken over by the Gloucester Yeomanry. The Regiment marched via Romani and Khirba, and on the 30th camped at Batar, an oasis near Hassaniya.

Something may be here said of the Railway, the Pipe Line, and the Wire Road.

In the early part of 1916 the laying of the broad gauge railway (4ft. 8½in.) was started at Kantara for Palestine. It practically followed the old caravan route to Syria—Darb Sultani. In was constructed by the Army engineers, the unskilled labour being furnished by the Egyptian Labour Corps. Volunteers with technical railway knowledge were called for from the Australian units and a limited number were attached for the duty of supervision on this railway construction. There were no engineering difficulties to be overcome and the railway was pushed on as rapidly as material could be supplied. The enemy aeroplanes frequently bombed the working parties with a view of delaying the construction, but on the whole, they did very little damage. Mounted troops were always some 20 miles ahead of the railhead protecting it from the interference by raiding parties of the enemy. We naturally gained great benefit from the proximity of the railway, as it meant that the camel convoys had only a day's march to go.

With the railway went the Pipe Line. This was a big water-main which started from the Sweet Water Canal at Kantara and finally finished up within a few miles of the Wadi Ghuzze, Palestine. Filtered water was forced through these pipes and was made available to those troops west of the Wadi Ghuzze, who had no good drinking water from other sources. This water was not used to any extent by the mounted troops, who, as above stated, were usually well ahead of the rail-head or were well out on the flanks and got their own water. Attempts were occasionally made by the enemy aeroplanes to bomb this line, and we know of one occasion when they landed well in rear of our front line in close proximity to the pipe line with a view of dynamiting it, but were chased off by a patrol before they could do any damage.

With the railway and pipe line ran the Wire Road. This consisted of four widths of three-foot wire netting laced together to make a 12-foot width and then pegged down on the sand. It formed a first-class road for infantry to march on and for light motors to drive on. This road was available to relieve the railway if the occasion ever required it. Branch roads were run off to the various infantry camps and garrison sites. As a matter of fact, the mounted troops never used it. The horses' shoes were liable to cut the netting.

It may be here remarked that the High Command were taking no risks in case of a possible offensive by the enemy. While waiting for the railway to be constructed, the energies of the infantry were employed at various places along the line of advance in preparing defensive systems in which millions of sand-bags were employed in rivetting the trenches and redoubts on the sand hills. As we now know, these defensive systems were not subsequently required, but "better be sure than sorry" is a good motto for soldiers as well as civilians.

In addition to the wire roads, experiments were made in other forms of roads in the desert. One was to make a road covered with palm leaves. It was too uneven for infantry to march on it, and it was not satisfactory for artillery to drive on. The palm leaves had big spikes which pricked the horses' feet; moreover, there were not enough palm leaves available within a reasonable distance in the desert to make many miles of road. Attempts were also made to make roads covered with brush. These, however, were not satisfactory, as they required too much attention.

For the next nine weeks the Brigade occupied the Hassaniya District, the headquarters of the Brigade being at the oasis of that name. The Brigade's duty was to watch the flank towards the Maghara Hills, past which the central route through the Sinai led to the Suez Canal. These hills were supposed to be occupied by Turkish parties, and unless watched, it was always possible that the enemy could send in a mobile column to interfere with our communications back to the Canal. The rest of the Anzac Mounted Division were operating out to the front, and during the period in question, the actions at Magdhaba and Rafa took place.

While in this area, the usual military precautions were adopted, the Regiment "standing to" and saddling up before dawn and remaining so until the "all clear" was reported.

Bivouacs were made in oases with the aid of palm leaves and old bags, tents not being available. Up to Christmas Day, the weather was good, but on that day it started to rain, and it rained off and on until the 7th January, 1917, when it again cleared up. There was usually a cold wind, and to prevent this adversely affecting the horses, wind-brakes were made of palm leaves across the oases.

From the 2nd December, 1916, to the end of the month, one squadron was detached to Gamal, being relieved every seven days, and while there, was placed under the orders of the C.O., 6th Light Horse Regiment at Bayud for operations only. While there, the squadron in question supplied night outposts and observation posts and short patrols. The only duties supplied by the Regiment at Batar was one day observation post and local outposts of two troops and camel escorts to Mageibra, Bayud and Gamal.

On the 12th December, 1916, the Regiment proceeded to Khirba for the purpose of being deloused. The original idea was to have the clothing of all ranks steamed and the men themselves put through a dip. On arrival at Khirba, it was ascertained that there was a shortage of water and the dip part of the operation was cut out, the men's clothing being put into a special railway truck and steamed for an hour.

During the month, Brigade sports took place at Hassaniya, consisting mostly of horse items, such as races, wrestling on horseback, etc., and a few items, such as jumping, the sand being too soft for foot running.

On the 2nd January, 1917, the Regiment, less two squadrons, moved to Geeila, the squadron at Gamal remaining there and coming back under the command of the C.O. One squadron was detached to Geisi, this Regiment taking over Geeila and Geisi from the 17th Camel Company.

On the 3rd January, 1917, the post at Geisi was reduced from a squadron to two troops owing to difficulty in watering the full squadron at that place.

On the 6th January a patrol of four men proceeded to El-Risha and brought in three Bedouin and 24 camels. These Bedouin and camels were let go shortly afterwards under instructions from Headquarters, as it was ruled that they were peaceful, and it was not desired to interfere with the few inhabitants more than necessary. We had our own ideas, however, about the peacefulness of these Bedouin, as on several occasions we found traces of their patrols having scouted our outpost lines. If these gentry's intentions were so peaceful, we wondered why they went to the trouble of coming 10 to 15 miles to peer into our camps.

On the 16th January, 1917, the Regiment was inspected by General Chauvel, the Divisional Commander, who expressed himself well satisfied with what he saw.

On the 24th January an inter-regimental football match between the 5th and 7th Regiments took place. It resulted in a tie, and both sides were satisfied.

During January, arrangements were made for a regimental relay race, each troop to supply 30 competitors, 200 yard laps, substantial prizes to be given from the Canteen Fund. These races created a lot of interest, and it meant that practically the whole Regiment went into training for the event, with excellent results to their staying power. As a matter of fact, the race did not come off as the Regiment moved before the day fixed for same.

During this month, training, particularly with the Lewis gun, was carried out. We had given special attention to the equipment of the Lewis gun with a view to its rapid coming into and going out of action. Special equipment was either made or purchased from Regimental Funds with the result that, although the guns were on their packs and moving at the gallop, they could be got into action and firing 20 seconds after the command "action" was given.

Up to this time no Turkish cavalry had been seen in the Sinai Desert. A few camels only had been noticed. It was now reported that the Turks were bringing into the Sinai a cavalry division of 3,000 sabres. The Regiment was drilled in preparing to meet cavalry attacks. As the Regiment was not equipped with the sword or lance, the training consisted

HISTORY OF THE 5th LIGHT HORSE REGIMENT. 91

chiefly of rapid dismounting by troops and forming rings of riflemen round the horses.

On the 20th January, 1917, the Regiment concentrated at Geeila, the squadron at Gamal and the detachment at Gesei being brought in. On the 2nd February, the Regiment left Geeila and arrived at Moseifig with the rest of the Brigade en route to Mazar. This was the first time we had been with our own Brigade since the previous April, having been camped away from them since that date. On the 3rd February, we arrived at Mazar, a place which most of us remembered from our experiences there in the previous September. The place had nothing to show for itself except a broken-down tomb—that of Abu Gilban. Our Brigadier very truly remarked that it looked like the remains of an old chimney.

We remained at Mazar for five days. On the 6th February, a mild excitement developed owing to the report that a squadron of Turkish cavalry had been noticed out on the sand hills to the east. Investigations, however, showed that there was no justification for the report. On the 8th February, we left Mazar and, marching via Bardawil, arrived at Mas'aid on the 10th February.

Mas'aid has a very large oasis near the beach. We remained in this camp until the 21st February. During this period we were supplied with tents, which were very acceptable, as it frequently rained. We were subsequently accused of cutting down palm trees in this oasis, and were made to pay damages for same out of Regimental Funds. As a matter of fact, it was one of the very few oases in which we did not cut down palm trees, as in this particular place, as above stated, we had tents and there was no need to use palm leaves for wind-brakes or shacks.

On the 17th February a rugby football match was arranged between the New Zealanders and the 2nd Brigade. This match the New Zealanders won by 6 points to nil.

CHAPTER 23.

RAFA (February and March, 1917).

On the 22nd February, 1917, we marched eastwards, passed through El Arish, crossed the Wadi El Arish, and arrived at Sheikh Zowaiid. We had now arrived on the border of the cultivated land. The country was under grass and crops and was beautifully green after the winter rains. For the first time since leaving the Delta, we saw wild flowers, poppies, daisies and lillies.

After remaining a few hours at Sheikh Zowaiid, we moved on on a reconnoissance towards Khan Yunus, the force consisting of the New Zealand Mounted Rifle Brigade (Chaytor) and the 2nd Light Horse Brigade (Ryrie). We moved at 1 a.m. on the morning of the 23rd, our Brigade in support of the New Zealanders. While the latter Brigade engaged the enemy about two miles south of Khan Yunus, this Regiment was posted on the flank as a guard towards the East facing Shellal, where the enemy had a large force of infantry. A few shots were exchanged with the enemy's patrols without casualties to this Regiment.. The Regiment acted as a left flank-guard to the force on its return to camp. The Regiment moved on to the beach opposite Sheikh Zowaiid with the rest of the Brigade.

On the 25th February, 1917, the Regiment was engaged on a reconnoissance to Rafa.

On the 27th the Brigade left camp at 6 a.m. and marched to El Badari, 15 miles to the east, and formed a screen while various parties surveyed the country.

On the march out our Regiment furnished one squadron (right flank-guard) and one squadron (left flank-guard). While the various parties were engaged in their tasks, the northern flank of the area (10 miles in length) was covered by "A" Squadron, and the southern flank of the area (10 miles) by "B" Squadron. While extended on these flanks, a few shots were exchanged with the enemy's cavalry patrols, but without casualties to this Regiment. One of our patrols of four tried to induce a Turkish cavalry troop to attack it. The Turks lowered lances and charged, but turned back after going a few yards, when their bluff was called.

We saw evidence of our friends, the "friendly" Arab. On the march out numerous smoke fires were seen arising which we had every reason to believe were messages to the Turkish force that we were coming. We also saw where the Bedouin had dug up the bodies of our men killed in the Rafa battle, presumably for the sake of their clothing, and left the bodies to the mercy of the numerous Jackals which infest this country.

On the 2nd March, 1917, the Brigade moved out form Khan Yunus with a view of having the country in that locality surveyed and reconnoitered. We left camp at 6 a.m., "A" Squadron moving along the beach road to Tel-el-Marakeb. The remainder of the Regiment formed the advance-guard to the east of the sand ridges. When the advance-guard passed east of Beni Sela, adjoining Khan Yunus, it was fired on from the eastward. Six snipers were taken prisoners here. The vanguard then moved on and occupied a line running east and west through Hill 30, gaining touch with the beach squadron.

Khan Yunus is a small native town in the middle of a big cultivated area. The fences of the allotments consist of cactus hedges. The town itself is full of very narrow lanes, so that we kept out of it as much as possible in our reconnaissances. There is a fine Crusaders' church in the town in a fair state of repair, said to have been built by Richard I. of England. While on this operation, Lieutenant Hicks made a reconnoissance of the sand hills from Rafa to Tel-el Marakeb. While at Khan Yunus, one long-range shell from Weli-Sheikh-Nuran, distant eight miles, dropped within a few yards of our main guard at Beni-Sela, but without doing any damage. The country moved over was covered with wheat and barley, interspersed with wild-flowers: poppies, lilies, buttercups, daisies and English clover. The Regiment returned to camp without any casualties.

On the 5th March, 1917, the Brigade moved out to make good Khan Yunus, El Fukhari and Abassan-el-Kebir. This Regiment formed the right flank-guard. A patrol was sent to El Fukhari, where an enemy patrol of 10 men was seen, but we did not get in touch with them. We duly returned to camp without any casualties.

On the 8th March the Regiment with the rest of the Brigade moved from Hamthala to Abu Shunnar, a distance of five miles along the beach. The reason for camping on the beach was the excellent water supply there. There was practically no water on the cultivated land to the east of the sand ridges, but between the sand ridges and the sea, good water could be obtained within a few inches of the surface.

On the 10th March, 1917, the Brigade proceeded to Belah to cover reconnaissances of roads and country. "A" Squadron of this Regiment formed the advance-guard, and proceeded three miles north of Belah. One troop of "C" Squadron formed the Brigade right flank-guard. Reconnaissances were duly made, but no enemy were seen.

On the 13th March another reconnaissance was made towards Weli-Sheikh-Nuran. This was a strongly fortified Turkish position, but it had now been evacuated, the enemy retiring across the Wadi Ghuzze. The position would have been very hard to have captured owing to the country being clear for some miles in front of it. We found their trenches in excellent order and in front of a lot of them were three rows of "wolf pits" in lieu of wire; these pits were about six feet deep, and the three rows were so close together that it was impossible to walk between them. The Nuran position was also well equipped with shell-proof shelters. The Turks, we subsequently ascertained, gave as their reason for vacating the position that they were short of men to hold such a large front, and that their expected reinforcement had not yet come down. They accordingly gave up the position without a blow. After examining the late Turkish positions, the Regiment returned to camp, after a 30-mile ride, without having seen any enemy. For the next ten days, the Regiment remained on the beach, the horses being sent out in the meantime on to the cultivated land east of the sand hills, where they were fed on the growing crops of barley and wheat. During one of the grazing excursions, 300 of the horses stampeded, and some of them galloped for ten miles before they were headed off.

At this period there took place a large increase in the mounted troops—two mounted divisions were formed. The Anzac Mounted Division under General Chauvel consisting of the 1st Light Horse Brigade (Cox). 2nd Light Horse Brigade

(Ryrie), New Zealand Mounted Rifle Brigade (Chaytor), and the 22nd Mounted (Yeomanry) Brigade (Fryer) and the Imperial Mounted Division under General Hodgson consisting of the 3rd Light Horse Brigade (Royston), 4th Light Horse Brigade (Meredith), 5th Mounted (Yeomanry) Brigade (Wiggins), and the 6th Mounted (Yeomanry) Brigade (Pitt).

To the Anzac Mounted Division were attached the Inverness, Ayrshire, Leicester and Somerset Batteries, and to the Imperial Division the Berks and Notts, and "A" and "B" of the H.A.C. Batteries.

CHAPTER 24.

GAZA (First)—March, 1917.

On the 25th March, 1917, the Brigade (Ryrie) moved at 2.30 a.m. to the operations which resulted in the First Battle of Gaza. We arrived next morning at Belah and left that place on the 26th in the evening with the rest of the Anzac Mounted Division (Chauvel). The scheme was that the infantry were to attack Gaza from the south and southeast at 6 a.m., the mounted troops in the meantime having broken through their thinly held line east of Gaza, closed the roads to the north, and so prevented the garrison from getting away. A thick fog covered the country in the early morning for some time after sunrise. This, the mounted troops thought rather an advantage, as it enabled them to get well on towards their objective before their presence was discovered by the enemy. Our men were quite capable of finding their way by compass. The infantry subsequently blamed the fog as the chief cause of their failure. The Division moved to Beit Durdis, the 2nd Brigade in the advance. Two troops of "A" Squadron of this Regiment formed the Brigade flank-guard. When Beit Durdis was reached, "B" Squadron was detached to outflank snipers who were firing on the advance-guard. That squadron moved out two miles and captured seven waggons and thirteen prisoners. Divisional Headquarters remained at Beit Durdis. The Brigade then moved on to west of Jabalie, about three miles northeast of Gaza, the 7th Regiment (Onslow) forming the advance-guard. When they came to the main Jafa-Gaza Road, they captured a Turkish Divisional Commander and his staff who were then moving into Gaza to take command at that post. The 7th Regiment, with two troops of "A" Squadron of this Regiment, moved on to the sand hills and the beach to block the prospective refugees. The 6th Regiment (Fuller) was posted some two miles to the northward to prevent Turkish reinforcements coming down the Jafa-Gaza Road.

The country, as it appeared from our position north-east of Gaza, was as follows:—A ridge ran from Jabalie to the Turkish position at Ali Muntar. Open sand ridges ran close to the beach and parallel to the last mentioned ridge. Between the Jabalie-Ali Muntar Ridge and the sand ridges was a valley running to the rear of the main Gaza town. The south-east side of this valley consisted of an olive grove, and the north-west side consisted of small allotments fenced with cactus hedges in which were numerous villages.

On occupying our position as above mentioned, a troop of "A" Squadron, with two troops of the Machine Gun Squadron, were sent forward some 300 yards as observation post. A body of Turkish infantry, estimated at one battalion, was seen marching towards our position through the cactus. The troop and the machine gun opened on them and inflicted numerous casualties, and the Turkish battalion dispersed amongst the hedges.

In the meantime, the main infantry attack by one division and one brigade on the south and south-east of Gaza was developing. The original intention of the Commander-in-Chief was that Gaza should be captured by the infantry and that the mounted troops in the rear should simply prevent the enemy from escaping. The scene in front of us was most spectacular. The infantry could be seen advancing to attack. The country was open and undulating, it afforded no cover. Our people were under a hail of Turkish shell, machine gun and rifle fire, and they were not making the progress that had been anticipated. At 2.30 p.m, the New Zealand Brigade arrived from Beit Durdis and moved on to the ridge running between our position and Ali Muntar. It had been decided that the mounted troops should attack the rear of Gaza to assist the infantry who were now held up in front.

General Ryrie's Orders to Lieutenant-Colonel Wilson,

the C.O. of this Regiment, were to co-operate with the New Zealanders in the attack on the rear of Gaza and to go in as far as possible. At this time, the 6th Regiment was watching the roads leading from Jafa, while the 7th Regiment was on the beach and the sand hills. Accordingly, at 2.30 p.m., the Regiment was ordered to fix bayonets, with the intention of galloping into the rear of the town of Gaza. Major Chatham with "C" Squadron galloped down the Jafa-Gaza Road, which runs through the olive grove mentioned, closely followed by "B" Squadron under Major Newton, and the remainder of the Regiment. As soon as we appeared in the open on the road, the Regiment was heavily shelled and fired on. Fire was opened from the cactus hedges and native villages to the right by remnants of the Turkish battalions that had been dispersed earlier in the day. Lieutenant Waite, who was on the right of the advance, at once wheeled his troop to the right, jumped the hedges still mounted, and got amongst the Turks. Lieutenant Wait used his revolver until shot through the body in five places, his men firing their rifles from their horses. The work was too fast and furious for the Turks. They either surrendered or scattered through the cactus hedges and hid. For Lieutenant Waite's brilliant action in this battle, he was subsequently awarded the Military Cross, and Shoeing-Smith T. Jones and Trooper S. L. Gofton (A.M.C. Details) were awarded the Military Medal.

The rest of the Regiment, supported by several guns from the Machine Gun Squadron, dismounted and opened fire on all enemy in sight or hearing. The men hacked their way through the cactus hedges with their bayonets and in a few minutes all opposition in our immediate neighbourhood ceased, and a large number of prisoners were taken.

While this operation was going on, Major Bolingbroke, with two troops of "A" Squadron which had originally gone to the beach, raided the Turkish artillery observation post at Sheikh Redwan, to the north-west of Gaza. With a few of his men, he crept up on to the Turkish artillery post who were directing fire on the infantry to the south and south-east of Gaza. Before this post knew its danger, Major Bolingbroke and his party rushed it, captured the observation party, four in number, together with their range-finding instruments and telephones. Fire was then opened on the raiding party with several machine guns. The raiding party accordingly withdrew with their prisoners and rejoined the Regiment.

After the north-east end of the cactus plantations had been cleared, the Regiment was reorganised and advance was made south-west on Gaza, "A" Squadron on the left in touch with the Wellington Mounted Rifles, "C" Squadron in the centre, and "B" Squadron on the right in touch with the 7th Regiment on the sand ridges. Owing to the more open nature of the country to the left, the left flank under Major Cameron was able to progress more rapidly than the remainder of the line. When this flank had advanced about two miles and within a few hundred yards of the main Gaza Mosque, the C.O. of the Wellington Mounted Rifles informed Major Cameron that he had captured two guns, but that the Turks were counter-attacking, and the C.O. of the Wellington asked for our assistance to hold the position and get the guns away. Some 200 yards from the guns there was a Turkish trench occupied by some 200 Turks. Major Cameron accordingly rushed this trench with 46 of "A" Squadron, under Major Bolingbroke, assisted by 25 of the New Zealanders, and captured it at the point of the bayonet, the charge being covered by two guns of our Machine Gun Squadron, under Captain Cain. "A" Squadron's Lewis gun and a New Zealand Lewis gun. The New Zealanders also firing two rounds into a hut from the captured field guns.

Lieutenant Graham entered into a bayonet contest with a burly Turk and received a bayonet wound in the stomach. Before the Turk could finish him off, however, one of our men shot the Turk with his revolver.

Another party of this squadron, consisting of Lieutenant Scott, Sergeant Gahan, Sergeant Hammond and Corporal Ogg, encountered in the scrub a party of Turks consisting of an officer and 15 other ranks. The Turks at once put up their hands in token of surrender, which was accepted, but seeing the numerical weakness of their captors, one of them fired at Sergeant Gahan and shot him through the body and another bayonetted Ogg through the leg. Scott and Hammond at once opened fire, the former accounting for five and the latter for one. The other nine disappeared in the scrub, but were subsequently rounded up.

HISTORY OF THE 5th LIGHT HORSE REGIMENT. 99

Our Squadron had captured one officer and 21 others, while 70 Turks were killed in the trench, and a large number seriously wounded.

For his gallant conduct on this occasion, Major Cameron received the D.S.O. and Major Bolingbroke received a similar distinction for his service on this occasion and for those earlier in the day, when he captured the Turkish artillery post at Sheik Redwan.

Our men stood by the captured guns until they were removed, and supplied an escort to the prisoners and assisted to bring the guns back to Divisional Headquarters.

While "A" Squadron was engaged as above, "C" Squadron and "B" Squadron were working through the prickly pear country and hacking their way through the hedges with their bayonets and killing or capturing various small parties of Turks. Owing to the difficult nature of the country, "C" Squadron was not able to keep in touch with "A," nor "B" with "C." "B" finally joined up with the 7th Regiment on their right on the sand hills. Shortly after sun-down, instructions were received from the Brigade that the whole mounted forces would withdraw back to the west side of Wadi Ghuzze, as large Turkish reinforcements had been reported coming from the direction of Beersheba, and it was considered very doubtful if the Imperial Mounted Division posted on that flank could keep them off. Accordingly, instructions were received for the Regiment to concentrate with a view to withdrawal. A most anxious time for the C.O. ensued. He knew the remainder of the Division might withdraw at any minute and that the Regiment was scattered through some square miles of cactus scrub, and it would take hours to collect all of them. "A" Squadron got clear of the cactus hedges by 9.30 p.m., and "B" Squadron rejoined Regimental Headquarters with "C" Squadron at 10 p.m.

The number of prisoners taken by the Regiment during the day's fighting amounted to 127. Our casualties amounted to 2 other ranks killed and 2 officers and 10 other ranks wounded. There is no doubt the comparative smallness of our casualties was due to the fact that the Turks were rushed as soon as they were located. They were given no time to do steady sniping. As soon as our men got within a few yards of them they became demoralised, their shooting was wild, and if they could not slip away among the prickly pear, they surrendered.

The Regiment left Jabalie with the Brigade at about 10.30 p.m. and arrived at Belah next morning after dawn. This ride will ever be remembered by those who took part in it. It was the third successive night without sleep.

That ended the first attack on Gaza. The casualties on the British side amounted to some 4,500. It was generally considered that if the mounted troops had stayed where they were, Gaza would have surrendered next morning. Prisoners subsequently informed us that orders had been issued for the surrender and preparations were made to that effect, but in the morning they found to their astonishment that our mounted troops had all gone.

The following letter was received by Major-General Chauvel, C.B., C.M.G., the G.O.C. Anzac and New Zealand Mounted Division, from Lieutenant-General Sir Phillip Chetwode, Bart., C.B., D.S.O., Commanding Desert Column, and was promulgated to all ranks:

"I wish to thank you personally for the very fine work accomplished by the Division under your command in the action of the 26th, and especially for the skilful way in which you withdrew the cavalry in the dark after their long day's work against the enemy. Will you express to all ranks under your command my admiration of their splendid behaviour before the enemy. It was no light task to delay the advance of greatly superior hostile forces throughout the whole day on a front of nearly 12 miles, and at the same time be able to put in a strong attack by two brigades to assist the infantry in the attack on Gaza. Two hours more daylight would have enabled the cavalry to finish the job, and it must have been most disheartening to your men after such a fine effort to have the prize snatched from their grasp by darkness.

"The harder the task I give to the mounted troops of the Desert Column, the better they carry it out, and no man could wish to command finer troops."

For the next three weeks, the Brigade remained in the

HISTORY OF THE 5th LIGHT HORSE REGIMENT. 101

neighbourhood of Belah, furnishing patrols, working parties and outposts, pending the next attack on Gaza, which was being arranged for.

On the 3rd April, 1917, "B" Squadron under Lieutenant Barwise, accompanied by Major Cameron, moved to Tel-el-Jemmi to cover a working party who were arranging for water for the next advance. Major Foster, accompanied by Major Cameron and Lieutenant Hansen's troop, proceeded as far as Armar to bring in an armoured-car which had been left in the recent operations, but owing to the threatened attack by a large body of Turks, they were unable to get the car away.

During our encampment at Belah, the camp was shelled with long-range guns from the Turkish Gaza position, but without severe casualties, as far as this Regiment was concerned.

CHAPTER 25.

GAZA (Second)—April, 1917.

On the night of the 16th April we left Belah for Shellal, and the following day with the Brigade moved to Hill 510, being the right flank of the operations comprising the Second Battle of Gaza.

On the 18th the Brigade (Ryrie) demonstrated against Hareira, this Regiment being in reserve.

On the 19th this Regiment left the east bank of the Wadi Ghuzee at 1 a.m. and marched to El Mendur. This Regiment was then sent to occupy a line, Erk to Dammath, this being the right flank of our attack. We entrenched this position. The 7th Light Horse Regiment (Onslow) and two armoured-cars were placed under command of the C.O. of this Regiment. In the afternoon, Turkish cavalry, numbering about 3,000 men and 4 guns approached to within 2,000 yards of our flank. They shelled our line and our armoured-cars, but did not seem inclined to come nearer than 2,000 yards. They were a motley lot, some riding donkeys. Our horses were sent to the rear and the field trenches which we dug were manned. The sending of our horses to the rear caused the Yeomanry Regiment on our right to believe that we had retired, and they at once retired, thus leaving our right flank open. The Turkish cavalry, however, did not advance any nearer, and we accordingly opened on them with our machine guns. They at once withdrew. At 9.30 p.m. we shortened our outpost line. This line we held the following day, and at dusk marched to Weli-Sheikh-Nuran where we took over an outpost line from the Wellington Rifles. Thus ended the second attack on Gaza. As far as our Regiment and Brigade were concerned, we got off very lightly, having had very little to do, and our casualties were nominal. The other brigades of the Light Horse, however, suffered very severely, particularly the 3rd, who had some 350 casualties. Our whole force is reported to have lost 14,000 men on this occasion.

CHAPTER 26.

WADI GHUZZE (April to July, 1917).

From April, 1917, on to the following October, the Regiment, as part of the Anzac Mounted Division, was operating on the Wadi Ghuzze pending the re-organization which was taking place with a view to a further attack on the Beersheba-Gaza line.

Shortly after the Second Gaza Battle, various changes took place in the Higher Commands. For some time past, the British force, operating east of the Canal, was called the Eastern Force (General Dobell). The troops in the field were known as The Desert Column (General Chetwode). In April, 1917, General Chetwode was appointed to command Eastern Force, General Chauvel to command The Desert Column, and General Chaytor to command the Anzac Mounted Division. In June General Murray was relieved of the Supreme Command and General Allenby took his place. On General Allenby's arrival, Eastern Force was abolished and one mounted corps known as the Desert Mounted Corps (General Chauvel), and two Infantry Corps, 20th and 21st, were constituted. The Desert Mounted Corps consisted of the Anzac, the Australian, and the Yeomanry Divisions.

For the first month or so, the whole of the mounted troops were busily engaged on patrols, reconnaissances, covering parties, making of roads, digging of water systems and trenches. After some time the infantry extended their line to the right and took over our trench systems and the mounted troops were then available for further reconnaissances, covering parties and raids. When this time had arrived, the three mounted divisions were employed one in the front line supplying day patrols, small raids, etc., the second division in support at Abassan, and the third division in reserve on the beach at Marakeb, within a few hours ride in case of need.

In April, 1917, the Hotchkiss Automatic Rifle was issued one per troop, in lieu of the Lewis Gun, three per regiment. The Hotchkiss proved itself a most excellent weapon.

The conditions during the summer of 1917 were most unpleasant. Palestine in spring is a regular land of promise, everything is beautifully green. As summer approaches, however, the crops are cut and any other vegetation is dried up and burnt off by the sun, and the country becomes a desert in appearance. In ordinary times this possibly would not be so bad, but would justify Sir Frederick Treve's definition of it as "The Land that is Desolate." Under war conditions, however, the country is much worse. Owing to the thousands of horses that were continually moving about the neighbourhood of the Wadi Ghuzze, the surface of the ground was tramped into powder and as soon as the sea breeze came up at 9 or 10 in the morning and thereafter until dusk, the whole country was one mass of dust. Occasionally there were hot winds from the desert which had the same effect of getting the dust moving. The water supply was poor, except for those troops that were actually camped on the banks of the Wadi. Owing to the water for all other troops having to be carried by water carts or camels, the supply was limited. On account of the presence of the large number of horses, the flies were extremely numerous and persistent. In addition to that, the whole ground itself was crawling with insects of all sorts, scorpions, spiders and beetles. As everybody slept on the ground, these insects became a real pest. Owing to the shortage of wood and water, the louse question was acute. Lice can only be got rid of by boiling, medical men say for two minutes. The wood issue, however, was so small that it was hardly sufficient to cook the meals of the men, and there was none to make boiling water for cleansing purposes. As the summer went on, septic sores and boils became prevalent in the force, this, no doubt, owing to insufficient supply of fresh vegetables. There were as many as 100 men a day attending our regimental medical officer for treatment in this respect.

For some period after the Second Battle of Gaza the Regiment was operating in the neighbourhood of the Wadi Ghuzze. While one squadron was holding an outpost line in the bed of the Ghuzze at Shellal, a Mosaic, which had formed the floor of a church dedicated to St. George, was uncovered. This Mosaic dates from the early Christian period—4th century. It was subsequenty taken over by the Rev. Maitland Wood, carefully removed and sent to Australia to be relaid at Canberra. Under the Mosaic there was an excavation in which were some human bones. Padre Wood reported to Division that he had found the bones of St. George. The D.A.Q.M.G. sent back a memo that he could find no record of this man and to at once forward his identity disc.

On the 23rd August, 1917, our patrols reached the Wadi Imlieh, where "A" Squadron was heavily shelled. On the 24th "C" Squadron was in action at Imara with a squadron of enemy cavalry, three prisoners being taken from the enemy. On this occasion a troop of the enemy cavalry got on the right flank of "C" Squadron and Lieutenant Webster's troop forced them to vacate their ground three times. This caused the enemy troops to work round to the neighbourhood of a 7th Light Horse squadron which was on our right flank. A troop of this squadron, after a gallop of three miles, cut them off and took them all prisoners—one officer and 16 other ranks. Our "C" Squadron was shelled during these operations.

On the 25th April, 1917, there was a similar reconnaissance by "B" Squadron to Hil 410, "C" Squadron being in support at Imara. "B" Squadron got into action with the enemy and both squadrons were shelled. We had two casualties and one horse killed and four wounded.

On the 26th April there was a reconnaissance to Hill 410 by "A" Squadron, "B" Squadron being in support at Imara. On this occasion we did not get into touch with the enemy. On the 27th, the Regiment moved to a position behind Nuran. Working parties were detailed for trench digging. On the 28th, "C" Squadron was engaged in filling water cisterns, and "B" in trench digging. On the 29th, the Regiment moved to a position near Nuran and Shellal. On the 30th April, "C" Squadron patrolled to Sausage Ridge and Sihan during which time they were heavily shelled by the enemy. One troop of "A" Squadron patrolled to 410. During the first week of May, we held daily patrols to Hill 410, the patrols usually being shelled. On the 9th May, the Brigade formed a covering party while the Army Commander made a reconnaissance of the country towards the Wadi Imlieh.

On the 11th May, 1917, the whole Brigade covered some 60-pounders while they shelled Wadi Sheria.

On the 17th May the Brigade moved camp and occupied the Gharbi-Gamli redoubts.

On the 22nd May, 1917, the Regiment handed these redoubts over to the 11th Light Horse Regiment and took part in the raid by the Anzac Mounted Division (Chaytor) and the Imperial Mounted Division (Hodgson) on the Turkish railway between Asluj and Auja. The Regiment, with the remainder of the Brigade, left its lines at 7.30 p.m. We formed the advance-guard to the column. We started off with a native guide, but he proved absolutely unreliable. When it was discovered that the advance-guard was marching straight into the rear-guard of the column, it was decided to do without this gentleman's services, he having led the column round in a circle. The remainder of the march was done on compass bearings. On our approach to Hill 820, this Regiment marched across the Wadi to take up the left half of the line between Gos Shelili and Hill 1240. On arriving at a point two miles east of the Wadi at 4.15 a.m., the advance-guard was fired on by enemy outposts. Two of the enemy were killed and two prisoners taken, while one of our horses was wounded. There was a fine duel between one of our scouts and a mounted Arab in the early dawn. Both on horseback, moving at a gallop at a few yards distance, both using their rifles, but neither scored a hit.

Our instructions were to gain touch with the New Zealanders on our left flank. As these had not put in an appearance, one squadron was sent a mile to the left flank and one a mile to the right at 7.15 a.m. The New Zealand Brigade subsequently joined up on our left, and "C" Squadron was sent to the right to gain touch with the 7th Regiment on our right. At 10.30 a.m., "C" Squadron reported that there was a body of enemy cavalry, at least one brigade in strength, moving out of the ridges and advancing in the direction of "C" Squadron, four miles away. About twenty minutes later a further report was received that the force last referred to consisted of two brigades of Turkish cavalry, but that they had turned north towards Beersheba. At 2.35 p.m., we were informed that our Brigade was retiring, and for us to conform. The Regiment accordingly retired, watering at Esani. We arrived back on our redoubts at 10.30 p.m. Our march for our old camp that night will be remembered for many a day by those that took part in it. We had difficulty in finding our bearings owing to the fact that the Yeomanry Division had in the meantime camped in the neighbourhood. They had not been there when we left the previous evening, and when we saw their camp in the dark wrong deductions were drawn, with the result that some miles of heedless marching were indulged in before we settled down for the night.

This raid had been a particularly successful one, as while we were holding the line, as above, the 1st Light Horse Brigade and the Camel Brigade had destroyed some 17 miles of the railway, blew up all the culverts, and cut every rail in that section with gun-cotton.

On the 29th May, 1917, the Regiment was relieved by part of the 53rd Infantry Division, and with the remainder of the Brigade moved to Tel-el-Marakeb on the beach opposite Kahn Yunus.

On the rolls being checked, it was ascertained there were at this time present with the Regiment 157 of those who had left Australia in December, 1914, when the Regiment embarked.

We remained at the beach until the 8th June, 1917. While here the time was put in bathing and resting. Mark VI ammunition was exchanged for Mark VII, Hotchkiss gun teams were exercised, and all ranks practised in bomb throwing.

On the 8th June, 1917, the Regiment with the remainder of the Brigade moved back to El Fukhari, as a support to the front-line division; while here, the commanding officer of the Regiment, Lieutenant-Colonel L. C. Wilson, C.M.G., was invested with the Croix-de-guerre by General Bailloud of the French Army. During our stay at Fukhari, a brigade rifle range was constructed, and the members of the Regiment exercised in musketry, bombing practice and Hotchkiss gun practice were also carried out. The Regiment remained at Fukhari until the 29th June, when it again went back to Tel-el-Marakeb.

The Regiment remained on the beach from the 29th June until the 5th July, during which period musketry, Hotchkiss gun practice and signal training were carried on. On the last-mentioned date the Regiment with the Brigade moved from el-Marakeb to Um Urgan on the Wadi Ghuzze, on which date the Brigade took part in forming a covering party while the Commander-in-Chief reconnoitered the country towards Beersheba.

CHAPTER 27.

WADI GHUZZE (July and August) MINOR ENTERPRISES.

The Higher Command now desired that the enemy should be harassed as much as possible, or as a divisional staff officer said, "the fear of God put into them." The regiments were accordingly invited to get up raids and ambushes for the enemy outposts, patrols and advanced posts. Schemes for these raids were drawn up by the Regimental Commander, submitted to the Brigade and, if approved, were then carried out. There was no lack of volunteers for these stunts, and it was the Commanding Officer's care to see that stunts were not taken on which might be carried out at too great a cost.

One of the first of these was carried out on the night of the 11th-12th July, 1917. The party left with the intention of raiding a Turkish trench on the western side of the Wadi Imlieh. This trench had been noticed by our patrols to be manned at various times, and it was anticipated that it would be manned at night. Accordingly, the raiding party left the Wadi Ghuzze at 7 p.m., moved out to Imara, there left an ambulance sand cart with an escort under Lieutenant Webster and 12 other ranks. The remainder of the party moved off towards the trench, the assaulting party consisting of Lieutenant Broughton with 20 other ranks and the supports under Lieutenant Boyd and 15 other ranks. They dismounted about two miles from the Wadi and there left their horses with an escort under Lieutenant Taylor. The assault party, followed by the supports at a distance of about 200 yards, marched on foot to within 400 yards of the hut opposite Hill 410, arriving there at 10 p.m. This party then moved due south of the hut. The assault party then advanced in single file, at three yards distance, two men in advance with fixed bayonets followed by four men and Lieutenant Broughton with bombs. All had their bayonets fixed and covered with cloth to prevent glistening. The assault troop was followed by the supports. The hut was first examined and then a move was made to the trench which starts about 25 yards from the hut and runs east and west, 150 yards long, 7 feet 6 inches deep, with fire-step and nine traverses. A party of five men was sent to block the communication trench, which it was reported extended between the trench and the Wadi, but it was found that no such trench existed. A party of men and bombers then got into the trench and worked along it from east to west, while another party worked along the top of the trench, but no enemy were seen. A patrol was sent to the bank of the Wadi, a distance of 200 yards, but no enemy were seen here. The raiding party then returned to their horses, arriving at them at 11.35 p.m., then picked up the other parties and returned to bivouac at 1.30 a.m. The night was cloudy and dark, no stars being visible. As it turned out, the raiding party met no opposition, but they might have had a very interesting evening. It was not their fault that they had not.

On the 14th July the Regiment took over the usual day patrols towards Beersheba.

On the night of the 15th July another minor enterprise was taken on with the intention of capturing a Turkish patrol which had been observed on several occasions to occupy the high ground south of Point 630, near the Abu Shawish Road. Accordingly, a troop of "A" Squadron under Lieutenant Webster left camp at 11.30 p.m. and proceeded to a point about a mile south of Hill 550. Here the horses were left under an escort of eight men, the remaining six other ranks and Lieutenant Webster occupying the ground about 2,000 yards to the south of Point 630. The hill had several firing positions dug in it. Lieutenant Webster's party concealed themselves in these, being in position at 3.45 a.m. At 4 a.m. a movement was seen in the Wadi, and at 4.15 six mounted men rode on to Point 630. Two of them then advanced half a mile towards Hill 550. Here they had a look round, went back to the rest of the party, then rode over the Wadi Hanafish, where they remained until our party withdrew. They were apparently suspicious of an ambush and were not taking any chances. Lieutenant Webster vacated his post at 6.15 a.m. and withdrew.

In the meantime, another troop under Lieutenant Graham had moved out from the outpost line at 3.5 a.m., as support to Lieutenant Webster. This patrol saw the Turkish patrol and it is possible that the Turks saw them. Lieutenant Graham's party was fired on by about 15 men at a range of 2,000 yards, but without any damage.

On the night of the 16th-17th July, a regimental enterprise to El-Buggar was carried out with the intention of capturing an enemy patrol which was reported to be in the habit of watering at the well at that place, and also to make a reconnaissance of the country east of Hill 810, near Sufi. Accordingly, a party of three officers and 80 other ranks left bivouac at 7 p.m. on the 15th. They arrived at the Chalk Pits at Khasif at 9.30 p.m. All here dismounted, the horses were concealed in the Chalk Pits and left with an escort with Lieutenant Taylor. The remainder of the party under Lieutenants Boyd and Broughton proceeded to El Buggar. Lieutenant Boyd and seven other ranks took cover in a hut there, while Lieutenant Broughton and 11 other ranks concealed themselves in a wash-out a few yards away from the well at which the Turks usually watered their horses. Shortly after 3 a.m. Lieutenant Boyd heard a patrol within a few yards of his hut, but it was too dark to take action against this body, which, from the noise they made, were in considerable numbers. One of the enemy came within a few yards of the hut but was not fired on, as it was hoped to catch the big patrol. Lieutenant Boyd saw through a hole he had drilled in the wall of the hut, a patrol of 38 at a distance of 900 yards. None of the patrols came near enough to Lieutenant Broughton's party to justify him firing on them. At 4.25 a.m. a patrol of 40 or 50 men came to Khasif, where the horses had been left under Lieutenant Taylor. Two of them rode up in the dark quite close to Lieutenant Taylor's party. They were called on to surrender and immediately tried to gallop off.

They were fired on and both their horses were killed. One man was wounded in the foot and both were taken prisoners. The remainder of this patrol kept well away from Lieutenant Taylor's party and sniped at it for a considerable time from the adjoining ridges. The remainder of the Regiment, together with two troops of the Machine Gun Squadron, arrived at Gos-el-Basal at 4 a.m. to act as a support to the ambushing party. This party remained at Basal till 8 a.m., as previously arranged. They then moved up the Khasif, drove off a partol of 20 that were sniping Taylor's party there, and then moved on to Buggar with the led horses of the ambushing party, and drove off a party that was sniping at the latter. The Regiment then moved on to Point 720, which was then occupied by enemy patrols. After exchange of rifle fire, these patrols retired.

Lieutenants Boyd, Broughton and Taylor with "C" Squadron then moved forward to Point 810 across the Wadi Hanafish. The ridges there were occupied by enemy patrols, but they retired on the approach of "C" Squadron. A troop of 20 enemy cavalry were observed at Taweil-el-Habari. Two machine guns and a troop were pushed out against these cavalry who immediately withdrew to Beersheba. "C" Squadron on Point 810 were now subjected to shell-fire, but without casualties. The Regiment then returned to camp, having taken note of the various tracks, gulleys, and matters of military interest in the country passed over.

On the 17th July, 1917, the Regiment had the usual day patrols. These patrols had left bivouac at 5 a.m. in a heavy fog. Almost immediately they passed through the barb-wire in front of the Wadi Ghuzze they were shelled by enemy guns in the direction of Point 705. The patrol on nearing Basal noticed Turkish cavalry at Khasif. These movements were reported to the Brigade and the whole of the Anzac Mounted Division moved out across the Wadi Ghuzze at 9 a.m. The enemy were in some strength, 4,000 infantry with 14 guns, it was afterwards learnt was their number. All our troops were heavily shelled. This Regiment formed the left flank of the Division. The Divisional artillery got into action and there was an artillery duel during the whole of the rest of the day. The Turks held the high ground. Our troops were in the open. We remained there till about 4 o'clock, when Lieutenant Broughton reported that the enemy were retiring and withdrawing their guns. Instructions were received from the Brigade to push forward parties to prevent this. The Regiment accordingly moved forward and to the left to cut off their retirement over the Wadi Imlieh. This, we were, however, not able to do. As soon as we advanced the enemy batteries from the direction of Hareira opened up on us. It was getting dark and they could not observe their fire. The enemy all retired over the Wadi. This Regiment withdrew to Gosel-Geleib (Ziklag of King David), where we remained on outpost till 2 a.m. and were then relieved by the New Zealanders. During these operations the Regiment was almost continuously under shell-fire from 9 a.m. till 7 p.m. We had only one casualty by shrapnel. The formation adopted by the Regiment was column of lines of troop columns at extended intervals and distances. When a troop found that the enemy shells were coming uncomfortably close, they moved quietly off to a flank and the enemy had the trouble of working out their ranges afresh. A large proportion of the shell used by the enemy was common percussion shell, and owing to the soft nature of the ground it had very local effect.

The Regiment got back to bivouac at 3 a.m. and moved out again at 6.30 a.m., as it was supposed the Turks might have again come across the Wadi Imlieh. They did not, however, and our people returned to bivouac at 11 a.m.

On the 22nd July, 1917, "A" Squadron went to Esani as an escort to a survey party. About 2 a.m. on the 23rd, a report was received that Beersheba had been evacuated by the enemy, and accordingly the Regiment with the remainder of the Brigade left bivouac at 6.30 a.m. to follow them up if they had done so. Our Brigade halted at Khasif as a reserve. Patrols were sent out towards Beersheba, when it was ascertained that there was no truth in the report.

On the 27th and 28th July, 1917, another regimental operation to El Buggar was carried out. It was known that enemy patrols came daily in to the El Buggar-Khasif-Karm District. It was proposed to capture these patrols. The scheme was to send one squadron some two miles to the right of Buggar, to send a second squadron to Hill 720 (some two miles to the left), and the remainder of the Regiment to go to Gos-el-Basal, thus forming a large triangle. It was hoped that the Turkish patrol would come into this triangle from the direction of Beersheba and that the three squadrons would then gallop in and surround and capture them. It was arranged that an aeroplane should co-operate in the operation. The 'plane was to fly over the district at 4.30 a.m. If any enemy patrols were visible they were to drop a smoke bomb. At this signal, the three squadrons were to gallop in and surround the enemy. In the event of a large number of the enemy going into the area, the 'plane was to drop two smoke balls and at once report to Regimental Headquarters at Basal. If it was considered that the enemy force were too much for us to attempt to surround, the 'plane was to rise again, drop three smoke balls and the flanking squadrons would withdraw. Accordingly, at 6 p.m. on the 27th, "A" Squadron under Major Bolingbroke, with two machine guns moved down to Esani, on the western side of the Wadi. On arriving there at 9 p.m., Sergeant Smith, who had been sent there in the afternoon to find a crossing, reported that he had seen a party of Bedouin on the east side of the Wadi near Esani. Major Bolingbroke accordingly sent Sergeant Smith and six dismounted men to deal with these Bedouin. They found 15 Bedouin with camels cutting and loading barley On Smith's approach the Bedouin fired on his party, but without casualties. The Bedouin were at once attacked. Two were killed with the bayonet and one by rifle fire. Several more were wounded. After its encounter at 9 p.m., "A" Squadron proceeded up the Wadi and took up a position at 2.50 a.m. in a depression two miles north-east of Rashid Bek. This squadron remained in concealment until 7 a.m., as no signal was given by the aeroplane to close in on El Buggar. In the meantime, "B" Squadron under Captain Nimmo and one machine gun troop, who were to form the left jaw of the trap, had taken up its position at Point 720 by 3 a.m. At 4.35 the advance scout of an enemy patrol approached Point 720 and gave what the writer considers one of the best exhibitions of scouting that he has heard. The concealed squadron was on the flat top of the hill and could not be seen from the slopes below. Observation posts were out and the place was half under fog. If the enemy scout had approached the hill in the usual manner, that is, slowly and carefully, he would have been marked down and either shot or captured. Instead of this, he galloped straight at the hill as hard as he could go, over the crest, saw "B" Squadron, turned round and was away before anybody understood what he was doing. Needless to say, he reported to his main body the presence of our squadron there, with the result that the Turks that day did not carry out their usual procedure of coming into Buggar. Captain Nimmo sent two of his troops after the Turkish cavalry, one south and one south-east, but the enemy had too good a start and got back to Tweil-el-Haberi, where they remained until our squadron retired.

The aeroplane which was co-operating with us reported at 5 o'clock that there were 50 enemy halted in the road two miles east of Haberi. This was outside the limit of our trap, and as we could do nothing, the aeroplanes machine-gunned them and dispersed them. The Regiment in due course retired to bivouac.

Sergeant A. V. Smith was recommended for a decoration in respect of his action at Esani on this operation, and same was suubsequently granted.

On the 29th July, 1917, the Regiment with the remainder of the Division formed a covering party while the Commander-in-Chief reconnoitered the country towards Beersheba.

On the night of the 30th July the 6th Regiment were operating towards Irgeig and the Wadi Hanafish. Information was received at Brigade Headquarters that a Turkish infantry division was marching along the Wadi Imleih towards Beersheba. It was most important that the 6th Regiment should be warned of this large body of infantry marching across their rear. Accordingly Lieutenant Broughton, of this Regiment, and one troop were sent out from Um Urgan at 11.10 p.m. for that purpose. Lieutenant Broughton noticed large bodies of Turkish infantry on the march near the Wadi Imlieh. He also noticed Turkish cavalry patrols marching along the flank of their infantry column towards Beersheba. Without raising their suspicion, he passed through their force and got in touch with the 6th Regiment and warned them of what was happening behind them. The 6th Regiment accordingly took the necessary precautions, and the Turks were unaware of the fact that a mounted regiment was out on their left. The 6th Regiment and Lieutenant Broughton duly returned to camp without any alarm being given.

On the 3rd August, 1917, the Brigade (Ryrie) undertook an operation to Sufi, a place at which there was a well about two miles in front of the Turkish position at Beersheba. It had been reported by natives that there was a Bedouin battalion some 300 strong encamped at this place. It was intended that the Brigade should proceed to Sufi, capture or destroy this battalion, and get back out of range of the Turkish guns at Beersheba before dawn. This last was imperative, as the Turks had a large number of guns mounted within 3,000 yards of Sufi. The Brigade accordingly left the east side of the Wadi Ghuzze at 7.30 p.m. on the 3rd August, "C" Squadron forming the advance-guard. The Brigade arrived at Taweil-el-Haberi at midnight, where it halted. This Regiment then moved on eastward until we arrived at a small wadi on the main Beersheba Road, half a mile west of the road running north and south from Sufi to Yahia. The last part of the Brigade march and the rest of the Regimental march was done by compass. The maps showed various roads and tracks, but these were the ones which were in existence prior to the war, and owing to the numerous military operations in this neighbourhood, fresh sets of tracks and roads had been made across the country. On approaching Sufi, "C" Squadron and two troops of machine guns moved northward up the wadi on Sufi, while "A" Squadron and one troop of machine guns moved half a mile on the right flank of "C" Squadron to protect it from any attack which might come from Beersheba defences. The remainder of the Regiment moved 400 yards in rear of and in support of "C" Squadron. "C" Squadron arrived at Sufi Well at 1 a.m., but found no trace of the enemy although it was noticed that a large number of stock had watered there the previous day. When the Regiment left Brigade Headquarters, we dropped a telephone line, so that we were in touch with the Brigade. On reporting that

HISTORY OF THE 5th LIGHT HORSE REGIMENT. 115

there was nothing at Sufi, we received instructions to send out patrols towards the railway and reconnoitre the enemy. Lieutenant Boyd and two troops of "C" Squadron accordingly moved north-east towards the railway. After proceeding 1¼ miles, they were fired on by Turkish outposts without suffering any casualties. The patrol returned to the Regiment. The Regiment rejoined the Brigade at 3.55 a.m. and the whole Brigade moved back to bivouac, where we arrived at 7.40 a.m.

On the 5th August, 1917, the Regiment carried out the usual day patrols and night outposts. The day patrols at Point 510 took one prisoner, while Lieutenant Graham and troop patrolled to Khasif and got into action with 30 Turks, one of whose horses was killed and one of whose men was wounded, but the latter was got away by his comrades.

On the 8th August the Regiment again carried out the usual day patrols and night outposts. Lieutenant Wetherell's troop were in action with the Turkish cavalry at Khasif. That officer had a rather interesting few minutes on the morning in question. The Turkish cavalry were seen some distance away and Lieutenant Wetherell moved towards them with a Hotchkiss rifle and three men, thinking that they might allow a small party like that to get within range. When he had proceeded some distance a troop of Turkish cavalry, who had been concealed in a dip in the ground on his flank, charged at a gallop, and were within 100 yards of him before they were seen. It was impossible, in the few seconds at his disposal, to get the Hotchkiss rifle into action, and it was a question of whose horses were the best. The party of four galloped back towards the remainder of the troop, over rough ground, with the Turkish cavalry in hot pursuit. The Turkish officer with his sword waving got within 30 yards of Corporal Axelson, the rear man of the four, he being handicapped by carrying the Hotchkiss rifle. The rest of the Turkish troop were strung out behind their officer. After a gallop of over a mile, Lieutenant Wetherell's men were getting back to their supports, who opened fire. The Turks wheeled about and retired; the Hotchkiss gunner at once halted and got his gun into action. Axelson's action in holding on to his Hotchkiss gun, which weighs over 27 lbs., while he was being pursued at a short distance by a Turkish officer on an Arab charger, was most commendable. Our day patrol on this occasion at Hill 510 had one man wounded by shell-fire.

On the night of the 10th August, 1917, a regimental operation was carried out with the purpose of capturing or destroying patrols visiting El Buggar and Khasif. The scheme was to put one squadron near Esani, two miles east of Rashid Bek, one squadron near Point 630, and the remainder of the Regiment at Karm. Telephone lines were laid from Regimental Headquarters at Karm to the flank squadrons. If any patrols came into the jaws of this trap, it was intended to cut them off and capture them. Accordingly "A" Squadron, under Major Bolingbroke, D.S.O., and one troop of Machine Gun Squadron, took up a position in the Wadi Esani, two miles east of Rashid Bek, at 2.30 a.m. on the 10th August. "B" Squadron, under Captain Nimmo, and one troop of machine guns at the same time occupied the entrenched hill one mile south of Point 630. The remainder of the Regiment occupied Karm by the same time. Telephone lines were run out to "A" and "B" Squadrons. Up till 9 a.m. no enemy patrols came within the danger zone. At dawn enemy observation posts were observed on the ridge east of El Buggar. At 9 a.m. a patrol was sent from Karm towards El Buggar to make sure there were no enemy patrols near the latter place. When our patrol reached Khasif, it was fired on at extreme range by three enemy cavalry from the ridge to the south-east of Khasif. This enemy patrol at once galloped off towards Habari. Word was then sent back to Karm of the enemy patrol's existence, and instructions were phoned through to "A" Squadron to cut it off. A troop was at once sent to do so, but the time occupied in getting the instructions from Khasif to Karm was sufficient to give the enemy patrol too big a start in the race for Habari. It was then found by Major Bolingbroke that, in addition to the patrol above-mentioned, there were two squadrons of enemy cavalry concealed in the ridges to the east of El Buggar. He at once brought up the remainder of his squadron and the machine gun troop at the gallop. The Turkish cavalry immediately departed, and kept at least 2,000 yards distance between themselves and any of Major Bolingbroke's men. Major Bolingbroke pursued them to within a mile of Habari, on the Beersheba Road. Shots were exchanged, but owing to the extreme range no casualties were inflicted on either side. Some of the enemy cavalry proceeded to Beersheba, while others galloped towards the south-east. Shortly after daylight, Major Bolingbroke had seen a patrol of 17 enemy cavalry riding from Beersheba towards Khalassa, but did not see them again. The Regiment returned to bivouac and arrived there at 3 p.m.

On the 11th August the Regiment occupied "X," "Y" and "Z" redoubts on the Ghabi-Gamli line.

On the 13th August, 1917, the Brigade (Ryrie) undertook an operation in the neighbourhood of Ingeig. This was one of those operations which it was very advisable to complete and be out of the enemy's gun-range before dawn. The Brigade left bivouac at 7.30 p.m., this Regiment forming the advance-guard to Point 770, east, of Khirbet Imlieh where it then formed the local protection to Brigade Headquarters and the horses of the other two regiments, and acted as support to those regiments. They went forward on foot to Wadi El Sufi, a distance of two miles. The intention of the operation was to raid the Beersheba railway, blow up certain bridges thereon and destroy any local Turkish posts. This was new country to the Brigade, and it was found to be very rough, with the result that the 6th (Fuller) and 7th (Onslow) Regiments did not make the progress on foot which had been anticipated, and by the time they got within 50 yards of the railway it was time to start back, as dawn was approaching, and it would have been disastrous if the Brigade had been caught out there at daylight right under the enemy's numerous guns on the Beersheba position. Accordingly the advance regiments returned to their horses without disclosing their presence, and the Brigade moved back to bivouac. It says very little for the Turkish outpost system, that there was a large body of dismounted men within 50 yards of the railway under one of their posts without their having observed same. No doubt their interest would have been aroused next morning when they saw the tracks of some 1,500 men close to their redoubts.

On the 18th August, 1917, the Regiment was relieved and moved with the rest of the Division back to the beach at Marakeb, the front line being taken over by the Yeomanry

Division. During the Division's last spell in the front line, it certainly got the upper hand of the Turks. Our G.S.O.1. was heard to remark to the Yeomanry G.S.O.1. that the former was handing over to the latter a lot of tame Turks. The Regiment remained at Marakeb from the 18th August to the 18th September. This was our last spell on the beach. These spells were the nearest approach to rests which the mounted troops enjoyed. There was an unlimited supply of fresh water there and unlimited sea bathing. We had no tactical duties to perform, but, of course, had our horses to look after. While there, training in signalling, gas respirators, Hotchkiss guns, musketry and bombing was carried out. Regimental funds were called on for the supply of fishing lines, but the results were not much good. It was found that Mills grenades were much better.

On the 29th August, 1917, the Regiment was inspected by the Divisional Commander, Major-General Chaytor. He was very complimentary in his remarks. On the 13th September the Regiment was inspected by the Corps Commander, Lieutenant-General Chauvel, who expressed himself as well satisfied with his inspection.

On the 18th September, 1917, the Regiment with the remainder of the Brigade moved from Marakeb to Kazar, near Abasan, the A. and N.Z. Division now being in support.

A census of the Regiment was taken, and it was found that there were only eight of the original members of the Regiment still with the Regiment who had never been away, i.e., sick, wounded, or on leave to England or Australia, of these the C.O. was one.

On the 24th September the Regiment was inspected by General Ryrie, and on the 28th by the Commander-in-Chief, General Allenby; on the 29th there was an inspection of horses by General Butler. These numerous inspections were the usual preliminary to a big forward movement.

We now received our first issue of donkeys—22 in number—big grey Egyptian ones. The War Establishments of a mounted regiment provided bicycles for the batmen. These "establishments" had evidently been prepared with a view to operations in country and under circumstances other than those in and under which we were campaigning. Bicycles were absolutely useless with us. The regiments were shifting their bivouacs so often that batmen wanted horses almost as much as the ordinary troopers. They acquired horses and disdained to ride on donkeys. We accordingly handed our donkeys over to the Brigade Band. Donkeys were of little use with a mobile mounted regiment, and were more trouble than they were worth.

On the 29th September the Brigade took part in tactical exercises in the neighbourhood of Gamli and Abreissa. It is interesting to note that documents were subsequently captured in the German headquarters, from which it was disclosed that the Turks at this time had a scheme by which they were to heavily attack the British right flank, i.e., the Gharbi-Gamli line, their idea being that if this line was attacked and shoved back it would block the British forward movement, which they anticipated would take place in October.

While we were in camp at Kazar, training in the form of physical exercises and musketry was carried out. On the 1st October the Regiment was practised going through a gas cloud. On the 5th there was a divisional staff ride; on the 12th a Brigade tactical exercise; and on the 18th another Brigade tactical exercise.

CHAPTER 28.

ASLUJ-ABDA (October, 1917).

The Commander-in-Chief's plan of operations was to break the Turkish centre at Sheria, first obtaining possession of Beersheba and attracting the Turkish general reserve to their left flank to prevent it being outflanked further. The necessary steps had been taken to lead the enemy to believe that the main attack would be at Gaza. Documents subsequently captured from the enemy proved that the enemy were deceived as to General Allenby's intentions. 31st October, 1917, was appointed for the attack on Beersheba—"Z" day. The preliminary operations for this offensive were to begin on the 20th October. It was intended to send the Desert Mounted Corps round to out-flank Beersheba and come in on the east thereof. The question of water was of vital importance. It was known that there was very little on the route which was to be taken by the mounted troops. The first thing, therefore, was to develop the water at Esani and Asluj, particularly at the latter place. This Regiment moved on the 21st to Esani. Large working parties were supplied to develop the water there and various patrols were sent out eastward. On the 24th October the Regiment with the rest of the Brigade left Esani at 5 p.m., and arrived next morning at Asluj at 4 a.m. The whole Brigade furnished working parties for the developing of water at this place. The Turks had done their best to destroy the water supply. There were several wells about 40 feet in depth. The pumping plant had been moved therefrom and the sides had been blown in with explosives, so that they were practically full of stones and rubbish. All ranks knew the importance of developing the water there, and the men worked with a will to remove the rubbish to get the wells in order again. While this was going on, the Commander-in-Chief personally visited the working parties and complimented them on their energy.

On the morning of the 26th October, news had been received that a party of enemy had been seen in the hills some 20 miles to the south of Asluj, near Matrade and in the neighbourhood of Abda, and this Regiment was ordered to operate against them. No British forces had been in this district before. The country was particularly broken, and it was extremely hard to march by compass bearings, as the whole place was intersected with deep gorges. Before moving off, arrangements had been made that an aeroplane should reconnoitre the enemy and drop a reconnaissance report to the Regiment. The aeroplane made its reconnaissance, but failed to find the Regiment, notwithstanding that the Regiment was on the open sand ridges some 4,000 to 5,000 feet below it. As a matter of fact, the Regiment at the time the aeroplane passed was stationary. The plane returned to Asluj and reported that they could not find any trace of the Regiment. This was an excellent example of the fact that it was not safe to depend on aerial reconnaissance alone. Simply because we were perfectly still at the time, the observers in the 'plane were unable to find us, notwithstanding that they knew that there was a mounted regiment somewhere in the neighbourhood. The Regiment arrived within a mile northwest of Murra. From here patrols were sent out as far as Abda, but no trace of the enemy was seen. Natives re-

HISTORY OF THE 5th LIGHT HORSE REGIMENT.   121

ported that 20 Turkish lancers had been at El Murra two days previously. The Regiment returned to bivouac at 8.45 p.m.

On the 27th October, 1917, orders were received that the commanding officer, Lieutenant-Colonel L. C. Wilson, C.M.G., had been appointed to command the 3rd Light Horse Brigade. He accordingly handed over the Regiment to Major D. C. Cameron, D.S.O., and took over the command of the 3rd Brigade, which was then at Esani.

CHAPTER 29.

GENERAL CONDITIONS—SINAI AND SOUTHERN PALESTINE.

Before concluding the history of the Regiment while under the command of Lieutenant-Colonel Wilson, a few remarks, in addition to those in previous chapters as regards general conditions and domestic economy in the Desert and Southern Palestine, might be of interest.

At this time, and for some considerable time prior thereto, this Regiment was numerically the strongest mounted regiment in the Desert Mounted Corps, and for a long time past had been the most healthy. The Regiment had marched out on the 21st October 530 all ranks in strength, although the establishment of the Regiment was 522. This state of affairs was due to the fact that we had very few evacuations for sickness and the personnel were thus available, also to the fact that we were over our establishment in horses. Full credit is to be given to our medical officer—Captain Fitzhardinge—for the most satisfactory healthy state of the Regiment, and to Farrier Q.M. Cook for the very satisfactory number of our horses, these two things—health of men and number of horses—enabling the Regiment to start operations over the full War Establishment. That the health was real is evidenced by the fact that during the succeeding three strenuous weeks, the Regiment evacuated seven men for sickness, while another mounted brigade in the same operation during the same period averaged 67 evacuations per regiment. General Chaytor, G.O.C. Anzac Mounted Division, informed the writer in December, 1917, that the Fifth was the strongest in numbers and the healthiest of all the regiments in the country.

With regard to our cover from the elements. Each man was supplied with a bivy sheet, two of which lashed together were supposed to make a cover for two men. The men could use their rifles for the necessary supports. The officers had small calico bivy tents, open at one end. These made a light cover about three feet high, and there was just room for a person to crawl in. These tents were not rainproof. If time permitted, in these tents a trench the length of the bivy and about one foot deep and one foot wide, was dug on one side. This enabled a person to sit down inside the cover. The Regiment carried three bell tents, one for the orderly room, one for the doctor, and one for the quarter-master's store. For practical purposes, we did not have tents during the campaign, although at Masaid in February, 1916, we had tents for a couple of weeks, and also when we came back to Dueidar in November, 1916, we had tents for the period we encamped there. As soon as it was seen that we were going to stop at any place for more than a few days, cover was improvised if there was any material available. While in the oases, palm leaves were used for the purpose of making shacks. Forage bags were also used for this purpose. In a few cases, holes were dug in the ground and cover put over the hole. As a substitute for a table, it was found that the digging of a round trench about one foot wide and one foot deep, leaving the earth in the centre undisturbed, formed an excellent table.

There was no spare fuel on this campaign. Timber was a very scarce commodity in Sinai, Palestine and Syria. What we had was brought from Egypt.

The matter of water supply has been dealt with in a previous chapter.

As regards foods, the scale thereof is set out in Appendix "E" to this narrative.

During our first stay at Dueidar, we, as previously stated, instituted a Regimental Canteen, but after leaving that place it was not practicable to have one. The matter of getting supplies was too difficult. Later on in the campaign, the Australian Canteen became a very useful institution, but up to the period on which we are now writing, we had obtained very little service from this.

HISTORY OF THE 5th LIGHT HORSE REGIMENT.   123

The cooking in standing camps was done usually regimentally or per squadron, as it was found that there was not sufficient fuel to issue out to the men to enable them to do their own cooking. On the line of march, and during operations, the men arranged for their own cooking, usually in small parties of about four, the men collecting what fuel they could for that purpose. As the cooking consisted principally of making tea, the requirements for fuel were not great.

Our friends in Australia had subscribed for travelling kitchens and sent several of them to Egypt, but so far as the Regiment itself was concerned, we received practically no benefit from them. These kitchens were placed at the bases at Cairo and Moascar and were no doubt of service there, but that was not the purpose for which they were sent. A light horse regiment has a certain establishment of horses. It was always short. Some of the horses were away in hospital. A travelling kitchen required at least four horses, and there were none available for the purpose. In any case, in the Sinai Desert these kitchens could not have been moved about. On our second visit to Dueidar in November, 1916, we got two of these kitchens out from Moascar and had the use of them in that standing camp for a couple of months, but this was the only occasion that the Regiment itself had the benefit of these kitchens.

There was a certain limited issue of dixies and meat dishes for cooking purposes issued as per Army Scale. Out of our Regimental Funds, however, we provided the cooks with further requirements in this direction. Before we left Australia, all ranks were supplied from Regimental Funds with "Jack Shays," i.e., quart pots, these being much more suitable than the Army Canteen issue. As these articles from time to time wore out or were lost, fresh ones were purchased from Regimental Funds and so tended to the extra comfort of the men.

With regard to our horses, the light horse regiment has a definite establishment. No spares were allowed, and in fact, no horses were allowed for batmen. In a mobile regiment, such as we were, horses were as necessary for batmen as for anyone else, and it meant that if we only had the authorised establishment of horses, some troopers would have to be left behind to enable the batmen to be mounted. As a matter of fact, some horses were always in hospital, and it took time to get them struck off the strength to enable us to requisition for fresh ones. Even then it took some time for the horses to come up from the base, and all this meant dismounted men. This difficulty, however, in our Regiment, was got over by collecting stray horses and looking after them. There were always thus a number of spare horses in the Regiment to make up for the horses which were on the strength, but were actually in hospital, or which had been struck off but not yet replaced.

Our experience was that the Australian well-bred horse was the best animal for the campaign. A number of horses taken from Australia were presentation horses and, as such, were over the average in breeding. It was found on taking a census of the original horses while in Palestine that there was a bigger percentage of these presentation horses surviving than of ordinary purchased troop horse, and the contention that the well-bred horse was the best stayer was supported.

In the winter of 1917-18 we clipped all our horses. There was a difference of opinion about the expediency of clipping, but we came to the conclusion that it was better to clip and go to the inconvenience of carrying a rug than have the horses with long hair full of dirt and, being sweaty, liable to chills. In the following winter, 1918-19, there was an Army Order against clipping except when authorised by the veterinary officer in case of lice or other special reason. It was remarkable how many horses came within the exceptions.

Questions arose from time to time as to the expediency of watering a horse two or three times in the day, but we finally came to the conclusion that it was quite sufficient to water them twice. The extra third watering meant a lot more work for the men, and the horses did not seem to gain any corresponding benefit from it. During our stay at Gharbi in May, 1917, when we were stationed seven miles away from the Wadi Ghuzze, we sent the horses down about 10 in the morning and brought them back about 3 in the afternoon, giving them two drinks while away. Even this meant 14 miles there and back to water, whereas two separate trips would have meant 28 miles, almost a day's work in itself.

Whenever practicable, we sent the horses out to grass. There was no grazing, of course, while they were in the Sinai Desert, but when we got on to the plains in Palestine there was excellent grazing on the growing crops which covered those plains.

With regard to amusements, there were much more of these in the latter part of the campaign than on Gallipoli, where there was practically none. A limited amount of leave to Egypt was available at times, but this leave was restricted, so far as the men were concerned, to Port Said. On one occasion about half the men, spread over a period of two months, got a week's visit to Alexandria. If there was any prospect of stopping in a place for any time, sports and race meetings were got up, and these afforded a very pleasant change to the ordinary camp routine. The Yeomanry regiments were particularly good at getting up race meetings, and their brigades vied with the Australians in seeing who could put up the best race meeting. Later on, these race meetings were equipped with the orthodox bookmakers and totalisators.

As regards training, it was our practice to do as much as reasonable when out of the front line, taking into consideration the necessity for giving the men proper rest. It was found from experience that they soon became very rusty if not kept up to the mark, particularly in rifle exercises and rifle shooting. As previously stated, we had several rifle competitions while at Dueidar, which resulted in keeping the men up to the standard of rapid shooting. As soon as we got into a back line, reserve squads for machine guns, Lewis guns and Hotchkiss rifles were put in training, and reserves for signallers were put through the necessary courses. All ranks were put through a course of gas exercises and bombing. Fortunately, the Turks did not use gas against us, but there was always the probability that they would do so at any moment.

Schools of instruction were from time to time held, chiefly in Cairo, and as many members of the Regiment as possible were sent to them.

The discipline of the Regiment had been most satisfactory from the point of view of the commanding officer. During the first three years of the existence of the Regiment, there had been, so far as the writer remembers, only two court-martials of members actually serving with the Regiment, the summary powers of the C.O. being quite sufficient to deal with the minor irregularities that one must expect with a regiment of high-spirited men on active service.

The medical organisation of the light horse is dealt with in Appendix "F" hereto. Our Regiment was particularly fortunate with its medical officers. As the result, our sick rate was comparatively low. For the purpose of transport, our medical units were supplied with sand carts, sledges and camel cacholets. The sand cart was the ordinary two-wheeled dray with wide iron tyres, a sledge was practically a sheet of galvanised iron turned up at the front and towed by a camel or a horse. Cachelots could be described as a pair of verandah chairs leashed one to each side of a camel. They were particularly uncomfortable to travel in, but in some places—rough hilly country—it was the only possible way of carrying a sick or wounded man.

PART II.

By CAPTAIN H. WETHERELL.

CHAPTER 30.

BEERSHEBA TO JERUSALEM.

(October to December, 1917)

On the departure of Lieutenant-Colonel Wilson, Lieutenant-Colonel D. C. Cameron took over the command.

The plan for the attack on Beersheba on October 31st, 1917, was briefly as follows:—The 60th and 74th Infantry Divisions were to attack the outer defences on the west and south-west and, having captured them, were to hold the high ground west of the town. Meanwhile, the Anzac and the Australian Mounted Divisions, starting respectively from Asluj and Khalasa were to march during the night right round the enemy left flank, and attack the town from the north-east. The 7th Mounted Brigade, marching direct from Esani, had the duty of masking the strongly entrenched southern end of the outer defences. To the cavalry, thus fell the task of seizing the town of Beersheba itself.

On the night of 30th October, the full Regiment ("B" Squadron having returned from outpost duty with the Camel Brigade) started with three days' rations from Asluj with the Anzac Division for the attack on Beersheba, a distance of 25 miles. The country traversed was difficult and was unknown to us and the maps lacked detail. But there was a bright moon, and no serious enemy opposition was encountered. At dawn next morning the Brigade attacked the entrenched Hill of Tel-el-Sakaty, which was captured about one o'clock, and half an hour later were astride the Hebron-Beersheba-Road. The general battle, however, lasted all day, and as the resistance increased the Division was reinforced by the 3rd Brigade under our old commanding officer. New reinforcements from Hebron had to be held up and the strong position of Tel-el-Saba was not captured by the Division until late in the afternoon. If Beersheba were not taken by nightfall, we should have been in serious straits—among other things—for water, but the brilliant charge of the 4th Brigade at dusk over successive lines of trenches finally captured the position.

Having watered our horses during the night at Beersheba wells, the Regiment was detached next morning and ordered to reconnoitre in the Judean Hills towards Hebron, in the direction of Dhaheriyeh. On reaching a point near Makruneh, the enemy were found to be holding the ridges in some strength and they opened fire with two guns and machine guns. They had created a new flank based on the commanding position of Khuweilfe. In the afternoon the Regiment moved forward to reconnoitre Deir Suideh, but found the enemy holding a strong position, which checked our advance. A withdrawal was made to B.H.Q. at dusk, where we watered and bivouaced for the night. The following days, from the 2nd November to the 5th November, further reconnaissances with the full Brigade were made, and at night touch was maintained with the enemy who were still holding the hills in strength. It had been the intention on the 3rd to attack if possible and work round the enemy's left flank. The country, however, was extraordinarily rugged and difficult, and in many places the horses had to be led up and down the hills. Enemy reinforcements could be seen hurrying down the Hebron Road in motor lorries. We were shelled most accurately during these days although we had good cover, and it was apparent that Bedouin spies were at work. On the 5th four guns concentrated their fire on us and caused casualties—nine men wounded, 14 horses killed and 17 horses wounded.

On the 6th we were withdrawn from the enemy's left flank (there was no water for our horses there) and we took up the pursuit more from the centre through El Sheria, which position had just fallen. Pressure and pursuit were our duties henceforth across the Philistine Plain. The enemy were holding fairly well to their left flank in the very rugged country, but now their centre had given way. The retreat, however, was not by any means a rout. Their artillery heavily shelled our advance and we were counter-attacked strongly on occasions.

HISTORY OF THE 5th LIGHT HORSE REGIMENT.   129

On the 8th two guns were captured by Lieutenant Ogg. For his gallant services on this occasion he was awarded the Military Cross. On the 9th at Kuridaba a large convoy was reported moving N.E., protected by infantry. The 5th Regiment, with the 7th on the right, after a gallop of seven miles, came up with the enemy at Suafie. Pursuit was continued to El Kustine and by this time 300 prisoners were taken and a large amount of booty. The advance continued from day to day, with strong opposition generally, and we had the experience on one occasion at nightfall of facing point blank shrapnel fire from two field guns. The artillery at all times was splendidly served by Austrians and Germans. On another occasion Corporal C. E. Cox was responsible for a fine individual effort. He was in advance with his section when two howitzer guns were come across apparently just abandoned. He immediately galloped over the brow of a hill in search of the gun teams and he there saw three men mounted and getting away. Corporal Cox was well mounted and out-distancing his own section and another section which had been sent to his support, accounted for all the three. After a gallop of more than a mile, he would fling himself from his horse when within range and, with bridle over his arm, bring his rifle to bear on horse or man, and then would mount again and continue the pursuit of the remainder. The last man's horse had been brought down, and he took cover behind a boulder, and then with his artillery rifle (he was an Austrian officer) fired at Corporal Cox at only about 20 yards range. Cox, however, was also ready with a second shot, and he won this duel even against these odds. Altogether, he had five shots in this pursuit and every one took effect. It was really as brilliant a piece of individual Light Horse work as one could imagine. He received the M.M.

The pursuit of the enemy continued until November 18th, when the objective was reached and an entrenched outpost line was taken up east of Jaffa and overlooking the river Auja.

Hotchkiss rifles were invaluable in the pursuit. The following is an instance how they could be used to deceive the enemy as to our strength. The advance troop (about 20 men) approached a village in which were probably 100 of the enemy endeavouring to get stores away by train. Without any definite target the Hotchkiss opened fire. When the troop advanced covered by this fire, the enemy dispersed and much booty was captured, including 1,500 rifles, without a casualty in the troop. From 30th October to the 18th November 120 miles of enemy country had been covered, 629 prisoners were taken, and four guns, 1,500 rifles and much other booty fell to the Regiment. This defeat of the Turkish Army and the pursuit up the Philistine Plains, over rolling downs country, was a tremendous change for us all. Gaza, of evil fame, was no more—the two disastrous battles there, with the months following of continuous dust, heat, road making, patrols, reconnaissances, etc., were in the limbo of the past. What a change had General Allenby wrought! Oranges obtained during the pursuit were a great treat.

The Turkish Army was now cut in two, and the Regiment's duty from 18th November was to assist in holding the left half of our line. The enemy were at all times active and made frequent attacks. Horses were sent to the rear, and it was trench warfare again. It was impossible to work on the trenches during daylight owing to enemy fire, and at night time every available man was kept digging and improving trenches. The Jewish village of Mulebbis was just in front of us, under enemy occupation. On the 6th December the Regiment was relieved by the Royal Scots Fusiliers and on the 7th bivouaced at Wadi Hanein, the weather then being wet and cold. On the 9th we heard that Jerusalem had fallen. The news came unexpectedly, for we had not known what was taking place on our right, and we could not but be stirred by this news. After four centuries of conquest the Holy City of Christendom was at last rid of the Turks.

The objective of the present advance had now been reached and there was now a lull in operations; a programme of training was then carried out at Esdud. Respirators were issued for the first time and all ranks received instructions thereon. Christmas Day was spent here in wet and cold weather. On the 28th December instructions were received to proceed north of Jaffa and report to the 52nd Division. On our arrival at Richon-le-Zion orders were received to rejoin the Brigade at Esdud, as it had been ascertained that it was impossible to carry out the work intended. The road passed over had been very heavy and in places boggy, especially on some black soil flats near Vebna. The last day

HISTORY OF THE 5th LIGHT HORSE REGIMENT.

of the year was marked for us by a disinfecting parade at Esdud railway siding.

On the 20th December, this day being the 3rd anniversary of the Regiment's departure from Australia, a census was taken of the original men and horses then with the Regiment. The result was as follows; and it curiously shows nearly the same proportion of casualties of men and horses.

Original strength, excluding M.G. Section 523
    Of these there were then with the Regiment .. 140
Original strength or horses, excluding M.G. Section .. 572
    Of these there were then with the Regiment .. 165

The C.O. of the Regiment, Lieutenant-Colonel Cameron, D.S.O., proceeded to England on private business and handed over to Major Bolingbroke, D.S.O., until the C.O.'s return in April. The lull in operations continued through January and February, 1918. This period was one of the very few real rests from military operations, but the weather was often very wet and conditions were far from comfortable. No rest from training was permitted, and the Hotchkiss guns sections were brought to a high stage of efficiency. On the 13th January a move was made from Esdud to Wadi Hanein on account of the wet weather. Squadrons were separated as a precaution against aircraft attack, and tents were camouflaged with red soil and water All ranks were innoculated here for cholera.

On the 14th March a move was made to Latron and from thence to Jerusalem, where parties of 10 under an officer were allowed to visit the city.

CHAPTER 31.

AMMAN RAID.

It now befell to the Regiment to take part in the raid to Amman, the object of which was to relieve the pressure on the Arab forces operating about Maan, to destroy the viaduct and tunnel on the railway near Amman, and if possible to draw the Turkish garrison from Maan.

On the 20th a move was made towards Jericho, which had been captured by Sir Philip Chetwode on the 21st February. We passed down the great winding metalled road, past the Good Samaritan Inn, and then crossed the Jordan on the 24th, and took up position on the right of the 60th Division, which was moving to attack Es Salt. The Jordan was crossed on the 24th, and for the night march through the hills the 5th Regiment formed the advance-guard with Lieutenant Broughton in charge of the screen. It was a very dark night, with pouring rain and a bitterly cold wind. Transport and guns were sent back as the road was impassable for them. The country rises 4,000 feet, and it took 24 hours to cover 16 miles to Ain Hekr. At Ain-es-Sir the Regiment cut the telephone line between Es Salt and Amman (the plateau of Gilead). On the plateau the ground was so boggy that it was impossible to move off the road. On the morning of the 25th a large motor convoy was observed on the Es Salt-Amman road and Major Bolingbroke, who was then commanding the Regiment, moved out to attack it with "B" and "C" Squadrons. The enemy on the ridges defending the convoy, estimated at about 50, dispersed as soon as the attack started and the captures included 12 prisoners, 19 motor lorries, 3 motor cars, 1 armoured car and 8 waggons. All forage had now been consumed and it was necessary to obtain a supply of doura from the Camel Brigade. The Regiment had now been marching for three consecutive nights under conditions of the utmost discomfort and fatigue. Amman was attacked on the 27th together with the rest of the forces, but the attack was unsuccessful. A number of shells burst among the led horses of "C" Squadron, killing 1 man, 10 horses, and wounding 1 man and 20 horses. Lance-Corporal McIndoe, showed conspicuous gallantry in this attack by lying on his back under heavy machine-gun fire and maintaining communication with B.H.Q. by signal flags. For this he was awarded the Military Medal. Orders had been given by General Chaytor to General Ryrie that an attempt be made to blow up a railway bridge to the north of Amman and cut communication with that place. It was recognised that this was a desperate undertaking, as the force dispatched would be out in "the blue," and no help could be given if it was attacked. Major Bolingbroke volunteered to do the job with the 5th Regiment (less "C" Squadron).

He was given a demolition party of New Zealanders. Accordingly, on the night of the 27th, the force moved out around the enemy flank to a railway bridge about five miles north of Amman. It was a most difficult march over rugged country, and great credit is due to Lieut. Jones, with a troop of "B" Squadron, who formed the advance troop. It wanted a good bushman to find the way, as detours had constantly to be made, and there was always the chance of meeting enemy patrols. The force did meet parties of Bedouins, who proved friendly, though it was feared they might inform the enemy of the movement. On arrival at the railway bridge it was found unguarded. All telegraph wires were cut and the bridge blown up. The force rejoined the Brigade without casualty. A telegram was received from General Chaytor, congratulating Major Bolingbroke and the Regiment on the achievement. It was subsequently ascertained that the Regiment narrowly escaped being cut off by a large enemy force which would have meant a stiff fight to get through.

On the 30th a further attack on Amman was unsuccessful, and on the 31st a withdrawal to the Jordan Valley commenced, the Regiment acting as rear-guard, but the enemy did not follow up with any vigour. On arrival on the 3rd April a line of outposts covering the Ghoraniyeh bridge head was taken over. The Amman operations were very severe on all ranks. The change from the heat of the Jordan Valley into the bitterly cold wet weather on the plateau was almost paralysing. Several natives in the Camel Transport Brigade died from exposure. The whole operation (owing to the delay from bad weather and the warning thus given) was successful only in so far as it drew off the Turkish troops who were operating against the Sherif Feisal and (what was most important) in persuading the enemy that our ultimate advance against Damascus would be made from our right flank. After the withdrawal from Amman, the enemy returned to his strong position in the foothills at Shunit Nimrin, facing our bridge head at Ghoraniyeh, and on 11th April attacked our position with 800-1,000 men and also attacked the Camel Brigade at Musallabeh. Both attacks were heavily repulsed. Before the attack the Regiment had erected 2,500 yards of single apron wire. Lieutenant-Colonel Cameron, D.S.O., now rejoined and resumed command from Major Bolingbroke, D.S.O. On the 15th the Jordan was crossed and the Brigade was joined at Tel-Es-Sultan on the Wadi Nuhemeir, three miles north of Jericho, with the Mount of Temptation overlooking the camp. The weather was now excessively hot, as much as 125 degrees in the shade. The valley had been churned into fine powder, and the dust rose so thickly that when riding one could not at times see one's horse's head.

CHAPTER 32.

ES SALT RAID.

General Allenby had now decided on another raid into the Land of Gilead. The objects of this raid were to cut off and destroy the force at Shunet Nimrin, to take Es Salt, and to hold it until the Arab forces could take it over, and generally to assist the Arabs. On the 27th April the Regiment crossed the Jordan on the pontoon bridge at Ghoraniyeh and bivouaced at Hajla. On the 29th three days' emergency rations were drawn for men and two days' forage for horses, all being carried on man and horse. On the 30th the Brigade marched from Es Salt up to the Um-Es-Shert track, a few miles to the north of Shunet Nimrin. The track up the hill was very rough and horses had to be led in single file a great part of the distance of 13 miles. Early next morning the Australian Mounted Division was joined about two miles from Es Salt, and we then learned that General Wilson with the 3rd Brigade had captured the town. Thereafter there were a very strenuous couple of days. The Regiment passed through the town and an outpost taken up at Ain Hemar at 4 p.m. Instructions were then received (May 2) to attack the rear of Shunet Nimrin position on foot. These instructions were then withdrawn and orders were issued to return to our horses and move against Amman reinforcements which attacked strongly during the night of 2nd-3rd May. "B" and "C" Squadrons were in front line between the 7th and 8th Regiments, with "A" Squadron in support. Another exposed ridge, known as Bald Hill, and about 700 yards in front of our position, was held with a troop (Lieutenant Ogg's). At dawn on the 3rd the enemy advanced and attacked strongly. Our reserve squadron ("A") then went into the line to assist the defence. The attack was repelled, and a number of the enemy (305) who had advanced so far that a machine gun from the 8th Regiment could attack them from the rear, surrendered and were just got in in time to prevent reinforcements reaching them that were coming at the double along the Amman Road. An instance of German treachery may be here related. The Turks were holding up rags, bushes, rifles, etc., in token of surrender, and Lieutenant Wetherell then stood up and waved to them to come in. At once a concealed machine gun, manned by Germans, fired a burst at him, but miraculously did not hit him, and they then walked in with their machine gun to a different part of the line. Every available man, nearly all the horse-holders, batmen, etc., were now put into the line and the general position of all our forces became very serious as the day progressed. The 4th Brigade, which was to hold the enemy from moving across the Jordan towards the Um-Es-Shert track, was forced to retire several miles with a loss of nine guns and some transport.

The enemy stronghold at Shunet Nimrin had not fallen— the Arabs had vanished into space and consequently the Ain Es Sir Road was left open to enemy reinforcements—and the Turks were strongly attacking on all sides of Es Salt. Our only line of retreat was down the Es Shert goat-track, and that might be closed at any time. The 1st Brigade had been deflected to defend the track, owing to the 4th Brigade's precarious position lower down, and consequently were not fully available at Es Salt. It was therefore decided to withdraw during the night. At midnight we held the ground to the west of Es Salt until the 3rd Brigade passed through the town and down the track. Corporal Simms had to be left behind in the Turkish hospital at Es Salt, as he was too badly wounded to ride. The Camel cacholets (dreadful torture to the badly wounded) were the only means of transport, and they had all left. (He was eventually recovered at Damascus quite fit again). The town's people were excited as we passed, and there was a good deal of scattered shooting in the rear of the column. Lieutenant Wetherell's troop was in the rear and he found it advisable to dismount a section to keep off the "jackals" who attack friend and foe when retreating, in the hope of loot. The track was with difficulty kept open long enough for us to reach the valley unmolested, except for ineffective shelling, and the camp across the Jordan was reached at 10 a.m. on the 4th May.

Want of sleep was the greatest hardship—for five days there was practically no sleep. Our feet, too, were very sore from clambouring about the stony hills. But our spirits were still buoyant. On reaching the valley, someone was

HISTORY OF THE 5th LIGHT HORSE REGIMENT. 137

heard to humorously repeat the plaintive question from Poe's "Raven":

> "Is there, is there, balm in Gilead?
> Tell me, I implore."

"Not a skerrik—for us, anyway," decidedly said someone else.

The whole operation was a very daring raid, and if the Es Shert track had not been kept open, the whole cavalry force in the hills would have found themselves in a very interesting position.

Our allies, the Arabs, for whose benefit the operation was mainly undertaken, vanished into thin air, but the final result was that the enemy lost over 900 men and was more than ever sure that the next big advance would take place from this flank. Thus a whole army was kept facing us in the Valley, giving General Allenby an opportunity on the Jaffa side, of which he was not slow to avail himself when the time was ripe.

CHAPTER 33.

JORDAN VALLEY (August).

From the 5th May to 22nd May it was the case of the "daily round, the common task," and a few extracts from the laconic Regimental War Diary may serve as illustrations of the variety of the light horseman's duties when not in the front line:

5th and 6th.—In bivouac south of Jericho.

7th.—Six enemy planes bombed Brigade camp. 7th L.H. had 8 men killed and 10 wounded in one troop. No casualties in this Regiment. Captain Boyd left with three troops to relieve 7th L.H. in outpost at Hajla Ford, Kasr and Yesud Henu.

8th.—Three enemy 'planes again over camp, but did not bomb Brigade area. Horses being watered in Wadi Kelt—watering arrangements not good.

9th.—Party proceeded to bridgehead at Ghoraniyeh to erect barbed wire. Weather extremely hot.

11th.—Regiment moved at 1415 to fresh bivouac dense cloud of dust.

12th.—Attached for duty Australian Mounted Division, working party of 1 officer and 50 other ranks sent out at 1700 forming and improving roads.

13th.—Working parties sent to Auja Crossing, digging fire trenches.

And so on, from day to day.

On the 22nd the Brigade took over section of the outpost line on Wadi Auja. On the 23rd stood to arms at 0330 (3.30 a.m.) and a patrol of 1 officer and 8 other ranks sent to Tel-el-Truny and remained in position until 1700 (5 a.m.). One or two more entries from the Diary give samples of the duties to the 6th June:

25th.—Stand-to 0330, patrol to Tel-el-Truny. Patrol fired on at 0830; one man killed. Working parties sent out for road-making.

26th.—Stand-to 0330. Usual patrol to Tel-el-Truny. One officer and 60 other ranks for erecting barbed wire report O.C. field troop. One officer and 50 men for road-making.

31st.—Stand-to 0330. Usual patrol to Tel-el-Truny. Three officers and 130 other ranks report O.C., Field Troop for road-making.

How well we remember the daily dawn patrol to Tel-el-Truny. We were nearly always fired on, and it surprised us greatly that the enemy never set a trap for us there.

On the 5th June orders were received that the Brigade would move that night to Solomon's Pools, in the Judean Hills near Bethlehem. This was very welcome news. Talaat-et-Dumm (Hill of Blood) was reached at 0145 (1.45 a.m.) next morning. The day was spent here; it was excessively hot, with stifling dust storms. The march was resumed at 1930. The night was hot until the column arrived near Bethany when the weather changed suddenly, and when Jerusalem was reached, a bitterly cold wind was blowing. The difference in temperature was 60 degrees, and, as at Amman, it was very trying. Men and horses were very tired. The Regiment stayed at Solomon's Pools (reservoirs of the ancient waterworks of Jerusalem supposed to have been constructed by King Solomon) until the 21st June, and the rest there in a beautiful climate was spent in training for bayonet-fighting, signalling and Hotchkiss rifle, with small leave parties to Jerusalem and Bethlehem. It was there that those exciting fights between a scorpion and a curious kind of tarantula spider first entertained us. On the 22nd June a return was made to the Jordan Valley. Descending the 3,000 feet by the old Roman road, the Valley beneath, 1,300 feet below sea level and covered with dust, looked like an inferno, and it did not belie its looks. It was truly a Valley of Desolation. Even the Bedouins clear out of it in the summer, and the only inhabitants who remained were a hybrid race descended from the African slaves who had been imported by the Arabs in their days of prosperity. Scorpions, spiders, snakes and sand-flies were plentiful and helped to while away one's leisure moments. Local authorities stated that it was impossible for Europeans to live there after 1st May on account of malaria of a most virulent type. The official military handbook of Palestine confirmed the local opinion by the statement that "Nothing is known of the climate of the lower Jordan Valley in summer time, since no civilized human being has yet been found to spend a summer there."

On the 23rd the Regiment took over the defence of a new series of detached posts in the Wadi Mellahah, west of the Jordan—"Shell," "Star," "Scrap," "Salt" and "Safe" were the names—the "S" series. The whole of the Valley was now defended by a series of detached, wired posts. It was not a strong defence, but was economical with troops. The enemy was in touch, and there was always "something doing." There was no rest here, apart from active offence and defence operations. A vigorous campaign was carried on against the mosquito, swamps were drained, and water confined to running channels; all this work falling on the troops, as the Egyptian Labour Corps was not to be employed in shelled areas. But one thing (and one only) was appreciated, and that was plenty of good water, and some of us experienced a swim in the weird waters of the Dead Sea.

Here are typical extracts from the Diary (1918):

>July 3rd.—At 2330 (11.30 p.m.) enemy patrols approached to high ground north of "Star" post. They

fired three flares, threw bombs and opened rifle-fire, with the evident intention of drawing our fire.

July 4th.—Patrol of 1 officer and 2 other ranks sent out from "Safe" post at 1930 and proceeded east of Jordan, with object of locating enemy who were supposed to draw water from the Jordan. Withdrew at 2145, no sign of enemy. No. 181 Sergeant Harrison evacuated to hospital. Eight reinforcements march in from Moascar. Garrisons in posts employed improving and strengthening positions.

July 6th.—The captured enemy gun, firing from — Regiment headquarters, did most effective shooting on enemy-wired positions N.E. of "Star" post.

(The gun referred to afterwards burst and killed some of its crew).

These extracts serve to illustrate the daily doings up to the 14th July, when the enemy made a real attack on the Valley positions. The attempt was to cut off our troops in the Jordan by penetrating between the Desert Mounted Corps and the 20th Corps of Infantry in the hills on our left. I will here give extracts from Colonel Cameron's report of the 14th July:

"At 0245 enemy artillery opened on Mussalabeh. At 0300 our listening-post in front of "Star" post was driven in. At 0315 enemy shelled high ground in rear of posts. At 0330 enemy were observed digging in on high ground 700 yards east of "Star" post. At 0400 the officer in charge of these men (a German major) was killed by one of our advance posts. At 0430 "A" Battery, H.A.C., fired on enemy who were digging in and they withdrew. A small patrol was then sent out by "C" Squadron from 'Star,' 'Shell' and 'Scrap' posts, and they reported 150-200 enemy sheltering under high bank east of Wadi Mellalah. Lieutenant J. D. Macansh and 14 men then moved out across the Wadi to drive them if possible from the high ground which dominated our position. They got within 20 yards of the enemy, whom they surprised, and who used bombs, which, however, were very local in effect. The retirement of our party was covered by fire from the posts and 15

German prisoners were brought back. At 0815 Lieutenant Macansh and 2nd Lieutenant Byrnes with 20 men again moved forward to dislodge the enemy, and on this occasion the attempt was a complete success. The enemy casualties were 26 prisoners, 25 killed, and 30 wounded. One machine gun, 4 automatic rifles, and a quantity of ammunition were captured. Our casualties, 1 officer and 2 other ranks slightly wounded. The enemy force consisted entirely of Germans; when they were surprised, those who were not captured, killed or wounded fled in wild disorder towards their wire, 1,000 yards in the rear. This is the first occasion when this Regiment has engaged a force comprised entirely of Germans. After providing a flank for protection and excluding the bombers, who crawled forward on the enemy's flank, Lieutenant Macansh's party, which finally attacked 150-200 Germans, consisted of no more than 12 men. All ranks engaged in this enterprise displayed great personal courage. The enterprise throughout was a fine example of able and gallant leadership, inspiring men to any undertaking, however hazardous."

For their services on this occasion Captain Boyd and Lieutenant Macansh were granted Military Crosses.

Throughout the day the enemy continued active. Snipers worked along the Jordan opposite the gap in the line between the 2nd and 4th Brigades. A party from the reserve squadron ("A"), under Lieutenant Ogg, drove them back, Sergeant W. Chaille being killed. A shot wounded both Lieutenant Broughton and Lieutenant A. V. Smith while in the R.H.Q. tent. The brunt of the enemy attack fell on the 1st Brigade holding the Abu Tellul Salient, a German battalion penetrating between the posts, but a counter-attack was most successful, and practically the whole battalion was accounted for. We were interested to learn later that Turkish troops were to have supported the attack, but for some reason, which, we understood, was friction with the Germans, they did not do so. In this we were fortunate! The posts were held until the 16th July, when the 6th L.H. took them over, and the Regiment moved to the reserve in the Wadi Auja, the duties comprising working parties for various posts, etc. The heat was at all times intense, but one favourable thing was that we were alongside water.

On the 28th the bivouac area was heavily shelled by 5.9, 4.2, and 77 m.m. batteries. The shooting was uncannily accurate, and our casualties were 2 men killed and 4 wounded, 19 horses killed and 16 wounded. It was a tragic day. A move was shortly afterwards made to the Corp's rest area at Solomon's Pools. The 25th August saw the Regiment back again in the Valley at the Auja bridgehead. The strain of the Valley conditions was now severely felt, and a Diary entry on the 31st August states: "Owing to malaria and other febrile complaints, the number of evacuated from the Regiment during August exceeded the total evacuations on account of sickness during the previous 18 months."

From the 25th August to the date of the great advance on 19th September, a great amount of reconnaissance work was carried out, nearly all under fire. On the 18th September Private S. Marshell was killed, Major Bolingbroke (second in command) and Corporal L. M. Case were wounded, and Private N. Wright reported missing, all on one small patrol. Germans were apparently encountered, as fire was withheld until the patrol was very close. Sergeant Solling here did gallant work in getting Major Bolingbroke, severely wounded in the face, back to our lines.

CHAPTER 34.

FINAL ADVANCE (September).

A few words may be given of General Allenby's plan for a great break-through. This plan was bold and ambitious, it was brilliant in execution, and it resulted in the greatest cavalry pursuit the world has possibly ever seen—an advance of 450 miles and the complete destruction of three Turkish armies.

The two trans-Jordan raids had given the enemy the impression that we intended to attack up the Jordan Valley, or east of it, and steps were taken to confirm that impression. The Anzac Division was to boldly reconnoitre across the Valley; the camps in the Valley vacated by the cavalry were left standing, and other camps were pitched there, and occupied by a few men to show signs of movement. New bridges were thrown across the Jordan, miles of Decauville railway were laid and hundreds of dummy horses were erected (a framework of sticks with bagging over them) on dummy horse-lines in the dummy camps. Every day for some considerable time a battalion or two of infantry marched down the Jerusalem-Jericho road, from Talaat-ed-Dumm, in view of the enemy at Shunet Nimrin, and were brought back at night in motor lorries. A German air reconnaissance report, dated 17th September, afterwards found among General Liman von Sander's papers at Nazareth, stated that "far from there being any diminution in the cavalry in the Jordan Valley, there are evidences of 23 more squadrons." The truth was that the force in the Valley was depleted to the great concentration on the coastal sector where the great attack was to take place. The Anzac Division were the only mounted troops left, the remainder being a composite infantry force composed of Indians, British West Indians, and two Jewish battalions. For the benefit of the native population, elaborate bogus preparations were made for the removal of General Allenby's headquarters to Jerusalem. Lastly, lest a chance word should reach a native enemy spy within our lines, everything was done to further the belief among our own troops that we were likely to attack from our east flank. A great factor in the secrecy maintained was the supremacy at last gained by our aerial forces. During a week in June 100 hostile aeroplanes had crossed our lines; only four ventured across during the period of concentration!

On the 19th September General Allenby, after a short intensive bombardment and an infantry attack, had broken through on the Coast, and three divisions of cavalry were galloping up the Plain of Sharon, shortly to reach the Plain of Esdraelon—Armageddon, of the ancient world. It was a terrific blow and it was soon felt in the Jordan Valley. The Turks' IV Army, which was facing our troops in the Jordan Valley and to the east of Jordan, must retreat or be cut off, and the duty of the Anzac Division was now to cross the Jordan for the third and last time, advance on Amman, and cut off the Turkish garrisons at Maan and in Arabia. The enemy held their positions until the 22nd September, and then commenced to withdraw. Before dawn on the morning of the 23rd, General Chaytor's Valley force advanced in strength from Hajla in the South (where our Brigade was) to Jisr ed Damieh in the North. The foot-hills were clear, except for scattered parties of cavalry, and by nightfall the Regiment was climbing up the Ain-Es-Sir track through Kajr Mujahid. The track was so rough and narrow that the enemy by the explosion of a few mines was able to check the Brigade for some hours during the night of the 23rd. Ain-Es-Sir was reached at noon on the 24th, and the Regiment was ordered to proceed to Ain Hemar and bivouac for the night. During the night orders were received that the Division would attack Amman the following morning. This Regiment led the Brigade with the New Zealanders on the left, detached posts were met and quickly overcome. Lieutenant B. R. Byrnes, with a weak troop, galloped 900 yards under machine gun and rifle-fire and attacked a position, resulting in the capture of 3 officers, 44 other ranks, 2 field guns and 2 machine guns. At the same time Lieutenant A. Currie advanced with his troop dismounted across a long stretch of exposed ground and under heavy fire. When within 80 yards of the position the white flag was raised, and as Lieutenant Currie and his men moved forward to take the surrender, the enemy reopened fire. Lieutenant Currie and all his men, except two, fell wounded, Lieutenant Currie mortally. Nevertheless, Sergeant P. Kelly with two men, one of them wounded, went on and seized the position with 33 prisoners. For this Sergt. Kelly was awarded the D.C.M. When the posts were overcome, the Regiment pushed forward to within 2,000 yards of Amman. All approaches were covered with machine gun fire, and shell-fire was encountered. Gradually pressing forward, with the Canterbury Rifles on the left and the 7th Regiment on the right, the resistance collapsed, and "C" Squadron entered the town at 1330 (25th Sept.). At 1520 Colonel Cameron sent the following message to Brigade: "Amman all clear, am sending one squadron to occupy high ground east of town. Our casualties throughout the day were 4 officers and 14 other ranks wounded and a number of horses wounded. Thirty officers, 552 other ranks, 3 field guns, 10 machine guns, 1 Hotchkiss rifle, 1 Lewis gun, 2 motor cars, and a considerable quantity of stores and equipment were captured." For his gallant con-

HISTORY OF THE 5th LIGHT HORSE REGIMENT.   145

duct on this occasion, Lieutenant B. R. Byrnes was awarded the M.C.

With Amman in his hands General Chaytor prepared for the destruction of the enemy force—5,000-6,000 strong—which had for some months been defending Maan against the Arabs, 120 miles to the south. The 1st Brigade followed up the enemy's rearguard, while our Brigade was diverted south to intercept this force. "A" Squadron of this Regiment was sent on the 26th with explosives to destroy the railway near Leban, some miles south of Amman. The line was destroyed in two places and touch was gained with the enemy troops at Leban.

CHAPTER 35.

THE SURRENDER AT ZIZA.

Now is reached the very remarkable incident of the surrender of the Maan force at Ziza—an incident probably unique in the whole annals of warfare. It was a case of defending enemies in the field from attacks by allies. Colonel Cameron's report is, therefore, given in full:

Report on operations on 29th September, 1918, culminating in the surrender of the Turkish force at Ziza.

Reference maps: Syria, Hafia and Jerusalem. Sheets, 1/250000.

At 0500 on 29th September, the Regiment, less one squadron, left camp near Amman, under orders to patrol south and get in touch with the enemy.

On arrival at Leban, natives reported that the enemy were holding Ziza with 600 cavalry and a considerable force of infantry.

"C" Squadron, under Captain J. M. Boyd, M.C., was in advance. El Kastel was found all clear.

We continued to push forward, our advanced troops halting within 700 yards of the Turkish position at Ziza.

At 10.30 a Turkish officer and 4 other ranks came out from Ziza on a trolley along the railway line, under the white flag. This officer handed me a note from the commandant of the Turkish force at Ziza. The commandant conveyed in this note that he wished to see me, and steps were immediately taken to arrange this meeting. At this time it was observed that the hills, east and west, were occupied by a large number of men mounted on horses and camels.

At 1100 I received a further communication from the commandant of the Turkish force at Ziza. He desired to surrender, but was afraid to do so. He maintained that if his force laid down its arms, we were not strong enough to protect him from the Bedouins. He also declined to personally leave his position and come out to interview us. I sent Captain J. M. Boyd, M.C., with a Turkish officer into Ziza to interview the commandant. He returned with an official surrender, couched in the following terms:

"To O.C., British Troops (Colonel Cameron):

"I hereby surrender unconditionally all my force, guns, ammunition, stores, etc., at Ziza, under my command, and in so doing claim your protection for the safety of my soldiers, wounded and sick."

(Sgd.) By the Turkish Commandant.
Ziza, 20/9/'18.

At this time one of our 'planes dropped the following message:

"Enemy have two field guns on track facing W at approx. 143/035. Rifle pits between you and station are occupied.

"Good luck to you,

"(Sgd.)   J. W. FOWLER."

I had now obtained direct communication with D.H.Q., my signallers having worked strenuously to repair the telephone line, which was broken in many places.

At this time mounted Bedouins and Arabs were concentrating from all directions with the intention of joining us in the attack on Ziza.

Fighting continued throughout the day between the Turks and Arabs on the east, south and west of their position, we holding the ground north of the Turkish position.

HISTORY OF THE 5th LIGHT HORSE REGIMENT. 147

The Turkish commandant expressed a claim that I should not attempt to enter Ziza with my two squadrons until sufficient reinforcements had arrived to protect the garrison from the hostile Bedouins.

D.H.Q. advised me that, unless the garrison surrendered, they would be bombed by 10 of our 'planes at 1500.

At 1445 hours after receiving the official surrender, D.H.Q. informed me that there was some doubt, as to whether the message, cancelling the raid, had reached the Royal Air Force. I immediately sent an officer, Lieutenant A. B. Crawford, with our Regimental Report Centre Sign and White Strips, instructing him to place them in the rear of the Turkish trenches. I also instructed him to explain the circumstances and advise the garrison to take cover.

I was greatly relieved to receive a communication from Division at 1515, notifying me that the raid had been cancelled. At intervals during the day I sent small parties under an officer into Ziza with instruction to re-assure the commandant that the Brigade was moving out with all haste and the situation would be cleared before dark.

At 1600 I sent Lieutenant J. D. Macansh, M.C., to the Turkish commandant, with instructions that, in the event of our not moving in before dark, he must keep his trenches manned.

Throughout the day I was surrounded by Arabs and Bedouins. They all enquired whether the Turks had surrendered. They maintained that, if so, they should be allowed to enter the position and take the rifles. If the Turks had not surrendered, they desired me to attack at once, promising to assist me. Several times during the day they moved forward, but were immediately driven back by Turkish machine gun and rifle-fire.

At 1600 I sent a message, by Arabs, to the Bedouins gathering round the position, to the effect that if they attempted to attack the Turks, I would attack them. This had the desired effect, and they began to withdraw.

Although throughout the day the situation appeared at times somewhat critical, fortunately, my men did not fire one shot at the Bedouins.

At 1715 the divisional commander arrived by motor car at my headquarters, 700 yards north of the Turkish trenches.

In company with a Turkish officer I immediately proceeded to the headquarters of the commandant at Ziza, located at the railway station. Captain Rhodes drove me in, and after some delay, we brought the Turkish commandant out to the divisional commander. He (the Turkish commandant) was most reluctant to leave Ziza, and expressed the greatest concern with regard to the Turkish garrison, particularly the sick and wounded.

The Regiment entered Ziza before dusk, the 7th Regiment co-operating on our right. I established my headquarters at the railway station, B.H.Q. in close proximity.

The trenches throughout the night were held by our men and the Turks, constituting, perhaps, an unique situation.

I was greatly struck by the fact, that the Turkish garrison, notwithstanding its superiority in numbers, was terrified of the Bedouins. Several instances occurred during the day of Bedouins capturing odd Turks. Though armed, the Turks seemed unable to protect themselves, and simply screamed like dying pigs.

The condition of the garrison on the whole was deplorable and, although they appeared to have food in quantity, they were evidently worn out.

DONALD C. CAMERON,
Lieutenant-Colonel,
Commanding 5th Light Horse Regiment, A.I.F.

In this dramatic way ended the Anzac Division's campaign east of the Jordan. The debacle to the Turkish forces there was complete. In nine days 10,300 prisoners, 57 guns, 132 machine guns, etc., were captured by the Anzac Division, with casualties to the whole Division of only 139. This Regiment's share, which includes the Ziza force of about 4,500, is recorded in the Regimental Diary as follows:—Prisoners, 5,186, guns 18, machine guns 40, railway engines 3, trucks 25.

The remainder of the Turkish forces east of the Jordan were cut off and destroyed before reaching Damascus.

CHAPTER 36.

WADI HANEIN, SEMAKH AND RAFA.

The Brigade now returned to the west of the Jordan. On the 2nd October the Regiment was at Ain es-Sir, the 3rd at Nimrin, 5th Hajla, 8th Talaat-ed-Dumm, 9th Mount of Olives, 12th Latron, and from the 13th October to 6th November at Wadi Hanein. A Diary note on the 31st October (date of Turkish Armistice) states: "of those original members of the Regiment who sailed from Australia in 1914, there remained 15 officers and 79 other ranks, of which 48 are N.C.O.'s Only two officers are now with the Regiment, who left Australia with commissioned rank. Of the men evacuated sick during the month, 35 were original members of the Regiment, and many of them had never been absent through sickness during their 47 months' service. There can be no doubt that the period of 6½ months spent in the Jordan Valley, during the unhealthiest time of the year, undermined the general health of the Regiment."

On the 7th November there was another move to Ras-el-Ain, thence to Tulkeram, Messudie, Jenin, Nazareth (watering horses at St. Mary's Well), Tiberias, and then to Semakh on the southern shore of the Sea of Galilee (Lake Tiberias), which was the camp from the 14th November to the end of February. A few items from the Diary will best serve to illustrate the life during this period:

14th Nov.—Morning spent in getting camp into order and generally settling down. Drying blankets, clothes, etc. Swimming horses in Lake Tiberias to get them clean—they were covered with mud.

15th Nov.—Party left on detachment to Jaaune for patrol work. Picquet duty in village.

20th Nov.—Tents arrived; very welcome. Usual village picquet.

22nd Nov.—All squadrons on roadmaking.

24th Nov.—S.S.-Cpl. Hayes and three shoeing-smiths left for Jisr-Benat-Yakub to shoe horses of "D" troop, Australian Engineers, who were stranded there.

26th Nov.—Party to escort prisoners to Tul Keram.

6th Dec.—General Allenby, C.-in-C., arrived Semakh.

12th Dec.—"B" Squadron obtained possession of person of Chief Sheik, causing Beisan trouble.

14th Dec.—Successful day's races.

1st Jan. (1919).—Gift of 500 oranges from Y.M.C.A., Haifa, distributed.

8th Jan.—Train in from Damascus for first time.

18th Dec.—Inspection of Regiment dismounted by C.-in-C.; address after inspection.

24th Dec.—Party searched Bedouin village near Jisr Majamie under supervision of Captain Kenny-Leveck (political officer). Sheik arrested and taken to Tiberias.

26th Dec.—Rosh Pinah patrol report all clear.

29th Dec.—220 other ranks left for Moascar to await embarkation (urgent reasons).

7th Feb.—Two officers and 50 other ranks to stand by at disposal of Military Governor, Tiberias.

14th Feb.—Recent reinforcements isolated on account of an outbreak of German measles at Moascar. Fifty worn-out horses destroyed.

17th Feb.—Issue of five bags sugar, 4,000 cigarettes, 400 tins tobacco, 100 packets candles, 250 lbs. coffee, from Mrs. Chisholm's fund.

On the 1st March, 1919, the return from the front was commenced and the 5th Regiment entrained at Nazareth for Rafa. The period—6th to 22nd—was spent at Rafa, cleaning saddlery, etc., and preparing for the return to Australia. Kantara was reached by rail on the 23rd, the horses having been previously sent to the remount depot at Moascar.

THE EGYPTIAN RISING.

But the dreams of Australia were not yet to be realised. An Egyptian rebellion had broken out, and so urgent at the outset was the call for mounted men that even the convalescents from the hospitals were enlisted. All Australian troops, except the 1st and 2nd L.H. Regiments (which had already embarked for Australia), were sent into the disturbed area.

HISTORY OF THE 5th LIGHT HORSE REGIMENT. 151

There was no actual organised fighting, but the rebellion took the form of murders of soldiers and European civilians, looting, tearing up railways, destruction of bridges, telegraph and telephone lines, etc., and there was a lot more patrolling to be done before it was quelled.

At Kantara on the 24th March, 150 horses and 150 mules were drawn from the remount depot, and by 6 p.m. that evening the Regiment was again fully equipped as a mobile column. On the 26th the Regiment entrained for Damanhour, where headquarters were established and from there squadron moved out on patrols. Many villages were searched, arms and ammunition were found, and arrests were made. The rebellion was crushed, and the end of May saw the Regiment again at Kantara, cleaning equipment for handing in to ordnance stores, prior to embarkation for Australia. Our horses, which had so splendidly served throughout the long years, were never to return to Australia, and were parted with with very real sorrow and affection. On the 28th June, 1919, all the men marched to the wharf at Kantara, each man got his kit bag from the stack facing the wharf, embarkation rolls were checked, and the members of the 5th L.H. Regiment (what were left of them) filed up the gangway of the "Madras" to return to their home country.

The Regiment arrived at Fremantle, W.A., on the 24th July, and at Melbourne on the 31st July, 1919.

Appendix "A."

SUMMARY OF CASUALTIES OF 1st TO 13th LIGHT HORSE REGIMENT, 1914-18.

L.H. Regiment	Deaths. Off.	O.R.	Wounded. Off.	O.R.	Pris. of War. Off.	O.R.	TOTAL. Off.	O.R.	Evacuated Sick. Off.	O.R.
1st	13	209	48	631	Nil	4	61	844	37	1111
2nd	15	189	29	443	Nil	10	44	642	37	1596
3rd	5	153	44	609	Nil	—	49	762	26	1496
4th	3	123	11	321	Nil	2	14	446	29	1059
5th	6	142	35	542	Nil	2	41	686	29	1075
6th	13	121	27	434	Nil	16	40	571	31	1234
7th	5	143	23	632	Nil	3	28	778	19	1548
8th	31	285	40	635	Nil	3	71	923	32	1249
9th	13	181	47	491	Nil	13	60	685	32	1356
10th	17	221	45	434	Nil	1	62	656	35	1315
11th	5	94	28	493	Nil	5	33	592	24	861
12th	4	63	27	374	Nil	1	31	438	19	822
13th	1	22	11	277	Nil	—	12	299	29	807

MISSING.—All Regiments: Nil.

Number of all ranks taken on strength of 5th Light Horse Regiment: 2436.

HISTORY OF THE 5th LIGHT HORSE REGIMENT.   153

Appendix "B"

NOMINAL ROLL OF OFFICERS TAKEN ON STRENGTH OF THE 5TH L.H.R., 1914-19.

Latest Rank.	NAME.	Rank at End of Service With 5th L.H.R.
Captain	ARCHER, A.	Lieutenant
Captain	ATKINSON, L. T.	Captain
Lieutenant	AYERS, H. B.	Lieutenant
Lieutenant	BAKER, L. J.	Lieutenant
Lieutenant	BANFF, F. W.	Lieutenant
Major	BARWISE, W. K.	Major
2nd-Lieutenant	BATHURST, G. W.	2nd-Lieutenant
Chap.-Captain	BERGIN, M (M.C.)	Chap.-Captain
Captain	BILLINGTON, R. S. (M.C.)	T.-Captain
Major	BOLINGBROKE, A. G. (D.S.O.)	Major
Major	BOYD, J. McC (M.C.)	Major
Lieutenant	BROUGHTON, D. B. R (M.C.)	Lieutenant
Captain	BROWN, H. S.	Lieutenant
Captain	BRUNDITT, T. J.	Captain
Lieutenant	BYRNES, B. R. (M.C.)	Lieutenant
Lieut.-Colonel	CAMERON, D. C. (C.M.G., D.S.O., Order of Nile)	Lieut.-Colonel
Lieutenant	CARNE, W. M.	Lieutenant
Major	CHATHAM, W.	Major
Lieut.-Colonel	CHRISTIE, R (D.S.O. and Bar, C. de G.)	Q.M. and Hon Lieutenant
Lieutenant	CRAWFORD, A. B	Lieutenant
Colonel	CROLL, D. G.	Major
Lieutenant	CROSBY-BROWNE, J.	Lieutenant
Lieutenant	CURRIE, A.	Lieutenant
Lieutenant	DAWSON, E. W. D. B.	Lieutenant
Lieutenant	DELPRATT, B. B.	Lieutenant
Lieut.-Colonel	DODS, J. E. (D.S.O., M.C.)	Captain
Major	DONOVAN, G. P.	Captain
Captain	FARGHER, T. B.	Lieutenant
Lieutenant	FREDERICKS, H. W. G.	Lieutenant
Lieutenant	GILLESPIE, E. W.	Lieutenant
Lieutenant	GRAHAM, R. D.	Lieutenant
Lieutenant	HAMMOND, H. A.	Lieutenant
Lieutenant	HANLY, J. M.	Lieutenant
Major	HANNAY, D. V.	Lieutenant
Lieutenant	HANSON, G. E.	Lieutenant
Lieut.-Colonel	HARRIS, H. J. I. (V.D.)	Lieut.-Colonel
Captain	HICKS, G.	Captain
Lieutenant	HEIDKE, G. A.	Lieutenant
Captain	IRVING, H. K.	Lieutenant
Major	JAMES, E. S. (O.B.E., M.C.)	Captain
Major	JOHNSTON, H. H.	Major
Lieutenant	JOHNSTONE, R. L. W.	Lieutenant
Lieutenant	JONES, J. C.	Lieutenant

Latest Rank.	NAME.	Rank at End of Service With 5th L.H.R.
Lieutenant	LAND, J. N.	Lieutenant
Lieutenant	LAURANCE, E. G.	Lieutenant
Hon. Major	LUXFORD, S.	Hon. Major
Captain	LYONS, W. M. J.	Captain
Lieutenant	MACANSH, J. D.	2nd-Lieutenant
Captain	MAHONEY, B.	Captain
2nd-Lieutenant	MARTYR, F.	2nd-Lieutenant
Lieutenant	MATTHEWS, J. V.	Lieutenant
Lieut.-Colonel	MIDGLEY, S. (C.M.G., D.S.O.)	Major
Lieutenant	MORGAN, A. C.	Lieutenant
Captain	MORT, H. C.	Lieutenant
Lieutenant	MORLEY, C. R.	Lieutenant
Major	McLAUGHLIN, H. F.	Captain
Captain	McNEILL, J. D. G.	Captain
Lieut.-Colonel	NEWTON, F. G. (C.B.E., D.S.O.)	Major
Captain	NICHOLSON, N. A.	2nd-Lieutenant
Major	NIMMO, R. H.	Major
Lieutenant	O'BRIEN, J. M.	2nd-Lieutenant
Lieutenant	OGG, E. G. (M.C.)	2nd-Lieutenant
Captain	ORR, J. E.	Lieutenant
Lieutenant	OWEN, F. S. B.	Lieutenant
Captain	PATERSON, L. L.	Captain
Major	PATRICK, W.	Major
Lieutenant	PAUL, W.	Lieutenant
Captain	PIKE, E. R. B.	Captain
Captain	PLANT, R. A. N.	Lieutenant
Lieutenant	RADCLIFF, B. H.	Lieutenant
Lieutenant	RICHARD, R. R.	Lieutenant
Lieut.-Colonel	RIDLEY, J. C. T. E. C. (D.S.O.)	Brig.-Major
Major	RIGHETTI, E. E.	Major
Captain	ROBINSON, P. D.	Captain
Captain	RUTHERFORD, D. W.	Captain
Captain	RYAN, A. M.	Captain
Lieutenant	SCOTT, C. E.	Lieutenant
Lieutenant	SMITH, A. V.	2nd-Lieutenant
Lieutenant	SOLLING, R. A. F.	Lieutenant
Captain	STANFIELD, E. A. F.	Captain
Lieutenant	TAYLOR, F. A. J. W.	Lieutenant
Captain	TOOTH, E. N.	Lieutenant
Lieutenant	TROUT, L. G.	2nd-Lieutenant
Captain	WAITE, F. M. (M.C.)	Captain
Lieutenant	WATSON, R. P.	Lieutenant
Lieutenant	WEBSTER, T.	Lieutenant
Captain	WETHERALL, H.	Captain
Lieutenant	WILLIAMS, T. H. B.	Lieutenant
Lieutenant	WILLIAMSON, R. B.	Lieutenant
Brig.-General	WILSON, L. C. (C.B., C.M.G., D.S.O., C. de G.)	Lieut.-Colonel
Lieutenant	WOOD, C. N.	2nd-Lieutenant
Major	WRIGHT, W. L. F.	Major
2nd-Lieutenant	YALDWIN, H. St. C.	2nd-Lieutenant

HISTORY OF THE 5th LIGHT HORSE REGIMENT. 155

Appendix "C."

DECORATIONS AWARDED TO MEMBERS OF 5TH LIGHT HORSE REGIMENT ON EASTERN FRONT. 1914-19.

C.B.	Brig.-General L. C. Wilson, C.M.G., D.S.O.
C.M.G.	Brig.-General L. C. Wilson, C.B., D.S.O. Lieutenant-Colonel S. Midgley, D.S.O. Lieutenant-Colonel D. C. Cameron, D.S.O.
D.S.O.	Brigadier-General L. C. Wilson, C.B., C.M.G. Lieutenant-Colonel D. C. Cameron, C.M.G. Major A. G. Bolingbroke. Lieutenant-Colonel F. G. Newton.
M.C.	Captain R. S. Billington. Major J. M. Boyd. Lieutenant D. R. B. Broughton. Lieutenant-Colonel J. E. Dods, D.S.O. Lieutenant, J. D. Macansh. Lieutenant E. G. Ogg. Captain F. M. Waite. Lieutenant H. L. Fraser. Lieutenant B. R. Byrnes.
C.B.E.	Lieutenant-Colonel F. G. Newton, D.S.O.
D.C.M.	329 Sergeant H. MacLean. 241 Lance-Corporal H. R. McGuigan. 355 Private W. E. Sing. 2901 S.-Smith A. A. Waters. 390 S.S.M. W. V. Dawson. 725 S.S.M. P. J. Kelly.
M.M.	Lieutenant A. Currie. 529 Sergeant J. E. Bourke. 283 Sergeant C. E. Cox. 2181 Private S. L. Gofton. 1113 Sergeant H. C. Hardwick. 214 Corporal E. Harrison. 180 Sergeant R. James. 876 Lance-Corporal H. A. Johnson. 525 Driver T. Jones. 1327 Corporal J. J. Kelly. 527 Driver T. Mahoney. 1333 Sergeant A. C. McIndoe. 2220 Corporal M. E. O'Connor. 174 Corporal F. E. G. Pullen. 1534 Lance-Corporal R. B. Richards. 523a Private J. Small. 482 Sergeant G. J. Smith 3013 Private R. Speed.
M.S.M.	315 W.O. A. J. McMullen.
Croix de Guerre (French)	Brig.-General L. C. Wilson, C.B., C.M.G., D.S.O.
Order of Nile	Lieutenant-Colonel D. C. Cameron, C.M.G., D.S.O.

Appendix "D."
RATION SCALES, GALLIPOLI, 1915.

The following is the normal scale of rations issued at GALLIPOLI when available.

Fresh Meat, per man (daily)	1 lb.	Was issued frequently; frozen mutton substituted occasionally.
Preserved Meat	¾ lb.	"Fray Bentos."
Bread	1 lb.	For first six weeks no bread received, afterwards issued on average four days a week, and then not always to scale.
Biscuits	¾ lb.	Issued when no bread available; also when shortage of bread ration.
Bacon	4 oz.	Issued regularly.
Potatoes	½ lb.	Rarely available, and seldom issued to scale.
Preserved Vegetables	2 ozs.	After first month troops would not use.
Sugar	3 ozs.	After two months reduced to 2 ozs.
Tea	½ oz.	Always to scale.
Cheese	3 ozs.	Always to scale.
Jam	4 ozs.	Often reduced to 2 ozs.
Pepper	3-8 oz.	
Mustard	3-5 oz.	
Condensed Milk	2 ozs.	Or eight to the tin; afterwards reduced to 1 oz.. Sixteen to tin milk only issued during last three months.
Rum	1-64 gal.	When issued.
Lime Juice	1-120 gal.	When issued; always available.
Cigarettes or Tobacco	2 ozs.	Weekly issue. During month of October issues were short.

Dried fruits, i.e., Raisins, Figs and Currants issued when Jam was not available.

Flour, at rate of 1 lb. for   , was occasionally issued in lieu of Biscuits, also Rice, which, with above-named fruits, made "spotted dog."

Water, normal issue 1 gallon per man, all purposes. This was reduced to a pint per day during November; often full issue of water was not available.

HISTORY OF THE 5th LIGHT HORSE REGIMENT.   157

Appendix "E."
RATION SCALES, 1916-19.

Ordinary: When in standing camps.
Mobile: When on march.
Special Emergency: Carried on march when on operations, not consumed unless mobile ration not to hand.
Iron: Always carried, but only used on special orders to that effect and when all other sources of supply fail.

ORDINARY RATION SCALE.

Meat, fresh or	12 ozs.
Preserved	9 ozs.
Bread, or	1 lb.
Biscuit	12 ozs.
Bacon	4 ozs.
Jam	3 ozs.
Milk	1½ ozs.
Vegetables, fresh, or	8 ozs.
Dried Vegetables	2 ozs.
Potatoes, or Onions	4 ozs.
Sugar	3 ozs.
Tea	½ oz.
Cheese	3 ozs.
Salt	1-100th oz.
Pepper	1-100th oz.
Mustard	1-100th oz.
Lime Juice, when dried vegetables	1-10th gill
Rum, when ordered by G.O.C.	½ gill
Cigarettes	2 ozs. weekly
Matches	3 boxes fortnight
Wood	2 lbs.

EXTRAS:—

Rice	2 ozs. three times week
Dried Fruit	2 ozs. weekly
Oatmeal	2 ozs. twice weekly
Flour	2 ozs. twice weekly

	Mobile.	Special Emergency.	Iron.
Preserved Meat	12 ozs.	9 ozs.	12 ozs.
Biscuits	12	13	16
Jam	4	3	—
Tea	½	½	½
Sugar	3	3	2

	Mobile.	Special Emergency.	Iron.
Milk	1 oz.	—	—
Cheese	3 ozs.	—	—

FORAGE SCALE.

	Ordinary.	Mobile.	Special E'cy.
Grain	10 lbs.	9 lbs.	9¼ lbs
Fodder	12	6	—
Draught, over 16 hands, extra grain	2	—	—

Appendix "F."

MEDICAL ORGANISATION.

Memorandum by Colonel Gifford Croll,
At one time Medical Officer to the 5th L.H. Regiment on Gallipoli and later A.D.M.S., Egypt.

MEDICAL ORGANISATION WITH MOUNTED TROOPS.

A Light Horse Field Ambulance was attached to each brigade. Its strength is 6 officers and 120 other ranks. It was divided into bearer, nursing and transport divisions In addition to this, each regiment had a medical officer and three medical orderlies Regimental stretcher-bearers, 12 to each regiment, were detailed from the combatant troops and were not A.M.C. men.

GALLIPOLI.

The bearer and nursing divisions of the 2nd Light Horse Field Ambulance accompanied the Brigade to Anzac, and after many vicissitudes, they finally settled at the foot of Victoria Gully and the nursing division established a field hospital there. The bearer division had a post on Shell Green. Patients were brought to this post by the regimental stretcher-bearers and the ambulance-bearers then took them to the field hospital. Here they were examined and any operations of immediate necessity performed. If the wound or illness was not of a serious nature, they were kept there until fit to return to duty. If the wound or illness was of a serious nature, they were taken by the ambulance-bearers to the casualty clearing hospital at Anzac Cove and transferred at the first opportunity to the hospital ship. They were not supposed to be held for treatment at the clearing hospital.

SINAI.

The three divisions of the ambulance accompanied the Brigade in this campaign. It was soon found necessary to subdivide the nursing division into mobile and immobile sections. The mobile section had light equipment and ample transport, and was expected to be able to keep up with mounted troops upon any operations. The immobile section of the nursing division was only able to move slowly from one camp to another, and often required the aid of L. of C. transport, but, of course, it was able to deal with a large number of patients and treat them more efficiently than the mobile section. Its functions was much the same as the hospital at the foot of Victoria Gully in the Gallipoli Campaign.

During minor operations, such as the earlier raids to Bayud and Bir el Abd, the bearer transport and mobile section of the nursing division accompanied the Brigade.

The nursing section used to be dropped in a suitable place a few miles before the objectve was reached, i.e., Hod Dababis in an attack on Bir el Abd. The bearer and transport divisions would halt when the attack commenced and mounted bearers would be detailed to push forward and keep in touch with the R.M.O.'s of each regiment. When casualties occurred, one of these bearers would ride back and fetch up the necessary sand cart or sledges. Other bearers accompanied the vehicles to assist in finding and loading the wounded. Bearers in the Sinai and Palestine Campaigns were never used for actually carrying the wounded, but for the purposes mentioned above. When a retreat was ordered, they were also to get in wounded without the aid of vehicles, and they found that much the best way to get in a wounded Light Horseman was to put him on a horse and lead it. Stretchers were practically never used to get in a wounded man, for even if he lay in an exposed position it was better to send a sand cart, which was no bigger target than two or three men with a stretcher, could move at a very much faster pace, and was much more easily distinguished if the enemy were inclined to refrain from firing on the Red Cross.

The casualties, when collected, were taken back to the nursing section, who, when the Brigade returned, packed up and accompanied it back to camp, where the patients were handed over to the immobile section of the nursing division.

Slight cases, such as heat exhaustions and mild diseases, were kept for a few days and then returned to their units. More serious diseases and casualties who required to go to hospital were evacuated from here by L. of C. Units.

At Romani, the first general action, the same procedure was adopted, i.e., the bearer, mobile nursing and transport division moved with the Brigade, but when our line was forced back on to the camp the sub-divisions became unnecessary, so they rejoined the immobile section and worked from there. At Katia and Bir el Abd, however, the plan worked so satisfactorily that it was adopted in all future engagements.

PALESTINE.

In this campaign the division was more frequently in action as a concentrated unit, and a further alteration of the medical organisation was made accordingly. Each brigade still retained the bearer and transport divisions of its ambulance, and if on detached duty the mobile section of the nursing division.

Generally, however, the three mobile sections of the nursing division were combined to form what was called the divisional collecting station and the three immobile sections were combined to form the divisional receiving station. The collecting station had its own transport, and could move with the division wherever it went; the receiving station was dependent upon the assistance of L. of C. transport to move it, but was capable of dealing thoroughly with cases of a serious nature and of retaining them if unfit to move further.

GIFFORD CROLL.

Appendix "G."

SPECIAL ORDER OF THE DAY.

Now that the Australian Mounted Division and Anzac Mounted Division are leaving my command, I wish to express to all ranks my admiration of and gratitude for the work they have done.

The units composing these divisions, landing in Egypt after gallant service in Gallipoli, have been constantly engaged with the enemy since the formation of the Egyptian Expeditionary Force, and have taken a leading part in all the victories won.

In the advance through the Sinai Desert; the capture of Beersheba; the pursuit of the enemy which ended in the taking of Jerusalem; the operations in the Jordan Valley, in the mountains to the east of Jordan; and in the final defeat and pursuit of the Turkish Army in September and October, 1918, Australian and N.Z. troops have been always in the forefront. They have borne with cheerful endurance the thirst and glare of the desert, the heat and dust of the Jordan Valley, and the fatigue of long and exhausting marches. They have responded to every call, and have fully earned the welcome which will reward them on their long-deferred return to their homes.

I send my congratulations, my thanks, and my best wishes.

EDMUND H. H. ALLENBY.
General.

General Headquarters,
  Egyptian Expeditionary Force,
    June 28th, 1919.

Appendix H.

NOMINAL ROLL OF FIFTH LIGHT HORSE REGIMENT, SECOND LIGHT HORSE BRIGADE, A.I.F., WAR, 1914-1919.

Showing Rank, Name in full (with Honours), Time of Service (from what source and time joined Regiment and to what Unit and when transferred or when discharged), and Casualties.

NOTE.—N.T.O.S. = Not Taken on Strength of Regiment.

ADAMS, Gunner Arthur: 11th Rfts., 1.3.16; 14/F.A.B., 27.3.16
ADAMS, Far/Cpl. George Edward: 2/L.H.R., 31.12.17; Discd., 29.9.19
ADAMS, Private Ireton William: 3rd Rfts., 29.7.15; Discd., 30.10.19
ADAMS, Corporal Joseph: 11/L.H R., 2.10.15; 11/L.H.R., 29.2.16
ADAMS, Private John Edward: 28th Rfts., N.T.O.S.; Discd., 1.2.18
ADDERLEY, Driver Richard Thomas: 13th Rfts., 19.2.16; 13/F.A.B., 27.3.16
AFFLECK, Private Claude Stanley: Original, 8.12.14; Discd., 28.12.15
AFFLECK, Private John Eric: Original, 8.12.14; Discd., 20.9.16
AHEARNE, Transport Sergeant John Frederick: 12th Rfts., 23.2.16; wounded, 5.8 16
AHERN, Private William Patrick: 19th Rfts., N.T.O.S.; Camel Corps, 7.9.16
AINSWORTH, Corporal Frederick: Original, 9.12.14; Discd., 5.3.18; wounded, 5 11.17
AITCHISON, Private John: 26th Rfts., 12.12.17; Discd., 4.9.19
ALBION, Driver Hughie: 12th Rfts., 7.1.16; 2/L.F.H. Amb., 25.1.16
ALBRECHT, Driver Albert: 11th Rfts., 23.3.16; Discd., 19.10.19
ALBRECHT, Private Ernest Charles: 2nd Rfts., 7.7.15; Discd., 11.8.19
ALDIS, Driver Lyle Henry: 13th Rfts., 19.2.16; 13/F.A.B., 27.3.16
ALLEN, Private Arthur Guy: Original, 8.12.14; Discd., 7.3.17; wounded, 5.11.15 and 9.8.16
ALLEN, T/Cpl. George: 7th Rfts, 19.11.15; Discd., 4.10.19
ALLEN, L./Cpl. Driver Michael John: 11th L.H.R., 29.8.15; 11th L.H.R. 22.2.16
ALLEN, E.R./2/Cpl. Percy Roland: 13th Rfts., 19.2.16; A. Prov. Cps., 25.5.18
ALLEN, Private William Graham: Camel Corps, 15.10.17; Discd., 21.5.19; wounded, 28.3.18
AMES, Private Reginald: 23rd Rfts., 15.4.18; Discd., 12.6.19
AMES, Gunner Sylvanus George: 13th Rfts., 19.2.16; 13/F.A.B., 27.3.16
AMOS, Private Walter Frederick: 11th Rfts., 10.2.16; Discd., 1.5.19
ANDERSEN, T/Sgt. Christian Adolph (Mentioned in Despatches): Original, 8.12.14; Discd., 26.2.19; wounded, 28.6.15
ANDERSEN, Private Lars Rodrick: Original, 8.12.14; Discd., 26.2.19; wounded, 26.3.17
ANDERSON, Private Arthur: 7th Rfts., 23.2.16; Discd., 4.10.19; wounded, 10.8.17
ANDERSON, S/Smth. Arthur Andrew: 25th Rfts., 28.7.17; Discd., 12.9.19
ANDERSON, Private Francis Edward: 3rd Rfts., N.T.O.S ; Discd., 1.3.15
ANDERSON, E.R./Sgt. George Otto: Original, 8.12.14; A. Prov. Cps., 9.2.17

HISTORY OF THE 5th LIGHT HORSE REGIMENT.   163

ANDERSON, R.S.M. (W.O. 1) James Francis (M.S.M.): 6th Rfts., 25.9.15; 14/F.A.B., 27.3.16
ANDERSON, Private George Venables: 29th Rfts., 28.2.18; Discd., 20.9.19.
ANDERSON, Private Hugh: 12th Rfts., 23.2.16; Discd., 27.9.19; wounded, 5.8.16.
ANDERSON, Driver Malcolm Roland: 12th Rfts., 7.1.16; 2nd L.H.F.A., 25.1.16; 2nd L.H.F.A., 14.5.17; Discd., 27.9.19.
ANDERSON, Corporal Robert: 4th Rfts., 22.5.15; Discd., 4.10.19.
ANDERSON, Private William: 20th Rfts., N.T.O.S.; Discd., 28.8.17.
ANDERSON, Driver William Jones: Original, 8.12.14; 31st Btn., 1.12.16; 31st Btn., 27.11.17; Discd., 2.4.19.
ANDERSON, Private William Robert: 5th Rfts., 12.10.16; A. Prov. Cp., 23.3.18.
ANDREWS, S.Q.M.S Arthur Algernon Irby: Original, 8.12.14; Discd., 26.2.19; wounded, 2.7.15.
ANDREWS, Private Benjamin Arthur: 15th Rfts., N.T.O.S.; 1/F.S.A.M.D., 25.6.16.
ANDREWS, Private Charles: 23rd Rfts., 18.6.18; Discd., 4.9.19.
ANSELL, Private Lance Herbert: 4th Rfts., 22.5.15; Discd., 4.6.17
ARCHER, Captain Alister: 15th Rfts., 25.6.16; 4th Cml. Rgt., 2.11.16.
ARCHIBALD, Private Thomas: 11th L.H.R., 29.8.15; 11th L.H.R., 22.2.16
ARCHIBALD, E.R./Corporal Walter Rothwell: 6th Rfts., N.T.O.S.; 14/F.A.B., 27.3.16.
ARENA, Private Antonio James: 27th Rfts., 10.9.18; Discd., 21.2.20.
ARMIT, E.R./Sergeant Harold Philip: 23rd Rfts., 20.10.17; Discd., 4.9.18.
ARMIT, 2 A.M. Richard John Edward: Original, 8.12.14; 2/L.H.B.-M.G.S., 24.7.16.
ARMOUR, Arm./S./Sgt. William James: Original, 8.12.14; A.A.O.C., 12.2.18; A.A.O.C. (attached), 12.2.18 to 11.10.18
ARMSTRONG, Private Alexander William: 30th Rfts., N.T.O.S., 11/L.H.R., 20.6.18.
ARMSTRONG, Driver George Walter: 5th Rfts., 25.9.15; Discd., 4.10.19.
ARNDT, Private Harry: 20th Rfts., 3.11.16; Discd., 1.6.19; wounded, 2.5.18.
ARNTZEN, L/Corporal Louis: Original, 8.12.14; killed in action, Gallipoli, 28.6.15.
ARTHUR, Private Sydney Thomas: 11th Rfts., N.T.O.S.; 4th Camel Rgt., 2.11.16.
ASH, T/Driver Richard Arthur: 6th Rfts., N.T.O.S.; 12th Coy I.C.C., 15.7.16.
ASHENDEN, Private Horace Edwin: 30th Rfts., 19.11.18; Discd., 28.8.19.
ASHWOOD, L/Corporal Percival George: Original, 8.12.14; 9th Btn., 30.7.18; wounded, 26.8.15.
ASKEW, Driver Edward: 12th Rfts., 7.1.16; 13/F.A.B., 27.3.16; died (lobar pneumonia), France, 8.9.16.
ASKEW, Private John Henry: 11th Rfts., N.T.O.S.; 2/M.G.S., 24.7.16.
ASPINALL, Private Arthur Clive Norman: 12th Rfts., 7.1.16; 14/F.A.B., 27.3.16.
ASPINALL, Driver Pearce: 13th Rfts., 19.2.16; 13/F.A.B., 27.3.16
ASHTON, Private Percy: 11th L.H.R., 29.8.15; 11th L.H.R., 22.2.16
ATFIELD, Private Bertie: 14th Rfts., 9.3.16; Camel Cps., 15.7.16; Camel Cps., 28.7.18; Discd., 27.8.19
ATFIELD, Gunner George: 13th Rfts., 19.2.16; 13/F.A.B., 27.3.16.
ATHERTON, Private Cecil Francis Spencer: 15th Rfts., N.T.O.S.; Camel Cps., 7.2.17; Camel Cps., 17.2.18; Discd., 27.9.19

164   HISTORY OF THE 5th LIGHT HORSE REGIMENT.

ATKINS, Gunner James: 9th Rfts., 16.2.16; 14/F.A.B., 27.3.16
ATKINSON, Captain Leslie Thomas: 6th Rfts., 13.11.15; Appt. Term., 4.10.19.
ATKINSON, Private Percy Arthur: 26th Rfts., N.T.O.S.; Discd., 23.11.18.
ATTHOW, Private Arthur George: 30th Rfts., 9.7.18; Discd., 28.8.19.
AUSTIN, Gunner Joseph: 6th Rfts., 14.11.15; 14/F A.B., 27.3.16.
AXELSEN, Corporal Francis George: 4th Rfts., 22.5.15; Discd., 4.10.19; wounded, 27.6.15.
AYERS, Lieutenant Harold Barton: Original, 8.12.14; 14/F.A.B., 27.3.16.
AYERS, Private Harry Leslie: 12th Btn., 22.8.15; Discd, 4.8.16; wounded, 29.11.15.
BABB, Private Ernest: 9th Rfts., 30.4.16; 2/L.H.B.M.G.S., 24.7.16.
BACKHOUSE, 2nd A.M. George: 12th Rfts., 7.1.16; 2/Sig. Troop., 1.4.16.
BAILEY, Private Cyril Carlyle: 12th Rfts., N.T.O.S.; 13/F.A.B., 27.3.16.
BAILEY, Gunner Lewis: 12th Rfts., 7.1.16; 14/F.A.B., 7.3.16.
BAIRD, Private Charles: 9th Rfts., N.T.O.S.; Aust., 21.1.15; 11/L.H.R., 12.10.16.
BAKER, Driver Arthur: 8th Rfts., 10.1.16; 13/F.A.B., 27.3.16.
BAKER, Private Ernest Walter: 15th Rfts., N.T.O.S.; 2/L.H.R., 24.4.16
BAKER, Corporal Fenwick Herbert (M.M.): 11th L.H.R., 29.8.15; 11th L.H.R., 22.2.16
BAKER, Driver John: 6th A.A.S.C., 26.3.16; Discd., 15.4.19.
BAKER, Driver Joseph Edward: 14th Rfts., 9.3.16; 14/F.A.B., 27.3.16.
BAKER, Lieutenant Leslie John: Original, 8.12.14; Appt. Term., 1.11.19.
BAKER, Driver Thomas Arnold: 12th Rfts., 7.1.16; 13/F.A.B., 27.3.16.
BAKER, Private Walter: 3rd Rfts., 29.7.15; Discd., 8.12.15; wounded, 12.8.15.
BALDERSON, Driver Ernest Alfred: Original, 8.12.14; Aust., 2.9.16; 23rd Rfts., N.T.O.S.; A.A.S.C., 30.7.17; wounded, 5.8.16
BALDWIN, L./Corporal Reginald John: 2nd Rfts., 7.7.15; Died 7.11.17; wounded, 26.3.17.
BALL, Private Harry Ernest Reginald: 25th Rfts., 28.7.17; Discd., 23.9.19.
BALL, Driver Joseph: 22nd Rfts., N.T.O.S.; "B" Trp., 1/M. Div., 22.2.17.
BALL, Corporal William Charles: 14th Rfts., 9.3.16; 14/F.A.B., 28.3.16.
BALSER, Private Frank: 30th Rfts., 25.7.18; Discd., 28.8.19.
BAMBERRY, Driver Edward Samuel: 13th Rfts., 19.2.16; 13/F A.B., 27.3.16.
BANFF, Lieutenant Frederick William: 4th Rfts., 22.5.15; Appt. Term., 2.5.16; wounded, 28.6.15.
BANISTER, Private Charles Thomas: 27th Rfts., 1.8.17; Discd, 27.9.19.
BANSGROVE, Private William: 1st Rfts., 19.10.15; Discd., 2.4.19.
BARBELER, Driver Sydney Cornelius: 13th Rfts., 19.2.16; 13/F.A.B, 27.3.16.
BARBOUR, Private Henry Albert: 10th Rfts., 31.12.15; 2/M.G.S., 24.7.16.
BARKE, Private Albert Ernest Lawrence: 7th Rfts., 14.11.15; 2/Dble Sqd., 6.7.16.
BARKER, Private Henry William: 17th Rfts., 20.8.16; Discd., 8.11.19.
BARKLEY, Private Victor (stated to be Victor Henry Provis): Original, 8.12.14; wounded, 16.7.15; died of wounds, 21.7.15
BARLOW, Private Reginald Rufus: 30th Rfts., N.T.O.S.; 11/L.H.R., 6.7.18.

BARNES, Private Henry Heathcote: 22nd Rfts., 14.3.17; Discd., 12.9.19.
BARNES, Private John Wilson: Original, 8.12.14; Discd., 1.12.15.
BARNES, Private Lesley Joseph: 25th Rfts., 9.7.17; Discd., 23.2.19.
BARNES, Private Thomas Messenger: 30th Rfts., 18.6.18; Discd., 28.8.19.
BARNES, Private William Albert: 11th L.H.R., 2.10.15; Discd., 13.9.16.
BARNES, Corporal William Henry: Original, 8.12.14; Discd., 12.9.18.
BARNES, Gunner William James: 12th Rfts., N.T.O.S.; 14/F.A.B., 27.3.16.
BARNETT, Private Harold Douglas: 23rd Rfts., 11.6.17; Discd., 12.8.19.
BARNETT, Private John Spencer: 18th Rfts., 20.11.16; Discd., 17.10.19; wounded, 11.4.18.
BARNETT, Corporal Harry Wallace: 11th L.H.R., 27.8.15; 11th L.H.R, 22.2.16
BARRON, Lieutenant, Percy Royd: 11th L.H.R., 2.10.15, 11/F.A.B., 1.4.16.
BARROW, Driver Charles: Original, 8.12.14; Discd., 26.2.19.
BARROWMAN, Private James Cockburn: 11th Rfts., 18.1.16; Discd., 4.10.19.
BARTLAM, Lieutenant Albert Youl (Mentioned in Despatches): 11th L.H.R., 29.8.15; 11th L.H.R., 22.2.16
BARTON, Sergeant Frederick John: 14th Rfts., N.T.O.S; Camel Cps., 2.11.16.
BARTON, Lieutenant Keith: 11th L.H.R., 29.8.15; 11th L.H.R., 22.2.16
BARWISE, Major, William Kenyon: 13th Rfts., 19.2.16; Appt. Term., 27.10.19; wounded, 9.11.17.
BASSE, Private George Thomas: Original, 8.12.14; Discd., 31.5.16; wounded, 12.7.15.
BATEMAN, Private Arthur Archibald: 10th Rfts., 23.2.16; Discd., 4.10.19; wounded, 9.8.16.
BATES, Private George Robert: 11th Rfts., 23.2.16; Discd., 23.4.19.
BATES, Private William Holdsworth: 4th Rfts., 22.5.15; wounded, 28.6.15; killed in action, Anzac, 2.9.15
BATHURST, 2nd Lieutenant George Waverley: 11th Rfts., N.T.O.S.; Dismissed, 1.7.16.
BATTIS, Private William Bernard: Original, 8.12.14, Aust., 4.11.15; 31st Btn., 14.6.17.
BATTS, Driver Alfred George: 16th Rfts., N.T.O.S.; 1/D.A.C., 24.9.17.
BAUER, Private Arthur: 2nd Rfts., 7.7.15; Discd., 4.10.19.
BAULCH, ER/2/Corporal Henry: Original, 8.12.14; A. Prov. Cps., 1.1.17.
BAUMGARTNER, Private William Francis: Original, 8.12.14; Discd., 26.2.19; wounded, 28.7.18.
BAXTER, Far./Sergeant Charles William: 29th Rfts., 23.12.17; Discd., 4.9.19.
BAXTER, Private Charles William F.: 19th Rfts., 2.10.16; Discd., 11.12.19.
BAXTER, Sergeant James Brown: Original, 8.12.14; Discd., 20.3.18; wounded, 28.6.15, 7.8.16, 8.11.17.
BAYFIELD, Private Herbert Reginald: 21st Rfts., N.T.O.S., A. Prov. Cps., 23.1.17.
BAYLEY, Private William Henry (stated to be Bert Bayley): 30th Rfts., N.T.O.S.; 2/L.H.R., 31.5.18.
BAYLISS, Private William Weaver: 1st Rfts., 16.5.15; Discd., 17.10.16.
BEATTIE, Driver Alexander: A.A.S.C., 26.3.16; Discd., 15.4.19.
BEATTIE, Private Frank: 11th Rfts., N.T.O.S.; 41st Btn., 24.11.16.
BEAZLEY, Sergeant Reginald Arthur: Original, 8.12.14; Discd., 26.2.19.
BEBBINGTON, Private Frederick John: 21st Rfts., 11.6.17; Discd., 19.9.19.

166 HISTORY OF THE 5th LIGHT HORSE REGIMENT.

BEBBINGTON, L./Cpl./Driver Samuel: 13th Rfts., 19.2.16; 14/F.A.B., 27.3.16.
BECK, Private Thomas James: 9th Rfts., 23.2.16; Discd., 4.8.19
BEDSER, S.S.M. Wilfred Harold: 11th L.H.R., 29.8.15; 2/L.H.R., 6.10.15.
BEGOURIE, Private Harry: Original, 8.12.14; 47th Btn., 26.3.16; wounded, 20.5.15; died of wounds, France, 8.8.16.
BEIRNE, Sergeant Edward John: 11th L.H.R., 29.8.15; 11th L.H.R., 2.2.16; wounded, 1.9.15
BELL, Private Edwin: 11th Rfts., N.T.O.S.; 2/M.G.S., 1.8.16; 2/M.G.S., 20.2.17, 2/M.G.S., 21.2.17
BELL, Corporal John George Kingsborrough: 15th Rfts., N.T.O.S.; 4/Camel Rgt., 2.11.16.
BELCHER, Far./Sergeant John Thornhill: Original, 8.12.14; Anzac Mtd. Div. H.Q., 12.8.17.
BENNETT, H./Lieutenant Francis Walter: Original, 8.12.14, 14/F.A.B., 27.3.16.
BENNETT, Private Frederick William: 10th Rfts., 23.6.16; Discd., 10.3.19.
BENNETT, Private Harold Edward: Original, 8.12.14; Demob., U.K., 16.4.16.
BENNETT, Private William: 4th Rfts., 25.5.15; Discd., 6.6.17.
BENNY, Private Alfred: 15th Rfts., N.T.O.S; 4th Camel Rgt., 2.11.16; 18th Coy., I.C.C., 7.7.17; Discd., 2.10.19.
BENNEY, Private Richard: 11th Rfts., 11.12.16; Discd., 19.10.19; wounded, 4.11.17.
BENTLEY, Private Phillip Arthur: 2nd Rfts., 7.7.15 Discd., 30.8.16.
BERESFORD, Driver Thomas Joshua: 1st Rfts., 29.7.15; 2/M.G.S., 23.7.16.
BERGIN, Chaplain Michael (M.C.): Chaps. Dept., 13.5.15; Chaps. Dept. (attached), 13.5.15 to 19.6.15; died of wounds, Belgium, 12.10.17
BERGIN, Private Michael Albert: 12th Rfts., 7.1.16; 14/F.A.B., 27.3.16.
BERRY, Driver Herbert James: 12th Rfts., N.T.O.S.; 14/F.A.B., 27.3.16.
BERRY, Driver Thomas William: 13th Rfts., 19.12.16; 13/F.A.B., 27.3.16.
BERWICK, Private Lawrence: 11th L.H.R., 2.10.17; 49th Btn., 21.1.17; killed in action, France, 2.4.17.
BEST, Lieutenant Eric Henry: 11th L.H.R., 29.8.15; Appt. Term., 16.5.16.
BETTENS, Driver Samuel John: 9th Rfts., N.T.O.S; 14/F.A.B., 27.3.16.
BETTENS, T/Corporal Frederick George: 18th Rfts., N.T.O.S.; Anzac Prov. Cps., 21.11.16.
BEVERIDGE, Driver John William Harold: 21st Rfts., N.T.O.S., 1st Sig. Sqdn., 10.6.17
BICKLE, Private Sydney Newman: 19th Rfts., N.T.O.S.; 2/M.G.S., 5.10.16.
BIDDLE, S/Smith William John: 13th Rfts., 19.2.16; 14/F.A.B., 27.3.16; killed accidentally, France, 18.1.17.
BIGGS, Lieutenant Aubrey Wilfred: 11th Rfts., N.T.O.S.; 2nd Btn., 21.3.16.
BILLINGTON, Captain Richard Stewart (M.C.): 2nd Rfts., 7.7.15; Appt. Term., 4.10.19.
BILLINGTON, Lieutenant William Hogarth: 11th L.H.R., 29.8.15; 11th L.H.R., 22.2.16
BIRKENSHAW, Private Sydney: 2nd Rfts., 16.5.15; Discd., 10.2.16; wounded, 28.6.15.

BIRT, Bombardier Robert Edward: 11th Rfts., 18.1.16; 14/F.A.B., 27.3.16; killed in action, Belgium, 22.7.17
BISHOP, Private James: Original, 8.12.14; Discd., 7.6.16.
BISHOP, Private John: 27th Rfts., 1.8.17; Discd., 4.9.19.
BISHOP, Driver Patrick: 12th Rfts., 7.1.16; 13/F.A.B., 27.3.16.
BLACK, Private Alan: 13th Rfts., 7.1.16; 13/F.A.B., 27.3.16.
BLACK, Private William: Original, 8.12.14; Discd., 29.3.16.
BLACKIE, L/Corporal Norman Robertson: Original, 8.12.14; wounded, 28.5.15; died of wounds (at sea), 31.5.15.
BLACKLEY, Gunner Matthew: 13th Rfts., 19.2.16; 13/F.A.B., 27.3.16.
BLACKMORE, Sergeant Herbert: Original, 8.12.14; 1st F.S. Engrs., 9.7.16
BLACKSHAW, W.O. (2) Oswald Roy: 6th A.S.C., 26.3.16; A.A.O.C., 4.8.16.
BLACKSHAW, Private William Eric: 6th A.S.C., 26.3.16; killed in action, Palestine, 8.11.17.
BLACKWELL, Private John Milton Roy: Original, 8.12.14; killed in action, Gallipoli, 28.6.15.
BLAIR, Private Sydney Ernest: 27th Rfts., 1.8.17; Discd., 4.9.19.
BLAKE, Driver Charles John: 26th Rfts., N.T.O.S.; A.Mtd Div.Trn , 20.8.17.
BLIGH, Corporal Maurice: 13th Rfts., 19.2.16; 13/F.A.B., 27.3.16.
BOBY, Driver Daniel Robert Morgan: 6th A.S.C., 26.3.16; 1/F.S.Engrs., 19.2.17.
BODEN, Gunner Frederic Charles: 13th Rfts., 19.2.16; 14/F.A.B., 27.3.16; died (influenza and bronchial pneumonia), France, 8.11.18
BOHRDT, Private Frederick William: 24th Rfts., 15.9.18; Discd., 4.5.19
BOLINGBROKE, Major Archdale George (D.S.O., Mentioned in Despatches): Original, 21.11.14; Appt. Term., 29.3.19; wounded, 8.10.15, 5.8.16; 17.9.18.
BOND, Private Thomas James: 30th Rfts., N.T.O.S.; 2/1.I.L.R., 12.7.18.
BONNER, Private Thomas: 8th Rfts., 14.11.15; Discd., 19.3.18.
BONSER, Private Walter Robert: 11th Rfts., 11.12.15; 4/Camel Rgt., 2.11.16.
BOOL, Private Harry: G.S. Rfts., 15.2.19; Discd., 19.8.19
BOOMER, Private Neil: Original, 20.12.14; 2/M.G.S., 1.8.16.
BOOTH, Private Frederick: 11th Rfts., 30.6.16; Discd., 25.10.16; wounded, 6.8.16.
BOSANQUET, Driver Arthur Eric Sidney: 6th A.S.C., 26.3.16; Discd., 24.2.19.
BOSTOCK, Driver Leslie: 12th Rfts., 7.1.16; 14/F.A.B., 27.3.16
BOSTOCK, Driver William Henry: 12th Rfts., 7.1.16; 14/F.A.B., 27.3.16.
BOTT, Gunner George Henry: 6th Rfts., 14.11.15; 13/F.A.B., 27.3.16.
BOTT, Sergeant George Lancelot: Original, 8.12.14; Discd., 26.2.19; wounded, 28.11.17.
BOTT, Private Percy Victor Ford: 11th L.H.R., 17.10.18; Discd., 4.10.19.
BOURNE, Corporal Alfred Edward: 15th Rfts., N.T.O.S.; 2nd Dble. Sqd., 1.7.16.
BOURNE, Corporal John: 11th L.H.R., 29.8.15; 11th L.H.R., 22.2.16
BOWCOTT, Private Clifford Owen: Original, 8.12.14; wounded, 27.6.15, 29.11.15; died of wounds, Alexandria, 5.12.15.
BOWKER, Gunner Sidney: 12th Rfts., 22.2.16; 14/F.A.B., 27.3.16.
BOWLY, Private Eustace Hamilton: 25th Rfts., 2.7.17; Discd., 10.9.19.
BOWLY, Private Francis William: 25th Rfts., 2.7.17; Discd., 24.5.19; wounded, 24.7.17.

168   HISTORY OF THE 5th LIGHT HORSE REGIMENT.

BOWMAN, Corporal Harold Macarthur: 11th L.H.R., 29.8.15; 11th L.H.R., 27.2.16
BOX, L/Corporal William Charles: 11th Rfts., 23.2.16; 15th Btn., 12.5.17.
BOYCE, Private Cecil Leonard Rodney: 11th Rfts., N.T.O.S.; Discd., 3.2.20.
BOYD, Private Ernest Joseph: 5th Rfts., 26.8.18; Discd., 28.1.20.
BOYD, Major John McClelland (M.C., twice Mentioned in Despatches): Original, 8 12.14; Appt. Term., 13.9.19; wounded, 16.11.15.
BOYLE, Private Joseph Patrick: 30th Rfts., 28.7.18; Discd., 9.5.19.
BOYLE, Private William Patrick: 18th Rfts., N.T.O.S.; Camel Cps, 7.9.16.
BOZIER, L/Sergeant Edward Basil: 14th Rfts., 9.3.16; 4th Camel Rgt., 2.11.16.
BRADBURY, Gunner Miles Coverdale: 12th Rfts., 7.1.16; 14/F.A.B., 27.3.16.
BRADLEY, Private John James: 11th Rfts., 28.12.15; Discd., 3.4.19; wounded, 25.9.18.
BRAND, Private Angus Duphney: Original, 8.12.14; Discd., 20.9.16; wounded, 7.6.15.
BRANGHAM, S.Q.M.S. Fred Dudley: 15th Rfts., N.T.O.S; 2/1..H.-M.G.S., 4.8.16.
BRANSON, T/Corporal John Edward: 17th Rfts., 20.8.16; Discd., 25.10.19.
BRAUNHOLZ, Private Eric William: 27th Rfts., 23.12.17; Discd., 8.4.19.
BRAZILL, Private Frank: 12th Rfts., 23.2.16; Discd., 27.9.19.
BRAZIL, Driver Michael: 11th Rfts., 2.1.16; Discd., 22 4.19.
BRECKENRIDGE, Private Robert William: 9th Rfts., 4.6.16; Discd., 1.5.19.
BREESE, Private Edward Stanley: 22nd Rfts., N.T.O.S ; Anzac Mtd D.H.Q., 9.4.17; Anzac Mtd. D.H.Q., 18.6.19; Discd., 12.9.19
BRENNAN, Private Charles Alma: Original. 8 12.14; Discd., 24.2.19
BRENNAN, Private Martin: 5th Rfts., N.T.O.S.; 2/L.H.R., 29.8.15.
BRENNAN, Private Stanley: 15th Rfts., N.T.O.S ; 2/M G.S., 12.9.16; died (broncho-pneumonia), Moascar, 14.2.19
BRENNAN, Driver William Vincent: 13th Rfts., 19.2.16; 13/F.A.B., 27.3.16.
BREWER, S Q.M.S. Albert Henry: Original, 8.12.14; Discd., 11.4.17; wounded, 21.11.15.
BREWER, Private Robert William Smythe: 23rd Rfts., N.T.O.S.; 8th San. Sec., 24.6.18.
BREWER, Private William Alfred: Original, 8.12.14; Discd., 9.11.16.
BRIERTY, Lieutenant Alwyn Robert (M.C.): 11th L.H.R., 29.8.15; 11th L.H.R., 22.2.16.
BRIMBLECOMBE, Sergeant Wilfred John: 15th Rfts., N.T.O.S.; 2nd L.H.B.M.G.S, 1.8.16
BROCKHURST, Driver Henry Thomas: 23rd Rfts., N.T.O.S.; 4/L.H.-Fld. Amb., 20.7.17
BRODIE, Private Arthur Einasleigh: 22nd Rfts., 11.4.17; Discd., 25.3.20.
BRODIE, Private Gordon Alexander: Original, 8.12.14; Discd., 10.5.16.
BRODIE, Private George William: 21st Rfts., 11.4.17; Discd., 14.10.19.
BRODIE, S.S.M. Reginald William Finch: 11/L.H.R., 29.8.15; 11th L.H.R., 22.2.16
BROOKS, Gunner George Edward: 2nd Rfts., 26.1.16; 13/F.A.B., 27.3.16.
BROOKS, Private Shirley: 4th Rfts., 25.5.15; Discd., 20.12.16; wounded, 9.8.16.

HISTORY OF THE 5th LIGHT HORSE REGIMENT. 169

BROUGHTON, Lieutenant David Blakeney Rhys (M.C., Mentioned in Despatches): Original, 8.12.14; Appt. Term., 15.3.19; wounded, 14.7.18.
BROWN, Driver Arthur Sylvester: 13th Rfts., 19.2.16; 13/F.A.B., 27.3.16.
BROWN, L/Corporal Charlie: 5th Rfts., 25.9.15; Discd., 11.5.19; wounded, 5.11.15, 8.11.17.
BROWN, Private Eric: 6th Rfts., 14.11.15; Discd., 1.8.19.
BROWN, Private Fred.: 2/L.H.R., 18.1.17; killed in action, Palestine, 28.3.18
BROWN, Private Fred. Clarence: 15th Rfts., N.T.O.S., 4th Camel Rgt., 2.11.16; 18th Coy. I.C.C., 27.6.17; Discd., 27.9.19
BROWN, Private Frederick James George: 10th Rfts., 23.2.16, killed in action, Sinai Peninsula, 17.9.16.
BROWN, Private George Ballangall: 11/L.H.R., 29.8.18; 11/L.H.R., 2.3.16.
BROWN, Private Herbert: Original, 4.11.14; Discd., 30.12.14.
BROWN, Captain Henry Samuel: 5th Rfts., 25.10.15; 4th Camel Rgt., 2.11.16.
BROWN, 2/A.M. Patrick (M.M.): 3rd Rfts., 29.7.15; A.F.C., 5.8.17.
BROWN, Private Robert: 11th Rfts., 17.1.16; 25th Btn., 5.2.17
BROWN, S/Smith Richard: 14th Rfts., 9.3.16; 14/F.A.B., 27.3.16.
BROWN, S/Smith William: 14th Rfts., 9.3.16; 14/F.A.B., 27.3.16.
BROWN, Private William John: 15th Rfts., 20.8.16; Discd., 27.9.19.
BROWNE, Private Roderic Stawell: Original, 8.12.14; killed in action, Anzac, 28.6.15
BROWNE, Private Sylvester Ulick: Original, 8.12.14; Discd., 13.8.15.
BROWNJOHN, Private William: 26th Rfts., N.T.O.S.; 4/L.H.F.A., 20.7.17
BROWNLESS, Corporal Charles Henry: 13th Rfts., 19.2.16; 14/F.A.B., 27.3.16.
BRUCE, Driver Ernest Leslie: 11/L.H.R., 29.8.15; 11/L.H.R., 22.2.16
BRUNDRIT, Captain Thomas Joseph (Mentioned in Despatches): Original, 28.9.14; killed in action, Anzac, 8.11.15
BRYANT, Driver Charles William: 30th Rfts., N.T.O.S.; 11/L.H.R., 21.6.18.
BRYANT, Sapper John McDonald: 11th Rfts., 14.1.16; 1st Fld. Sqdn., 29.6.16.
BRYSON, Gunner Joseph: 12th Rfts., 7.1.16; 13/F.A.B., 27.3.16.
BRYCE, Private James: G.S. Rfts., 21.1.19; Discd., 19.8.19.
BUCHANAN, Driver George: 5th Rfts., 25.9.15; 14/F.A.B., 27.3.16.
BUCHANAN, Driver Hugh: 11th Rfts., 5.2.16; 13/F.A.B., 27.3.16
BUCHANAN, L/Corporal Thomas: 3rd Rfts., 29.7.15; Discd., 9.10.19.
BUCK, Private William: 3rd Rfts., 29.7.15; Discd., 4.10.19; wounded, 26.3.17.
BUCKBY, S/Smith James Alfred: 11th L.H.R., 29.8.15; 11th L.H.R., 22.2.16
BUCKLAND, Private Francis Henry: 21st Rfts., 11.6.17. Discd, 29.10.19.
BUDD, Private Edward Amos: 27th Rfts., 1.8.17; Discd., 24.5.19.
BUDD, Driver Reginald English: 11/L.H.R., 2.10.15; 11/L.H.R., 22.2.16
BUDDEN, Corporal Norman Wilfred (Mentioned in Despatches): Original, 8.12.14; Discd., 15.4.19; wounded, 9.8.16
BULFIN, Private William: 15th Rfts., 10.8.16; Discd., 23.4.19; wounded, 3.5.18.
BULL, Private Ernest Aaron: 17th Rfts., N.T.O.S.; Camel Cps., 7.9.16; Camel Cps., 7.11.16; Discd., 19.9.19
BULL, S/Smith Thomas Edward: 16th Rfts., N.T.O.S.; 2/L.H.R., 9.5.16.
BULL, Private George Isaac: 17th Rfts., 20.8.16; Discd., 19.9.19.

HISTORY OF THE 5th LIGHT HORSE REGIMENT.

BULL, Private Ruben: 15th Rfts., N.T.O.S.; 4th Camel Rgt., 2.11.16.
BUNCH, E.R./2nd/Corporal William Thomas: 8th Rfts., 10.1.16; A. Prov. Cps., 30.10.17.
BUNT, Private William: 15th Rfts., N.T.O.S.; Camel Cps., 2.11.16.
BUNTON, T/S.S.M. Henry Albert: Original, 8.12.14; Discd., 26.2.19.
BURCHILL, Driver Alan: 12th Rfts., N.T.O.S.; 14/F.A.B. 27.3.16.
BURCHILL, Private John Galloway: 14th Rfts., 9.3.16; Discd., 29.10.19; wounded accidentally, 16.7.18.
BURCHILL, Private Samuel John: 11/L.H.R., 29.8.15; 11/L.H.R., 22.2.16; wounded, 8.10.15
BURDEKIN, Private Arthur Hugh: Original, 8.12.14; Demob., U.K., 27.7.15.
BURDON, Private Frederick: Original, 8.12.14; Discd., 15.7.15
BURKE, Private Daniel: 11/L.H.R., 2.10.15; Discd., 5.7.16; wounded, 8.11.15.
BURKE, Private John: Original, 8.12.14; Discd., 11.3.17
BURKE, Sergeant James Ernest (M.M.): Original, 8.12.14, Discd., 26.2.19; wounded, 5.11.15.
BURKE, Private Patrick: 5th Rfts., 25.9.15; 2/M.G.S., 10.7.17.
BURNETT, T/Corporal (Hon./Sergeant) Thomas William: 10th Rfts., 23.2.16; Discd, 4.3.20.
BURNEY, Private William: 12th Rfts., 23.2.16; Discd., 27.9.19
BURNS, Private Edward: 6th Rfts, 25.9.15; Discd., 18.3.19
BUROWS, Private Sidney: 27th Rfts., 1.8.17; Discd., 19.9.19.
BURRELL, Private Thomas Frederick: 6th Rfts., 25.9.15; Discd., 30.10.19.
BURROWS, Private Colin George: 24th Rfts., 15.7.17; Discd., 22.4.18.
BURROWS, Gunner Stanley: 11th Rfts., 16.1.16; 13/F.A.B., 27.3.16.
BURT, Private Frank Gregory: 19th Rfts., N.T.O.S.; Camel Cps., 7.9.16.
BURTON, T/Sergeant Alfred Mark: 12th Rfts., 7.1.16; Discd., 27.9.19.
BUTCHER, Private Alexander Charles: 11/L.H.R., 29.8.15; 11/L.H.R., 22.2.16
BUXTON, Private Horace: 14th Rfts., 9.3.16; Camel Cps, 2.11.16.
BUXTON, Driver William Henry: 12th Rfts., N.T.O.S.; 14/F.A.B., 27.3.16
BYERS, Private Hugh Wason: 30th Rfts., 28.7.18; Discd, 19.4.19
BYERS, Private Leslie Ross: 3rd Rfts., 29.7.15; Discd, 6.12.16; wounded, 2.12.15, 5.8.16.
BYERS, Corporal Thomas Leslie: 15th Rfts., N.T.O.S.; Camel Cps., 2.11.16
BYERS, Sapper William: 17th Rfts., N.T.O.S.; 1/Sig. Sqdn., 22.7.16.
BYRNE, Gunner Gladstone William: 5th Rfts., 25.9.15; 13/F.A.B., 28.3.16; wounded, 11.11.15; killed in action, Belgium, 30.9.17.
BYRNE, Driver John James: 13th Rfts., 19.2.16; 14/F.A.B., 27.3.16
BYRNE, Private John Wall: Original, 8.12.14; Discd., 26.2.19
BYRNES, Lieutenant Bernard Richard (M.C.): Original, 8.12.14; Appt. Term., 12.4.19.
BYROM, Private Francis William: 11th Rfts., 18.1.16; Discd., 4.10.19.
CAGNACCI, Corporal Curzio: 10th Rfts., 26.1.16; 13/F.A.B, 27.3.16.
CAIN, Major John Robert (M.C., Mentioned in Despatches): Original, 8.12.14; 2/A.M.G.S., 23.7.16
CAIRNS, L/Corporal William: 7th Rfts., 10.1.16; Discd., 4.10.19
CALDWELL, Corporal Joseph William: 13th Rfts., 19.2.16; 13/F.A.B., 27.3.16.
CALLANAN, Private John Joseph: 5th Rfts., N.T.O.S.; Discd., 9.2.16.
CAMERON, T/Sergeant Archibald: Original, 8.12.14; Discd., 29.3.19; wounded, 28.6.15, 5.8.16.
CAMERON, T/Far./Corporal Donald: 22nd Rfts., 25.2.17; Discd., 12.9.19.

HISTORY OF THE 5th LIGHT HORSE REGIMENT. 171

CAMERON, Lieutenant-Colonel Donald Charles (C.M.G., D.S.O., Order of Nile 3rd Class, three times Mentioned in Despatches): Original, 30.9.14; Appt. Term., 4.10.19; wounded, 9.6.15, 28.6.15
CAMERON, Driver Ethelbert Allan: 19th Rfts., 12.10.16; 1st Fld. Sqdn. Engrs., 28.6.17.
CAMERON, Private Harry Westropp: 5th Rfts., 2.8.15; wounded, 5.11.17; killed in action, Palestine, 28.7.18.
CAMERON, Far./Sergeant John: Original, 8.12.14; Discd., 26.2.19.
CAMERON, Private James Edward: 15th Rfts., N.T.O.S.; 4th Camel Rgt., 2.11.16.
CAMERON, Private William Charles: 4th Rfts., 25.5.15; Discd., 5.4.16.
CAMP, Private William Spencer: 28th Rfts., N.T.O.S.; 2/1.H.B. Supply Sect., 29.7.17.
CAMPBELL, Private Alexander Buchanan: 19th Rfts., N.T.O.S.; 2/1.H.B. M.G.S., 6.10.16.
CAMPBELL, Gunner Charles, Junr. (M.M.): 8th Rfts., N.T.O.S.; 14/F.A.B., 27.3.16; died of wounds (broncho-pneumonia), France. 26.10.18.
CAMPBELL, Driver Claude: 12th Rfts., 7.1.16; 14/F.A.B., 27.3.16.
CAMPBELL, Private Frederick William: 10th Rfts., 23.2.16; Discd., 15.10.19
CAMPBELL, T/S.S.M George Finlay: Original, 8.12.14; Discd., 15.4.19; wounded, 25.4.17.
CAMPBELL, Private John: 15th Rfts., N.T.O.S.; 12/Coy. I.C.C., 7.9.16; died of wounds. Egypt, 11.1.17
CAMPBELL, Private John Gordon Leslie: 18th Rfts., 20.8.16; Discd., 19.9.19; wounded, 6.4.18.
CAMPBELL, Private Thomas: 11/L.H.R., 29.8.15; 11/L.H.R., 6.3.16
CANNAVAN, Private Patrick: 5th Rfts., 25.9.15; Discd., 17.1.20.
CANNAVAN, Corporal Thomas Francis: 5th Rfts., 25.9.15; Discd., 14.10.19.
CANNING, Driver William: 16th Rfts., N.T.O.S.; 13/F.A.B., 31.3.17
CANTWELL, Driver Herbert Douglas: 23rd Rfts., N.T.O.S.; 33/Coy., A.S.C., 13.8.17.
CAPPER, A./Bombardier Vivian Ashby: 1st Rfts., 7.7.15; 14/F.A.B., 27.3.16
CARBERRY, Private Charles Sebastian: 11th Rfts., 23.2.16; Discd., 27.9.19.
CARBERRY, Gunner John: 14th Rfts., 9.3.16; 14/F.A.B., 27.3.16; killed in action, France, 5.8.17.
CARD, Private Herbert: 5th Rfts., 28.8.15; Discd., 4.10.19; wounded, 19.7.17.
CARDEW, Private James Joseph Hunter: 23rd Rfts., 27.11.17; Discd., 4.7.19.
CARDNO, Corporal John Lindsay: 10th Rfts., 23.2.16; Discd., 30.10.19; wounded, 10.8.16.
CAREY, Private John Thomas Henry: 27th Rfts., N.T.O.S.; Discd., 6.10.19
CARLETON, Driver Arthur Herbert: 12th Rfts., 7.1.16; 13/F.A.B., 27.3.16; killed in action, France, 24.4.18.
CARMODY, E.R./2/Corporal Peter: 15th Rfts., 20.8.16; A. Prov. Cps., 25.5.18.
CARNE, S/Smith Pery Kerr: 12th Rfts., 8.1.16; Discd., 27.9.19; wounded, 25.9.18.
CARNE, Lieutenant Walter Mervyn (Mentioned in Despatches, Silver Medal, Serbia): 2/1. H.F.A., 19.2.19 (attached strength); Appt. Term., 19.9.19.
CARNIE, Private William Andrew Craze: 26th Rfts., N.T.O.S.; 4/1.H.B. Supply Sec., 30.7.17.

CARPENTER, Private George William: 15th Rfts., N.T.O.S.; Discd., 7.9.16.
CARPENTER, Driver Ernest Doel: 16th Rfts., N.T.O.S.; 5/D.A.H.Q., 12.9.16
CARR, Private Arthur Percy: 11th L.H.R., 29.8.15; 11th L.H.R., 22.2.16
CARR, Gunner Cecil Godfrey: 9th Rfts., N.T.O.S.; 13/F.A.B., 27.3.16; killed in action, France, 18.7.16.
CARR, Private Charles Roland: 11/L.H.R., 29.8.15; 11/L.H.R., 3.4.16
CARR, Driver Edgar Norman: 11/L.H.R., 29.8.15; 11/L.H.R., 8.3.16
CARR, Private John Edward: 15th Rfts., N.T.O.S.; 13/L.H.R., 2.6.16
CARROLL, Private William: Original, 8.12.14; Discd., 18.4.19.
CARSON, Private William Henry: 10th Rfts., N.T.O.S.; Discd., 27.3.16.
CARSTEN, Private Hans: 16th Rfts., N.T.O.S.; 15th Btn., 12.6.17.
CARTEN, Private Angus Bruce: 15th Rfts., 20.8.16; Discd., 27.9.19; wounded, 8.11.17.
CARTER, Private Andrew: 30th Rfts., N.T.O.S.; 11/L.H.R., 8.6.18.
CARTER, A/Corporal Allan Thomas: 29th Rfts., N.T.O.S.; Discd., 29.11.19.
CARTER, Driver Frederick Ernest: 4th Rfts., 25.5.15; 13/F.A.B., 27.3.16; died of wounds, France, 19.8.17.
CARTER, Driver George Davis: 26th Rfts., N.T.O.S.; 35/Coy., A.S.C., 21.8.17.
CARTER, Private John: 9th Rfts., 23.2.16; Discd., 4.10.19; wounded, 28.3.18
CARTER, Driver Lawrence Stanley: 12th Rfts., 7.1.16; 13/F.A.B., 27.3.16.
CASE, Corporal Lionel Matthew: 8th Rfts., 10.1.16; Discd., 29.7.19; wounded, 17.9.18
CASELLS, Gunner Charles: 16th Rfts., N.T.O.S.; 2nd L.H.R., 9.5.16
CASEY, Driver Eugene: Original, 8.12.14; Discd., 26.2.19
CASSELL, Private John: 29th Rfts., 18.5.18; Discd., 7.6.19
CASTLE, Private George: 29th Rfts., 12.5.18; Discd., 24.5.19
CASTLE, Private William George: 20th Rfts., N.T.O.S., 2/M.G.S., 5.10.16
CATON, Private William: 21st Rfts., 27.11.17; Discd., 3.4.19
CATON, Corporal William John: 11th Rfts., 23.2.16; Discd., 4.10.19
CAVANAGH, Private John James: 15th Rfts., N.T.O.S.; 4/Camel Rgt., 2.11.16
CAVANAGH, Driver William: 12th Rfts., 7.1.16; 13/F.A.B., 27.3.16
CAVE, L./Cpl. Frank: Original, 8.12.14; Discd., 4.7.19
CAVE, Private Stanley Thomas: 25th Rfts., 2.7.17; Discd., 12.9.19
CHAILLE, Sergeant Wilfred M.: Original, 8.12.14; wounded, 27.6.15; killed in action, Palestine, 14.7.18
CHALK, Corporal Alfred Titmarsh: 17th Rfts., 24.8.17; Discd., 9.5.18; wounded, 6.12.17
CHAPMAN, Private Harry Mulga: 24th Rfts., 15.7.17; Discd., 2.12.19
CHAPMAN, Private Richard Lance: Original, 8.12.14; Discd., 13.9.16; wounded, 27.6.15
CHARD, Sergeant Albert Arthur: 15th Rfts., N.T.O.S.; Camel Corps, 2.11.16; killed in action, Palestine, 4.12.17
CHARLES, Sergeant James Henry: 14th Rfts., 9.3.16; 18/Coy. I.C.C., 7.2.17
CHARLES, Driver Samuel McKay: 13th Rfts., 19.2.16; 13/F.A.B., 27.3.16
CHARLES, Private Thomas: Original, 8.12.14; Discd., 26.2.19
CHATHAM, Major William (Mentioned in Despatches): Original, 14.11.14; Appt. Term., 28.4.20; wounded, 5.8.16
CHAVE, Private William: Original, 8.12.14; 13/M.G.C., 3.5.17; wounded, 3.9.16

HISTORY OF THE 5th LIGHT HORSE REGIMENT. 173

CHEFFINS, 2/A.M. Archibald: Original, 8.12.14; 2/L.H.M.G. Sqdn., 24.7.16
CHEYNE, Gunner Wallace Gordon: 3rd Rfts., 29.7.15; 13/F.A.B., 27.3.16
CHIDLOW, Private Robert Joseph: 7th Rfts., 14.11.15; Discd., 28.10.19
CHISHOLM, S/Smth. Alexander Sanderson: 13th Rfts., 19.2.16; 13/F.C.E., 6.3.16
CHRISTIANSEN, Private Charles: Camel Cps., 26.7.18; Discd., 19.9.19
CHRISTIANSEN, Private John: 6th Rfts., 3.10.15; killed in action, Anzac, 22.11.15
CHRISTENSEN, T/Sgt. Thomas: Original, 8.12.14; 2/L.H.M.G. Sqdn., 24.7.16
CHRISTIE, Driver Carl Johan: 20th Rfts., 12.10.16; Discd., 19.9.19
CHRISTIE, Lieut.-Col. Robert (D.S.O. and Bar, C. de G., Belgium, Mentioned in Despatches twice): Original, 8.12.14; 51st Bn., 26.3.16
CHRISTISON, Private Robert McIlroy, 11th Rfts., 23.2.16; Discd., 4.10.19
CLANCY, T/Dvr. John: 28th Rfts., N.T.O.S.; 30/Coy. A.S.C., 21.8.17
CLANCY, Driver James Thomas: 11th Rfts., N.T.O.S.; 1st Fld. Sqdn., 25.6.16
CLANCHY, Private Steve: 27th Rfts., N.T.O.S.; 8th L.H.R., 31.8.17
CLARE, Private Joseph: 25th Rfts., N.T.O.S.; 2/L.H.R., 24.5.17
CLARK, Private Albert: 11th Rfts., N.T.O.S.; died (mastoiditis), Ghezireh, Egypt, 27.1.16
CLARK, Driver David Laing: Original, 8.12.14; Discd., 14.2.19
CLARK, Private Robert: 7th Rfts., 14.11.15; Discd., 30.10.19
CLARK, Private John: 3rd Rfts., 29.7.15; Discd., 15.4.16; wounded, 9.11.15
CLARK, Private William: 1st Rfts., 16.5.16; Discd., 24.5.16
CLARK, Corporal William Ord: Original, 8.12.14; Discd., 24.1.19; wounded, 5.11.15
CLARKE, Private Charles: 5th Rfts., N.T.O.S.; 2/L.H.R., 25.10.15
CLARKE, Driver Edward Patrick: 12th Rfts., 7.1.16; 14/F.A.B., 27.3.16
CLARKE, Private John: 11th L.H. Rgt., 29.8.15; 11th L.H. Rgt., 22.2.16
CLARKE, Gunner Theodore Talbot: Original, 8.12.14; 14th F.A. Bde, 27.3.16; died after discharge (motor accident), 14.12.20
CLARKSON, Sapper Patrick: 17th Rfts., N.T.O.S.; 2nd M.G. Sqdn., 12.9.16
CLARRIS, Private Charles William: 20th Rfts., 12.10.16; Discd., 19.9.19
CLAYSON, Private Ardren Vernon: 11th L.H. Rgt., 29.8.15; Cml. Cps., 5.8.16
CLAYTON, 2/Lieut. Frank Basil Stewart: Original, 8.12.14; Aust., 31.10.15; 6th L.H.R., 26.7.16; A.F.C., 24.7.18; wounded, 28.6.15
CLAYTON, Gunner Philip Henry: 11th Rfts., N.T.O.S. 13th F.A. Bde., 27.3.16
CLEMENTS, Private Sydney Vincent: 19th Rfts., 12.10.16; Discd., 8.10.19
CLOUGH, Corporal Richard Henry: Original, 8.12.14; died of wounds at sea, 2.6.15
CLYDE, Driver George: 12th Rfts., N.T.O.S.; 1st F.C. Eng., 23.11.16
COBB, Lieut. Henry Lackie: Original, 8.12.14; 41st Btn., 8.8.18; wounded, 21.10.15
COCKERILL, Private Benjamin James: 6th Rfts., 25.9.15; 12th I.C.C., 15.7.16
COCKRANE, Private Ben Smith: 1st Rfts., N.T.O.S.; Discd., 8.2.15
COFFILL, Sergeant Frank: Original, 8.12.14; Discd., 26.2.19; wounded, 5.8.16, 19.4.18
COLE, E.R/Corporal George Fleming: 23rd Rfts., N.T.O.S.; Postal Cps., 4.6.18

COLE, Private Richard John Henry: Original. 8.12.14; 31st Btn., 1.12.16.
COLEMAN, T/S.Q.M.S. Joseph: 14th Rfts., N.T.O.S.; 2nd M.G.S., 4.8.16; 2nd M.G.S., 20.2.17; 2nd M.G.S., 21.2.17
COLEMAN, Private William Charles: 29th Rfts., 28.2.18; Discd., 21.9.19; wounded, 28.8.18.
COLGAN, Corporal Robert Phillip (C. de G., Belgian): 16th Rfts., N.T.O.S.; 12th F.A.Bde., 9.4.17.
COLLIE, Private William Thomas: 4th Rfts., 29.7.15; Aust., 19.1.16; Anzac Prov. Cps., 23.1.17; killed in action, Palestine, 26.11.17.
COLLINS, Sergeant Alfred John Edward: 4th Rfts., 25.5.15, Discd., 4.10.19; wounded, 25.4.17.
COLLINS, R.S.M. Bernard Joseph: Original, 7.12.14, Aust., 31.1.16; Aust., 7.10.16; Discd., 28.9.19; wounded, 27.6.15.
COLLINS, Private Gerald Robert: 30th Rfts., 17.8.18; Discd., 28.8.19, wounded, 25.9.18.
COLLINS, Private Harold Frederick: 19th Rfts., N.T.O.S.; Camel Cps., 7.9.16
COLLINS, Private Patrick: 11/L.H.R., 29.8.15; Discd., 2.5.16.
COLLINS, Driver Percy: 11th Rfts., 31.12.15, 14/F.A.Bde., 27.3.16.
COLQUHOUN, Sapper James: 14th Rfts., N.T.O.S.; 4th Camel Rgt., 2.11.16.
COMPTON, Sergeant Clarence Henry: A.A.S.C., 26.3.16; died (suicide), Marakeb, Palestine, 3-5.9.17.
COMPTON, Private Frederick David: 11/L.H.R., 19.9.17; Discd., 4.9.19
CONAGHAN, Private Charles Joseph: 7th Rfts., 14.11.15; 2/L.H.B H.Q., 14.4.17; 2/L.H.B H.Q., 16.10.17; A.I.F. Canteens, 18.10.17, died (pneumonia and influenza), Kantara, Egypt, 4.1.19
CONMEE, Corporal James Timothy (M.M.): 5th Rfts., 25.9.15, 13/F.A.Bde., 27.3.16.
CONNEW, Private John Alfred: 15th Rfts., N.T.O.S; 4th Camel Rgt., 2.11.16.
CONNOLLY, Private Alfred Henry: 1st Rfts., 25.6.15; killed in action, Gallipoli, 28.6.15.
CONNOLLY, Gunner George Andrew (M.M.): 11th Rfts., N.T.O.S.; 13/F.A.B, 27.3.16
CONNOLLY, T/Sergeant John Morris: 5th Rfts., 25.9.15; 14/F.A.B., 27.3.16.
CONNOR, Driver John Patrick: 14th Rfts., 9.3.16; 14/F.A.B., 27.3.16.
CONNOR, Private William Alfred: 7/L.H.R, 4.12.17 (attached strength); Discd., 29.12.19.
CONNOR, Private William John: 15th Rfts., N.T.O.S.; 4th Camel Rgt., 2.11.16.
CONNORS, Private James Wallace: 11/L.H.R., 2.10.15; 11/L.H.R, 22.2.16.
CONRIDGE, T/Sergeant Percy: Original, 8.12.14; Discd., 19.8.19.
CONSIDINE, Private James Henry: 11/L.H.R., 29.8.15; 11/L.H.R., 11.3.16.
CONWAY, Private John Cornelius (served with 19th Btn. as 5069 Pte. WALKER, John): 12th Rfts., N.T.O.S., 19th Btn., 11.12.15; killed in action, France, 23.12.16.
COOK, F/Q.M.S. Alfred Woodburn (D.C.M.): Original, 8.12.14; Discd., 12.4.19.
COOK, T/Bdr. Colin Stewart: 14th Rfts., 9.3.16; 13/F.A.B., 28.3.16.
COOK, Private James: 11th Rfts., 20.1.16; 13/F.A.B., 27.3.16; killed in action, Belgium, 19.10.17.
COOK, Major Leonard Roy (Mentioned in Despatches): A.A.M.C. (attached), 3.10.15 to 4.11.15.

COOK, Private Samuel: 5th Rfts., 25.9.15; wounded, 29.10.15, 5.11.15; died of wounds, Alexandria, 14.11.15.
COOKE, Gunner Arthur Dixon: 16th Rfts., N.T.O.S.; 5/D.A.C., 19.9.16.
COOKE, Bdr. Alfred Ernest: 16th Rfts., N.T.O.S.; 2/D.A.C., 18.5.17.
COOKE, Gunner Allan Stewart (M.M.): 15th Rfts., N.T.O.S.; 12th F.A.B., 9.4.17.
COOKE, Sergeant Harry Alexander (M.M., M.S.M.): 16th Rfts., N.T.O.S.; 12/F.A.B., 29.3.17.
COOKE, Private William: 21st Rfts., N.T.O.S.; Discd., 21.7.20.
COOKE, Sergeant William Robert: 11th Rfts., 23.2.16; Discd., 17.12.19.
COOMS, Sergeant John Joseph (Mentioned in Despatches): 16th Rfts., N.T.O.S.; 4/D.A.C., 14.12.16.
COOMS, Private Walter: 11/L.H.R., 29.8.15; 11/L.H.R., 9.3.16; wounded, 2.9.15.
COONAN, Private Thomas Jeremire: 26th Rfts., 27.11.17; Discd., 3.6.19.
COONEY, Private Thomas: 17th Rfts., N.T.O.S.; 2/L.H B.M.G.S., 1.8.16.
COOPER, T/Corporal Clyde William Stanley (D.C.M.): 11 L.H.R., 29.8.15; 11/L.H.R., 24.2.16.
COOPER, George Thomas: 13th Rfts., 19.2.16; 14/F A.B., 27.3.16.
COOPER, Sergeant George Thomas: 13th Rfts., 19.2.16; 13/F.A.B.,
COOPER, S/Smith/Corporal John Joseph: 13th Rfts., 19.2.16; 13th F.A.B., 27.3.16.
COOPER, Private William: 1st Rfts., N.T.O.S., Discd., 21.7.20.
COOPER, Gunner William Joseph: Original, 8.12.14; 14/F.A.B, 27.3.16; wounded, 28.6.15.
CORBETT, Private Cecil Angus: 14th Rfts., N.T.O.S.; 12th Coy. I.C.C., 15.7.16.
CORBETT, Gunner George Percy: 13th Rfts., 19.2.16; 13/F.A.B., 27.3.16.
CORNELL, L/Corporal Edward Arnold: 11th Rfts., 23.2.16; Discd., 14.6.19.
CORNER, Temp /Sergeant Edward Elgie: Original, 8.12.14; Discd, 26.2.19.
CORY, Private Charles Barnes (M.M.): 11/L.H R., 2.10.15; 11/L.H.R., 22.2.16.
CORY, T/Sergeant Thomas Barnes: 11/L.H.R., 29.8.15; 11/L.H.R., 22.2.16.
COSTELLO, Gunner Victor Charles: 16th Rfts., N.T.O.S.; 12/F.A.B, 29.3.17.
COTT, T/Corporal Charles Frederick: 27th Rfts., 23.12.17; A Prov. Cps., 25.5.18.
COUCHY, Driver Walter: 16th Rfts., N.T.O.S.; 9/F.A B., 10.11.16.
COULTER, Private Arthur: 15th Rfts., N.T.O.S.; Camel Cps., 7.9 16.
COULTER, Private David: 11th Rfts., N.T.O.S.; 2/L.H F. Amb., 25.1.16
COUNSELL, Driver Albert Vincent: 11th Rfts., N.T.O.S.; 14/F.A.B., 27.3.16.
COWAN, Private James Henry: 24th Rfts., 15.7.17; Discd., 12.9.19
COWAN, Driver Thomas: 13th Rfts., 19.2.16; 13/F.AB., 27.3.16.
COWDROY, Private Albert Herbert George: 23rd Rfts., 27.11.17; Discd., 4.9.19
COTTEW, Private Edward Arthur Lewis: Original, 8.12.14; A.A.M.C., 21.2.16.
COWELL, Private Edwin Thomas: 12th Rfts., 7.1.16; Camel Cps., 7.9.16.
COWEN, Private Denzil Rupert: 18th Rfts., N.T.O.S.; A. Prov. Cps., 26.7.16; A. Prov. Cps., 16.4.17; Discd., 19.9.19.

COWLEY, Private Maurice Alfred: 3rd Rfts., 29.7.15; Discd., 16.8.16
COWLISHAW, Lieutenant Bob Thompson (M.C.): 5th Rfts., 25.9.15; 14/F.A.B., 27.3.16
COWLISHAW, Corporal Leo: 5th Rfts., 25.9.15; 14/F.A.B., 27.3.16
COX, Sergeant Charles Edward (M.M.): Original, 8.12.14; Discd., 29.3.19.
COX, Bombardier George: 12th Rfts., 7.1.16; 14/F.A.B., 27.3.16.
COX, Private John: 14th Rfts., N.T.O.S.; 12/Coy. I.C.C., 15.7.16.
CRAIG, Corporal James Richardson: 18th Rfts., 15.6.16; 15th Btn., 3.8.16.
CRAMB, Sergeant Nathaniel Alexander: 9th Rfts., 8.1.16; 13th F.C.E., 21.3.16.
CRAMP, Private Ernald Ventry: 29th Rfts., 28.2.18; Discd., 4.9.19.
CRANE, L/Corporal Richard Warren: Original, 8.12.14; Discd., 28.6.16.
CRAVEN, Private Frank: 11th Rfts., 30.6.16; Demob., U.K., 20.5.19.
CRAWFORD, Gunner Archibald: 13th Rfts., 19.2.16; 13/F.A.B., 27.3.16
CRAWFORD, Lieutenant Arthur Bruce: 3rd Rfts., 29.7.15; Appt. Term., 17.3.20; wounded, 28.3.18.
CRAWFORD, Driver Leo: 14th Rfts., 9.3.16; 14/F.A.B., 27.3.16.
CRAWFORD, Private Mervyn Alexander: Original, 8.12.14; Discd., 14.3.16.
CRAWFORD, Private William: 27th Rfts., N.T.O.S.; Discd., 16.2.19.
CREAGHE, Private John Weldon: 3rd Rfts., 29.7.15; Demob., Egypt. 12.3.17; wounded, 10.8.15.
CRESSWELL, Private Walter James: 18th Rfts., N.T.O.S.; 10/L.H.R., 26.5.16.
CREW, Private John: 11th Rfts., 23.2.16; Discd., 27.9.19.
CRISP, Driver Alexander John: 15th Rfts., N.T.O.S.; 4th Camel Rgt., 2.11.16.
CRISP, L/Corporal William Charles: 20th Rfts., N.T.O.S.; 2/M.G.S., 5.10.16.
CROCKETT, Private William George: 28th Rfts., 17.8.18; Discd., 21.9.19.
CROFT, Private Samuel Freestone: 7th Rfts., 14.11.15; Discd., 4.10.19.
CROMBIE, Private Alexander George Leslie: 23rd Rfts., N.T.O.S.; 10/L.H.R., 29.11.17.
CROSBY-BROWNE, Lieutenant John: 16th Rfts., 12.5.16; Appt. Term., 27.9.19.
CROSS, Gunner Charles Isaac: 16th Rfts., N.T.O.S.; 2/L.H.R., 9.5.16
CROSSMAN, T/S/Smith. Charles Henry: Original, 8.12.14; Discd., 24.2.19.
CROWE, Corporal Arthur Sidney: Original, 21.12.14; Discd., 14.3.19.
CROZIER, Bombardier Arthur Albert (M.M.): 6th Rfts., 14.11.15; 13/F.A.B., 27.3.16.
CRUTCHFIELD, L/Corporal George Albert: 2nd Rfts., 7.7.15; Discd., 9.10.19; wounded, 10.11.17.
CULLEN, Driver Edward: 13th Rfts., 19.2.16; 13/F.A.B., 27.3.16
CULLEN, Private George Edward: 20th Rfts., N.T.O.S.; 2/L.H.B. M.G.S., 6.10.16.
CULLEN, Private James (M.M.): 9th Rfts., 23.2.16; Discd., 3.10.19
CUMES, T/S.Q.M.S. Sidney Owen: 10th Rfts., 23.2.16; Discd., 16.6.19.
CUMMING, Private Thomas: 12th Rfts., 7.1.16; Discd., 23.8.16.
CUMMINGS, T/Sergeant John Joseph: 27th Rfts., N.T.O.S.; 8/Coy A.M.D. Trn., 6.9.17
CUNNEEN, Private Maurice Patrick: 11/L.H.R., 29.8.15; 11/L.H.R., 6.3.16.
CUNNEEN, Saddler Sergeant Urban James: Original, 8.12.14; Discd., 6.6.16.

HISTORY OF THE 5th LIGHT HORSE REGIMENT.

CUNNINGHAM: Private Alfred George: 11th Rfts., 31.12.15; Discd., 4.10.19.
CUNNINGHAM, Private Patrick: 11th Rfts., 18.1.16; Discd., 4.10.19.
CUNNINGTON, Private William: 19th Rfts., N.T.O.S.; Camel Cps., 7.9.16.
CUPPAIDGE, Driver Loftus Russell: 13th Rfts., N.T.O.S.; 13/I.B.H.Q., 14.3.16.
CUREL, Private John: 11/L.H.R., 29.8.15; 11/L.H.R., 22.2.16.
CURRIE, Lieutenant Archibald (M.M.): Original, 8.12.14; wounded, 25.9.18; died of wounds, Palestine, 25.9.18.
CURRIE, A/2/Corporal Frederick (stated to be CURRIE, Ernest Edward): 15th Rfts., N.T.O.S.; 12/Coy. I.C.C., 15.7.16.
CURRIE, Private Thomas: Original, 8.12.14; Discd., 24.1.19.
CURRY, Private Samuel Hugh: 12th Rfts., 7.1.16; wounded, 5.8.16; died (pneumonia and malaria), Jeruaslem, 24.10.18
CURWEN-WALKER, Private Maxwell Christian: 23rd Rfts., 1.8.17; Discd., 30.8.19.
CUSSEN, Private Fletcher: 1st Rfts., N.T.O.S.; Discd., 13.8.15
CUTLER, Private Percy John B.: 11/L.H.R., 29.8.15; Discd., 20.7.16
DALE, Private John: Original, 8.12.14; Discd., 24.1.19; wounded, 26.6.15, 13.11.15.
DALLOW, Private Joseph: 14th Rfts., 9.3.16; Postal Cps., 24.4.16.
DALTON, Private John: 21st Rfts., N.T.O.S.; 3/L.H.R., 18.1.17.
DALTON, Private Victor Oliver: 19th Rfts., 12.10.16; Discd., 3.4.19.
DALY, Sergeant Geoffrey Dunsandle (Medaille Barbatie Si Credinta, 3rd Class, Roumania): 2nd Rfts., 13.11.15; Discd., 4.10.19.
DANCOCKS, Private John Thornton: 6th Rfts., 25.9.15; Discd., 27.3.17.
DANIEL, Driver Alexander: 8th Rfts., 10.1.16; Discd., 23.4.19.
D'ARCY, Private Charles: 29th Rfts., N.T.O.S.; 2/M.G.S., 3.2.18.
DARCEY, Private James: 3rd Rfts, N.T.O.S.; Discd., 4.1.16.
DARLING, Private William: 14th Rfts., 9.3.16; 15th Btn., 4.8.16.
DAUBERN, Private William: 11th Rfts., 21.1.16; Discd., 18.5.16.
DAVIDSON, Private Varro Clarke: 4th Rfts., 25.5.15; 47th Btn., 3.10.16.
DAVIE, Gunner James: 9th Rfts., 18.1.16; 13/F.A.B., 27.3.16.
DAVIES, Private Idawl Llewellyn: Original, 8.12.14; Demob., U.K., 7.1.16.
DAVIES, Private James Judge: 17th Rfts., N.T.O.S.; 2/M.G.S., 1.8.16; died (pneumonia), Port Said, 22.10.18.
DAVIES, Sapper Thomas Edward: 9th Rfts., 23.2.16; 2/Sig. Troop, 1.4.16.
DAVIS, Private Edward: 26th Rfts., 1.8.17; wounded, 8.11.17; died of wounds, Palestine, 9.11.17.
DAVIS, O.R./Sergeant William Ernest Francis: Original, 8.12.14; Discd., 3.12.18.
DAVISON, Driver Ernest Charles: 4th Rfts., 25.5.15; Discd., 9.12.19; wounded, 24.8.15.
DAVISON, A/Sergeant Thomas: 11th Rfts., 18.1.16; 14/F.A.B., 27.3.16
DAWES, Driver Bernard Conrad: A.A.S.C., 26.3.16; Discd., 23.1.19.
DAWSON, Lieutenant Erskine William D. H.: 7th Rfts., 7.1.16; 11th Coy. I.C.C., 1.7.16; died of wounds, Palestine, 6.11.17.
DAWSON, Private Henry: Original, 8.12.14; Discd., 24.1.19; wounded, 9.8.16.
DAWSON, Private Herbert Selwyn: Original, 8.12.14; died (heart failure), Anzac, 28.6.15.
DAWSON, Gunner Lindsay: 8th Rfts., 14.11.15; 14/F.A.B., 27.3.16.
DAWSON, Private Matthew William: G.S. Rfts., 13.1.19; drowned accidentally, Lake Tiberias, 27.1.19.

178 HISTORY OF THE 5th LIGHT HORSE REGIMENT.

DAWSON, E.R./C.S.M. William Vesey (D.C.M.): Original, 8.12.14 (attached strength); Camel Transport Corps, 11.11.16.
DAY, S.Q.M.S. Darcy: 5th Rfts., 25.9.15; I.C.Bde., 20.2.17.
DAY, Private Michael James: 28th Rfts., 27.2.18; Discd., 17.4.19.
DAY, Sergeant Sylvester: Original, 8.12.14; Anzac Mtd. Div., 24.3.16
DAYTON, L/Corporal Elmer: 8th Rfts., 10.1.16; Discd., 25.10.16; wounded, 9.8.16.
DEACON, Private Robert Percy: 21st Rfts., 28.7.17; Discd., 19.9.19.
DE BATHE, 2/Lieutenant Henry Michael: 3rd Rfts., 29.7.15; Appt. Term., 28.10.15; died after Term. of Appt.; (Granted Commission Imperial Army).
DECENT, Private Leslie Stanley: 2/L.H.F. Amb., 25.10.15; 8/L.H.R., 27.1.16; wounded, 15.11.15.
DE CRESPIGNY, Private Philip Champion: 30th Rfts, N.T.O.S.; 2nd L.H.R., 12.7.18; killed in action, Palestine, 14.7.18.
DEGOTARDI, Private Francis Delimere (Medaille Barbatie Si Credinta, 3rd Class, Roumania), subsequently served as No. 3753, 2nd Btn.: 2nd Rfts., N.T.O.S.; Discd., 13.8.15.
DELANEY, S/Smith. John Abraham: 30th Rfts., 10.6.18; Discd., 23.9.19.
DELANEY, Driver Patrick: 6th Rfts., 14.11.15; Discd., 23.6.19.
DELPRATT, Lieutenant Bertram Barnard: 49th Btn., 2.4.16; Appt. Term., 30.4.19.
DELPRATT, Sergeant Maurice George: Original, 8.12.14; Discd., 16.1.19; prisoner of war, Turkey, 28.6.15.
DELVES, Private Arthur Bentley: 4th Rfts., 6.8.15; Discd., 7.3.18; wounded, 26.3.17.
DENNY, Private John Keighley: 9th Rfts., 18.1.16; 2/L.H.B. M.G.S., 23.7.16; 2/L.H.B. M.G.S., 22.8.16; Discd., 4.10.19; wounded, 28.3.18.
DENNY, Private Henry Thomas: 29th Rfts., 23.2.18; Discd., 4.9.19; wounded, 14.7.18.
DENT, Driver Frank: 16th Rfts., N.T.O.S.; 1st D.A.C., 20.1.17.
DENT, Captain Rowe Clyde: 2/L.H.F. Amb. (attached), 25.3.19 to 27.3.19.
DENT, Private Spencer William: Original, 8.12.14; Discd., 10.8.15.
DE VILLIERS, Private Henry Daniel: 9th Rfts., 18.1.16; Discd., 4.10.19.
DEVLIN, Driver Bernard Murvyn: 13th Rfts., 19.2.16; Discd., 16.8.16.
DEVLIN, T/S/Sergeant Joseph: 8th Rfts., 14.11.15; 2/L.H.F. Amb., 25.1.16.
DE WARREN, Corporal Francis Joseph: 2nd Rfts., 7.7.15; killed in action, Suez Canal Zone, 9.8.16.
DE WINTON, Private Cuthbert Lechmere S.: 8th Rfts., N.T.O.S.; Camel Transport Corps, 9.2.16; Camel Cps., 18.3.16; Camel Cps., 26.5.16 (attached strength).
DIBLEY, Private Alfred William: 10th Rfts., 27.1.16; Discd., 8.11.19.
DICKASON, Private Charles Birfield: 8th Rfts., 25.10.15; Discd., 4.10.19.
DICKINSON, Driver Albert Norman: 27th Rfts., N.T.O.S.; H.Q., A.A.S.C., 20.8.17.
DICKINSON, A/Sergeant Harry Dudley: 9th Rfts, 18.1.16; 14/F.A.B., 27.3.16.
DICKSON, Sergeant Samuel: Original, 8.12.14; Discd., 7.6.16; wounded, 28.6.15.
DILLON, Gunner Edward James: 16th Rfts., N.T.O.S.; 2/D.A C., 7.9.17.
DILLON, Private John Clarence Michael: 26th Rfts., 21.9.17; Discd., 19.7.19; wounded, 6.4.18.
DILLON, Private William: 27th Rfts., 17.8.18; Discd., 30.8.19.

HISTORY OF THE 5th LIGHT HORSE REGIMENT. 179

DINGWALL, Driver Malcolm Barker: 14th Rfts., 9.3.16; Discd., 13.6.19.
DIPROSE, Corporal Frederick Augustus: 12th Rfts., 7.1.16; 2/L.H.F. Amb., 16.1.16.
DIXON, Corporal Charles Chisholm (M.M.): 12th Rfts., 7.1.16; 14th F.A.B., 27.3.16; died (influenza), France, 23.12.18.
DIXON, Private Edward Cameron: 24th Rfts., 28.7.17; Discd., 12.9.19.
DOBBINS, Private William John: 3rd Rfts., 29.7.15; 2/M.G.S., 18.9.18.
DOBBS, Private William Wright: Original, 8.12.14; Discd., 19.1.16; wounded, 26.6.15.
DOBE, Private James: 15th Rfts., N.T.O.S.; 4th Camel Rgt., 2.11.16.
DOCKERY, Private Leonard: 28th Rfts., N.T.O.S.; 1/L.H.B. Supply Sec., 30.7.17
DODS, Lieut.-Colonel Joseph Espie (M.C., D.S.O., twice Mentioned in Despatches): Original, 2.10.14; Appt. Term., 28.4.17; wounded, 29.8.15.
DOHERTY, Private Andrew James: 17th Rfts., 12.10.16; wounded, 25.9.18; died of wounds, Palestine, 28.9.18
DOHERTY, Private William: 11/L.H.R., 29.8.15; 11/L.H.R., 22.2.16; wounded, 4.9.15.
DOHERTY, Private William: 17th Rfts., 20.8.16; Discd., 19.9.19.
DOIG, Far./Corporal Andrew: Original, 8.12.14; Discd., 15.4.19.
DOLAN, Driver Hugh: 11th Rfts., 9.2.16; 4th Caml Rgt., 2.11.16
DONALDSON, Private Alexander: 11/L.H.R., 2.10.15; 11/L.H.R., 22.2.16; killed in action, Palestine, 25.9.18
DONALDSON, Driver Leonard: 16th Rfts., N.T.O.S.; 12/F.A.B., 29.3.17
DONALDSON, Driver Robert Smith: 16th Rfts., N.T.O.S.; 4/D.A.C., 1.11.16; killed in action, France, 29.9.18
DONALDSON, L/Corporal Thomas: 2nd Rfts., 7.7.15; 2/M.G.S., 12.9.16.
DONNELLAN, Driver John Michael: Original, 8.12.14; Discd., 24.2.19.
DONNELLY, Lieutenant Charles Edward: 2nd Rfts., 7.7.15; 2/Pnr. Btn., 11.3.16.
DONOVAN, Major George Peter (Mentioned in Despatches): Original, 28.9.14; Appt. Term., 29.10.19; wounded, 28.6.15
DONOVAN, Private Herbert Albert: 15th Rfts., 11.12.16; Discd., 2.11.19.
DOOLAN, Private James Francis: Original, 8.12.14; Discd., 15.4.19.
DOPSON, Sergeant, John Joseph: 14th Rfts., 30.4.16; Camel Corps, 7.9.16.
DORMAN, Sapper Cecil George: 14th Rfts., 9.3.16; 13/F.A.B., 27.3.16.
DOUGHERTY, Sergeant Charles Robert G.: 11/L.H.R., 2.10.15; 11/L.H.R., 22.2.16.
DOUGALL, Private George Henry: 26th Rfts., 27.11.17; Discd., 8.12.19.
DOUGLAS, Private John William: 18th Rfts., 12.10.16; Discd., 18.9.19.
DOWIE, Sergeant Harry (stated to be DOWEY, Harry): 11/L.H.R., 29.8.15; 11/L.H.R., 20.3.16; killed in action, Palestine, 4.7.17.
DOWLEY, T/Sergeant Gordon Frank: Original, 8.12.14; Demob., U.K., 4.4.19; wounded, 26.3.17.
DOWNES, Private Henry Edward: 21st Rfts., 2.6.17; Discd., 20.10.18.
DOWNIE, Private Alexander Mark: 11/L.H.R., 2.10.15; 11/L.H.R., 22.2.16; killed in action, Palestine, 14.7.18.
DOWNIE, Private Thomas William: 6th Rfts., N.T.O.S.; Aust., 3.9.15; 4/L.H.R., 11.8.16.
DOYLE, Private Harry: 8th Rfts, 14.11.15; 12/Coy. I.C.C., 15.7.16
DOYLE, Lieutenant John Clifton: 10th Rfts., N.T.O.S.; 14/F.A.B., 27.3.16.
DOYLE, Far./Corporal James Edward: 23rd Rfts., N.T.O.S.; 32/Coy. A S.C., 7.8.17.

DRAKE, Private Cedric George: G.S. Rfts., 17.10.18; Discd., 20.8.19.
DRANEY, L/Corporal John: Original, 8.12.14; killed in action, Suez Canal Zone, 9.8.16.
DREGHORN, Driver Peter: 12th Rfts., 7.1.16; 14/F.A.B., 27.3.16.
DREW, Driver Cecil: 16th Rfts., N.T.O.S.; 4/F.A.B., 17.12.16.
DREYER, T/Far./Sergeant William Charles: 11/L.H.R., 29.8.15; 11/L.H.R., 22.2.16
DROCHMAN, Sergeant Frederick: 6th Rfts., 25.9.15; Discd., 4.10.19; wounded, 8.11.17.
DRURY, Private Albert Matthew: 4th Rfts., 25.5.15; Discd., 19.10.19; wounded, 10.11.15.
DRYSDALE, Private Robert McAlpine: Original, 8.12.14; Discd., 4.5.16; wounded, 2.7.15.
DUCE, L/Cpl. Driver Frank Charles: 11th Rfts., 23.2.16; Discd., 1.5.19.
DUCE, Driver John: 9th Rfts., 23.2.16; Discd., 30.10.19.
DUCHATEL, Major Charles Francis (M.C., Mentioned in Despatches): Original, 8.12.14; 13/M.G.C., 8.4.16.
DUFFY, Private John: 11/L.H.R., 29.8.15; 11/L.H.R., 21.3.16.
DUFFY, Private John James: 14/Coy. I.C.C., 15.2.19; Discd., 19.9.19
DUKE, Corporal Allan Duncan: Original, 8.12.14; Discd., 25.10.16; wounded, 5.8.16.
DUNCAN, Private Charles Stewart: Original, 8.12.14; Discd., 23.6.19; wounded, 28.6.15, 11.7.15.
DUNCAN, Private Walter John: 17th Rfts., 12.10.16; Discd., 19.9.19
DUNCOMBE, Private Robert William: 22nd Rfts., 11.4.17; Discd., 12.9.19.
DUNN, Private Oscar Thomas: Original, 8.12.14; killed in action, Anzac, 28.6.15
DUNN, Private Robert Armstrong: 20th Rfts., 12.10.16; Discd., 13.8.19.
DUNN, S/Smith William Alexander: 11/L.H.R., 2.10.15; 11/L.H.R., 26.3.16.
DUNNING, Private William: 20th Rfts., N.T.O.S; 2/L.H.B. M.G.S., 6.10.16.
DUTTON, Driver Ernest Christian: 14th Rfts., 9.3.16; 13/F.A.B., 27.3.16.
DWYER, Private Thomas: 4th Rfts., 29.7.15; 49th Btn., 16.2.17; wounded, 12.12.15; killed in action, France, 5.4.18.
DWYER, Private Walter Ernest: Original, 8.12.14; 2/A.M.G.S., 20.9.17.
DYOS, Hon./Captain (Lieutenant) Albert Edward: 2nd Rfts., 17.2.16; 13/I.B.H.Q., 17.3.16.
DYSON-HOLLAND, Gunner Fenton Mervyn: 1st Rfts., 16.5.15; A. Prov., Cps. 9.11.16.
EADY, Private Charles Robert: Original, 8.12.14; Discd., 31.3.19
EARDLEY, Private Edward Godfrey Cyril: 11th L.H.R., 29.8 15; 11th L.H.R., 22.2.16
EARL, Private John Speight: Originla, 8.12.14; 31st Bn., 7.12.16
EDGINTON, S.S.M. John Patrick: Original, 8.12.14: Discd., 23.1.19
EDMONDS, Private Charles Henry: 16th Rfts., N.T.O.S.; Discd., 21.7.20
EDNEY, Private James Darcy: Original, 8.12.14; Discd., 7.4.18
EDWARDS, Private Arthur Francis: Original, 8.12.14; Discd., 12.4.16
EDWARDS, T/Sergeant Ernest (stated to be Ernest Waldemar Hammond): 11th L.H.R., 29.8.15; 11th L.H.R., 22.2.16
EDWARDS, Sergeant James Henry: Original, 8.12.14; Discd., 26.2.19
EGERTON, Bombdr. Francis Victor (M.M.): 4th Rfts., 22.5.15; 14/F.A.B., 27.3.16; wounded, 9.7.15
EGGAR, Private Jonathan Seymour: 3rd Rfts., 29.7.15; A. Prov. Cps. 3.4.16

HISTORY OF THE 5th LIGHT HORSE REGIMENT. 181

EGGINS, Corporal Harold James: Original, 8.12.14; killed in action, Anzac, 28.6.15
EGLINTON, Private Alvin: 18th Rfts., N.T.O.S.; Camel Cps., 5.8.16
ELCOATE, S.Q.M.S. Aubrey Tom Johnstone: 24th Rfts., 5.6.17; Discd., 31.3.21
ELLIOT, T/S.Q.M.S. Leslie Ernest: 4th Rfts., 25.5.15; Discd., 4.10.19; wounded, 28.7.15, and 9.8.16
ELLIOTT, Private Alwyne: 6th Rfts., 14.11.15; Discd., 23.8.16
ELLIOTT, Private David: 26th Rfts., N.T.O.S.; Discd., 6.10.19
ELLIS, Driver George Arthur: 23rd Rfts., N.T.O.S.; 32/Coy. A.S.C., 7.8.18
ELLIS, Private Jack: Original, 8.12.14; wounded, 18.11.15, and 3.5.18; died of wounds, Palestine, 3.5.18
ELLIS, Sergeant Roy Joseph Francis: 12th Rfts., 7.1.16; 14th F.A.B., 27.3.16
ELMES, Private George Alfred: 11th Rfts., 23.2.16; Discd., 4.10.19
ELWYN, Lieut. Maundy Garth: 10th Rfts., 23.2.16; A.F.C., 17.11.16
EMERSON, T/Sgt. Henry: Original, 8.12.14; Demob., U.K., 9.9.19
EMMONS, Private William John: 22nd Rfts., 11.4.17; Discd., 27.1.19
ENGLISH, S/Smth. Charles Edward (M.S.M.): 22nd Rfts., N.T.O.S.; 5th Sig. Troop, 23.4.17
ENRIGHT, Private Michael James: 19th Rfts., N.T.O.S.; Camel Cps., 7.9.16
ENSOR, Private Ernest Edwin: Original, 8.12.14; wounded, 19.4.18; died of wounds, Palestine, 20.4.18
ETHERINGTON, E.R./2/Cpl. George Lord: 4th Rfts., 25.5.15; A. Prov. Cps., 3.4.16
EVANS, T/Driver David: 25th Rfts., N.T.O.S.; A.S.C., 20.8.17
EVANS, Private Esmond: 27th Rfts., 15.4.18; Discd., 4.9.19
EVANS, E.R./2/Cpl. George: 11th L.H.R., 29.8.15; 11th L.H.R., 22.2.16; wounded, 19.9.15
EVANS, Sergeant John Caradoc: 11th L.H.R., 29.8.15; Discd., 6.9.16
EVANS, Private John Thomas: 11th L.H.R., 29.8.15; 11th L.H.R., 22.2.16; wounded, 5.11.15
EVANS, Private Thomas Robert: Original, 8.12.14; wounded, 28.6.15; killed in action, Anzac, 26.11.15
EVANS, Corporal William: 2nd Rfts., 16.5.15; 3/D.H.Q., 1.8.16; wounded, 28.7.15
EVANS, Gunner William John: Original, 8.12.14; 13/F.A.B., 27.3.16
EVERDELL, L/Cpl. William James: 20th Rfts., N.T.O.S.; 2/M.G. Sqdn., 6.10.16
EWEN, Private Bruce Skinner: 29th Rfts., 6.1.19; Discd., 4.9.19
EWING, Sergeant Thomas Campbell: Original, 8.12.14; Discd., 2.2.16; wounded, 28.6.15
FAGAN, Private Hugh Robinson: 22nd Rfts., 11.4.17; Discd., 2.9.19
FAIRHALL, Private James: Original, 8.12.14; Discd., 23.1.19
FAIRHALL, Sergeant John Huntley: Original, 8.12.14; Discd., 28.6.16
FAIRLEIGH, Gunner Edgar: 9th Rfts., N.T.O.S.; 13th F.A. Bde., 27.3.16
FALCONER, T/Cpl. John: 11th L.H. Rgt., 29.8.15; 11th L.H. Rgt., 22.2.16
FALLON, Private Stephen: 11th L.H. Rgt., 29.8.15; 15th Btn., 4.10.16
FANNING, Gunner John Rogers: 12th Rfts., 7.1.16; 13th F.A. Bde., 27.3.16
FANNON, Driver Frederick Arthur: 12th Rfts., 7.1.16; 13th F.A. Bde., 27.3.16
FARGHER, Captain Thomas Beswick: Original, 11.11.14; Appt. Term., 4.10.19
FARLOW, Lieut. Frederick Garnet (M.C., Mentioned in Despatches): 11th L.H. Rgt., 29.8.15; 11th L.H. Rgt., 22.2.16; killed in action, Palestine, 25.9.18

FARMER, Private Percy: 12th Rfts., 7.1.16; Discd., 5.6.16
FARRELL, Gunner Albert William: 16th Rfts., N.T.O.S.; 2nd D.A.C., 7.9.17
FARRELL, Private Peter James (alias Oswald Faulkiner): 1st Rfts., N.T.O.S.; Discd., 28.10.15
FELL, Private Alfred: 11th Rfts., 23.2.16; Discd., 18.4.17; wounded, 9.8.16
FELMINGHAM, E.R./2/Cpl. Benjamin: 6th Rfts., 25.9.15; A. Prov. Cps., 25.5.18
FENNER, Private John Adrian: 8th Rfts., N.T.O.S.; Discd., 21.7.17
FENWICK Private Thomas Abraham: 12th Rfts., 7.1.16; Discd., 5.4.19
FENWICKE, Lieut. Christopher Rupert: 10th Rfts., 4.1.16; R.F.C., 4.12.16
FERGUS, Private John Joseph: 11th L.H. Rgt., 29.8.15; 11th L.H. Rgt., 22.2.16
FERGUSON, Private Arthur: Original, 8.12.14; Anz. Prov. Cps., 26.3.17
FERGUSON, Gunner Cleveland Harold: 12th Rfts., N.T.O.S.; 13th F.A. Bde., 27.3.16
FERGUSON, Private Charles Stuart: 6th Rfts., 25.9.15; died (bronchopneumonia), Moascar, 25.2.19
FERNANDEZ, Driver John (M.M.): 14th Rfts., 9.3.16; 13th F.A. Bde., 27.3.16
FERRAR, Private George: 8th Rfts., 10.1.16; Discd., 6.2.18
FERRIE, Private Albert Edward: 3rd Rfts., 7.7.15; Discd., 28.3.17
FERRIS, Private Leslie: Original, 8.12.14; 14th F.A. Bde., 27.3.16; wounded, 29.5.15, and 14.9.15
FINES, Private Percy: 21st Rfts., 11.4.17; died (acute nephritis), Egypt, 3.4.19
FINLAY, Gunner Arthur: 16th Rfts., N.T.O.S.; 4th D.A.C., 25.10.16
FINLAY, Sergeant Hunter: 15th Rfts., N.T.O.S.; 4th Camel Rgt., 2.11.16
FINLAY, Private Nigel Lyall George: 11th L.H. Rgt., 29.8.15; 11th L.H. Rgt., 24.2.16
FIRTH, Bombdr. Charles Edward: Original, 8.12.14; 13th F.A. Bde., 27.3.16
FISHER, Driver Charles John: 14th Rfts., 9.3.16; 13th F.A. Bde., 27.3.16
FISHER, Private David: 8th Rfts., 10.1.16; Discd., 26.4.18; wounded, 6.12.17
FITZGERALD, Driver Joseph Francis: Original, 8.12.14; 2/L.H.B. M.G. Sqdn., 24.7.16
FITZGERALD, Private Robert James: 10th Rfts., 23.2.16; Discd., 4.5.19
FITZGERALD, Private William Thomas: 11th Rfts., N.T.O.S.; 4/Camel Rgt., 2.11.16
FITZ HANNAM, Private Charles Edgar: Original, 8.12.14; wounded, 26.6.15; killed in action, Anzac, 27.8.15
FITZHARDINGE, T/Major John Fortescue G. (M.C., Mentioned in Despatches): 2/L.H. Fld. Amb., 16.10.16; Appt. Term., 1.1.20; wounded, 25.9.18
FLAHERTY, Corporal Francis John: Original, 8.12.14; 12/Coy., I.C.C., 15.7.16; wounded, 7.6.15
FLAHERTY, Private Herbert Walter: Original, 8.12.14; killed in action, Anzac, 25.11.15
FLANAGAN, Private John Henry: 13th Rfts., 19.2.16; Discd., 27.9.19
FLANAGAN, Corporal Thomas: 13th Rfts., 19.2.16; 14th F.A.B., 27.3.16
FLEISCHFRESSER, Private Carl: 29th Rfts., N.T.O.S.; 2/A.M.G. Sqdn., 3.2.18
FLEMING, Gunner Frederick William: 13th Rfts., 19.2.16; 14th F.A.B., 27.3.16

HISTORY OF THE 5th LIGHT HORSE REGIMENT. 183

FLOHR, Driver Martin: 3/Bn. I.C.C., 28.7.18; Discd., 27.9.19
FLYNN, Gunner John: 11th Rfts., N.T.O.S.; 14th F.A.B., 27.3.16
FOGARTY, Private Alfred George: 1st Rfts., 16.5.15; 1st D.H.G., 1.6.17
FOLEY, Private Patrick: Original, 8.12.14; killed in action, Anzac, 2.6.15
FOLEY, Bombdr. William James: 8th Rfts., 10.1.16; 14th F.A.B., 27.3.16
FOOT, Private Alexander Madden: Original, 8.12.14; killed in action, Anzac, 22.11.15
FOOT, Sergeant George Peirce: Original, 8.12.14; 2/M.G. Sqdn., 24.7.16
FOOT, Sergeant Vivian Cyril: 15th Rfts., N.T.O.S., 4/Camel Rgt., 2.11.16
FORD, Private Arthur Ernest: 8th Rfts., 10.1.16; Discd., 23.6.19; wounded, 5.8.16
FORD, T/Sgt. Michael Joseph: Original, 8.12.14; killed in action, Anzac, 14.11.15
FORDE, Private Robert Assheton: Original, 8.12.14; Demob., Egypt, 6.12.15 (granted Commission, Imperial Army).
FORREST, Lieut. Roy Everard: Original, 8.12.14; Camel Cps., 31.1.16
FORSTER, Private Peter Aitken: 24th Rfts., N.T.O.S.; Discd., 12.9.19
FOSTER, Private John: 3rd Rfts., 29.7.15; Discd., 30.6.19
FOX, Corporal Claude Douglas: Original, 8.12.14; 3rd A.G.H., 11.4.17
FOX, Private Herbert James: 11th L.H.R., 29.8.15; Discd., 11.9.16; wounded, 13.12.15
FOX, Private James: 27th Rfts., N.T.O.S.; A.A.S.C., 13.8.17
FOX, Private Thomas Celsus: 8th Rfts., 10.1.16; Discd., 30.10.19
FOX, Private Walter John: 8th Rfts., 10.1.16; Discd., 9.9.19; wounded, 30.3.18
FOXTON, T/Sgt. Eric Gilson: 14th Rfts., 9.3.16; 13th F.A.B., 27.3.16
FRANCIS, Private Reginald John: 14th Rfts., 9.3.16; Dental Service, 31.8.17
FRANCIS, Corporal William John: 5th Rfts., 25.9.15; 1/Fld. Sqd. Engrs., 25.6.16
FRANCIS, Driver William Leslie Claude: 1st Rfts., 16.5.15; Discd., 24.2.19; wounded, 16.7.15
FRANKLIN, Driver William Edgar: Original, 8.12.14; 1/Fld. Sqdn. Engrs., 19.2.17
FRASER, Corporal David: Original, 8.12.14; Discd., 16.4.19; wounded, 27.11.17
FRASER, Lieut. Donald Lovat: Original, 8.12.14; 42nd Bn., 20.11.16
FRASER, Private Douglas Martin: G.S. Rfts., 4.10.18; Demob., Egypt, 21.3.19
FRASER, Lieut. Harold Livingstone (M.C.): 5th Rfts., 25.9.15; A.F.C., 7.4.17; wounded, 5.8.16
FRASER, Private Jack Hughie Belmore: 15th Rfts., N.T.O.S.; 2/L.H. M.G. Sqdn., 1.8.16
FRASER, A/Cpl. John Lawrence: 13th Rfts., 19.2.16; Discd., 29.5.17
FRASER, Private Victor Douglas: G.S. Rfts., 4.6.19; Discd., 20.8.19
FRASER, Private William Albert: 11th L.H.R., 25.10.15; wounded, 8.11.15; died of wounds at sea (off Gallipoli), 9.11.15
FREDERICKS, Lieut. Harold William Gordon: Original, 8.12.14; Appt. Term., 15.4.19
FREDERICKS, Private Stanley Harry: Original, 8.12.14; Discd., 31.5.16; wounded, 18.6.15
FREDERICKS, Gunner Walter Richard E.: 14th Rfts., 9.3.16; 13th F.A.B., 27.3.16
FREEMAN, Private Reuben: 7th Rfts., 10.1.16; 2/L.H.B.M.G. Sqdn., 1.8.16
FREESTONE, Driver Frank William: Original, 8.12.14; 2/L.H.B.M.G. Sqdn., 24.7.16; killed in action, Palestine, 10.11.17

FRENCH, T/Bombdr. Albert Lester: 13th Rfts., 19.2.16; 14th F.A.B., 27.3.16; killed in action, France, 29.1.17
FRENCH, Gunner William George B.: 14th Rfts., 9.3.16; 13th F.A.B., 27.3.16
FRISBY, Private Albert John: 8th Rfts., 10.1.16; Discd., 26.12.19; wounded, 9.8.16
FRY, Private Harry: Original, 8.12.14; Discd., 12.4.16; wounded, 28.6.15
FUGE, Private Arthur Seth: Original, 8.12.14; 7/A.M. Vet. Sec., 20.9.18; wounded, 28.7.15
FULLER, Private Andrew: Original, 8.12.14; A. Prov. Cps., 1.1.17; wounded, 28.6.15
FULLER, Private George Edward: 15th Rfts., 6.7.16; 4/Camel Rgt., 2.11.16
FULLER, Private George Richard: 4th Rfts., N.T.O.S.; Discd, 13.8.15
FULLER, 1/A.M. Shered Francis: Original, 8.12.14; A.F.C., 10.1.18
FULLER, Private Vivian George: 9th Rfts., 8.1.16; Discd., 4.10.19
FULLOON, Gunner Percy Charles: 11th L.H.R., 2.10.15; 11th L.H.R., 22.1.16
FULTON, Lieut. Hugh (Mentioned in Despatches): 23rd Rfts., N.T.O S.; 34/Coy. A.S.C., 31.8.17
FURNISS, Sergeant Walter (D.C.M.): 13th Rfts., 19.2.16; 14th F.A.B., 27.3.16; killed in action, France, 8.10.18
FUSSELL, Private Edgar Coldham: 21st Rfts., N.T.O.S.; 9/M. Vet. Sec., 21.8.17
GABY, L/Cpl. Henry Richard (stated to be Henry Richard Biggs): 30th Rfts., N.T.O.S.; 2nd L.H.R., 31.5.18
GAHAN, Sergeant Joseph: Original, 8.12.14; wounded, 27.6.15; killed in action, Palestine, 26.3.17
GAHAN, T/Bdr. Lawrence: 12th Rfts., 7.1.16; 13th F.A.B., 27.3.16
GALLAGHER, T/Cpl. James Augustine: 18th Rfts., 5.8.16; Discd., 19.9.19
GALLAGHER, Shoe/Smith. Oliver Jacob: 16th Rfts., N.T.O.S.; 2nd D.A.C., 24.11.16
GALLAGHER, T/Cpl. Patrick John: 18th Rfts., 20.8.16; Discd., 19.9.19
GALLAGHER, Private Virgil Vincent Patrick: 26th Rfts., 16.2.18; Discd., 4.9.19
GALLIGAN, Driver Edmund Andrew: 16th Rfts, N.T.O.S.; 4th D.A.C., 24.9.16
GALLIGAN, Private John Bennett: 6th Rfts., 25.9.15; killed in action, Palestine, 26.3.17
GALVIN, Private Thomas: 11th L.H.R., 2.10.15; 11th L.H.R., 22.2.16; wounded, 11.11.15
GALVIN, Driver William Bede: 26th Rfts., N.T.O.S.; A A.S.C., 20.8.17
GALVIN, Private William Patrick: Original, 8.12.14; Discd., 19.7.16; wounded, 14.7.15
GAMES, Private Robert Sumerton: 11th Rfts., 18.1.16; 4/Camel Rgt., 6.7.16
GANNON, Private Herbert: Original, 8.12.14; A. Prov. Cps., 1.1.17
GANNON, Private John: 28th Rfts., N.T.O S.; Discd, 12.7.19
GANNON, Private Jerry Thomas: Original, 8.12.14; A. Prov. Cps., 1.1.17; A. Prov. Cps., 30.5.17; Discd., 2.4.19
GANNON, Private Victor: Original, 8.12.14; Discd., 24.1.19
GANT, Sergeant Robert Samuel: 19th Rfts., N.T.O.S.; Camel Cps., 10.9.16
GANZER, Private Terence Joseph: 24th Rfts., 15.7.17; Discd., 23.9.19
GARD, Private Sidney Charles: Original, 8.12.14; Discd, 26.2.19
GARDNER, Gunner James (M.M.): 7th Rfts., 14.11.15; 14th F.A.B., 27.3.16; killed acc., 8.11.16, France

GARDNER, Private Thomas Hamilton: Original, 8.12.14; Discd., 4 4.16; wounded, 28.6.15, and 6.11.15
GARNER, Gunner Wesley Diamond: 13th Rfts., 19.2.16; 14th F.A.B., 27.3.16
GARNER, Private Wilfred Immanuel: 20th Rfts., N.T.O.S., 2/L.H.B. M.G. Sqdn., 6.10.16
GARTON, Private William Henry: 17th Rfts., N.T.O.S.; 2 L.H B. M.G. Sqdn., 1.8.16
GAULD, L./Cpl. Ronald Leslie: 5th Rfts., 25.9.15; Discd., 18.3.19; wounded, 19.4.18
GAUNT, Driver Gustave Simpson: Original, 8.12.14; Discd., 26.2.19; wounded, 4.9.15
GAUT, Private Oliver: 11th L.H.R., 29.8.15; 11th L.H.R., 22.2.16
GAVIN, Private George: 12th Rfts., 7.1.16; Discd., 3.4.19
GAVIN, Gunner John Joseph: 16th Rfts., N.T.O.S.; A. Prov. Cps., 1.1 17
GAVIN, Private Patrick Joseph: 26th Rfts., 1.8.17; Discd., 29.9.19; wounded, 2 5.18
GAVIN, Private Stephen: 26th Rfts., N.T.O.S.; A.A.S.C., 12.10.17
GAZZARD, Sapper George: Original, 8.12.14; 1st Fld Sqdn., 12.10.16
GEDDES, C.Q.M.S. William (Mentioned in Despatches): 7th Rfts., 25.9.15; Imp. Cml. Cps., 1.7.16
GEE, Captain Herbert John (M.C., Mentioned in Despatches twice): 11th L.H. Rgt., 29.8.15; 11th L.H. Rgt., 22.2.16; wounded, 3.9.15, and 3.11.15; killed in action, Palestine, 25.9.18
GEES, Driver Archie: 13th Rfts., 19.2.16; 13th F.A. Bde., 27 3.16
GEES, Driver Walter James: 13th Rfts., 19.2.16; 14th F.A. Bde., 27.3.16
GEORGE, Private Roy, 15th Rfts., N.T.O.S.; 2nd L.H.B M.G.S., 4.8.16; died of wounds, Ismara, Palestine, 8.11.17
GEORGE, Private James: 11th L.H. Rgt., 29.8.15; Aust., 11.4 16; 26th Btn., 18.6.17; died of wounds, France, 20.4.18
GERAGHTY, Private James: 15th Rfts., N.T.O.S.; 2nd L H.B.M.G.S., 4.8.16
GERRARD, Private Thomas: 11th L.H. Rgt., 2.10.15; 11th L.H. Rgt., 2 2.16; died (enteric, collapse and heat-stroke), Tel-el-Kebir, 21.6.16
GIBBON, Private Harold: 11th L.. Rgt., 2.10.15; 11th L.H. Rgt., 22.2.16; killed in action, Sinai Peninsula, 7 8.16
GIBBONS, L Cpl Horace Walter, 11th L.H. Rgt., 29.8 15; 11th L.H. Rgt., 1.3 16
GIBBS, S/Smith Arthur Henry Archibald: 14th Rfts., 9.3.16; 14th F.A. Bde., 27.3.16
GIBBS, Gunner Percival: 14th Rfts., 9.3.16; 14th F.A Bde., 27.3.16
GIBSON, Private Alexander: 17th Rfts., N.T.O.S.; 2nd M.G. Sqdn., 1.8.16
GIBSON, Lieut. Archibald Dickson Lockhart: 14th Rfts., 9 3.16; 13th F.A. Bde., 27.3.16
GIBSON Private James: 22nd Rfts., N.T.O.S.; Discd., 11.11.19
GIBSON, Sapper Robert: Original, 8.12.14; 1st F. Sqn. Eng., 12.6.17
GIBSON, Lieut. Robert Clarence: Original, 8.12.14; Anz. Prov. Cps., 9.2.17
GIBSON, Private William: 12th Rfts., 7.1.16; Discd., 4.10.16
GIELIS, T/Sgt. Henry Francis: 11th L.H. Rgt., 29.8.15; 11th L.H. Rgt., 22.2.16
GILBERT, Driver Charles: 8th Rfts., 10.1.16; 14th F.A. Bde., 27.3.16
GILBERT, T/S/Smth. William: 15th Rfts., N.T.O.S.; 1st F.S. Eng., 25.6.16
GILBY, Gunner Andy Albury: Original, 8.12.14; 14th F.A. Bde., 27.3.17; wounded, 8.7.15
GILES, Private Monte William: Original, 8 12.14; Discd., 15.4.19

GILHESPY, S./Sm./Cpl. John William: 11th Rfts., 23.2.16; died (pneumonia), Abbassia, 12.11.18
GILHOOLY, Gunner Bernard Benedict (M.M.): 13th Rfts., 19.2.16; 13th F.A. Bde., 27.3.16; killed in action, France, 9.8.18
GILL, Far./Sgt. Ernest: 11th L.H. Rgt., 29.8.15; 11th L.H. Rgt., 22.2.16
GILL, Gunner Frederick Palmer: 16th Rfts., N.T.O.S.; 2nd D.A.C., 22.8.17
GILL, Private George Henry: Original, 8.12.14; 4th Mob. Vet. S, 22.3.16; wounded, 28.6.15
GILLES, Gunner William John: 7th Rfts., 14.11.15; 14th F.A. Bde., 27.3.16; died of wounds, Outreau, France, 4.11.17
GILLESPIE, Lieut. Eric Walter: Original, 8.12.14; Appt. Term., 4.10.19
GILLIS, Private George: 21st Rfts., N.T.O.S.; 2nd M.G Sqdn., 7.6.17
GILLS, Private Christopher: 7th Rfts., 23.2.16; Discd., 4.10.19; wounded, 5.8.16
GILMORE, Private James: 3rd Rfts., 29.7.15; Discd., 26.7.16
GILMORE, Gunner William Sylvesta: Original, 8.12.14; 13th F.A. Bde., 27.3.16
GLANVILLE, L./Cpl. Charles Henry (M.M.): Original, 8.12.14; Discd., 24.2.19
GLEESON, Driver George Henry: 12th Rfts., N.T.O.S.; 13th F.A. Bde., 27.3.16
GLIDDON, Driver George: 16th Rfts., N.T.O.S.; 4th D.A.C., 8.2.17
GLOVER, Private George: 22nd Rfts., 27.11.17; Discd., 12.9.19
GOFF, Private Alfred William: 15th Rfts, N.T.O.S.; Discd., 3.3.17
GOFFIN, Private Arthur: Original, 8.12.14; Discd., 26.2.19
GOFTON, Private Septimus Laws (M.M., Mentioned in Despatches): 15th Rfts., 20.8.16; 2/L.H.F. Amb., 18.1.17; 2/L.H.F. Amb.. 1.2.18; 2/L.H.F. Amb., 8.6.18; wounded, 28.3.18
GOLDEN, Private William: 24th Rfts., 2.7.17; Discd., 12.9.19
GOLDING, F.Q.M.S. Charles Henry: 12th Rfts., 27.1.16; Discd., 27.9.19
GOLDING, Driver Charles Leo: 22nd Rfts., N.T.O.S.; 1st Sig. Sqn., 27.4.17
GOLDING, T/Driver Frederick Charles: 12th Rfts., N.T.O.S.; 14th F.A. Bde., 27.3.16
GOLDSWORTHY, Sapper Edwin Thomas: 22nd Rfts., N.T.O.S.; 4th Sig. Trp., 22.2.17
GOMERSALL, Private Harold Bowman: 29th Rfts., 12.5.18; Discd., 4.9.19
GOOCH, Driver Albert Edward: 13th Rfts., 19.2.16; 13th F.A. Bde., 27.3.16
GOOD, Private Edward John: 26th Rfts., 1.8.17; Discd., 27.4.18; wounded, 7.11.17
GOODE, Private Richard Hillary: Original, 8.12.14; Discd., 10.8.15
GOODMAN, Sergeant Ernest Aloysius: Original, 8.12.14; Discd., 26.2.19
GORDON, Driver Douglas: 15th Rfts., N.T.O.S.; 1st Fld. S.E., 19.2.17
GORDON, Private Frank: 4th Rfts., 25.5.15; Discd., 4.10.19
GORDON, Driver James: 11th Rfts., N.T.O.S.; 14th F.A. Bde., 27.3.16
GORDON, Private Kenneth: 15th Rfts., N.T.O.S.; 4th Cml. Rgt., 2.11.16
GORMAN, Private Charles: Original, 8.12.14; Discd., 15.4.19
GORMAN, Gunner James Aloysius: 13th Rfts., 19.2.16; 13th F.A. Bde., 27.3.16
GORMAN, Driver Thomas: 4th Rfts., 28.7.15; 13th F.A. Bde., 27.3.16
GOULD, L./Cpl. Robert: 5th Rfts., 25.9.15; Aust., 3.1.16; Aust., 20.8.16; Discd., 4.10.19
GOYMER, Lieut. Robert Clifford: 12th Rfts., 7.1.16; Appt. Term., 31.5.16
GRADY, Private James Michael: 1st Rfts., N.T.O.S.; Discd., 13.8.15
GRAFF, Private Alfred Edward: 20th Rfts., 15.7.17; Discd., 27.9.19
GRAHAM, Private Alfred Charles: Original, 8.12.14; Discd., 25.10.16

HISTORY OF THE 5th LIGHT HORSE REGIMENT.

GRAHAM, Private Archibald George: 4th Rfts., 25.5.15; Discd., 2.8.16
GRAHAM, Private David Hutchinson: 19th Rfts., N.T.O.S.; Cml. Cps., 7.9.16
GRAHAM, Driver John: 13th Rfts., 19.2.16; 13th F.A. Bde., 27.3.16
GRAHAM, Sergeant John Archibald: Original, 8.12.14; Discd., 24.2.19
GRAHAM, Lieut. Robert Davie: Original, 8.12.14; Appt. Term., 30.9.19; wounded, 9.11.15, 9.8.16, and 26.3.17
GRAHAM, Sergeant Victor Carlyle: 8th Rfts., 10.1.16; Discd., 4.8.19
GRAHAM, Sergeant Victor William: 11th L.H.R., 29.8.15; 11th L.H.R., 22.2.16
GRAHAM, Gunner William: 2nd Rfts., 16.5.15; 13th F.A.B., 27.3.16; wounded, 27.6.15, and 14.11.15
GRALOW, Bombdr. Sydney Hector: Original, 8.12.14; 13th F.A.B., 27.3.16
GRANT, Gunner Francis Robert: 13th Rfts., 19.2.16; 13th F.A.B., 27.3.16
GRAVES, Private Frederick Lyle: 30th Rfts., 28.7.18; Discd., 28.8.19
GRAY, Driver Alfred James: 16th Rfts., N.T.O.S.; 1st D.A.C., 13.3.17
GRAY, Corporal Thomas Craig: 2nd Rfts., 7.7.15; Discd., 11.8.19; wounded, 25.9.18
GREEN, Driver Frederick Arthur: 12th Rfts., 7.1.16; 14th F.A.B., 27.3.16
GREEN, M.T./Driver John: 16th Rfts., N.T.O.S.; 2nd L.H.R., 9.5.16
GREEN, Driver Newbury Hine: 11th Rfts., 18.1.16; 14th F.A.B., 27.3.16
GREENE, Corporal Joseph Bertram: Original, 8.12.14; Demob., U.K., 13.12.15 (granted Commission, Imperial Army)
GREENE, Lieut. William: Original, 8.12.14; 10th F.A.B., 19.4.16
GREENE, Private William Merton: 30th Rfts., N.T.O.S.; 11th L.H.R., 31.7.18
GREENWOOD, Driver Charles Frederick: 14th Rfts., 9.3.16; 14th F.A.B., 27.3.16
GREER, Gunner Cleveland Hawthorn: 3rd Rfts., 29.7.15; 14th F.A.B., 27.3.16
GREER, Private Ernest: 29th Rfts., 4.5.18; Discd., 4.9.19
GREEVY, Gunner Thomas Fitzpatrick: 13th Rfts., 19.2.16; 14th F.A.B., 27.3.16; died of wounds, France, 9.3.17
GREGORY, Driver Benjamin Montague: 12th Rfts., 7.1.16; 13th F.A.B., 27.3.16
GRENDON, Private George Jack: 8th Rfts., 10.1.16; Discd., 16.6.19
GRIESBACH, Gunner James: 9th Rfts., 4.2.16; 14th F.A.B., 27.3.16
GRIEVE, Driver John William: 21st Rfts., N.T.O.S.; 2nd Sig. Troop, 28.2.17
GRIEVES, Sergeant Joseph: Original, 8.12.14; Discd., 26.2.19; wounded, 5.8.16
GRIFFIN, Driver John Thomas: 14th Rfts., 9.3.16; 14th F.A.B, 27.3.16; killed in action, Belgium, 20.7.17
GRIFFITH, Private Hugh: 17th Rfts., 12.10.16; Discd., 8.5.19
GRIFFITH, Private John Joseph: Original, 8.12.14; 1st Fld. Sqdn., 29.6.16
GRIFFITH, Private William Henry: Original, 8.12.14; Discd., 16.8.16; wounded, 10.11.15, and 20.11.15
GRIFFITHS, Sergeant Harold: Original, 8.12.14; Discd., 3.3.18
GRIFFITHS, Driver Rollo James: 23rd Rfts., N.T.O.S.; A.S.C., 20.8.17
GRIGG, Private William Hannaford: 21st Rfts., 25.12.16; Discd., 21.3.18
GRIMLEY, Gunner William Arthur: 11th Rfts., N.T.O.S.; 13th F.A.B., 27.3.16
GUNSTON, Private James: 11th L.H.R., 2.10.15; 11th L.H.R., 22.2.16
GWYNNE, A./Sgt. John: Original, 8.12.14; killed in action, Anzac, 31.10.15

GWYNNE, Private James: 11th Rfts., 23.2.16; Discd., 16.6.19; wounded, 14.7.18
HAASE, Private William: 28th Rfts, N.T.O.S.; A. Mtd. D.H.Q., 20.8.17
HACK, E.R./Sgt. Herbert Cecil: 10th Rfts., N.T.O.S.; Discd., 28.9.19
HADFIELD, Corporal Charles David: 6th Rfts., 25.9.15; Discd., 8.10.19; wounded (acc.), 1.12.18
HAGEN, Private Charles: 18th Rfts., 20.8.16; Discd., 19.9.19; wounded (acc), 15.10.17
HALL, Private Colin Fleming: 11th L.H. Rgt., 12.10.16; Prov. Cps., 25.5.18; Prov. Cps., 26.3.19; Discd., 17.9.19
HALL, T/S.S M. Donald: 11th Rfts., 18.1.16; Discd., 4.10.19
HALL, Private: Joseph Edward: 11th L.. Rgt., 29.8.15; 11th L H. Rgt., 22.2.16
HALL, Private Job Joseph Victor: Original, 8.12.14; 14th F.A. Bde., 27.3.16; wounded, 1.11.15, and 21.11.15
HALL, L/Cpl. Raymond Lester: Original, 8.12.14; Discd., 26.2.19; wounded, 26.3.17
HALL, Private Stanford Sydney: 6th Rfts., 25.9.15; A.A.O.C., 9.9.16
HALLER, Gunner Frederick: 5th Rfts., 25.9.15; 13th F.A. Bde., 27.3.16
HALLETT, Private William Burnard: 7th Rfts., 14.11.15; Discd., 26.4.16
HALLIGAN, Gunner Ernest Harold: 11th Rfts., N.T.O.S.; 14th F.A. Bde., 27.3.16
HAMBLETON, Private Sidney Thomas: 29th Rfts., 15.4.18; Discd., 24.3.21; wounded, 25.9.18
HAMILTON, Driver John Charles Sutton: 14th Rfts., 9.3.16; 14th F.A. Bde., 27.3.16
HAMILTON, Sergeant Kenneth Macleod: Original, 8.12.14; Aust., 21.1.16; 18th Rfts., 20.8.16; Discd., 26.4.19
HAMILTON, Private William Ernest: Original, 8.12.14; Anz. Prov. C., 3.4.16; Anz. Prov. C., 10.6.18; Discd., 23.1.19
HAMMOND, Lieut. Henry Armstrong: Original, 8.12.14; 3rd L.H. Bde., 6.4.18
HAMMOND, Private Robert Moline: 25th Rfts., 2.6.17; Discd , 30.11.18
HANCOCK, Driver George: 16th Rfts., N.T.O.S.; 4th D.A.C., 24.11.16
HANDLEY, Private Robert: 6th Rfts., 14.11.15; Discd., 18.12.19
HANFLING, Private Thomas: 28th Rfts., N.T.O.S.; Discd., 14.7.17
HANKINSON, Private Arthur James: Original, 8.12.14; Discd., 1.5.16; wounded, 28.6.15, and 8.8.15
HANLON, Private David: 18th Rfts., 20.8.16; Discd., 19.9.19
HANLY, Lieut. John Matthew: Original, 30 9.14; killed in action, Anzac, 6.6.15
HANLY, Sergeant Paul: Original, 8.12.14; Imp. Cml. C.. 1.7.16
HANNAN, Driver Timothy George: 11th L.H. Rgt., 2.10.15; 11th L.H. Rgt., 1.7.16
HANNAY, Major Denis Vincent: 8th Rfts., 18.1.16; 47th Btn., 12.3.16
HANSEN, Private Frank Barnard: 21st Rfts.. 4.7.18; Discd., 16.9.19
HANSEN, Driver Nero: 5th Rfts.. 25.9.15; 13th F.A. Bde., 27.3.16
HANSEN, Private Thomas Edward: 11th L.H. Rgt., 29.8.15; 49th Btn., 18.1.17
HANSEN, Driver Oluf Thorval: 15th Rfts., N.T.O.S.; 1st F. Sqd. E., 7.6.16
HANSON, Lieut. Gordon Edward: Original, 8.12.14; Appt. Term., 9.4.19
HARCOURT, Private Maurice Albert: 2nd Rfts., 25.9.15; Discd., 29.3.16
HARCUS, Gunner James Norman: 13th Rfts., 19.2.16; 13th F.A. Bde., 27.3.16; killed in action, France, 4.10.17
HARDING, Private Arthur Henry: G.S. Rfts., 21.1.19; Discd., 19.8.19
HARDING, Private George: 7th Rfts., 25.9.15; Discd., 23.8.16; wounded, 5.11.15
HARDWICK, T/Sgt. Herbert Charles (M.M.): 7th Rfts., 14.11.15; Discd., 4.10.19; wounded. 25.9.18

HISTORY OF THE 5th LIGHT HORSE REGIMENT. 189

HARDY, Private Charles Percival: 14th Rfts., 9.3.16; Discd., 17.7.19
HARDY, Private Haymond James Basil: 11th L.H. Rgt., 29.8.15; 11th L.H. Rgt., 22.2.16
HARKIN, Private William: 24th Rfts., 15.7.17; 2nd M.G. Sqdn., 18.9.18; wounded (acc.), 22.2.18
HARLEY, Corporal John (C. de G., Belgian): 13th Rfts., 19.2.16; 13th F.C. Eng., 21.3.16
HARNAN, Private Frederick Alexander: 18th Rfts., 23.8.16; Discd., 19.9.19
HARPER, Gunner Walter Thomas: 16th Rfts., N.T.O.S.; 4th D.A.C., 24.11.16
HARPHAM, L/Cpl. Leonard Wilson: Original, 8.12.14; Com. Imp. Army, 29.12.15
HARRINGTON, Private Patrick Francis: 27th Rfts., N.T.O.S.; 7th San. Sec., 20.7.17; 7th San. Sec., 28.2.18; Discd., 21.11.18; wounded, 26.6.18
HARRIS, Gunner Eric Brentnall: 12th Rfts., N.T.O.S.; 14th F.A. Bde., 27.3.16
HARRIS, Lt.-Col. Hubert Jennings Imrie: Original, 28.10.14; killed in action, Gallipoli, 31.7.15
HAMLYN-HARRIS, Private Thomas: Original, 8.12.14; Discd., 26.2.19
HARRIS, Private Thomas: 24th Rfts., 17.12.17; Discd., 12.9.19
HARRIS, Gunner William: 11th L.H. Rgt., 2.10.15; 11th L.H. Rgt., 22.2.16; died after discharge.
HARRISS, Private Arthur Frederick: 12th Rfts., N.T.O.S.; 21st A.S.C., 5.3.16
HARRISON, Gunner Augustus Thomas Edward: 6th Rfts., 25.9.15; 14th F.A. Bde., 27.3.16
HARRISON, Corporal Eric (M.M.): Original, 8.12.14; Discd., 12.8.19
HARRISON, Driver William Robert: 27th Rfts., N.T.O.S.; 7th San. Sec., 20.7.17
HARTWELL, Driver Bertram Nigel: 13th Rfts., 19.2.16; 13th F.A. Bde., 27.3.16; died of wounds, France, 24.4.18
HARVEY, Private Edward Benjamin Waldron: Original, 8.12.14; Prov. Cps., 26.4.16
HARVEY, Driver Herbert Victor: 14th Rfts., 9.3.16; 14th F.A. Bde., 27.3.16
HARVEY, Driver Percy: Original, 8.12.14; 13th F.A. Bde., 27.3.16
HASSALL, T/S.Q.M.S. Richard Arthur: 9th Rfts., 23.2.16; 2nd B.M.G. Sqn., 23.7.16; 2nd B.M.G. Sqn., 28.7.17; Discd., 3.10.19
HASSED, Private Martin James: 11th Rfts., 23.2.16; Discd., 8.4.19; wounded, 3.5.18
HASSON, Private William James: 26th Rfts., 4.5.18; Discd., 10.10.19
HATFIELD, T/Cpl. Leslie: 11th L.H. Rgt., 2.10.15; 11th L.H. Rgt., 22.2.16
HATFIELD, Driver Reginald: 25th Rfts., 2.7.17; Discd., 8.4.19
HAUSKNECHT, Private Henry: 9th Rfts., 20.11.15; 12th Co. I.C.C., 15.7.16; Cml. Cps., 26.8.18; Discd., 2.11.19; wounded, 25.12.15
HAWES, Sapper Robert Ernest: 17th Rfts., N.T.O.S.; Anz. D. Sig. S., 22.7.16
HAWTHORN, Private William: 2nd Rfts., 7.7.15; Anz. Pol. Cps., 3.4.16
HAWTHORNE, S.Q.M.S. Lindsay Ivan: 7th Rfts., 23.2.16; Discd., 15.10.19
HAY, Private John Story: Original, 8.12.14; Discd., 24.1.19
HAY, Private Thomas: 3rd Cml. Btn., 28.7.18; Discd., 19.9.19
HAYES, F/Sgt. Charles Daniel: 21st Rfts., 11.6.17; Discd., 18.9.19
HAYES, Private Eugene: 26th Rfts., N.T.O.S.; 2nd M.G. Sqdn., 18.9.18
HEALY, L/Cpl./Dvr. James: 11th L.H. Rgt., 29.8.15; 11th L.H. Rgt., 22.2.16
HEALY, Private Nicholas Dillon: Original, 8.12.14; Discd., 23.7.16

HISTORY OF THE 5th LIGHT HORSE REGIMENT.

HEALY, Private Thomas Eugene: 11th L.H. Rgt., 29.8.15; 4th L.H. Rgt., 3.3.17
HEANEY, Private Harry Raymond: Original, 8.12.14; Discd., 12.2.17; wounded, 9.8.16
HEAP, Driver Albert John: Original, 8.12.14; 13th F.A. Bde., 27.3.16
HEASLOP, Private Alexander: 18th Rfts., N.T.O.S.; Imp. Cml. Cps., 7.9.16; died (cerebro-spinal meningitis,) Rafa, Palestine, 1.7.17
HEATH, Driver James Lindsay: 14th Rfts., 9.3.16; 14th F.A. Bde., 27.3.16
HEERS, Private Edward Roland: Original, 8.12.14; Aust., 14.11.15; 16th Rfts., 11.12.16; Discd., 4.10.19
HEGARTY, Corporal John Joseph: 11th Rfts., 23.2.16; Discd., 4.10.19
HEIDKE, Lieut. Gustave August: Original, 8.12.14; Appt. Term., 26.2.19; wounded, 26.3.17
HEILBRONN, Sapper Henry Lewis: 11th L.H. Rgt., 2.10.15; 11th L.H. Rgt., 22.2.16; wounded, 8.10.15
HEMSLEY, Private Horace: 15th Rfts., 26.7.16; Discd., 20.12.18; wounded, 28.7.18
HENDERSON, Driver James: 10th Rfts., 31.12.15; 14th F.A. Bde., 27.3.16
HENDERSON, L./Cpl. Kenneth Selby: Original, 8.12.14; Comm. Imp. Army, 25.11.15
HENDERSON, S/Smth. William Shaw Staines: Original, 8.12.14; 2nd L.H.F. Amb., 4.5.15
HENDY, Gunner James Melbourne: 16th Rfts., N.T.O.S.; 3rd D.A.C., 16.9.17
HENNEGAN, Far./Sgt. Robert: Original, 8.12.14; Discd., 27.4.19
HENNEGAN, Private Samuel: Original, 8.12.14; 2nd M.G. Sqdn., 10.7.17
HENNESSEY, T/Cpl. Arthur Francis: 11th Rfts., 23.2.16; died of wounds (P.O.W.), 3.10.18, Palestine
HENNESSEY, Private Leopold Victor: 14th Rfts., 9.3.16; Discd., 29.3.19
HENNINGSEN, Driver Hans Peter: 2nd Rfts., 4.10.15; 2nd L.H.F. Amb., 25.1.16
HENRICKSON, Private Henry Norman: G.S. Rfts., 17.10.18; Discd., 20.8.19
HENRY, Private Clement Samuel: 2nd Rfts., 7.7.15; Anz. Pol. Cps., 26.4.16; Anz. Pol. Cps., 15.7.17; Discd., 4.10.19
HENSLEY, Driver Sydney: 6th Rfts., 25.9.15; Discd., 4.10.19
HERBERT, Wheeler Arthur: 6th Rfts., 25.9.15; Aust., 3.1.16; 16th Rfts., N.T.O.S.; 14th F.A. Bde., 8.11.16
HERBERT, Private James Courtney: 1st Rfts., 16.5.16; Discd., 26.2.19; wounded, 9.8.16
HERBERT, Sapper Joseph Louis: 11th Rfts., 3.2.16; Discd., 7.1.19
HERBERT, Private William Thomas: Original, 8.12.14; Discd., 13.9.16; wounded, 28.6.15
HERRING, Private John: Original, 8.12.14; Discd., 2.2.16
HERRON, Private George Knight: 15th Rfts., N.T.O.S.; 15th Btn., 16.10.16
HERTH, Sergeant Henry Roy: 11th L.H. Rgt., 29.8.15; 11th L.H. Rgt., 10.3.16; wounded, 11.11.15
HESSION, Driver Harold: 8th Rfts., 14.11.15; 13th F.A. Bde., 27.3.16
HETHERINGTON, Private Frank Adair: 29th Rfts., 23.5.18; Discd., 24.5.19
HETHORN, Driver William Harding: Original, 8.12.14; 14th F.A. Bde., 27.3.16; died of wounds, France, 31.8.18
HEUGH, Private Samuel George Bruce: Original, 8.12.14; 1st M.G. Sqdn., 23.10.16; 1st M.G. Sqdn., 3.11.16; Discd., 25.2.19; wounded, 27.6.15, 5.8.16, and 8.11.17
HEWETSON, T/Cpl. Thomas Arthur: Original, 8.12.14; Discd., 24.2.19; wounded, 27.6.15

HISTORY OF THE 5th LIGHT HORSE REGIMENT. 191

HEWITT, Gunner Hubert Deane: 12th Rfts., N.T.O.S.; 14th F.A. Bde., 27.3.16
HEYDON, Private Wattie: 8th Rfts., 23.2.16; Discd., 2.10.19
HICKS, Captain George: Original, 8.12.14; Appt. Term., 26.2.19; wounded, 4.8.16
HICKS, Private William James: 11th L.H. Rgt., 29.8.15; 11th L.H. Rgt., 22.2.16
HIGGINS, Private Joseph: 1st Rfts., 16.5.15; 3/L.H.B.H.Q., 29.10.17
HIGGINS, Private Thomas John: Original, 8.12.14; killed in action, Gallipoli, 28.6.15
HILL, Gunner Frederick Thomas: 4th Rfts., 25.5.15; 13th F.A. Bde., 27.3.16
HILL, Gunner George: 16th Rfts., N.T.O.S.; 4th D.A.C., 9.8.16
HILL, Private Sydney Granfield: 11th L.H. Rgt., 29.8.15; 11th L.H. Rgt., 22.2.16
HINGST, Private Frank Albert: 23rd Rfts., 27.11.17; Discd., 4.9.19
HINTON, Sergeant Frederick William: 3rd Rfts., 29.7.15; 2nd L.H.B. M.G.S., 24.7.16
HIRON, Lieut. Frank (stated to be Francis Thomas Hiron): 11th L.H. Rgt., 29.8.15; 11th L.H. Rgt., 22.2.16
HITCHCOCK, Private John: 17th Rfts., N.T.O.S.; 2nd L.H.B.M.G.S., 12.9.16
HJELM, Driver Henry Edward: 23rd Rfts., N.T.O.S.; 8th San. Sec., 30.7.17
HOARE, Driver William James: 14th Rfts., 9.3.16; 14th F.A. Bde., 27.3.16
HOBBS, Private Kenneth Charles Stuart: 8th Rfts., 10.1.16; 2nd L.H.B. M.G.S., 6.12.16
HOBBS, Private Reginald Thomas: 8th Rfts., N.T.O.S.; died (cerebro-spinal meningitis), Alexandria, 29.11.15
HOCKINGS, Lieut. Eric Raymond: 3rd Rfts., 25.9.15; 52nd Btn., 22.1.17
HODGE, Private Cyril Kingsley: 6th G.S. Rfts., 15.2.19; Discd., 19.8.19
HODGES, Driver George Douglas: 3rd Cml. Bn., 14.10.18; Discd., 16.6.19
HODGES, Private Percy Charles: 22nd Rfts., N.T.O.S.; Sig. Sqn. Mtd. Div., 13.5.17
HOERLEIN, Driver Victor Henry William: 14th Rfts., 9.3.16; 14th F.A. Bde., 27.3.16
HOFFMAN, Captain George Henry: 11th L.H. Rgt., 29.8.15; 11th L.H. Rgt., 22.2.16; wounded, 11.11.15, and 20.12.15
HOGAN, Private Harold Michael: 14th Rfts., 9.3.16; 4th Cml. Rgt., 2.11.16; killed in action, Gaza, Palestine, 19.4.17
HOGDEN, Private Albert Dunstan: Original, 8.12.14; Discd., 30.8.16; wounded, 31.7.15
HOGG, Corporal Robert: 12th Rfts., 7.1.16; Discd., 27.9.19
HOJEL, Gunner Augustus James: 12th Rfts., N.T.O.S.; 13th F.A. Bde., 27.3.16
HOLCROFT, Bombdr. James William (Mentioned in Despatches): 14th Rfts., 9.3.16; 14th F.A. Bde., 27.3.16
HOLDGATE, Private Henry Albert: 20th Rfts., N.T.O.S.; 2nd M.G. Sqdn., 6.10.16; killed in action, Palestine, 10.11.17
HOLLIS, Sapper Russell George: 21st Rfts., N.T.O.S.; 2nd Sig. Sqn., 28.6.19
HOLMES, Private William Francis Henry: 11th L.H. Rgt., 2.10.15; 11th L.H. Rgt., 22.2.16
HOLTON, Private Alfred James (stated to be Alfred Holton Symons): 19th Rfts., N.T.O.S.; Cml. Cps., 7.9.16
HOLYER, Private Sidney: 15th Rfts., N.T.O.S.; 4th Cml. Rgt., 2.11.16
HOMER, Private Arthur Charles: Original, 8.12.14; killed in action, Gallipoli, 28.6.15

HOOD, Private Edward Leslie: 3rd Rfts., 29.7.15; Discd., 25.10.16
HOOD, Private William Frederick: 3rd Rfts., 29.7.15; Com. Imp. Army, 7.11.15; wounded, 2.9.15; served as 2/Lieut. R.F.A., Imperial Army
HOOPER, Private Gordon Trescott: 22nd Rfts., 11.4.17; 2nd M.G. Sqdn., 18.9.18
HOPKINS, T/Cpl. Charles Raymond: 20th Rfts., 12.10.16; Discd., 19.9.19
HOPPER, Sergeant David Lewin: 11th Rfts., 16.1.16; 14th F.A. Bde., 27.3.16
HOPPER, Private John Joseph: 11th Rfts., 23.2.16; 4/L.H.F. Amb., 3.5.17; 4/L.H.F. Amb., 10.7.17; Discd., 4.10.19
HOPPER, Lieut. Joseph Stewart: 6th Rfts., 25.9.15; 14th F.A. Bde., 27.3.16; killed in action, France, 6.8.17
HORE, Private Benjamin: 25th Rfts., 9.7.17; Discd., 24.5.19
HORSLEY, Lieut. Ralph Drummond: 5th Rfts., 25.9.15; 2nd F.S. Eng., 24.10.17
HORSWOOD, Private Herbert Edward: 15th Rfts., 20.8.16; Discd., 27.9.19
HORSWOOD, Private Thomas Samuel: 15th Rfts., 20.8.16; Discd., 27.9.19
HORT, Private Robert Alfred: 10th Rfts., 23.2.16; Discd., 6.9.19; wounded, 9.8.16
HOSIE, Private Henry: Original, 8.12.14; Anz. Pol. Cps., 26.4.18; Anz. Prov. C., 2.4.17; Discd., 26.1.18; wounded, 28.6.15
HOUNSLOW, Private Herbert: 1st Rfts., 16.5.15; Discd., 24.1.19; wounded, 27.7.15
HOWARD, Private Edgar Joseph: Original, 8.12.14; Discd, 24.1.19; wounded, 27.6.15
HOWLING, Private William John: 12th L.H. Rgt., 14.7.16; Discd., 16.5.19
HOWARTH, Private Alan: 25th Rfts., 9.7.17; wounded, 8.11.17; killed in action, Palestine, 25.5.18
HOY, Driver Hunter Maitland: G.S. Rfts., 17.10.18; Discd., 14.9.19
HUBBARD, Private James Alfred: 11th Rfts., 22.10.15; 2nd Rmt. Unit, 16.2.16
HUGGINS, Private Charles Frank: 10th Rfts., 23.2.16; wounded, 2.5.18; died of wounds, Palestine, 4.5.18
HUGHES, L/Cpl. Albert Edward: 22nd Rfts., 15.7.17; Discd., 12.9.19
HUGHES, Sergeant Archibald George: 2nd Rfts., 16.5.15; Discd., 23.6.19
HUGHES, Private Alfred Lloyd: 7th Rfts., 30.6.16; Discd., 9.1.20
HUGHES, Private Charles Montease: 15th Rfts., N.T.O.S.; 1st Fld. Sqdn., 5.7.16; Aust., 2.9.16
HUGHES, Private Eric: 16th Rfts., N.T.O.S.; 4th D.A.C., 9.8.16
HUGHES, Private Frank Cameron: G.S. Rfts., 9.10.18; Discd., 20.8.19
HUGHES, C.Q.M.S. George (Mentioned in Despatches): Original, 8.12.14; 4th Camel Rgt., 2.11.16
HUGHES, Private James: 11th Rfts., 18.1.16; wounded, 9.8.16; died of wounds, Kantara, Egypt, 10.8.16
HUGHES, L/Cpl. Robert Francis: 19th Rfts., N.T.O.S.; Camel Cps., 18.9.16
HUGHES, Private William: 20th Rfts., N.T.O.S.; 2/L.H.B.M.G. Sqdn., 6.10.16
HUGHES, Gunner William David: 12th Rfts., N.T.O.S.; 13th F.A.B, 27.3.16
HUGHES, Sapper William Walter: 15th Rfts., N.T.O.S.; 1st Fld. Sqdn., 25.6.16
HUISH, Private Harold Arthur F.: 12th Rfts., 23.2.16; Discd., 27.9.19

HISTORY OF THE 5th LIGHT HORSE REGIMENT. 193

HUISH, Corporal Raymond Douglas: 12th Rfts., 23.2.16; 2/Sig. Trp., 26.2.17; wounded, 5.8.16
HULBERT, Driver William Edward: 14th Rfts., 9.3.16; 14th F.A.B., 27.3.16
HUMPHREY, Private Percy: 22nd Rfts., N.T.O.S.; H.Q.A. Mtd. Div., 20.7.17; H.Q.A. Mtd. Div., 13.4.19; Discd., 15.11.19
HUMPHRIES, Private Cecil Conick: 8th Rfts., 10.1.16; Discd., 4.10.19
HUNT, Private Reginald Charles: 11th Rfts., N.T.O.S.; 4/Camel Rgt., 9.1.17
HUNT, Private Stephen William: 4th Rfts., 25.5.15; died (enteric fever), Malta, 18.7.15
HURSE, Private George: 9th Rfts., N.T.O.S.; Discd., 7.6.16
HUTTON, Sergeant Falconer Holt: 11th L.H.R., 29.8.15; 11th L.H.R., 22.2.16; wounded, 19.9.15
HYDE, Sergeant Harold Walter: Original, 8.12.14; A.I.F. Hqrs., 28.10.15
HYDE, Private Norman Cropley: 3rd Rfts., 29.7.15; killed in action, Anzac, 9.11.15
HYNES, Bombdr. John: 16th Rfts., N.T.O.S.; 1st D.A.C., 24.5.17
HYNES, Driver John Edward: 12th Rfts., N.T.O.S.; 13th F.A.B., 27.3.16
HYNES, Driver Martin Francis: 13th Rfts., 19.2.16; 13th F.A.B, 27.3.16
HYSSETT, Private John Cecil: 2nd Rfts., 7.7.15; Discd., 24.5.16
IDRIESS, Private Ion Llewellyn: Original, 8.12.14; Discd., 10.5.18; wounded, 5.9.15, and 2.12.17
IGNATIUS, Sergeant James: 9th Rfts., N.T.O.S.; 14th F.A.B., 27.3.16
INSCH, S.S.M. Edward Bland: Original, 8.12.14; 2/M.G. Sqdn., 21.4.18; wounded, 4.12.15
IRBY, Private Arthur Algernon: 15th Rfts., N.T.O.S.; 18/I.C.C., 7.2.17
IRVINE, Private William: 27th Rfts., 17.12.17; Discd., 3.10.19
IRVINE, Gunner Wallace Robert: Original, 8.12.14; 4th F.A.B., 25.1.16; wounded, 28.6.15
IRVING, Captain Henry King: Original, 14.11.14; 14th F.A.B., 27.3.16
IRVING, T/Cpl. William Howe: 19th Rfts., N.T.O.S.; Camel Cps., 7.9.16; killed in action, Palestine, 6.11.17
IRWIN, Sdlr./Sgt. Richard: 11th L.H.R., 29.8.15; 11th L.H.R., 22.2.16; wounded, 11.11.15
IVORY, Gunner Alexander Donnell: 13th Rfts., 19.2.16; 13th F.A.B., 27.3.16
IVORY, Corporal Wilham Michael Francis: 11th L.H.R., 2.10.15; 1st Fld. Sqdn., 14.6.16
JACKSON, Sergeant Ernest: Original, 8.12.14; Discd., 26.2.19
JACKSON, T/Cpl. Johnny: 2nd L.H. Rgt., 24.11.16; Discd., 2.12.19; wounded, 2.12.17
JACKSON, Private Fred: 16th Rfts., N.T.O.S.; 4th Cml. Rgt., 2.11.16
JACKSON, Lieut. Robert George (M.C.): Original, 8.12.14; 2nd F.A. Bde., 6.8.15
JACKSON, Driver William: 7th Rfts., 24.1.16; 14th F.A. Bde., 27.3.16
JACKSON, Private William James: 18th Rfts., 20.8.16; Discd., 19.9.19
JAMES, Gunner Albert John (M.M.): 12th Rfts., 7.1.16; 13th F.A. Bde., 27.3.16
JAMES, Major Edward Stewart (O.B.E., Mentioned in Despatches twice): Original, 17.10.14; 4th Mob. Vet. S., 22.3.16
JAMES, Driver John Herbert: 2nd L.H.F. Amb., 9.9.15; Discd., 18.8.16
JAMES, Private John William Joseph: 15th Rfts., N.T.O.S.; Cml. Cps., 15.7.16
JAMES, Sergeant Richard (M.M.): Original, 8.12.14; Discd., 20.6.18; wounded, 5.11.17, and 19.11.17
JAMES, Driver Richard, 1st Rfts., 16.5.15; 2nd L.H. Rgt., 11.6.16; 2nd L.H. Rgt., 27.7.17; Discd., 26.2.19
JAMES, T/S.S.M. Richard Seddon: 8th Rfts., 10.1.16; Discd., 4.10.19

JAMIESON, Private Alexander: Original, 8.12.14; Discd., 10.5.16
JAMIESON, Corporal Arthur William: 12th Rfts., 7.1.16; 2nd L.H. Rgt., 27.8.16
JARDINE, Private Frank Alexander Lascelles: Original, 8.12.14; Discd., 17.5.16; wounded, 28.5.15
JARMAIN, Private Claude Henry: Original, 8.12.14; Discd., 25.4.19
JARMAN, Private Herbert: 11th L.H. Rgt., 29.8.15; 11th L.H. Rgt., 22.2.16
JARRETT, Private Roy: 15th Rfts., N.T.O.S.; 4th Cml. Rgt., 2.11.16
JEFFERIS, Far./Sgt. Arthur: Original, 8.12.14; 2nd M.G. Sqdn., 1.8.16
JEFFERY, Private William Henry: 25th Rfts., 21.9.17; Discd., 31.5.19
JENKINS, Private Andrew James: 4th Rfts., 22.5.15; Discd., 8.5.19; wounded, 10.8.15
JENKINS, Gunner Charles: 13th Rfts., 19.2.16; 14th F.A. Bde., 27.3.16
JENKINS, E.R./2/Cpl. Rupert Lewis: 21st Rfts., N.T.O.S.; Anz. Prov. Cps., 23.1.17
JENNS, Sapper Stanley Cresswell: Original, 8.12.14; 3rd L.H.B.H.Q., 29.10.17
JENSEN, Gunner Frederick Charles J.: 13th Rfts., 19.2.16; 13th F.A. Bde., 27.3.16; killed in action, France, 8.10.18
JENSEN, Private Peter: 11th Rfts., 18.1.16; Discd., 9.10.18; wounded, 8.11.17
JENSEN, Lieut. Rennie Hendri: Original, 8.12.14; 1st Btn., 4.12.16
JIBSON, Private Fred.: 3rd Cml. Bn., 28.7.18; Discd., 24.9.19
JOHNS, Private Herbert Stanley: Original, 8.12.14; Cml. Cps., 15.7.16
JOHNSTON, Private Albert: 7th Rfts., 10.1.16; Discd., 19.9.17; wounded, 26.3.17
JOHNSTON, Gunner Alfred Joseph: 13th Rfts., 19.2.16; 13th F.A. Bde., 27.3.16; killed in action, France, 12.12.17
JOHNSON, Private Charles Frederick: 11th L.H. Rgt., 29.8.15; 11th L.H. Rgt., 22.2.16
JOHNSON, Private Charles Hinson: 28th Rfts., 23.12.17; Discd., 4.9.19
JOHNSON, T/Sgt. Charles Tudor: Original, 8.12.14; 2/L.H.B.M.G. Sqdn., 23.8.16
JOHNSON, Driver Eric: 11th Rfts., 23.2.16; 2/L.H.B.M.G. Sqdn., 1.8.16
JOHNSON, Sergeant Elmo Morris: 7th Rfts., 14.11.15; Discd., 4.10.19
JOHNSON, L/Cpl. Harold Ambrose (M.M.): 4th Rfts., 25.5.15; Discd., 2.11.18; wounded, 19.4.18
JOHNSON, Sergeant Richard Cecil: Original, 8.12.14; Discd., 19.9.20; wounded, 25.9.18
JOHNSTON, Sergeant Harold Francis: 11th L.H.R., 29.8.15; 11th L.H.R., 22.2.16; wounded, 30.8.15
JOHNSTON, Major Herbert Hall (Mentioned in Despatches): Original, 28.9.14; Appt. Term., 18.10.16; wounded, 9.8.16
JOHNSTONE, E.R./Cpl. John Francis: 25th Rfts., N.T.O.S.; Discd., 4.11.20
JOHNSTONE, Lieut. Robert Leonard Willox: Original, 8.12.14; Appt. Term., 24.5.16; wounded, 9.11.15
JOHNSTONE, Corporal William George: Original, 8.12.14; 2/L.H.B. M.G. Sqdn., 24.7.16
JOMARTZ, Private Ernest: 2/Vet. Sec., 16.5.15; Aust., 21.1.16; attached strength, 4th L.H.R., 10.6.16
JONES, Private Benjamin Thomas: 14th Rfts., 9.3.16; 4/Camel Rgt., 2.11.16
JONES, Private Clarence George H.: 5th Rfts., 28.8.15; Discd., 27.9.16
JONES, Private Cyril Jack: 15th Rfts., N.T.O.S.; 4/Camel Rgt., 2.11.16
JONES, Driver Charles William: 14th Rfts., 9.3.16; 13th F.A.B., 27.3.16
JONES, Private Daniel: 10th Rfts., 8.1.16; Discd., 4.10.19; wounded, 14.7.18

HISTORY OF THE 5th LIGHT HORSE REGIMENT. 195

JONES, Private Daniel Thomas: 13th Rfts., 19.2.16; 13th F.A.B., 27.3.16
JONES, Private Frederick Edward: 12th Rfts., 7.1.16; 2/L.H. Fld. Amb., 25.1.16
JONES, Private George Wellesley: Original, 8.12.14; Discd., 13.8.15
JONES, Sapper Henry: 5th Rfts., 25.9.15; 14th F.A.B., 27.3.16
JONES, Private Howen: 28th Rfts., N.T.O.S.; 2/M.G. Sqdn., 6.12.17
JONES, Lieut. John George: Original, 21.12.14; Appt. Term., 26.2.19
JONES, Bombdr. Lamington Meyrick: 16th Rfts., N.T.O.S.; 4th D A.C., 19.11.16
JONES, Private Richard: Original, 8.12.14; 14th F.A.B., 27.3.16
JONES, T/S.S.M. Samuel Reginald: 26th Bn., 23.10.15; Discd., 4.10.19
JONES, Driver Thomas (M.M.): Original, 8.12.14; Discd., 22.2.19
JONES, Driver Thomas Rodger: 13th Rfts., 19.2.16; 13th F.A.B., 27.3.16
JONES, Private Thomas William: 24th Rfts., N.T.O.S.; Aust. Airline Sec., 18.9.17; 2/Sig. Sqdn., 26.3.19; Discd., 4.9.19
JONES, Private William Alan: 11th L.H.R., 29.8.15; Camel Cps., 9.7.16
JORGENSEN, Far./Cpl. Peter Martin: 14th Rfts., 9.3.16; 14th F.A.B., 27.3.16
JOSE, Driver Thomas: Original, 8.12.14; Discd., 22.2.19
JOYCE, Corporal Frederick James: 4th Rfts., 22.5.15; 2/M.G. Sqdn., 10.1.18; wounded, 8.8.17
JUDD, Private Gerald Christopher: Original, 24.12.14; Discd., 10.11.15 (granted Commission, Imperial Army)
KADEL, Private John Allan: Original, 8.12.14; Discd., 24.12.15
KANE, Private John: 25th Rfts., 2.7.17; Discd., 12.9.19
KANE, Driver John Joseph: Original, 8.12.14; Discd., 26.2.19
KAYE, L/Cpl. Charles Roy: 24th Rfts., 15.7.17; Discd., 12.9.19
KEAL, Driver Ernest Alfred: 12th Rfts., 7.1.16; 14th F.A. Bde., 27.3.16
KEANE, Sergeant John Donnelly: Original, 8.12.14; Discd., 24.2.19; wounded, 5.11.15
KEARSLEY, Driver William: 6th Rfts., 2.8.15; Discd., 30.10.19
KEATING, Gunner Richard Wallace: 16th Rfts., N.T.O.S.; 4th D.A.C., 1.11.16
KEBBLEWHITE, Driver Edward Allan: 5th Rfts., 25.9.15; 14th F.A. Bde., 27.3.16
KEEGAN, Private Matthew: 28th Rfts., 14.10.18; Discd., 4.9.19
KEELAN, Private William: 3rd Rfts., 29.7.15; killed (motor accident), England, 27.11.15
KEENE, Prviate Gilbert Sydney: 15th Rfts., 20.8.16; Discd., 27.7.19
KEHOE, L/Cpl. Edward Joseph: 19th Rfts., N.T.O.S.; Cml. Cps., 7.9.16
KELLAND, Driver Alfred Henry: 13th Rfts., 19.2.16; 14th F.A. Bde., 27.3.16
KELLAND, Driver Claude Demarshay: 13th Rfts., 19.2.16; 14th F.A. Bde., 27.3.16
KELLAND, Driver Francis James: 13th Rfts., 19.2.16; 14th F.A. Bde., 27.3.16
KELLEHER, T/Sgt. John: 11th Rfts., 23.2.16; wounded, 8.11.17; died of wounds, Palestine, 9.11.17
KELLY, Private Alexander Matthew: 11th Rfts., 23.2.16; Discd., 27.9.19
KELLY, L/Cpl. David: Original, 8.12.14; 31st Btn., 15.10.16
KELLY, Gunner Ernest Mathew: 13th Rfts., 19.2.16; 14th F.A. Bde., 27.3.16
KELLY, Private James Edward: Original, 8.12.14; Discd., 19.7.16
KELLY, Corporal James Joseph (M.M.): 10th Rfts., 6.1.16; Discd., 4.8.19
KELLY, Driver Patrick Edward: 2nd Rfts, 16.5.15; A. Mtd. D. Trn., 20.8.17
KELLY, T/S.S.M. Patrick Joseph (D.C.M.): 2nd Rfts., 7.7.15; Discd.. 9.6.19

KELLY, Private Thomas: 29th Rfts., N.T.O.S.; 2nd M.G. Sqdn., 24.5.18
KELLY, Private William John: 12th Rfts., 7.1.16; Discd., 27.9.19
KEMP, Private Edward William George: 5th Rfts., 25.9.15; Anz. Pol. Cps., 26.4.16; Anz. Prov. Cps., 3.12.18; Discd., 17.10.19
KEMP, T/Cpl. Reginald Norman: 5th Rfts., 25.9.15; Anz. Pol. Cps., 3.4.16
KEMP, Private William Henry: Original, 8.12.14; wounded, 31.5.15; killed in action, Gallipoli, 28.6.15
KENNEDY, Private Gordon Laurie: 12th L.H.F. Amb., 1.6.16; 2nd L.H.F. Amb., 2.12.16; 4th Cml. Rgt., 21.1.17; 2nd L.H F. Amb., 9.2.17
KENNEDY, S,'Smith John Alfred: Original, 8.12.14; 7th Mob. Vet. S., 3.8.18
KENNEDY, Captain Malcolm Stuart: Original, 3.11.14; 52nd Btn., 20.10.16; wounded, 7.8.15; died of wounds, France, 2.1.18
KENNEDY, Sergeant William: 12th Rfts., 7.1.16; Discd., 27.9.19
KENNETT, Private Lewis Alfred: 15th Rfts., N.T.O.S.; 4th Cml. Rgt., 2.11.16
KENNIFF, Private Gwydir: 24th Rfts., N.T.O.S.; Discd., 1.8.17
KERR, Driver David John: 2nd Rfts., 29.7.15; Discd., 4.10.19
KERR, Driver James Henry: 4th Rfts., 22.5.15; Discd., 29.9.19
KERR, Sergeant Leo Arthur: 11th L.H. Rgt., 29.8.15; 11th L.H. Rgt., 22.2.16
KERR, Private Peter William: 19th Rfts., 11.12.16; Discd., 1.6.19
KERSHAW, Private Reginald: 12th Rfts., 7.1.16; Discd., 12.7.16
KESSLER, L/Cpl./Dvr. Christopher John: Original, 8.12.14; 2/L..H.B. M.G.S., 24.7.16
KEYLAR, T/F.Q.M.S. Harry: Original, 8.12.14; Discd., 26.2.19
KEYS, Private Edward: 6th Rfts., 25.9.15; Discd., 4.10.19
KILGOUR, L/Cpl. Arnold: Original, 8.12.14; Discd., 22.4.19; wounded, 3.9.15
KILLEN, Private Ernest: 3rd Rfts., N.T.O.S.; Discd., 23.7.15
KILPATRICK, Driver James Eric: 16th Rfts., N.T.O.S.; 4th D.A.C., 19.11.16
KINEAVY, Private Michael Joseph: 24th Rfts., N.T.O.S.; Discd., 8.10.19
KING, Private Amos Glen: Original, 8.12.14; Anz. L H. Rgt., 5.7.17; wounded, 28.5.15
KING, W.O. (2) Frederick Neebone: Original, 8.12.14; Discd., 29.10.19; wounded, 4.8.16
KING, Driver James: 11th L.H. Rgt., 29.8.15; 11th L.H.R., 4.3.16
KING, Driver Joseph Francis: Original, 8.12.14; 2nd L.H.B.M.G.S., 24.7.16; wounded, 27.6.15
KING, Private John Osborne: 1st Rfts., N.T.O.S.; Discd., 13.8.15
KING, Private Percy Gains: 4th Rfts., 22.5.15; Discd., 16.8.16
KING, Private Percival James: 2nd Rfts., 29.7.15; Discd., 12.4.16
KING, Sergeant Rooper (M M.): 11th L.H. Rgt., 2.10.15; 11th L.H. Rgt., 22.2.16
KING, Private Thomas Alfred: Original, 8.12.14; wounded, 5.9.15; died of wounds at sea, 8.9.15
KING, Corporal William Edward: 21st Rfts., 14.5.17; A. Mtd. Div. Trn., 6.9.17
KINGSBURY, Lieut. Ernest Lionel (M.C.): Original, 8.12.14; 14th F.A. Bde., 27.3.16
KINGSTON, Private Frederick Charles: 3rd Rfts., 29.7.15; Discd., 6.9.16; wounded, 23.8.15
KINRED, Private Claude Douglas: 2nd Rfts., 7.7.15; Discd., 30.8.16
KIRBY, Private Alexander: 1st Rfts., 16.5.16; Discd., 12.4.19; wounded, 5.7.15
KIRK, T/Cpl. John: 26th Rfts., N.T.O.S.; 4th L.H.B. Sply S., 30.7.17

HISTORY OF THE 5th LIGHT HORSE REGIMENT. 197

KIRKLAND, Sergeant Hugh Kenneth: Original, 8.12.14; Discd., 23.1.19; wounded, 27.6.15
KIRKLAND, Corporal William Henry Harold: 14th Rfts., 9.3.16; 4th Cml. Rgt., 2.11.16
KIRKMAN, Private Henry: 15th Rfts., N.T.O.S.; 4th Cml. Rgt., 2.11.16
KIRKMAN, Private James: 15th Rfts., N.T.O.S.; 4th Cml. Rgt., 2.11.16
KIRKUP, Private Fredrick John: 22nd Rfts., 9.7.18; Discd., 16.6.19
KITCHING, Driver Harry: 26th Rfts., 9.10.18; Discd., 21.9.19
KLAUKE, Private Herman: 20th Rfts., 12.10.16; Discd., 21.1.20
KLAUKE, Private Rudolph: 12th Rfts., 23.2.16; Discd., 27.5.19
KLUVER, Driver Henry: 3rd Rfts., 29.7.15; Discd., 26.7.16
KNICKEL, Gunner Ernest August: 16th Rfts., N.T.O.S.; died (Bright's disease), England, 24.7.17
KNIGHT, Private Alfred James: 11th Rfts., 5.1.16; H.Q. 13/L.H.R., 2.6.16
KNIGHT, Corporal Cecil Charles: 16th Rfts., N.T.O.S.; 2nd F.A.B., 12.12.17
KNIGHT, Private George Henry: 2nd Rfts., N.T.O.S.; Discd., 10.5.15
KNIGHT, Corporal John Hope Hamilton: Original, 8.12.14; 4/Camel Rgt., 2.11.16
KNIGHT, Gunner John Percival: 4th Rfts., 22.5.15; 14th F.A.B., 27.3.16
KNIGHT, T/Cpl. Phillip: Original, 8.12.14; H.Q.A. Mtd. Div., 24.3.16; wounded, 27.6.15
KNIGHT, Private Sydney Victor Spencer: 27th Rfts., N.T.O.S; 36/Coy. A.A.S.C., 13.8.17
KNIGHT, Private William Francis: 12th Rfts., 7.1.16; Discd., 2.10.19
KNOBEL, T/S/Smth. Charles: 26th Rfts., N.T.O.S.; 38th Coy. A.S.C., 28.9.17; 38th Coy. A.S.C., 28.7.18; Discd., 3.4.19
KNOWLES, Private Walter Henry Joseph: 28th Rfts., N.T.O.S.; 2nd L.H.R., 4.8.17; 2nd L.H.R., 17.8.18; Discd., 4.9.19
KNOX, Private John: 14th Rfts., 9.3.16; 4/Camel Rgt., 2.11.16
KOCH, Major William Francis J. (Mentioned in Despatches): 11th L.H.R., 29.8.15; 11th L.H.R., 22.2.16; wounded, 3.9.15
KOHLER, Private Louis: 11th Rfts., 23.2.16; Discd., 12.7.19
KRAUSE, L/Cpl. Paul: 11th L.H.R., 2.10.15; 11th L.H.R., 1.3.16
KREIG, Lieut. Louis Paul: 11th L.H.R., 29.8.15; 11th L.H.R., 22.2.16; killed in action, Palestine, 19.8.18
KRUGER, Private Charles Edward: 11th L.H.R., 29.8.15; Discd., 12.4.16
KUNKEL, T/Dvr. Matthew David John: 28th Rfts., N.T.O.S.; 32/Coy. A.S.C., 7.8.17
LACE, Private William Henry: 17th Rfts., N.T.O.S.; 2/L.H.B.M.G. Sqdn., 12.9.16
LAING, Private Andrew David: 26th Rfts., 23.12.17; Discd., 4.9.19
LAING, L/Cpl. Daniel James: 2nd Rfts., 7.7.15; 1st Fld. Sqdn., 29.6.16
LAKE, Private John: Original, 8.12.14; 7/M.G. Coy., 17.8.16
LAKE, Private Walter Miles: 11th Rfts., 23.2.16; Discd., 4.10.19
LAMBERT, Private Matthew: 7th Rfts., 19.11.15; Discd., 20.10.18
LAMBERT, Gunner Rowley (M.M.): 16th Rfts., N.T.O.S.; 12th F.A.B., 29.3.17
LANCASTER, Corporal Ernest Edward: 11th Rfts., 18.1.16; 14th F.A.B., 27.3.16; killed in action, France, 17.10.17
LAND, Lieut. John Norman: 9th Rfts., 18.1.16; Appt. Term., 26.2.20
LAND, Lieut. Nicholas Lisle (M.M.): 13th Rfts., 19.2.16; 14th F.A.B., 27.3.16
LANDON, Private Hubert: 12th Rfts., 7.1.16; Discd., 9.2.17
LANE, Private Edward Joseph Frank: Original, 8.12.14; Demob., UK, 4.2.18; wounded, 28.6.15
LANE, Private John: 7th Rfts., 10.1.16; Discd., 20.9.16
LANGE, T/Cpl. Henry: 3rd Rfts., 29.7.15; A.M.D.H.Q., 20.7.17; A.M.D.H.Q., 28.2.18; Discd., 4.10.19; wounded, 8.8.15, 9.11.15

LANGSTON, Private Frederick George: 11th L.H.R., 29.8.15; 11th L.H.R., 22.2.16
LARCOMBE, Private Benjamin: 10th Rfts., Camel Cps., N.T.O.S., 5.8.16
LARSEN, Private Soren Christian: 11th L.H.R., 29.8.15; 11th L.H.R., 22.2.16; wounded, 25.10.15
LARTER, Private Thomas: 28th Rfts., N.T.O.S.; A.S.C., 21.8.17
LASCELLES, Private Evelyn Herbert: Original, 8.12.14; Demob., U.K., 25.12.15 (granted Commission, Imperial Army).
LAURANCE, Lieut. Ethelbert Glenn: Original, 8.12.14; Appt. Term., 16.1.20; wounded, 30.3.18
LAVENDER, T/S/Smth. Andrew: Original, 8.12.14; 2/M.G. Sqdn., 24.7.16
LAVER, Lieut. Albert (M.C.): Original, 8.12.14; 2nd Btn., 4.3.16; wounded, 7.11.15
LAVER, Private Alexander James: 22nd Rfts., 15.7.17; Discd., 13.10.19
LAVERTY, Driver Albert Charles: 12th Rfts., 7.1.16; 14th F.A.B., 27.3.16
LAW, Private Frederick Charles: Original, 8.12.14; killed in action, Anzac, 26.11.15
LAW, B.Q.M.S. Henry Pohlman: 12th Rfts., N.T.O.S.; 14th F.A.B., 27.3.16
LAWLESS, Private Ivan Desmond: 11th Rfts., 23.2.16; Discd., 4.10.19; wounded, 11.4.18
LAWLESS-PYNE, Private Clement Lumley: 30th Rfts., 4.7.18; Discd., 28.8.19
LAWLESS-PYNE, T/R.S.M. John Lindsay: 11th Rfts., 23.2.16; Discd., 4.10.19; wounded, 28.3.18, and 14.7.18
LAWLOR, Private James John: 11th Rfts., N.T.O.S.; 4/Cml. Rgt., 2.11.16
LAWRENCE, Private Herbert Henry: 11th L.H.R., 29.8.15; 11th L.H.R., 24.2.16
LAWRENCE, Private William Edward: 23rd Rfts., 23.12.17; Discd., 4.9.19
LAWRENCE, Driver William George: 12th Rfts., 7.1.16; 13th F.A.B., 27.3.16
LAWRIE, Private David McCall: 21st Rfts., N.T.O.S.; Discd., 30.9.16
LAWSON, Private George Adam: 20th Rfts., N.T.O.S.; 2/M.G. Sqdn., 6.10.16
LAWSON, Driver William: 22nd Rfts., N.T.O.S.; 4/M.G. Sqdn., 19.3.17
LAWTON, Private William Wallace: 13th Rfts., 19.2.16; Discd., 26.4.19
LAXTON, Sergeant Frank Pierpoint: 11th L.H.R., 29.8.15; 11th L.H.R., 22.2.16; died of wounds, Palestine, 19.4.17
LEA, Private Henry Cecil: 14th Rfts., 9.3.16; 14th F.A.B., 27.3.16
LEAMON, Private George Leslie: 16th Rfts., N.T.O.S.; Discd., 13.9.16
LEAROYD, Private Walter: 15th Rfts., N.T.O.S.; 12/Coy. I.C.C., 15.7.16
LEDGER, Private Frederick: 14th Rfts., 9.3.16; 13th F.A.B., 27.3.16
LEDLIE, T/Sgt. John Malcolm: 11th L.H.R., 2.10.15; 11th L.H.R., 22.2.16
LEDLIE, Driver William Bell: 13th Rfts., 19.2.16; 14th F.A.B., 27.3.16
LEE, L./Cpl. Albert Hezekiah A: 12th Rfts., 7.1.16; 1st Fld. Sqdn., 25.6.16
LEE, Lieut.-Colonel Charles Arthur (Mentioned in Despatches): 11th L.H.R., 25.10.15; 11th L.H.R., 22.2.16; died after term. of appt.
LEE, Private George: 8th Rfts., 14.11.15; Discd., 26.3.20
LEE, Driver John: 11th Rfts., 17.2.16; 14th F.A.B., 27.3.16
LEE, Private Thomas: Original, 8.12.14; A. Prov. Cps., 22.4.17; wounded, 14.7.15
LEEKE, Private Henry: Original, 8.12.14; Demob., U.K., 24.7.16
LEEN, Driver John: 14th Rfts., 9.3.16; 13th F.A.B., 27.3.16

HISTORY OF THE 5th LIGHT HORSE REGIMENT. 199

LEGH, Corporal Thomas: 11th L.H.R., 29.8.15; 11th L.H.R., 22.2.16
LEIGH, Private Frederick John: Original, 8.12.14; 4/Fld. Amb., 25.11.15
LEMASS, Private Joseph Charles: 11th L.H.R., 29.8.15; 11th L.H.R., 27.10.15
LEISHMAN, Sergeant Robert: 2nd Rfts., 7.7.15; killed in action, Anzac, 9.3.16
LENIHAN, Private Malachi: 11th L.H.R., 2.10.15; 11th L.H.R., 22.2.16.
LENIHAN, Private Michael: 7th Rfts., 14.11.15; Discd., 4.10.19
LEONARD, L/Cpl. Gerald James F.: Original, 8.12.14; Demob., U.K., 12.11.15 (Granted Commission Imperial Army); wounded, 27.6.15.
LESWELL, Private Jack: 11th L.H.R., 2.10.15; 11th L.H.R., 22.2.16; killed in action, Canal Zone, Egypt, 15.10.16.
LEWIS, Gunner Cyril Henry: 14th Rfts., 9.3.16; 13th F.A.B., 27.3.16.
LEWIS, Driver Clive William: 12th Rfts., 7.1.16; 13th F.A.B., 27.3.16
LEWIS, Private Ernest George: 21st Rfts., N.T.O.S.; Discd., 25.9.19
LEWIS, Private Hurtle John: Original, 8.12.14; 2/M.G. Sqdn., 6.10.16.
LEWIS, Private Henry Mansfield: 10th Rfts., 19.1.16; Discd., 29.11.17.
LIDDELL, Private Alfred Charles T.: Original, 8.12.14; Discd., 5.4.16; wounded, 27.5.15.
LIDDLE, Private Thomas: 23rd Rfts., 6.6.19; Discd., 4.9.19.
LINDSAY, Driver James Bruce: Original, 8.12.14; Sig. Sqd. A.M.D., 25.4.17.
LINDSAY, Private Robert: 3rd Rfts., 29.7.15; Discd., 21.7.20.
LINDSAY, Private Samuel Sydney: 25th Rfts., 28.7.17; Discd., 9.10.18.
LINGARD, Sergeant Henry Arthur: 11th L.H.R., 29.8.15; 11th L.H.R., 22.2.16.
LINNANE, Private John Austin: 8th Rfts., 2.1.16; died (pneumonia), Kantara, 1.5.16.
LINNANE, Gunner Peter John: 13th Rfts., 19.2.16; 14th F.A. Bde., 27.3.16; died of wounds, Belgium, 23.11.17.
LIPPIATT, Private William Arthur: Original, 8.12.14; Discd., 27.3.16.
LIPSTINE, Private Eric John Simon: 28th Rfts., 10.6.19; Discd., 4.9.19.
LISLE, S/Smith Robert: 15th Rfts., 26.7.16; Discd., 27.9.19.
LITTLE, 2/Lieut. Nevill Montague: Original, 8.12.14; 49th Btn., 26.3.16; wounded, 31.5.15; killed in action, France, 3.9.16.
LITTLE, Private Robert James: Original, 8.12.14; Discd., 26.2.19.
LLOYD, Gunner David: 11th Rfts., N.T.O.S.; 13th F.A.Bde., 27.3.16.
LLOYD, Private William Vernon: 11th Rfts., 30.6.16; Discd., 18.12.19.
LOCKHART, T/Sgt. William Edward Clarence J.: Original, 8.12.14; Discd., 12.4.19.
LOGAN, Private Graham: Original, 8.12.14; Discd., 24.1.19.
LOGIE, L/Cpl. Norman William: Original, 8.12.14; Discd., 29.11.16; wounded, 16.7.15 and 9.8.16.
LONG, Driver Edward Richard: 8th Rfts., 18.1.16; 3rd D.A.C., 18.7.17.
LONG, Private Frederick Edmund: 23rd Rfts., N.T.O.S.; 26th D.U.S., 30.7.17.
LONG, T/2/Cpl. John: 12th Rfts., 7.1.15; 13th F.A.Bde., 27.3.16.
LONG, Private Norman Joseph: 12th Rfts., 7.1.16; 2nd L.H.F.Amb., 25.1.16.
LONG, L/Cpl. William: 11th L.H.R., 2.10.15; 11th L.H.R., 22.2.16.
LONGLEY, Gunner William: 12th Rfts., 7.1.16; 14th F.A.Bde., 27.3.16.
LONGWILL, Gunner William Matthew: 13th Rfts., 19.2.16; 14th F.A.Bde., 27.3.16; killed in action, France, 8.10.18.
LOOSE, Private Charles Ernest: 20th Rfts., 12.10.16; Discd., 12.10.19.
LORD, E.R./S/Sgt. Charles James: Original, 8.12.14; A.I.F. Canteens, 23.10.16.
LOVE, Private Guylford Wilton: 1st Rfts., 7.7.15; Discd., 31.12.15.

LOVELL, Private Clyde: 1st Rfts., 16.5.15; killed in action, Gallipoli, 28.6.15.
LOVELL-SHORE, Sergeant Ernest Edward: Original, 8.12.14; Discd., 15.4.19; wounded, 27.6.15.
LOWE, Private Harold Dudley Gaden: 11th L.H.R., 29.8.15; 11th L.H.R., 26.2.16; wounded, 5.11.15.
LUBOMIRSKI, Private August: 29th Rfts., 15.4.18; killed in action, Palestine, 28.7.18.
LUCAS, Private Charles Edward: 8th Rfts., N.T.O.S.; 2nd L.H.Rgt., 13.11.15.
LUCAS, Private James: 5th Rfts., 25.9.15; killed in action, Gallipoli, 7.11.15.
LUCAS, E.R./Cpl. Joseph Hamilton: 12th Rfts., 7.1.16; 2nd L.H.F. Amb., 25.1.16.
LUCAS, Driver Milton: 14th Rfts., 9.3.16; 4/Caml Rgt., 2.11.16.
LUCK, Private John Gordon: 21st Rfts., 9.7.17; Discd., 12.9.19.
LUMLEY, Private Arthur Charles: 19th Rfts., 12.10.16; Discd., 11.7.19.
LUMLEY, L/Cpl. Percy Hampden: 8th Rfts., 10.1.16; wounded, 28.3.18; died of wounds, Palestine, 30.3.18
LUTHER, Private Donald: G.S. Rfts., 15.2.19; Discd., 19.6.19.
LUXFORD, Major Sydney (Mentioned in Despatches): Original, 8.12.14; Appt. Term., 9.11.19.
LYALL, Gunner John: 12th Rfts., 20.1.16; 14th F.A.B., 27.3.16.
LYNAM, Driver John Kevin: 14th Rfts., 9.3.16; 14th F.A.B., 27.3.16.
LYNAM, Driver Michael Joseph: 14th Rfts., 9.3.16; 13th F.A.B., 27.3.16; died of wounds, Belgium, 20.10.17
LYON, Private Leonard: 15th Rfts., N.T.O.S.; Camel Cps., 2.11.16.
LYONE, Corporal John Martin: Original, 8.12.14; Discd., 25.2.19; wounded, 7.8.15, 5.8.16 and 24.9.18.
LYONS, Captain Leon Maurice: Original, 21.11.14; 49th Btn., 10.3.16
LYONS, Captain William Michael: Original, 8.12.14; Appt. Term., 29.1.18.
MACANSH, Lieut. John Donald (M.C.): Original, 8.12.14; Appt. Term., 30.4.19; wounded, 14.7.18.
MACARTNEY, Private Harold Eric Joseph: 6th Rfts., N.T.O.S.; died (meningitis) at sea, 5.7.15.
MACDONALD, T/Sgt. Angus Bernard: 3rd Rfts., 29.7.15; 2/M.G. Sqdn., 24.7.16
MACDONALD, Sergeant Claude Hamilton: Original, 8.12.14; Discd., 10.1.17; wounded, 28.6.15, 8 11.15 and 5.8.16.
MACDONALD, Private John: 7th Rfts., 23.2.16; Discd., 26.12.19; wounded, 31.3.18.
MACDONALD, Private Leslie: Original, 8.12.14; wounded, 28.5.15; killed in action, Anzac, 28.6.15.
MACFARLANE, T/Sgt. Neil Archibald: 11th Rfts., 23.2.16; Discd., 4.10.19.
MACINTOSH, L/Cpl. Hector: 11th L.H.R., 2.10.15; 11th L.H.R., 14.3.16.
MACKAY, L/Cpl. Arthur Norman: 11th Rfts., 23.2.16; Discd., 7.11.19.
MACKENZIE, Private George Harry: 22nd Rfts., 11.6.17; Discd., 12.9.19; wounded, 8.11.17.
MACKIE, Corporal Andrew: 14th Rfts., 9.3.16; 13/F.A.B., 27.3.16.
MACKIE, Private Eric Francis: Original, 8.12.14; Discd., 17.5.16.
MACKIE, Driver Thomas: 14th Rfts., 9.3.16; 13th F.A.B., 27.3.16.
MACLEAN, Major Hector Rath: A.A.M.C. (attached), 8.1.16 to 23.2.16.
MACMASTER, Private Joseph Hassell: 23rd Rfts., 27.11.17; Discd., 18.7.19.
MACPHERSON, Corporal Bruce (M.M.): 16th Rfts., N.T.O.S.; 5th D.A.C., 19.9.16.

HISTORY OF THE 5th LIGHT HORSE REGIMENT.

MACPHERSON, Private George Henry: 16th Rfts., N.T.O.S.; 2/M.G. Sqdn., 4.8.16.
MACPHERSON, Lieut. Norman Saladin: Original, 8.12.14; A.I.F. H.Q., 25.8.15; wounded, 28.6.15.
MACHIN, Private Thomas: 4th Rfts., 29.7.15; Discd., 28.9.19.
MADDEN, Gunner Albert John (M.M.): 16th Rfts., N.T.O.S.; 4th D.A.C., 5.8.16.
MADDISON, Sapper Archibald George: 15th Rfts., N.T.O.S.; 1st Fld. Sqn. Eng., 25.6.16.
MADDISON, Bombdr. Hastings Elms: 6th Rfts., 14.11.15; 14th F.A.Bde., 27.3.16.
MAGARRY, L/Cpl. Walter: Original, 8.12.14; died (enteric fever), Mudros, 12.10.15.
MAGUIRE, Driver Robert Michael: 16th Rfts., N.T.O.S.; 1st Fld. Sqn. Eng., 27.6.16.
MAHER, Sapper John Hugh: 14th Rfts., N.T.O.S.; A.Mtd.Div.Sig S., 22.7.16.
MAHONEY, Captain Bernard: 2nd Rfts., 7.7.15; Appt. Term., 29.3.20; wounded, 28.11.17.
MAHONEY, Driver Eugene: 14th Rfts., 9.3.16; 13th F.A.Bde., 27.3.16.
MAILE, T/Sgt. Alfred William: 10th Rfts., 23.2.16; Discd., 4.10.19.
MAILE, T/Dvr. Henry Vincent: 23rd Rfts., N.T.O.S.;; 4th L.H.F.Amb., 22.9.17.
MAISHMAN, Private Thomas Alfred: Original, 8.12.14; 49th Btn., 27.3.16.
MALONEY, Private George Henry: 22nd Rfts., 2.7.17; Discd., 12.9.19
MALPAS, Driver Cedric Gower: 12th Rfts., 13.1.16; 13th F.A.Bde., 27.3.16.
MALVINE, Private Joseph: 10th Rfts., 22.1.16; Discd , 4.10.19.
MANCKTELOW, Private Sydney Thomas Edward: 15th Rfts., 18.4.16; Discd., 1.11.16.
MANNING, Private Frank Clive: 16th Rfts , 20.8.16; Discd., 27.9.19.
MANSON, Private Andrew Turton: Original, 8.12.14; Discd., 19.7.16; wounded, 28.6.15.
MANTTON, Private Reginald Porter: Original, 8.12.14; Discd., 25.8.16; wounded, 24.9.15.
MARGETTS, R.Q M.S. Leonard Ross: 10th Rfts., 23.2.16; Discd., 4.10.19.
MARKS, S/Smith Peter Henry: 12th Rfts., 1.2.16; 14th F.A.Bde., 27.3.16.
MARKWELL, Gunner John Thomas: 8th Rfts., 14.11.15; 14th F.A.Bde., 27.3.16.
MARLEY, Private Ernest George: Original, 8.12.14; killed in action, Gallipoli, 28.6.15.
MARNANE, Private Maurice William: 11th L.H.Rgt., 2.10.15; Cml. Cps., 9.9.16.
MAROSKE, Driver Albert: 12th Rfts., 7.1.16; 13th F.A.Bde., 27.3.16.
MARR, Private Justin: 4th Rfts., 22.5.15; Discd., 25.4.19.
MARSDEN, Sdlr./Sgt. Harold Bertie: Original, 8.12.14; Discd., 4.10.19.
MARSH, Private Arthur Herbert: 7th Rfts., N.T.O.S.; Discd., 23.3.16.
MARSH, Private Charles William: 2nd L.H.Rgt., 28.6.17; Discd., 12.9.19; wounded, 5.11.17.
MARSH, Lieut. Hugh Walter (M.C.): Original, 8.12.14; 13th F.A. Bde., 27.3.16.
MARSH, L/Cpl. John James: 11th Rfts., 23.2.16; wounded, 5.11.17; died of wounds, Palestine, 6.11.17.
MARSHALL, 2/Lieut. Harold Guyer: Original, 8.12.14; 2nd D.A.C., 13.9.16.
MARSHALL, Private John: 11th Rfts , 30.4.16; 4th Cml. Rgt., 2.11.16.

MARSHALL, Corporal Rex Lawson: Original, 8.12.14; 15th F.A.Bde., 4.5.16.
MARSHALL, Private Sidney: 10th Rfts., 15.12.15; 2nd L.H.B.H.Q., 21.3.17; killed in action, Palestine, 17.9.18.
MARSHALL, Corporal Sydney Augustus: Original, 8.12.14; 14th F.A.Bde., 27.3.16; 2nd L.H.B.H.Q., 21.1.18.
MARSON, Driver Joseph William: 14th Rfts., 9.3.16; 13th F.A.Bde., 27.3.16.
MARSON, S/Sm./Cpl. Lowson Emanuel: 14th Rfts., 9.3.16; 13th F.A.Bde., 27.3.16.
MARTIN, Private Horace Victor: 29th Rfts., 23.2.18; Discd., 12.1.19.
MARTIN, Private James Garrett: Original, 8.12.14; Discd., 12.4.16.
MARTIN, Private Leslie Albert: G.S. Rfts., 15.2.19; Discd., 19.8.19.
MARTIN, Private Robert: 1st Rfts., 16.5.15; wounded, 5.6.15; died (peritonitis) at sea, 27.8.15.
MARTYR, 2/Lieut. Frederick: 14th Rfts., 9.3.16; 15th Btn., 1.4.16; killed in action, France, 8.8.16.
MASKELYNE, Private Henry: Original, 8.12.14; Discd., 10.12.14; 9th Rfts., 20.11.15; 13th F.A.Bde., 27.3.16.
MASON, Gunner Francis: 11th Rfts., N.T.O.S.; 13th F.A.Bde., 27.3.16.
MASON, Private John: 26th Rfts., N.T.O.S.; Discd., 30.7.19.
MASON, Gunner Lawrence Hillerby: 10th Rfts., 28.12.15; 14th F.A.Bde., 27.3.16.
MASON, Lieut. Robert Edward: Original, 8.12.14; Cml. Cps., 13.8.16.
MASSY, Driver Charles Bute: Original, 8.12.14; killed in action, Suez Canal Zone, 5.8.16.
MASTERSON, L/Cpl. William George: Original, 8.12.14; Discd., 26.2.19.
MATHIESON, Gunner Donald David: 12th Rfts., 7.1.16; 13th F.A.Bde., 27.3.16.
MATSON, Gunner Claw: 2nd L.H.Rgt., 7.1.16; 14th F.A.Bde., 27.3.16
MATHEWS, Lieut. John Victor: 4th Rfts., 26.5.15; Appt. Term., 4.10.19; wounded, 14.7.18.
MATTOCKS, O.R./Sgt. Edward Albert: 12th Rfts., 7.1.16; Discd., 27.9.19
MAUDSLEY, Gunner Leonard Richard: 13th Rfts., 9.2.16; 14th F.A.Bde., 27.3.16.
MAXWELL, S.Q.M.S. Anthony: Original, 8.12.14; Discd., 26.2.19; wounded, 9.8.16.
MAYNE, Bombdr. Charles Sebra: 14th Rfts., 9.3.16; 13th F.A.Bde., 27.3.16.
MAYNE, Driver Edgar Christopher: 13th Rfts., 19.2.16; 13th F.A.Bde., 27.3.16.
MAYNE, Private Stanley: 15th Rfts., N.T.O.S.; 4th Cml. Rgt., 2.11.16.
MAZLIN, Private Frederick Robert: 1st Rfts., 7.7.15; Discd., 18.2.16.
MEAGHER, Driver William: 30th Rfts., 21.10.18; Discd., 23.9.19.
MEALING, Private William Richard: 3rd Rfts., 29.7.15; 13th F.A.Bde., 27.3.16.
MEIKLE, Private Robert: 2nd Rfts., 7.7.15; Discd., 23.2.16.
MEIKLE, Private William Leslie: 22nd Rfts., 2.7.17; accidentally wounded, 17.7.17; died (pneumonia), Rafa, Syria, 26.7.17.
MEIKLEJOHN, Private John: 11th Rfts., 23.2.16; Discd., 4.10.19.
MEIKLEJOHN, Private Joseph William: 11th Rfts., 23.2.16; Discd., 8.11.19.
MEIKLEJOHN, Private William Robert: 11th Rfts., 23.2.16; Discd., 4.10.19.
MEILLEAR, Private Arthur Johann: 11th Rfts., 23.2.16; Anz.Mtd.Div. H.Q., 22.10.16.
MELVILLE, Private James: Original, 8.12.14; Discd., 4.11.15.

HISTORY OF THE 5th LIGHT HORSE REGIMENT. 203

MELVILLE, Private John Hill: 24th Rfts., 15.7.17; Discd., 13.8.19; wounded, 19.11.17.
MENHINICK, Private Richard Orams: 26th Rfts., N.T.O.S.; Anzac Mtd.Div.Trn., 31.8.17.
MERRITT, Sergeant Harold Waldron: 11th L.H.Rgt, 2.10.15; 11th L.H.Rgt., 22.2.16.
MERRITT, Driver Walter: 8th Rfts., 10.1.16; 13th F.A.Bde., 27.3.16.
MIDDLETON, Private John: 11th L.H.Rgt., 29.8.15; 11th L.H.Rgt., 22.2.16.
MIDGLEY, Private Alfred Norman: Original, 8.12.14; Discd., 26.2.19; wounded, 17.9.16.
MIDGLEY, Lt./Col. Stephen (C.M.G., D.S.O., three times Mentioned in Despatches): Original, 30.9.14; 54th Btn., 5.9.16; wounded, 9.11.15.
MILES, E.R./2/Cpl. John William: 20th Rfts., N.T.O.S.; 3rd Cml Btn., 6.10.17; 3rd Cml. Btn., 28.7.18; Anz. Prov. Cps., 10.2.19.
MILLAR, Private Ernest Robert: Original, 8.12.14; Aust. Mtd. Div. H.Q., 18.4.16; Aust. Mtd. Div. H.Q., 19.9.17; Discd., 22.2.19; wounded, 5.11.15.
MILLAR, Lieut. George Simpson: Original, 8.12.14; Com. Imp. Army, 25.12.15.
MILLER, Private Edwin Andrew: 18th Rfts., 21.6.16; Cml. Cps., 7.9.16.
MILLER, Private James: 17th Rfts., N.T.O.S.; 2nd L.H.B.M.G.S., 12.9.16.
MILLER, Driver Oswald Roy: Original, 8.12.14; Discd., 26.2.19.
MILLER, Private Percy: 15th Rfts., 26.7.16; Discd., 3.11.19.
MILLER, L/Cpl. Robert Percival: Original, 8.12.14; Discd., 26.2.19; wounded, 6.9.15 and 16.11.15.
MILLER, Driver Robert Stanley: 3rd Cml. Btn., 28.7.18; Discd., 4.9.19.
MILLER, Driver William: 11th Rfts., 27.2.16; 13th F.A.Bde., 27.3.16.
MILLS, Gunner William Vaughan: 3rd Rfts., 29.7.15; 14th F.A.Bde., 27.3.16.
MILNE, Private Thomas Ernest Orton: 6th Rfts., N.T.O.S.; Imp. Cml. Cps., 1.7.16.
MILSON, Private Alfred Douglas: 3rd Rfts., 29.7.15; Discd., 9.11.19.
MILSON, Private Innis Vivian: 3rd Rfts., 29.7.15; Discd., 3.10.19.
MILTON, Private Herbert George: 14th Rfts., N.T.O.S.; 2nd M.G.Sqdn., 4.8.16.
MINAHAN, Bombdr. Edward Redmond: 11th Rfts., 28.12.15; 13th F.A.Bde., 6.4.16.
MINNION, Private William James: 1st Rfts., 16.5.15; Discd., 26.2.19.
MITCHELL, Private Allan Archibald: Original, 8.12.14; Discd., 26.1.18.
MITCHELL, Private Clarence: Original, 8.12.14; Discd., 12.5.19; wounded, 28.6.15 and 10.11.17.
MITCHELL, Gunner Charles Andrew: 13th Rfts., 19.2.16; 14th F.A.Bde., 27.3.16.
MITCHELL, Private Frederick Langdon: 12th Rfts., 7.1.16; 2nd Bde. H.Q., 18.4.16; 2nd Bde. H.Q., 21.3.17; Discd., 1.11.18.
MITCHELL, Private Harold Lawson: 15th Rfts., N.T.O.S.; 4th Cml. Rgt., 2.11.16; 4th Cml. Rgt., 23.12.16; Discd., 27.9.19.
MITCHELL, Private Laurence: 11th L.H.Rgt., 25.9.15; 13th L.H.Rgt., 27.3.16; 13th L.H.Rgt., 27.2.18; Demob., U.K., 5.10.19.
MITCHELL, Private Thomas: 12th Rfts., 7.1.16; 14th F.A.Bde., 27.3.16.
MOBBS, Driver William Arthur: 16th Rfts., N.T.O.S.; 3rd D.A.C., 4.8.17.
MOFFAT, Private Hugh: 7th L.H.Rgt., 5.10.18; Discd., 29.7.20.
MOLONEY, Private James: 15th Rfts., N.T.O.S.; 4th Cml. Rgt., 2.11.16.

MONAGHAN, Private John: 6th Rfts., 14.11.15; died (malaria), with
E.E.F., 12.12.18.
MONAGHAN, Private Patrick, 15th Rfts., 20.8.16; Discd., 27.9.19;
wounded, 8.11.17.
MONCRIEFF, 2/Lieut. John Bain: Original, 8.12.14; 13th M.G. Coy.,
26.5.16; killed in action, France, 3.9.16.
MONROE, Private James Gavin: 21st Rfts., 11.4.17; Discd., 26.11.19.
MONTGOMERY, Private Herbert Sydney: 27th Rfts., 1.8.17; Discd.,
20.9.19.
MOODY, Sapper Charles Arthur Langden: 10th Rfts., 23.2.16; 2nd
Sig. Trp., 1.4.16.
MOONEY, Private James Thomas: 6th Rfts., 23.2.16; Discd., 4.10.19.
MOORE, Private Daniel Celestine: Original, 8.12.14; Discd., 6.8.15.
MOORE, Driver Joseph Charles: 4th Rfts., 22.5.15; Discd., 4.10.19.
MOREY, T/Sgt. Frederick Edmund: 18th Rfts., 20.8.16; Discd., 19.9.19.
MORGAN, Lieut. Arthur Clinton: 11th L.H.Rgt., 29.8.15; 11th
L.H.Rgt., 22.2.16.
MORISON, Private John Arthur: 16th Rfts., N.T.O.S.; 2nd M.G.Sqdn.,
6.10.16.
MORLEY, Lieut. Charles Reginald; Original, 8.12.14; Aust., 9.2.16;
18th Rfts., 20.8.16; wounded, 8.11.17; died of wounds, Palestine,
8.11.17.
MORRIS, S/Smith Henry James: 24th Rfts., N.T.O.S.; 1st Sig. Sqn.,
10.6.17.
MORRIS, Private Walter Robert: 24th Rfts., 15.7.17; Discd., 31.3.19.
MORRISON, Private Archibald Maclaine: Original, 8.12.14; Discd.,
26.7.16; wounded, 27.6.15
MORISON, Private Donald Rutherford: Original, 8.12.14; killed in
action, Gallipoli, 28.6.15
MORRISON, Private Frank Alton: 1st Rfts., 16.9.15; Discd., 26.2.19.
MORRISSEY, Private Jack: 10th Rfts., 23.2.16; Discd., 9.10.19;
wounded, 28.3.18.
MORSCHEL, Private Gordon Adalbert: 10th Rfts., N.T.O.S.; Discd.,
13.12.15.
MORT, Capt. Henry Chisholm: 16th Rfts., 25.5.16; 4th Cml. Rgt.,
2.11.16.
MORTIMER, Private Cecil Selby: 11th Rfts., 30.12.15; Discd., 16.1.20
MOSLEY, Private James: 15th Rfts., 26.4.16; 49th Btn., 1.8.16.
MOSS, Private Frederick Arnold Wrench: 2nd Rfts., 7.7.15; Discd.,
3.12.19.
MOUGHTY, A/Sgt. Hugh: 15th Rfts., 20.8.16; Discd., 27.9.19.
MOURITZ, Corporal Ernest Arthur Richard (M.M.): 1st Rfts., 16.5.15;
Discd., 18.4.19; wounded, 28.3.18 and 25.9.18
MOY, A/Bombdr. Francis Michael: 14th Rfts., 9.3.16; 13th F.A Bde.,
27.3.16; killed in action, France, 24.4.18.
MUIR, Lieut. Albert Stanley: Original, 8.12.14; 2/M.G. Sqdn., 24.7.16;
wounded, 21.8.15; killed in action, Palestine, 5.11.17.
MUIRHEAD, L/Cpl. Henry: 9th Rfts., 20.11.15; 2nd L.H.B.M.G.S.,
21.9.16.
MULHOLLAND, Private James William: 3rd Cml. Btn., 28.7.18; Discd.,
27.9.19.
MULLER, Driver Albert Henry: 29th Rfts., 28.2.18; Discd., 24.5.19.
MULLINS, Sergeant Daniel: Original, 8.12.14; Discd., 26.2.19.
MULLINS, Chaplain Thomas (M.C., twice Mentioned in Despatches):
Chaplain (attached), 2.11.15 to 24.4.19.
MULQUEENEY, Private Herbert John: 11th Rfts., 23.2.16; Postal Cps.,
28.11.16; Postal Cps., 11.4.17; Discd., 11.2.19.
MUNDON, Private Harold John: 15th Rfts., N.T.O.S ; 2nd M.G.Sqdn.,
4.8.16.
MUNNS, Corporal Leonard Clarence: Original, 8.12.14; Discd., 20.4.19.

HISTORY OF THE 5th LIGHT HORSE REGIMENT. 205

MUNRO, Private Angus: Original, 8.12.14; 11th L.H.Rgt., 15.4.17.
MUNRO, Major Charles Alexander Richmond: 11th L.H.R., 29.8.15; 11th L.H.Rgt., 22.2.16.
MUNRO, Driver Edgar Charles: 11th L.H.Rgt, 29.8.15; 11th L.H.Rgt., 22.2.16.
MUNRO, Private John: 18th Rfts., N.T.O.S.; 2nd M.G.Sqdn., 12.9.16.
MUNRO, Private Keith Ross: Original, 8.12.14; Com. Imp. Army, 3.2.16; wounded 28.6.15.
MUNRO, Sergeant Victor Albert Clarence: Original, 8.12.14; 11th L.H.Rgt., 12.3.18; wounded, 21.5.15.
MUNRO, Private William: 18th Rfts., N.T.O.S.; 2/M.G.Sqdn., 12.9.16.
MUNSON, Private Arthur: 2nd Rfts., N.T.O.S.; Discd., 9.2.15.
MURDOCH, T/Cpl. David: 9th Rfts., 18.1.16; 4th Cml. Rgt., 2.11.16.
MURDOCH, Gunner James: 16th Rfts., N.T.O.S.; 4th D.A.C., 27.4.17.
MURPHY, Driver George: 12th Rfts., 7.1.16; 14th F.A.Bde., 27.3.16.
MURPHY, Sergeant John Joseph: 2nd Rfts, 7.7.15; 2nd L.H.B.M.G.S., 24.7.16.
MURPHY, Private Michael Ernest: 15th Rfts., N.T.O.S.; 4th Cml. Rgt., 2.11.16.
MURPHY, Private Patrick: 4th Rfts., 22.5.15; Discd., 4.4.16; wounded, 28.6.15.
MURPHY, Pr.vate Robert: 11th L.H.Rgt., 6.9.16; Cml. Cps., 7.9.16.
MURRAY, Private Alfred Archibald: 15th Rfts., N.T.O.S.; Discd., 13.9.16.
MURRAY, Private David James: Original, 8.12.14; wounded, 30.5.15; died of wounds at sea, 30.5.15.
MURRAY, Corporal Ernest John: Original, 8.12.14; Discd., 26.2.19.
MURRAY, Private James Martin: Original, 8.12.14; wounded, 10.7.15; died of wounds, Gallipoli, 10.7.15.
MURRAY, E.R./S/Sgt. Thomas (M.M.): 14th Rfts., 9.3.16; 14/F.A.B., 27.3.16.
MURTHA, Private James: 14th Rfts., 9.3.16; Discd., 3.10.19; wounded, 28.3.18.
MURTHA, Gunner John Henry: 1st Rfts., 16.5.15; Aust., 8.10.15; 16th Rfts., N.T.O.S.; 25th F.A.Bde., 25.10.16; wounded, 28.6.15.
McALISTER, 2nd/A.M. Con: Original, 8.12.14; 67th Sqn. A.F.C., 18.12.16.
McALPINE, Private Charles Steele: 15th Rfts., 26.7.16; Discd., 3.4.19.
McBRIDE, S/Smith Allison Thomas: 12th Rfts., 7.1.16; 13th F.A.Bde., 27.3.16.
McBRYDE, Private Isaac Ruddell: 6th Rfts., 25.9.15; Aust., 21.1.16; 9th Btn., 17.11.16; killed in action, Belgium
McCABE, Private Alexander Edward James: 17th Rfts., N.T.O.S.; 2nd L.H.B.M.G.S., 1.8.16.
McCABE, Gunner Richard: 12th Rfts., 7.1.16; 13th F.A.Bde., 27.3.16; killed in action, Belgium, 29.8.17.
McCADDEN, Driver Patrick: 12th Rfts., 7.1.16; 14th F.A.Bde., 27.3.16.
McCAIG, Private Francis John: 9th Rfts., 26.1.16; 12th Coy. I.C.C., 15.7.16.
McCALLUM, S/S/Cpl. Harold Coogee: 7th Rfts., 18.9.15; Discd., 12.5.20.
McCANN, Private Joseph: 24th Rfts., 21.9.17; Discd., 12.9.19.
McCONNELL, Private David: Original, 8.12.14; 25th Btn., 5.2.17; died (appendicitis), England, 1.11.18.
McCONNEL, Lieut. Kenneth Hamlyn: 2nd Rfts., 7.7.15; 1st Btn., 2.3.16.
McCORMICK, Private Cornelius: Original, 8.12.14; Anz. Mtd. D.H.Q., 20.7.17; Anz. Mtd. D.H.Q., 28.2.18; Discd., 12.4.19; wounded 28.3.18.

McCORMICK, Private Thomas: 12th Rfts., 7.1.16; 47th Btn., 3.10.16; killed in action, France, 11.4.17.
McCROHAN, Private Edwin: 11th Rfts., 16.2.16; Discd., 30.7.16.
McCULLOCH, Private Vivian William: 9th Rfts., 23.2.16; Discd., 4.10.19.
McDERMOTT, Private Thomas Francis: 16th Rfts, 3.11.16; Discd., 10.10.17.
McDIARMID, Driver Duncan: 11th Rfts., 23.2.16; Discd., 5.8.19; wounded, 5.11.17.
McDIARMID, Corporal James: 12th Rfts., 7.1.16; Discd., 27.9.19.
McDONALD, Driver Croxford Cross: 13th Rfts., 19.2.16; 14/F.A.Bde., 27.3.16.
McDONALD, Private Francis Aubrey: 9th Rfts., N.T.O.S.; Cml. Cps., 8.9.16; Cml. Cps., 17.8.18; Discd., 28.8.19.
McDONALD, Private George: Original, 8.12.14; Discd., 26.2.19; wounded, 11.9.15.
McDONALD, Private Jack: 17th Rfts., N.T.O.S.; 2nd M.G.Sqdn., 12.9.16.
McDONALD, Gunner Leith John: 11th Rfts., 14.12.15; 14th F.A. Bde., 27.3.16
McDONALD, Private Stanley Gordon: 24th Rfts., 6.6.19; Discd., 12.9.19
McDONNELL, Driver John Joseph: 11th L.H. Rgt., 29.8.15; 11th L.H. Rgt., 22.2.16
MacDONNELL, L/Cpl. Valentine Vincent: 18th Rfts., N.T.O.S.; Cml. Cps., 5.8.16
McDOWALL, Private William Gill: 6th G.S. Rfts., 21.1.19; Discd., 27.8.19
McDUFF, Private Hugh Alexander: 21st Rfts., N.T.O.S.; 2nd Sig. Trp., 26.2.17
McELLIGOTT, Lieut. Joseph (Mentioned in Despatches): 11th L.H. Rgt., 29.8.15;; 11th L.H. Rgt., 22.2.16
McENIRY, Private Noel: 13th Rfts., 19.2.16; Discd., 27.9.19; wounded, 14.7.18
McGEE, T/Cpl. Michael: 3rd Rfts., 29.7.15; Discd., 9.10.19; wounded, 29.3.18
McGEE, Driver Percy Edward: 12th Rfts., 27.2.16; 13th F.A. Bde., 27.3.16
McGILL, Private Archibald Fredrick: 26th Rfts., N.T.O.S.; Discd., 4.9.18
McGOWAN, L/Cpl. Samuel Crichton: 10th Rfts., 19.12.15; wounded, 5.8.16; died of wounds, Etmaler, 7.8.16
McGRATH, Pte. Henry James: Original, 8.12.14; Anz. Mtd. D.H.Q., 30.6.17
McGRATH, Gunner James Clyde: 11th Rfts., N.T.O.S.; 14th F.A. Bde., 27.3.16; killed in action, France, 22.10.18
McGRATH, Corporal John Paul (D.C.M., Mentioned in Despatches): 11th L.H. Rgt., 2.10.15; 11th L.H. Rgt., 22.2.16
McGRATH, Driver Richard: 13th Rfts., 19.2.16; 14th F.A. Bde., 27.3.16; killed in action, France, 12.12.17
McGRATH, Private William Francis (M.M., Mentioned in Despatches): 11th L.H. Rgt., 2.10.15; 11th L.H. Rgt., 22.2.16
McGREGOR, S.S.M. George: 11th L.H. Rgt., 29.8.15; 11th L.H. Rgt., 22.2.16
McGREGOR, Private Rob Roy: 16th Rfts., N.T.O.S.; 1st D.A.C., 2.8.16
McGREGOR, Gunner Walter: 16th Rfts., N.T.O.S.; 1st D.A.C., 29.3.17
McGUIGAN, L/Cpl. Horace Robert Young (D.C.M.): Original, 8.12.14; 1st Fld. Sqdn. A.M.D., 22.11.16
McGUIRE, Pte. Vallan Henry: 11th Rfts., 23.2.16; Discd., 4.10.19
McINDOE, T/Sgt. Alexander Clarke (M.M.): 10th Rfts., 23.2.16; Discd., 4.10.19; wounded, 25.9.18
McINDOE, Driver Hugh: 10th Rfts., 30.12.15; 14th F.A. Bde., 27.3.16

HISTORY OF THE 5th LIGHT HORSE REGIMENT. 207

McINNERNEY, Private Thomas Joseph: 20th Rfts., 12.10.16; Discd., 3.12.19
McINTOSH, Private Arthur: 11th L.H. Rgt., 29.8.15; 11th L.H. Rgt., 22.2.16
McINTOSH, Far./Sgt. Frank Stewart: Original, 8.12.14; Discd., 11.7.19
McINTOSH, Gunner William: 6th Rfts., 25.9.15; 13th F.A. Bde., 27.3.16
McINTYRE, Driver Bruce Kingsley: 15th Rfts., N.T.O.S.; Cml. Cps., 7.9.16
McINTYRE, Driver Peter: Original, 8.12.14; 14th F.A. Bde., 27.3.16
McIVOR, Private Thomas: 7th Rfts., 14.11.15; Discd., 21.6.16; wounded, 16.11.15
McKAVANAGH, Private Charles William: 16th Rfts., N.T.O.S.; 15th Btn., 7.3.17
McKAY, Private Alfred Arnot: 12th Rfts., 7.1.16; Discd., 7.6.16
McKAY, Private Lewis Fordyce: 11th L.H. Rgt., 29.8.15; 11th L.H. Rgt., 22.2.16; killed in action, Sinai Pen., 10.8.16
McKAY, Private William: 8th Rfts., 12.1.16; Discd., 29.1.18
McKAY, Private William John: Original, 8.12.14; Discd., 28.6.16; wounded, 8.11.15
McKEE, Private Edward (Mentioned in Despatches): 2nd L.H. Rgt., 21.7.17; Discd., 30.10.19
McKEE, Private Thomas Joseph: 12th Rfts., 7.1.16; Discd., 17.8.16
McKENNA, Private Francis: 23rd Rfts., 6.6.19; Discd., 4.9.19
McKENZIE, R.S.M. Hector: 11th L.H. Rgt., 29.8.15; 11th L.H. Rgt., 22.2.16
McKEOWN, Private Charles Gordon: 30th Rfts., N.T.O.S.; 1st F.S. Engrs., 14.6.19
McKERIHAN, Gunner Roland George: 11th Rfts., 11.2.16; 14th F.A. Bde., 29.8.16
MACKEY, Driver William (stated to be Edward Meyers): 9th Rfts., 7.1.16; Discd., 22.6.19
McKILLOP, E.R./Sgt. Harley John: 27th Rfts., 16.2.18; Discd., 11.7.19
McKINLAY, Driver Duncan William: 14th Rfts., 9.3.16; 13th F.A. Bde., 27.3.16
McKINNON, Private Alexander John Dugald: 7th Rfts., 14.11.15; Discd., 18.12.19
McKINNON, Private Claude Selby: 12th Rfts., 7.1.16; Discd., 25.10.16; wounded, 9.8.16
McKINNON, Corporal Lachlan: Original, 8.12.14; Discd., 26.2.19
McKINNON, Private Sydney: 14th Rfts., 9.3.16; 12th I.C.C., 15.7.16
McKISSON, Private Albert: 23rd Rfts., 6.6.19; Discd., 3.9.19
McKNOULTY, Driver Michael Roy: Original, 8.12.14; 14th F.A. Bde., 27.3.16; wounded, 27.6.15
McLACHLAN, Captain John McKenzie: 23rd Rfts., N.T.O.S.; Dental Cps., 24.3.18
McLAREN, Private Frank Cromwell: 11th L.H. Rgt., 2.10.15; 11th L.H. Rgt., 22.2.16
McLAREN, Private Thomas McLean: 11th L.H. Rgt., 29.8.15; killed in action, Gallipoli, 8.9.15
McLAUGHLIN, Major Herbert Francis: Original, 21.11.14; 47th Btn., 12.3.16
McLEAN, Private Alexander: 11th L.H. Rgt., 2.10.15; 11th L.H. Rgt., 22.2.16
McLEAN, Corporal Donald Stuart Lethbridge: Original, 8.12.14; Discd., 24.1.17
McLEAN, Sergeant Hector (D.C.M., Mentioned in Despatches): Original, 8.12.14; Discd., 17.1.17; wounded, 9.8.16
McLEAN, Private James: 4th Rfts., 22.5.15; killed in action, Gallipoli, 28.6.15

McLELLAN, Bombdr. Alexander: 5th Rfts., 24.11.15; 13th F.A. Bde., 27.3.16
McLENNAN, Private Kenneth John Kennedy: 30th Rfts., N.T.O.S.; 2nd L.H. Rgt., 26.7.18
McLENNAN, Sapper Thomas: 25th Rfts., N.T.O.S.; A. Mtd. Div. Sig. S., 27.4.17
McLEOD, Driver Henry: 10th Rfts., N.T.O.S.; 13th F.A. Bde., 27.3.16
McLEOD, Private William Kendall: 12th Rfts., 7.1.16; 25th Btn., 4.8.16
McMAHON, Driver Patrick Joseph: 14th Rfts., 9.3.16; 13th F.A. Bde., 27.3.16
McMAHON, Sergeant Stuart Moubray: 11th L.H. Rgt., 29.8.15; 11th L.H. Rgt., 22.2.16
McMAHON, Gunner Thomas Joseph: 6th Rfts., 25.9.15; 14th F.A. Bde., 27.3.16; died (meningitis), Egypt, 14.5.16
McMILLAN, Corporal Leslie William: Original, 8.12.14; 31st Btn., 15.10.16
McMILLAN, Driver Robert: Original, 8.12.14; 7th Mob. V.S., 17.11.16
McMULLEN, E.R./W.O. 1 Alexander John (M.S.M.): Original, 8.12.14; Discd., 15.4.19; wounded, 7.7.15
McMULLEN, T/S.S.M. Roy Victor: Original, 8.12.14; Discd., 26.2.19
McMULLIN, Driver William: 19th Rfts., 3.11.16; Discd., 24.9.19
McMURTRIE, Pte. Thomas Walter: 1st Rfts., 16.5.15; Discd., 24.12.15; 21st Btn., 28.5.17; killed in action, France, 5.10.18
McNAMARA, Private Francis Augustine: Original, 8.12.14; Discd., 16.4.19; wounded (acc.), 25.8.15
McNAMARA, Gunner Patrick Joseph: 12th Rfts., 7.1.16; 13th F.A. Bde., 27.3.16
McNAMEE, 2/Cpl. William: 11th L.H. Rgt., 29.8.15; 11th L.H. Rgt., 22.2.16
McNEILL, Captain John George Donald: Original, 11.11.14; Appt. Term., 17.1.17; wounded, 28.6.15, 1.12.15, and 5.8.16
McNULTY, Private John Joseph: 13th Rfts., 19.2.16; 13th F.A.B., 27.3.16
McPHAIL, L/Cpl. Leslie: 15th Rfts., N.T.O.S.; 12th Coy. I.C.C., 15.7.16
McPHERSON, T/Dvr. Donald Charles: 16th Rfts., N.T.O.S.; 4/Camel Rgt., 21.12.16
McPHERSON, Private George Alexander: 7th Rfts., 10.1.16; Discd., 4.10.19
McRAE, Private John David: 8th Rfts., 10.1.16; killed in action, Suez Canal Zone, Egypt, 9.8.16
McTIGUE, T/Dvr. Joseph: 8th Rfts., 14.11.15; 1st Fld. Sqdn., 15.6.17
McWILLIAM, Private Robert: 11th Rfts., N.T.O.S.; 5/A.S.C., 16.1.16
NEATE, 2nd A.M. Reginald Charles: Original, 8.12.14; 68th Sqn. A.F.C., 17.11.16
NEIGHBOUR, Private Leslie: 8th Rfts., 10.1.16; 13th F.A. Bde., 27.3.16
NEILSON, Gunner Charles: 12th Rfts., 7.1.16; 13th F.A. Bde., 27.3.16
NEILSON, Gunner Daniel Leslie: 11th Rfts., 20.1.16; 13th F.A. Bde., 27.3.16
NELSON, Private John: 7th Rfts., 14.11.15; Discd., 4.4.17; wounded, 17.11.15
NELSON, Private William Charles: Original, 8.12.14; Discd., 26.2.19
NESS, Private Frederick William: 2nd Rfts., 29.7.15; Discd., 3.1.16
NEVILL, Sergeant Stanley Cecil: 13th Rfts., 19.2.16; 13th F.A. Bde., 27.3.16
NEVILLE, Private Charles: Original, 29.12.14; Discd., 24.5.16; wounded, 28.6.15
NEWELL, Private Herbert Langley: 6th Rfts., 25.9.15; Discd., 13.9.16; G.S. Rfts., 17.8.18; Discd., 30.5.19; wounded, 8.10.15, 9.11.15
NEWTON, Private Francis: 11th Rfts., 23.2.16; Discd., 27.9.19; wounded, 9.11.17

HISTORY OF THE 5th LIGHT HORSE REGIMENT. 209

NEWTON, Lt.-Col. Frank Graham (C.B.E., D.S.O., Mentioned in Despatches twice): Original, 16.12.14; Appt. Term., 31.7.19
NEWTON, Driver Robert: 13th Rfts., 19.2.16; 13th F.A. Bde., 27.3.16
NEWTON, Private William Henry: 7th Rfts., N.T.O.S.; 2nd M.G. Sqdn., 5.10.16
NEYLON, Driver John: 12th Rfts., 7.1.16; 13th F.A. Bde., 27.3.16
NICHOLAS, L/Cpl. Stanley Sylvester: Original, 8.12.14; Discd., 12.7.16
NICHOLLS, Sergeant Leopold: 14th Rfts., 9.3.16; 2nd L.H. Rgt., 16.1.17
NICHOLLS, Driver Terence Patrick: 28th Rfts., N.T.O.S.; A. & N.Z. Dvl. Trn., 13.8.17
NICOL, Private Archibald: 7th Rfts., N.T.O.S.; Aust., 10.7.16; 29th Rfts., N.T.O.S.; 2nd M.G. Sqdn., 10.1.18
NICOLSON, Captain Norman Alexander (Mentioned in Despatches): 14th Rfts., 9.3.16; 13th F.A. Bde., 27.3.16
NIELSEN, Private Christie: 7th Rfts., 14.11.15; Discd, 25.4.17; wounded, 9.8.16
NIELSEN, T/Driver Thomas: 4th Rfts., 22.5.15; 2nd M.G. Sqdn., 5.8.17; wounded, 16.7.15
NILSON, Private William Martin: 16th Rfts., N.T.O.S.; 4th Cml. Rgt., 2.11.16; killed in action, Palestine, 8.11.17
NIMMO, Private John Robertson: 4th Btn., 17.7.16; Discd., 13.10.17
NIMMO, Major Robert Harold (Mentioned in Despatches): Original, 3.11.14; Appt. Term., 19.6.19
NIX, Sergeant George Thomas: Original, 8.12.14; Discd., 26.2.19
NOAH, E.R./Cpl. Bernard William: 2nd Rfts., 29.7.15; 1st F.A. Bde., 11.10.18
NOAKES, Private Lawrence Walter W.: Original, 8.12.14; Discd., 12.4.19
NOLAN, Driver William: 11th L.H. Rgt., 29.8.15; 11th L.H. Rgt., 22.2.16
NOLLER, Private William Arthur: 5th Rfts., 25.9.15; killed in action, Gallipoli, 8.11.15
NORGATE, Private William Crankyn: 19th Rfts., 12.10.16; Discd., 19.9.19; wounded, 5.11.17
NORMAN, Private Andrew: 4th Rfts., 29.7.15; 2nd Bde. M.G.S., 24.7.16
NORRIE, Private Arthur George: 2nd Rfts., 7.7.15; Discd., 25.3.19
NORRIS, Private James Henry: 5th Rfts., 11.4.17; Discd., 15.6.19
NORTH, Gunner Thomas: 13th Rfts., 19.2.16; 14/F.A.B., 27.3.16
NORTON, Private Ernest John: 17th Rfts., N.T.O.S.; 2nd M.G. Sqdn., 1.8.16; killed in action, Gaza, Palestine, 19.4.17
NOTT, Private Frederick Graham N.: 11th L.H.R., 2.10.15; 2nd L.H. Rgt., 17.10.15
NUDD, Private William Joseph: 2/L.H.F. Amb. (attached), 8.6.18 to 1.11.18
NUGENT, Private Reginald: 4th Rfts., 29.7.15; Discd., 7.6.16
OAKLEY, Gunner William Henry: 12th Rfts., 23.2.16; 14/F.A.B., 27.3.16
O'BRIEN, Sapper Frederick Charles: 15th Rfts., N.T.O.S.; 1/F.S.E., 19.2.17
O'BRIEN, Lieut. John Murdoch: 5th Rfts., 25.9.15; 12/Coy. I.C.C., 15.7.16
O'BRIEN, Driver James Roy: 17th Rfts., 20.8.16; A.S.C., 21.8.17
O'BRIEN, Private Martin: 11th L.H.R., 29.8.15; 11th L.H.R., 22.2.16
O'BRIEN, Private William James: 11th L.H.R., 29.8.15; wounded, 23.9.15; died (pneumonia), England, 2.11.15
O'CALLAGHAN, F/Cpl. Leslie: Original, 8.12.14; Discd., 29.3.19; wounded, 9.8.16
O'CONNOR, Driver Arthur: 16th Rfts., N.T.O.S.; 4/D.A.C., 24.8.16; died of wounds, France, 9.6.17

210 HISTORY OF THE 5th LIGHT HORSE REGIMENT.

O'CONNOR, Driver Edmund James: 11th Rfts., 30.6.16; Discd., 4.10.19; wounded, 9.8.16; died after discharge
O'CONNOR, Driver Joseph: 16th Rfts., N.T.O.S.; 4/D.A.C., 19.11.16
O'CONNOR, Private Michael: Original, 8.12.14; Aust., 3.3.16; 20th Rfts., 4.5.18; Discd., 18.4.19
O'CONNOR, L/Cpl. Maurice Edward (M.M.): 15th Rfts., 20.8.16; Discd., 19.5.19; wounded, 2.5.18
O'CONNOR, Driver William: 11th L.H.R., 29.8.15; 11th L.H.R., 22.2.16
O'DONNELL, Private George: Original, 8.12.14; Discd., 20.9.16
O'DONNELL, Private Stephen: 9th Rfts., 23.2.16; 2/M.G. Sqdn., 10.7.17
O'DONOGHUE, Driver Francis Joseph: 12th Rfts., 7.1.16; 14th F.A.B., 27.3.16
O'DONOHUE, Corporal Denis John: 5th Rfts., 25.9.15; 14/F.A.B., 27.3.16
O'DONOHUE, L/Cpl. Richard: 7th Rfts., 10.1.16; Discd., 3.5.19; wounded, 25.9.18
O'DONOHUE, Pte. William Joseph: 7th Rfts., 23.2.16; Discd., 4.10.19
O'DOWD, Private Peter Matthew: 11th L.H.R., 29.8.15; 11th L.H.R., 22.2.16; wounded, 19.9.15; killed in action, Gaza, Palestine, 19.4.17
O'DWYER, Private Stanley: 8th Rfts., 14.11.15; 14th F.A.B., 27.3.16; died of wounds, France, 13.12.16
O'FLANAGAN, L/Cpl. Denis Gerald: 11th L.H.R., 29.8.15; Discd., 6.9.16; wounded, 6.11.15
O'FLYNN, Sergeant Gerard: 12th Rfts., 7.1.16; 2/L.H.B. Sup. Sec., 9.9.16
OGDEN, Private Herbert Edwin: Original, 8.12.14; Discd., 15.4.19
OGG, Lieut. Edward Gordon (M.C.): Original, 8.12.14; Appt. Term., 6.5.19; wounded, 26.3.17, and 25.9.18
OGG, Driver Gordon Alexander: Original, 8.12.14; 14/F.A.B., 27.3.16
OGILVIE, Driver Henry Harvey: 16th Rfts., N.T.O.S.; 4/D.A.C., 9.8.16
OGILVY, Driver Reginald: 14th Rfts., 9.3.16; 13th F.A.B., 27.3.16
O'GRADY, Private William Joseph: 7th Rfts., N.T.O.S.; Discd., 16.8.16
O'HARA, Lieut. Denis: Original, 8.12.14; 2/L.H.M.G. Sqdn., 24.7.16
OLDHAM, Gunner William: 5th Rfts., 25.9.15; 14th F.A.B., 27.3.16
O'LEARY, Private Patrick Bernard: 1st Rfts., 16.5.15; 49th Bn., 5.10.16; wounded, 28.6.15, and 19.7.15
OLIVER, Private Thomas William: 17th Rfts., 26.7.16; Discd., 6.11.19
O'LOUGHLIN, Sergeant Thomas Charles: 3rd Rfts., 29.7.15; Aust., 3.1.16; 39th Bn., 1.4.16
OLSEN, Private Andrew: 2nd Rfts., 16.5.15; Discd., 9.5.17
OLSEN, Private Clarence Richmond: 2nd L.H.R., 4.2.16; Discd., 3.4.19
OLSEN, Driver Charles Gustav: 18th Rfts., N.T.O.S.; 2/M.G. Sqdn., 5.10.16
OLSEN, Private George Philip: 9th Rfts., 23.2.16; Discd., 4.10.19
OLSEN, Private Ivan Lender Eric: G.S. Rfts., 9.10.18; Discd., 20.8.19
O'MARA, Private John: 11th Rfts., 21.1.16; Discd., 30.10.19
O'MARA, Private Stephen: 2/L.H.R., 10.5.18; Discd., 28.8.19
O'MEARA, Private Hugh: 11th Rfts., 23.2.16; Demob., U.K., 25.10.19
O'NEILL, L/Cpl. William: Original, 8.12.14; wounded, 28.6.15; killed in action, Anzac, 5.11.15
O'NEILL, Private William James: 29th Rfts., 9.7.18; died (diphtheria), Gaza, Palestine, 8.8.18
O'REILLY, Bdr. John Joseph: 13th Rfts., 19.2.16; 14/F.A.B., 27.3.16
O'REILLY, Gunner John William: 14th Rfts., 9.3.16; 14/F.A.B., 27.3.16
O'REILLY, Bdr. Thomas: 13th Rfts., 19.2.16; 14/F.A.B., 27.3.16
O'ROURKE, L/Cpl. Patrick Michael: 12th Rfts., N.T.O.S.; 13/F.C.E., 21.3.16
O'ROURKE, Private Francis James (M.M.): 9th Rfts., 4.3.16; Camel Cps., 16.11.16
ORR, Private George Ronald: 11th Rfts., 4.6.16; A.A.S.C., 12.11.18

HISTORY OF THE 5th LIGHT HORSE REGIMENT. 211

ORR, Captain John Edward (M.C.): Original, 8.12.14; 1/Div. Engrs., 26.5.15
ORR, Corporal William Arthur (M.M.): 12th Rfts., 7.1.16; 14/F.A.B., 27.3.16
OSBORNE, Private Arthur: 4th Rfts., 22.5.15; Discd., 19.1.16; wounded, 28.6.15
OSBORNE, Private Jack Arthur: 18th Rfts., N.T.O.S.; A. Prov. Cps., 2.8.16
OSBORNE, T/Cpl. Maurice: 11th Rfts., 23.2.16; 2/Sig. Troop, 8.4.16
O'SULLIVAN, Private John: 1st Rfts., 16.5.15; killed in action, Anzac, 28.6.15
OWEN, Lieut. Francis Stephen B. (Mentioned in Despatches twice): Original, 8.12.14; 2/L.H.R., 22.4.16
OWEN-JONES, Lieut. Robert Gregory: Original, 8.12.14; 2/L.H.M.G. Sqd., 16.7.16; wounded, 13.7.15
OXENHAM, Private Reginald John: 15th Rfts., 26.7.16; Discd., 27.9.19
OXFORD, Sergeant Arthur Robert French: 15th Rfts., N.T.O.S.; 4/Cml. Rgt., 2.11.16; killed in action, Palestine, 6.11.17
OXFORD, Private Walter: 11th Rfts., N.T.O.S.; Discd., 12.4.16
PACKER, M.T./Dvr. Percy Frederick: 10th Rfts., 23.2.16; A.M.T.S., 30.1.17
PAGE, Private Charles: 14th Rfts., 9.3.16; 49th Btn., 19.8.16
PAGE, L/Cp. Douglas: 11th L.H. Rgt., 29.8.15; Discd., 10.5.16
PAGE, Driver Hugh Murray: 8th Rfts., 10.1.16; 13th F.A. Bde., 27.3.16
PALMER, Private Cecil Spunner: 30th Rfts., N.T.O.S.; Discd., 21.7.20
PALMER, Sapper James Ernest (M.M.): 13th Rfts., 19.2.16; 13th F.C. Engrs., 21.3.16
PALMER, Private Reginald Nutfield: 11th L.H. Rgt., 29.8.15; 11th L.H. Rgt., 25.2.16
PANKHURST, Driver Christopher William: 12th Rfts., 7.1.16; 13th F.A. Bde., 27.3.16
PARGETER, Private William: Original, 8.12.14; Discd., 1.1.16
PARKER, Driver Charles Allen: Original, 8.12.14; Com. Imp. Army, 25.12.15; died after discharge
PARKER, Private Harry: 6th Rfts., 25.9.15; Discd., 4.10.19
PARKER, Private John James: 11th L.H. Rgt., 29.8.15; 11th L.H. Rgt., 22.2.16; wounded, 6.11.15
PARKER, Private Michael John: 11th L.H. Rgt., 2.10.15; 11th L.H. Rgt., 26.2.16
PARKER, Driver Percy: 25th Rfts., N.T.O.S.; A.A.S.C., 13.8.17
PARKER, Private Richard Austin: 11th L.H. Rgt., 29.8.15; 11th L.H. Rgt., 28.3.16
PARKER, Private Trevor: 12th Rfts., 7.1.16; 2nd L.H.F. Amb., 25.1.16
PARR, Private Arthur Joseph Cameron: 21st Rfts., 11.6.17; Discd., 19.9.19
PARRY, Private Gwydir Ballford: 11th Rfts., 30.12.15; 13th F.A. Bde., 27.3.16
PARSONS, Driver John Vincent: 11th Rfts., N.T.O.S.; 14th F.A. Bde., 27.3.16
PASCOE, Corporal Joseph Henry: 11th L.H. Rgt., 29.8.15; killed in action, Gallipoli, 22.9.15
PASCOE, S.Q.M.S. William: 25th Rfts., N.T.O.S.; 1st Sig. Sqdn., 14.8.17
PASLEY, Private Robert Henry: 6th Rfts., 2.8.15; 2nd M.G. Sqdn., 20.9.17
PATCH, Driver Albert Reuben: 12th Rfts., 7.1.16; 2nd L.H.F. Amb., 15.3.17
PATCH, L/Cpl./Dvr. Henry William: 12th Rfts., 7.1.16; 2nd L.H.F. Amb., 15.3.17
PATEN, Private Norman Frances: 1st Rfts., 16.5.15; Discd., 29.8.19

212   HISTORY OF THE 5th LIGHT HORSE REGIMENT.

PATERSON, Private Alexander Learmonth: 11th L.H. Rgt., 2.10.15; 11th L.H. Rgt., 22.2.16; died (bronchitis and pneumonia), Beirut, 6.11.18
PATERSON, Captain Laurence Lindley (Mentioned in Despatches): A.A.V.C. (attached), 25.2.16 to 22.3.16
PATERSON, Private Sidney Lekberg: Original, 8.12.14; Discd., 2.2.16
PATRICK, Major William: 10th Rfts., 23.2.16; Appt. Term., 4.10.19
PATTERSON, Driver Percy Andrew: 13th Rfts., 19.2.16; 14th F.A. Bde., 27.3.16
PAUL, Lieut. William (Mentioned in Despatches): Original, 8.12.14; Appt. Term., 4.10.19
PAVEY, Private William Alexander: 8th Rfts., 10.1.16; 14th F.A. Bde., 27.3.16; died of wounds, France, 1.5.18
PAYNE, Driver Joseph George: 12th Rfts., 7.1.16; 13th F.A. Bde., 27.3.16
PAYNE, Private Thomas: Original, 8.12.14; Discd., 2.3.17
PAYNTER, Driver George Alfred: 11th Rfts., N.T.O.S.; 14th F.A. Bde., 27.3.16
PEARCE, Private Arthur: 15th Rfts., N.T.O.S.; 4th Cml. Rgt., 2.11.16
PEARCE, Private Charles Albert: 14th L.H.R., 17.8.18; Discd., 27.3.19; wounded, 21.9.18
PEARCE, T/Sgt. Harry: 16th Rfts., 24.10.16; 2nd M.G. Sqdn., 20.7.17
PEARCE, Private Henry: 28th Rfts., 14.10.18; Discd., 4.9.19
PEARSE, Private Edward James: 11th L.H. Rgt., 29.8.15; 4th Cml. Rgt., 2.11.16
PEARSON, Driver Edward Henry: 3rd Rfts., 29.7.15; 14th F.A. Bde., 27.3.16
PEARSON, Driver Harold Joseph (M.M.): 14th Rfts., 9.3.16; 14th F.A. Bde., 27.3.16
PEEL, Private Robert Pugh: 28th Rfts., 18.6.18; Discd., 30.8.19
PEGG, Private George Edgar: 29th Rfts., N.T.O.S.; 2nd M.G. Sqdn., 8.3.18
PELLING, 2/A.M. John Edward: 10th Rfts., 8.1.16; A.F.C., 17.11.16
PENDOCK, Private Charles: 11th L.H. Rgt., 29.8.15; 49th Btn., 20.2.17
PENN, Private Charles James: Original, 8.12.14; Discd., 2.5.16; wounded, 2.7.15
PENNY, Private Francis Robert: 3rd Rfts., 29.7.15; Discd., 24.4.16; 9th Btn., 29.8.17; died of wounds, France, 5.7.18
PENNY, A/Bombdr. Philip Alfred: 14th Rfts., 9.3.16; 13th F.A. Bde., 28.3.16
PENO, Private Charles: 16th Rfts., N.T.O.S.; 2nd L.H.B.M.G.S., 12.9.16
PENROSE, Private Herbert Henry: 30th Rfts, N.T.O.S.; 2nd L.H. Rgt., 12.7.18
PERES, Driver James Francis: 27th Rfts., N.T.O.S.; 36th Coy. D.T., 21.8.17
PERRET, T/C.Q.M.S. George Edward Julien: Original, 8.12.14; Demob., U.K., 18.2.19
PERRIE, Private Samuel Lauder Capie: 24th Rfts., N.T.O.S.; Discd., 17.4.17
PERRY, Private George: 15th Rfts., N.T.O.S.; 18th Co. Cml. C, 7.2.16
PERRY, Driver Michael: 11th L.H. Rgt., 29.8.15; 11th L.H. Rgt., 29.2.16
PERRY, Sergeant Morton John: 11th L.H. Rgt., 2.10.15; 11th L.H. Rgt., 24.2.16
PETERSEN, Private James: 5th Rfts., 25.9.15; Discd., 9.10.19
PHILLIPS, Private Frederick Freestone: 11th Rfts., 23.2.16; Discd., 27.9.19; wounded, 6.4.18, and 19.4.18
PHILLIPS, T/S/S/Cpl. William Thomas: 11th Rfts., 23.2.16; Discd., 16.6.19
PHILP, Driver Arthur Francis: 12th Rfts., 7.1.16; 13th F.A. Bde., 27.3.16

HISTORY OF THE 5th LIGHT HORSE REGIMENT. 213

PHILP, Sergeant Edward George: 11th L.H. Rgt., 29.8.15; 11th L.H. Rgt., 6.3.16
PHILP, T/Cpl. Edmund Henry Haldon: 28th Rfts., 27.11.17; 2nd M.G. Sqdn., 18.9.18; 2nd M.G. Sqdn., 9.10.18; Discd., 4.9.19
PHILP, Private Richard Stewart: 27th Rfts., 28.7.17; Discd., 24.5.19
PHIPPS, Driver Colin: 14th Rfts., 9.3.16; 14th F.A. Bde., 27.3.16
PICKSTONE, Private William George: 19th Rfts., N.T.O.S.; Cml. Cps., 7.9.16
PIDD, S/Smith Stanley Lloyd: 12th Rfts., 23.2.16; Discd., 27.9.19
PIGRAM, Private Harold James: 28th Rfts., 18.6.18; Discd., 26.12.19
PIKE, Captain Eustace Royston Baum: Original, 8.12.14; Appt. Term., 8.9.16
PIKE, Private George Walter: Original, 8.12.14; Discd., 22.3.16; wounded, 30.5.15
PIPER, Driver William Henry (correct name, William Henry Richards): 9th Rfts., 18.1.16; 13th F.A. Bde., 27.3.16
PITCEATHLY, L/Cpl. Robert: 15th Rfts., N.T.O.S.; 4th Cml. Rgt., 2.11.16
PITCHER, Major Cyril Frederick: A.A.M.C. (attached), 30.8.15 to 9.9.15
PLANT, Captain Reginald Arthur Neville: Original, 8.12.14; Appt. Term., 17.4.17; Aust., 19.11.18; Appt. Term., 22.1.20; wounded, 9.11.15, 9.11.15, and 5.8.16
PLAYER, Driver Albert Edward: Original, 8.12.14; Discd., 15.4.19; wounded, 5.11.15, and 5.8.16
PLEDGER, Private Robert Portway: 11th L.H. Rgt., 29.8.15; 11th L.H. Rgt., 22.2.16; killed in action, Palestine, 25.9.18
PLOWMAN, Driver Donald: 11th L.H. Rgt., 29.8.15; 11th L.H. Rgt., 22.2.16
PLUMB, Private John Robert: 12th Rfts., 7.1.16; Cml. Cps., 5.8.16
POHLMAN, Private John: 18th Rfts., 20.8.16; Discd., 4.10.19
POINTON, Sergeant Abel Sydney (M.M.): 11th L.H. Rgt., 2.10.15; 11th L.H. Rgt., 22.2.16
POINTON, L/Sgt. Percy Charles: 11th L.H. Rgt., 2.10.15; 11th L.H. Rgt., 22.2.16
POINTON, Private William Joseph: 18th Rfts., N.T.O.S.; 2nd M.G. Sqdn., 1.8.16
POKARIER, Private George Gustav: 23rd Rfts., 1.8.17; Discd., 4.9.19
POLLITT, Private Arthur: 29th Rfts., N.T.O.S.; 2nd M.G. Sqdn., 3.2.18
PONSFORD, Private Dudley Walter: 2nd Rfts., 29.7.15; Discd., 27.10.16; wounded, 23.8.15
PONT, Private Henry John: 30th Rfts., N.T.O.S.; 11th L.H. Rgt., 17.6.18
PONTON, Private Charles John: 11th L.H. Rgt., 29.8.15; 49th Btn., 19.11.16
POOL, Private Herbert Frederick: Original, 8.12.14; Discd., 12.4.19
POOLE, Gunner Alfred Henry: 13th Rfts., 19.2.16; 13th F.A. Bde., 27.3.16
POPE, Private Alexander: 15th Rfts., 15.7.17; Discd., 4.2.19
PORTER, Private Robert: 12th Rfts., 7.1.16; Discd., 28.3.17; died after discharge, 29.3.19 (pneumonic influenza)
PORTER, Private Robert Beattie: 14th Rfts., 9.3.16; Discd., 21.3.17
POSTLETHWAITE, Private John Joyce: 11th L.H. Rgt., 29.8.15; killed in action, Gallipoli, 2.11.15
POTTER, Private Arthur Laurence: 26th Rfts., 27.11.17; wounded, 2.5.18; died of wounds, Palestine, 3.5.18
POTTER, Bombdr. Llewellyn Henry: Original, 8.12.14; 13th F.A. Bde., 27.3.16
POUNTNEY, Private David: 5th Rfts., N.T.O.S.; Discd., 5.1.16
POUNTNEY, Private Leslie Raymond: Original, 8.12.14; wounded, 28.6.15; died of wounds, at sea, 28.6.15

214 HISTORY OF THE 5th LIGHT HORSE REGIMENT.

POWELL, Private Ernest: 8th Rfts., 23.2.16; Discd., 1.10.18
POWELL, Private Sidney George: 21st Rfts., 9.7.17; Aust. Mtd. Div. T., 18.9.17
POWELL, Sergeant Thomas: 11th L.H.R., 29.8.15; 11th L.H.R., 22.2.16
POWER, Gunner Paul: 16th Rfts., N.T.O.S.; 1st F.A.B., 30.3.17
POWIS, A/Sgt. Michael: Original, 8.12.14; wounded, 1.6.15; killed in action, Anzac, 28.6.15
POXON, Driver Reuben Joseph: 17th Rfts., N.T.O.S.; 2/L.H.M.G. Sqdn., 12.9.16
POYNTING, S.Q.M.S. Arthur Henry: Original, 8.12.14; Discd., 26.2.19
PRATT, Private Arthur Rex: Original, 8.12.14; Discd., 31.5.16
PRATT, Private Cedric Belford: 11th Rfts., 23.2.16; Discd., 27.10.19; wounded, 17.9.16
PRENTICE, Private John Richard: 11th L.H.R., 29.8.15; died (dysentery), Port Said, 1.10.15
PRESHO, Driver Wesley: 26th Rfts., N.T.O.S.; A. Div. Trn., 20.8.17
PRICE, Private Arthur Ernest: 1st Rfts., 16.5.15; Discd., 26.2.19
PRICE, Private Benjamin Henry Eyles: 3rd Rfts., 7.7.15; Discd., 14.7.19
PRICE, T/Cpl. Thomas Charles: 20th Rfts., 12.10.16; Discd., 19.9.19; wounded, 5.11.17
PRIDDLE, Private Eustace Randolph: Original, 8.12.14; wounded, 27.6.15; died (pneumonia), Brisbane, Q'ld, 21.11.15
PRIDDLE, Gunner Laurie Ernest Adam: 16th Rfts., N.T.O.S.; 5/D.A.C., 19.9.16
PRINGLE, Private John Ernest: 5th Rfts., 25.9.15; Discd., 4.10.19
PRINGLE, Gunner Vivian James: 5th Rfts., 25.9.15; 14/F.A.B., 27.3.16
PRITCHARD, Pte. Thomas: 15th Rfts., N.T.O.S.; 4/Cml. Rgt., 2.11.16
PROCTOR, Private Basil Ernest: 6th Rfts., 23.2.16; Discd., 11.1.17
PROCTOR, L/Sgt. Mervyn John: Original, 8.12.14; 2/L.H.F. Amb., 8.9.15
PROCTOR, Corporal Norman James: Original, 8.12.14; A. Prov. Cps., 7.4.16
PULLEN, Corporal Frank Ernest Gordon (M.M.): Original, 8.12.14; Discd., 12.4.19
PULLEN, Private Robert: 2nd Rfts., 7.7.15; 25th Bn., 5.2.17
PUNCH, Lieut. Joseph James Raphael (M.C. and Bar): 11th Rfts, 4.2.16; 13th F.A.B., 27.3.16
PURVIS, Private Julian Amourous: 19th Rfts., N.T.O.S.; Camel Cps., 7.9.16
PYNE—See Lawless-Pyne.
PYNEGAR, Bombdr. Edgar Sylvanus: 5th Rfts., 25.9.15; 13/F.A.B., 27.3.16; died (broncho-pneumonia), France, 30.10.18
QUINN, Private George: 26th Rfts., N.T.O.S.; 27/D.U.S., 1.8.17
QUINN, Private James: 12th Rfts., 23.2.16; wounded, 5.11.17; died of wounds, Palestine, 5.11.17
QUINN, Sergeant Walter Herbert (D.C.M.): 11th L.H.R., 29.8.15; 11th L.H.R., 22.2.16
RABY, Private William: Original, 8.12.14; died (enteric), Heliopolis, 21.3.16
RADCLIFF, Lieut. Bernard Radcliff (Mentioned in Despatches): Original, 8.12.14; Appt. Term., 18.4.19; wounded, 21.11.15
RADCLIFFE, Pte. Joseph Bernard: 15th Rfts., 26.7.16; Discd., 23.1.17
RADCLIFFE, Private Thomas: 15th Rfts., 26.7.16; killed in action, Suez Canal Zone, 9.8.16
RAE, Private Donald: 11th Rfts., 23.2.16; Discd., 6.9.16
RAE, Private George Alexander: 11th L.H. Rgt., 2.10.15; 11th L.H. Rgt., 22.2.16
RAFF, Driver George Wyven: 11th Rfts., 23.2.16; Discd., 27.9.19
RANGER, Gunner Bertram Harold (M.M.): 10th Rfts., 1.3.16; 14th F.A. Bde., 27.3.16

HISTORY OF THE 5th LIGHT HORSE REGIMENT. 215

RANN, Private Alfred Charles: 11th L.H. Rgt., 29.8.15; wounded, 5.11.15; died of wounds, Malta, 26.11.15

RASMUSSEN, Driver Alfred: 12th Rfts., 7.1.16; 14th F.A. Bde., 27.3.16

RAYNER, Gunner Frederick Robert: 16th Rfts., N.T.O.S.; Prov. Cps., 1.1.17

RAYSON, Gunner Sydney: 16th Rfts., N.T.O.S.; 4th D.A.C., 2.8.17

READ, Private Percival Cornelius: Original, 8.12.14; A.M.D.H.Q., 10.4.17; wounded, 28.6.15

REARDON, Private Denis Glendon: Original, 8.12.14; Discd., 1.4.19; wounded, 28.6.15

REARDON, Private James: 15th Rfts., N.T.O.S.; 4th Cml. Rgt., 2.11.16

REDDICLIFFE, Bombdr. William Henry: 5th Rfts., 25.9.15; 14th F.A. Bde., 27.3.16

REDFERN, Driver Ernest Edward: 8th Rfts., 9.1.16; 14th F.A. Bde., 27.3.16

REDMAN, Driver Roy: Original, 8.12.14; 2nd L.H.B.M.G.S., 24.7.16

REECE, Driver James Aubrey: 19th Rfts., N.T.O.S.; Cml. Cps., 7.9.16

REED, Corporal Fredrick William: 8th Rfts., 14.11.15; Discd., 2.8.16; 30th Rfts., N.T.O.S.; Discd., 25.6.18

REEMAN, Driver Harry William: 27th Rfts., N.T.O.S.; 33rd Coy. A.S.C., 31.3.18

REEVE, Driver Nathan: 13th Rfts., 19.2.16; 14th F.A. Bde., 27.3.16

REGAN, Private Daniel Thomas: 15th Rfts., N.T.O.S.; 4th Cml. Rgt., 2.11.16

REGAZZOLI, Private Santo: 11th L.H. Rgt., 2.10.15; 11th L.H. Rgt., 3.4.16

REID, Private Robert James: 11th L.H. Rgt., 29.8.15; 11th L.H. Rgt., 6.3.16

REIS, Sergeant Victor Lamington: 2nd Rfts., 7.7.15; Discd., 27.7.19

RENDELL, T/Cpl. William: 17th Rfts., 26.7.16; Discd., 19.9.19

RENSHAW, Sergeant Frank Armitage: 4th Rfts., 22.5.15; 13th F.A. Bde., 27.3.16

REYNOLDS, Private Bertie: 12th Rfts., 23.2.16; Discd., 27.9.19

REYNOLDS, T/Sgt. Ernest: 12th Rfts., 7.1.16; Discd., 16.5.19

REYNOLDS, Private Edward Thomas: Original, 8.12.14; wounded, 28.6.15; killed in action, Gallipoli, 25.7.15

REYNOLDS, Driver James Henry: 11th Rfts., 1.2.16; 14th F.A. Bde., 27.3.16; died of wounds, France, 7.5.18

REYNOLDS, Corporal William: 11th L.H. Rgt., 29.8.15; 11th L.H. Rgt., 2.2.16

RHODES, Gunner Victor John (correct name, Conway Morris): 14th Rfts., 9.3.16; 13th F.A. Bde., 27.3.16

RHODES, Driver William Henry: 8th Rfts., N.T.O.S.; 13th F.A. Bde., 27.3.16

RICE, Driver George Harold: 14th Rfts., 9.3.16; 13th F.A. Bde., 27.3.16

RICHARD, Lieut. Roland Rolf: 7th Rfts., 14.11.15; 5th F.A. Bde., 10.3.16

RICHARDS, Driver John: Vet. Cps., 11.7.15; Vet. Cps., 1.2.16

RICHARDS, T/Sgt. Roy Barton (M.M.): 12th Rfts., 7.1.16; Discd., 25.10.19

RICHARDS, Private William Louis: 2nd A. Vet. C., 15.5.15; 2nd A. Vet. C., 1.2.16 (attached strength)

RICHARDSON, Driver Aubrey: 29th Rfts., N.T.O.S.; A. & N.Z. Dvl. Trn., 24.2.18

RICHARDSON, Private Alfred Frederick: 11th L.H.R., 29.8.15; Discd., 1.2.17; wounded, 6.11.15

RICHARDSON, Private Claude: Original, 8.12.14; Discd., 6.1.15

RICHARDSON, Private George Henry: 16th Rfts., N.T.O.S.; 1st D.A.C., 13.3.17

216 HISTORY OF THE 5th LIGHT HORSE REGIMENT.

RICHMOND, Driver Thomas: 16th Rfts., N.T.O.S.; 9th F.A. Bde., 10.11.16; killed in action, Belgium, 19.10.17
RICKETTS, Private Harold Stanley: 8th Rfts., 13.12.15; 13th F.A. Bde., 27.3.16; killed in action, Belgium, 15.10.17
RIDLEY, Lt.-Col. John Cecil Thomas E. C. (D.S.O., Mentioned in Despatches): Original, 20.11.14; 13th I.B.H.Q., 4.3.16
RIELLY, T/Cpl. Edward Charles: 10th Rfts., 23.11.15; 1st F.S. Engrs., 5.3.18
RIELLY, Driver James: 25th Rfts., N.T.O.S.; A.A.S.C., 31.8.17
RIGBY, Private John Robert: Original, 8.12.14; Discd., 9.8.16
RIGHETTI, Major Edmund Edward: Original, 1.11.14; Appt. Term., 6.9.16
RILEY, Gunner Charles: 10th Rfts., N.T.O.S.; 14th F.A. Bde., 27.3.16
RILEY, Pte. George Herbert: 11th Rfts., 23.2.16; 1st Sig. Sqn., 15.4.17
RILEY, Private Terence: 16th Rfts., N.T.O.S.; 15th Btn., 16.10.16
RIPPON, Private Leslie Ernest: 19th Rfts., N.T.O.S.; Cml. Cps., 7.9.16
RITCHIE, Driver Ernest Charles: 14th Rfts., 9.3.16; 13th F.A. Bde., 27.3.16
ROACH, Private Cyril Gordon: 25th Rfts., 2.7.17; Discd., 24.4.20
ROACH, Driver Herbert: 13th Rfts., 19.2.16; 14th F.A. Bde., 27.3.16
ROACH, Private Thomas Joseph: 11th L.H. Rgt., 29.8.15; 11th L.H. Rgt., 22.2.16
ROBERTS, Private Frederick: 9th Rfts., 23.2.16; Discd., 4.10.19
ROBERTS, Private Harry: G.S. Rfts., 9.10.18; Discd., 20.8.19
ROBERTS, Private James John: 1st Rfts., 16.5.15; Discd., 6.9.16; 13th Btn., 18.8.18
ROBERTS, S.Q.M.S. Lewis David: 11th L.H. Rgt., 2.10.15; 11th L.H. Rgt., 22.2.16
ROBERTS, Private Philip: 16th Rfts., N.T.O.S.; Cml. Cps., 7.9.16
ROBERTS, Private Sid: 30th Rfts., 18.6.18; Discd., 28.8.19
ROBERTSON, S.S.M. James: 2nd Rfts., 16.5.15; Discd., 30.10.19
ROBERTSON, Gunner James: 13th Rfts., 19.2.16; 14th F.A. Bde., 27.3.16
ROBERTSON, Private John: 25th Rfts., 2.6.17; Discd., 7.10.19
ROBERTSON, Gunner John Crawford: 13th Rfts., 19.2.16; 13th F.A. Bde., 27.3.16
ROBERTSON, Gunner James McDonald: 14th Rfts., 9.3.16; 13th F.A. Bde., 27.3.16
ROBERTSON, Private Leonard John: 8th L.H. Rgt., 14.5.17; A.A.S.C., 4.8.17; A.A.S.C., 28.2.18; Discd., 19.8.19
ROBERTSON, Private Ralph: Original, 8.12.14; killed in action, Gallipoli, 28.6.15
ROBINS, Private Angus Bruce: Original, 8.12.14; killed in action, Gallipoli, 14.11.15
ROBINSON, Private Alfred Henry: Original, 7.12.14; Discd., 29.12.16; wounded, 28.5.15
ROBINSON, Private Blakiston: 5th Rfts., 25.9.15; Discd., 16.8.16
ROBINSON, Private Charles Knight: 4th Rfts., 22.5.15; Discd., 16.8.16
ROBINSON, S/Smith Herbert Sidney: 16th Rfts., N.T.O.S.; 1st D.A.C., 21.11.16
ROBINSON, Private John James: 5th Rfts., 25.9.15; Discd., 24.5.17; wounded, 5.11.15
ROBINSON, Private James Patrick: 6th Rfts., 14.11.15; Discd., 4.10.19; wounded, 28.7.18
ROBINSON, Captain Paul Degge: Original, 14.11.14; Cml. Rgt., 2.11.16
ROBINSON, Private Robert Hall: 25th Rfts., N.T.O.S.; 2nd M.G. Sqdn., 7.6.17
ROBINSON, Corporal Vincent Davy: Original, 8.12.14; 13th F.A. Bde., 27.3.16
ROCHE, Private James: 23rd Rfts., 28.7.17; Imp. Cml. Cps., 29.8.17

HISTORY OF THE 5th LIGHT HORSE REGIMENT. 217

RODERICK, Private Cyril Randall: 28th Rfts., 27.11.17; Discd., 4.9.19
RODGERS, Private Galbraith Phillip: 28th Rfts., 23.5.18; Discd., 4.9.19
ROGERS, Private Arthur William: 28th Rfts., 23.12.17; Discd., 4.9.19
ROGERS. Driver Francis Amos: 17th Rfts., 26.7.16; 1st F.S. Engrs., 19.2.17
ROGERS-HARRISON, Sergeant Kenneth Berkeley: Original, 8.12.14; Discd., 11.3.19
ROOKS, E.R./Cpl. Joseph Henry: 4th Rfts., 22.5.15; Anz. Po! Cps., 3.4.16
ROONAN, Driver Alfred Victor: 16th Rfts., N.T.O.S.; 1st D.A.C., 11.17
ROONEY, T/Far./Cpl. George William: 29th Rfts., 15.4.18; Discd., 17.5.19
ROSE, Private Albert Ernest: 2nd Rfts., 7.7.15; 53rd Bn., 13.4.17
ROSE, Sergeant Gordon: 5th Rfts., 25.9.15; Discd., 23.6.19
ROSE, Gunner George: 11th Rfts., N.T.O.S.; 14th F.A. Bde., 27.3.16
ROSE, Private George William: 2nd Rfts., 14.11.15; killed in action, Gallipoli, 29.11.15
ROSER, Driver Octavius: 13th Rfts., 19.2.16; 13th F.A. Bde., 27.3.16
ROSS, Lieut. Byron John (M.C.): Original, 8.12.14; 12th F.A. Bde., 24.4.16; wounded, 27.6.15, and 7.11.15
ROSS, Gunner Clive Hall: Original, 8.12.14; Discd., 9.12.14; 13th Rfts., 19.2.16; 14th F.A. Bde., 27.3.16
ROSS, Corporal John Henry Zoudo: Original, 8.12.14; Discd., 29.5.16
ROSS, Private Joseph James: 15th Rfts., N.T.O.S.; 13th L.H.R., 2.6.16
ROSS, Gunner Kenneth Stewart: 12th Rfts., 28.12.15; 24th F.A.B., 27.3.16
ROSS, Private Nigel Grafton: Original, 8.12.14; Discd., 26.2.19; wounded, 6.4.18
ROSS, Private Wilfred Wallace: Original, 8.12.14; wounded, 22.5.15; killed in action, Tel-Abu-Dilakh, Palestine, Turkey Asia, 8.11.17
ROUSE, Lieut. Claude Martin: 11th L.H.R, 29.8.15; 11th L.H.R., 22.2.16
ROWE, Private Charles Edward: Original, 8.12.14; Discd., 5.4.16
ROWE, Private Frederick: 4th Rfts., 28.5.15; Discd., 2.4.19; wounded, 28.6.15, and 28.7.18
ROWE, Private Frederick William: 1st L.H.F.A., 25.5.16; 2nd L.H.F.A., 2.12.16; A.A.M.C. (attached), 2.12.16 to 17.2.17
ROWE, Sergeant Thomas William: 11th L.H.R., 29.8.15; 11th L.H.R., 22.2.16
ROWLANDS, Private Thomas Llewellyn: Original, 8.12.14; accidentally killed, Sinai Peninsula, 27.8.16
ROWLEY, Private Arthur William: 7th Rfts., 14.11.15; Discd., 29.10.19
ROWLEY, Private Charles: Original, 8.12.14; Discd., 21.7.20
RUDD, Corporal William Henry: 11th L.H.R, 29.8.15; Demob., U.K., 11.8.16; wounded, 25.9.15
RUDKIN, Sergeant Percy (Mentioned in Despatches): Original, 8.12.14; Demob., U.K., 26.2.19; wounded, 28.6.15, and 15.9.15
RUMMEL, Private Arthur James: Original, 8.12.14; Discd., 6.9.16
RUMMEL, Private Edward: Original, 8.12.14; A.M.D. H'qrs., 21.3.16; A.M.D., H'qrs., 13.7.17; wounded, 27.11.17; died of wounds, 45th Stationary Hosp., El Arish, Egypt, 20.12.17
RUSHWORTH, Corporal Dennis William: 1st Rfts., N.T.O.S.; Aust., 4.10.15; 2nd L.H.R., 6.3.16
RUSSELL, Private Albert: Original, 8.12.14; Discd., 15.4.19
RUSSELL, Private James: 20th Rfts., 12.10.16; Discd., 19.9.19
RUSSELL, Private Michael: 1st Rfts., 7.7.15; 14th F.A.B., 27.3.16; accidentally killed, St. Sylvestre, Cappel, France, 2.9.17
RUSSELL, Driver William: 29th Rfts., N.T.O.S.; 2nd M.G.S., 30.5.18
RUSSELL, L/Cpl. William Cathro Tait: Original, 8.12.14; Discd., 18.7.17
RUSTELL, T/Cpl. William: 16th Rfts., N.T.O.S.; 4th D.A.C., 24.11.16

RUTHERFORD, Captain Douglas Wallace: 1st Rfts., 16.5.15; A.F.C., 25.8.16; wounded, 28.6.15
RUTLEDGE, Private Francis Brian: 10th Rfts., 23.2.16; Discd., 16.6.19
RUTLEDGE, Private Henry Lawrence: 10th Rfts , 23.2.16; Discd., 4.8.19
RUTLEDGE, Private Thomas Richard: 10th Rfts., 23.2.16; wounded, 9.11.17; killed in action, Palestine, 19.4.18
RUTTLEY, Private John George: 30th Rfts., N.T.O.S.; 11th L.H.R., 29.5.18
RYAN, Private Albert: Original, 8.12.14; Discd., 25.7.16; wounded, 16.10.15
RYAN, Captain Augustus Maxwell: Original, 21.11.14; Appt. Term., 19.7.19
RYAN, Private Cornelius James: 20th Rfts., N.T.O.S.; 2nd M.G.S., 6.10.16; died of wounds, Palestine, 4.5.18
RYAN, Far./Sgt. Harold Albert: 3rd Rfts., 29.7.15; Discd., 4.10.19
RYAN, Private Henry Salisbury: 29th Rfts., 4.7.18; Discd., 4.9.19
RYAN, Gunner Joseph: 12th Rfts., 7.1.16; 13th F.A. Bde., 27.3.16
RYAN, Driver James: 18th Rfts., N.T.O.S.; 2nd M.G. Sqdn., 1.8.16
RYAN, Private James Edward: 3rd Rfts., N.T.O.S.; Aust., 13.9.15; 14th L.H.R., 8.5.16
RYAN, Private John Francis: 11th L.H. Rgt., 29.8.15; Discd., 31.5.16
RYAN, Private John Joseph: 12th Rfts., 7.1.16; Discd., 1.3.18
RYAN, E.R./2/Cpl. John Shepherd: 11th L.H. Rgt., 29.8.15; 11th L.H. Rgt., 22.2.16
RYAN, Private John Vallantyne: Original, 8.12.14; Discd., 30.10.18; wounded, 11.9.15
RYAN, Gunner Leslie James: 16th Rfts., N.T.O.S.; 1st D.A.C., 25.6.17
RYAN, Gunner Owen John: 16th Rfts., N.T.O.S.; 3rd D.A.C., 4.8.17; killed in action, Belgium, 11.9.17
RYAN, Driver William: 14th Rfts., 9.3.16; 13th F.A.B., 27.3.16
RYAN, Private William: 14th Rfts., 9.3.16; Cml. Cps., 7.9.16
RYCEN, Sergeant John Henry: 13th Rfts., 19.2.16; 13th F.A. Bde., 27.3.16
RYDER, Private Francis William: 7th Rfts., 10.1.16; Discd., 4.10.19
RYNNE, Gunner Michael: 16th Rfts., N.T.O.S.; Discd., 22.6.17
RYNNE, Driver William Edward: 16th Rfts., N.T.O.S.; 4th D.A.C., 19.11.16
SAIT, Corporal Charles Frederick: 11th L.H. Rgt., 2.10.15; 11th L.H. Rgt., 29.2.16
SALES, Corporal Albert Edward: 1st Rfts., 7.7.15; Demob., U.K., 4.4.19
SANDEMAN, Private John: 9th Rfts., 28.12.15; Discd., 19.2.19
SANDERCOCK, Private James Walter: 6th Rfts., 25.9.15; Discd., 30.11.19; wounded, 9.8.16
SANDERSON, Gunner Isaac John: 9th Rfts., 7.1.16; 13th F.A. Bde., 29.3.16
SAUNDERS, L/Cpl. Joseph Henry John: 18th Rfts., N.T.O.S.; 2nd L.H.B M.G.S., 5.10.16
SAUNDERS, C.S.M. James Leslie: Original, 8.12.14; 26th Btn., 23.5.15; died (cerebro-spinal meningitis), 1.2.16, Egypt.
SAUNDERS, Private Richard William: 28th Rfts., 21.9.17; Discd., 4.9.19
SAUNDERS, T/Cpl. Thomas Henry: Original, 8.12.14; killed in action, Gallipoli, 5.11.15
SAUNDERSON, T/Cpl. Arthur Rodney: 5th Rfts., 23.2.16; 2nd L.H.B. M.G.S., 24.7.16
SAWYER, Private Arthur: 4th Rfts., 22.6.15; Discd., 10.5.16
SCANLAN, Private Lewis William Charles: 11th L.H. Rgt., 29.8.15; Discd., 13.3.16
SCHAFER, Pte. George Conrade: 26th Rfts., N.T.O.S.; Discd., 14.3.19
SCHAFER, Private William Henry: 11th Rfts., 23.2.16; Discd., 4.10.19

HISTORY OF THE 5th LIGHT HORSE REGIMENT.   219

SCHMID, Private John Frederick: 11th L.H. Rgt., 29.8.15; 11th L.H. Rgt., 22.2.16
SCHUCHARD, W.O. (1) Carl (M.S.M., Mentioned in Despatches): Original, 8.12.14; Discd., 4.6.20
SCHWENKE, Private Cyril Clement: 15th Rfts., N.T.O.S.; 4th Cml. Rgt., 2.11.16
SCOTT, 2/Lieut. Andrew Anderson: Original, 8.12.14; Aust., 4.11.15; 25th Btn., 8.8.16; killed in action, Belgium, 4.10.17
SCOTT, Private Alfred Charles: 18th Rfts., 20.8.16; Discd., 19.9.19
SCOTT, Lieut. Cyril Ernest: Original, 8.12.14; Appt. Term., 30.4.19; wounded, 27.6.15
SCOTT, Private Oliver Benjamin: 30th Rfts., 9.7.18; Discd., 28.8.19
SCOTT, Private William Davis: 2nd Rfts., 7.7.15; Discd., 4.10.19; wounded, 6.11.15
SCOTT, Private Wallace Oakhampton: 11th Rfts., 23.2.16; Discd., 30.10.19; wounded, 6.4.18
SEABROOK, Private Harry Reginald: Original, 8.12.14; A.A.O.C., 27.8.17
SEANEY, Private Henry James: 3rd Rfts., 29.7.15; wounded, 5.10.15; killed in action, Gallipoli, 14.11.15
SEANIGER, T/Cpl. Alfred Ernest: 9th Rfts., 23.2.16; Discd., 4.10.19
SEXTON, Sergeant Arthur Richard: 22nd Rfts., 14.3.17; Discd., 12.9.19
SEXTON, A/Bombdr. Norman Charles Robert: 14th Rfts., 9.3.16; 13th F.A. Bde., 27.3.16
SEYMOUR, T/Cpl. George: 21st Rfts., N.T.O.S.; A. Prov. Cps., 15.12.16
SHACKLETON, S.Q.M.S. Robert Wilson: Original, 8.12.14; Discd., 4.10.16
SHADWELL, Pte. Richard James: 11th Rfts., 23.2.16; Discd., 4.10.19
SHAMBROOK, E.R./2/Cpl. Bernard Edward: 14th Rfts., 9.3.16; 13th F.A. Bde., 27.3.16
SHARP, Private David Lindsay: Original, 8.12.14; 25th Btn., 9.4.17; died of wounds, France, 28.4.18
SHARPE, Private Frank: Original, 8.12.14; Discd., 13.9.16
SHAW, Private George Albert: 15th Rfts., 26.7.16; Discd., 27.9.19
SHAW, Driver Harold Herbert: 5th Rfts., 25.9.15, 14/F.A.B., 27.3.16; killed in action, France, 24.4.18
SHAW, Private Hubert William: 25th Rfts., 18.6.19; Discd., 12.9.19
SHEEHAN, Gunner Roy Allen: 16th Rfts., N.T.O.S.; 4/D.A.C., 24.9.16; killed in action, France, 12.5.17
SHEEHAN, Private Thomas: 1st Rfts., 16.5.15; Discd., 29.3.16; wounded, 25.8.15
SHELVEY, Private James: 24th Rfts., N.T.O.S.; 8/Mob. Vet. Sec., 10.3.18
SHEPHERD, Private Raymond Pownall: 22nd Rfts., 11.6.17; Discd., 18.10.19
SHERATON, T/Cpl. Sidney William: 9th Rfts., 3.2.16; Discd., 4.10.19
SHERIDAN, Private Henry Bradley: 28th Rfts., N.T.O.S.; died (fractured skull), Moascar, 24.1.18
SHERIDAN, Private Stanley Henderson: Original, 8.12.14; killed in action, Anzac, 28.6.15
SHERLOCK, Driver Charles: 12th Rfts., 7.1.16; 2/L.H.F. Amb., 25.1.16
SHERWIN, Private Harold Phillip: Original, 8.12.14; killed in action, Gallipoli, 7.11.15
SHERWIN, Private Herbert Vicary: Original; 8.12.14; Discd., 18.8.15
SHORT, Driver John Henry: 13th Rfts., 19.2.16; 14/F.A.B., 27.3.16
SIDDINS, T/Dvr. Joseph Clyde: 20th Rfts., 5.11.16; Discd., 18.9.19
SIDDINS, Sergeant Oswald Threlkeld: 10th Rfts., 28.12.15; Discd., 4.10.19
SIDNEY, T/Tnspt Sergeant Robert Varney D.: Original, 8.12.14; Discd., 26.2.19

SILVERLOCK, T/Sgt. Albert Edward: Original, 8.12.14; Discd., 25.1.20
SIMMS, Corporal William Herbert: 11th Rfts., 28.12.15; Discd., 10.3.19; wounded, 8.11.17; wounded and prisoner of war, 3.5.18
SIMONSON, Private Alfred William G.: 11th Rfts., 23.2.16; Discd., 16.5.19
SIMPSON, Private Cecil Raymond: 7th Rfts., 9.1.16; Discd., 9.10.16
SIMPSON, Private Harry: 3rd Rfts., 29.7.15; wounded, 8.11.15, and 21.11.15; killed in action, Suez Canal Zone, 9.8.16
SIMPSON, Driver William Clyde: 11th L.H.R., 29.8.15; 11th L.H.R., 22.2.16
SINCLAIR, Lieut. Leslie Duncan: Original, 8.12.14; 4/M.G.C., 4.5.17
SING, Private William Edward (D.C.M., C. de G., Belgian, Mentioned in Despatches): Original, 8.12.14; 31st Bn., 4.1.17; wounded, 25.8.15
SINNOT, Private James John Woods: 22nd Rfts., N.T.O.S.; 2/M.C. Sqdn., 21.5.17
SIZER, Driver William Edward: 11th Rfts., 23.2.16; A. Mtd., Div. Trn., 18.2.18
SKETCHLEY, Driver George Ernest: 13th Rfts., 19.2.16; 14/F.A.B., 27.3.16
SKIMMINGS, Bombdr. Martin James: 16th Rfts., N.T.O.S.; 2/D.A.C., 11.12.17
SKIPPER, Private Edmund Gibson: 27th Rfts., 27.11.17; Discd., 4.9.19
SLADEN, Driver Frederick Thomas: 11th Rfts., N.T.O.S.; 2/L.H.R., 8.11.15
SLATTERY, Private John Patrick: 1st Rfts., 16.5.15; 26th Bn., 6.9.16
SLEEMAN, 2nd A.M. Walter Montague: 11th Rfts., 23.2.16; 67th Sqn. A.F.C., 7.10.17
SMALL, Private James (M.M.): 2nd L.H.F. Amb., 2.10.15; Discd., 16.1.20; wounded, 25.9.18
SMALL, Corporal John Lyons Lindesay: 21st Rfts., N.T.O.S.; A.A.S.C., 13.8.17
SMART, Sergeant John (M.M.): 11th Rfts., N.T.O.S.; 14th F.A. Bde., 27.3.16
SMELTZER, Sergeant Thomas: 15th Rfts., N.T.O.S.; 2nd L.H.B.M.G.S., 4.8.16
SMETZER, Private Charles Selby: 21st Rfts., 14.3.17; killed in action, Palestine, 2.5.18
SMITH, Private Albert Edward: 9th Rfts., 23.2.16; Discd., 4.10.19
SMITH, Lieut. Arthur Vincent (Mentioned in Despatches): Original, 8.12.14; Appt. Term., 26.2.19; wounded, 14.7.18
SMITH, L./Cpl. Charles: 24th Rfts., 15.7.17; Discd., 21.8.19
SMITH, E.R./Sgt. Claude Eric: Original, 8.12.14; Aust., 15.11.15; 9th Btn., 7.9.16
SMITH, Sergeant David Kenneth: 28th Rfts., 8.9.17; Discd., 4.9.19
SMITH, T/Cpl. Ernest: 12th Rfts., 23.2.16; Discd., 14.1.20
SMITH, Private Frederick (stated to be F. H. Smithenbecker): 13th Rfts., 19.2.16; 56th Bty., 27.3.16
SMITH, Sergeant Frederick George Leslie: 24th Rfts., 2.7.17; Discd., 12.9.19
SMITH, Gunner Frederick Pentland: 7th Rfts., 14.11.15; 5th F.A. Bde., 10.3.16
SMITH, T/Cpl. George Glenrock: 2nd L.H. Rgt., 8.2.16; Discd., 14.1.20
SMITH, Sergeant Greville James (M.M.): Original, 8.12.14; Discd., 17.12.18; wounded, 6.9.15, and 16.7.17
SMITH, Private Herbert John: G.S. Rfts., 15.2.19; Discd., 19.8.19
SMITH, Driver Henry William: 3rd Rfts., 29.7.15; 32nd Co. A.S.C., 19.2.18
SMITH, Private Henry William: 11th L.H. Rgt, 2.10.15; 11th L.H. Rgt., 6.3.16

HISTORY OF THE 5th LIGHT HORSE REGIMENT. 221

SMITH, Private Harold William: 18th Rfts., N.T.O.S.; Discd., 11.10.16
SMITH, Gunner John Armstrong: 12th Rfts., 25.1.16; 13th F.A. Bde., 27.3.16
SMITH, Private John Henry: 6th Rfts., 1.8.15; 2nd L.H.B.M.G.S., 24.8.16
SMITH, Captain John William: A.A.M.C. (attached), 26.9.18 to 28.10.18, 7.11.18 to 10.1.19, 14.2.19 to 6.3.19
SMITH, Private Richard Robert: 24th Rfts., 15.7.17; Prov. Cps., 13.8.18
SMITH, Private Samuel Stanley: Original, 8.12.14; killed in action, Gallipoli, 29.11.15
SMITH, Private Thomas James: 9th Rfts., 23.2.16; Discd., 21.2.17
SMITH, Driver Thomas Watson: 13th Rfts., 19.2.16; 14th F.A. Bde., 27.3.16
SMOOTHY, Corporal Leslie (Mentioned in Despatches): 11th L.H. Rgt., 2.10.15; 11th L.H. Rgt., 22.2.16
SNEATH, Gunner Robert: 16th Rfts., N.T.O.S.; 12th F.A. Bde., 9.4.17
SNOW, Driver Charles Thomas: Original, 8.12.14; 2nd L.H.F. Amb., 12.8.17
SNOW, Private Francis Charles: Original, 8.12.14; Discd., 29.2.16; wounded, 15.7.15
SNOWDON, Pte. Frederick Thomas: 4th Rfts., 22.5.15; Discd., 5.12.16
SOLLING, Lieut. Rex Aubrey Fritz (M.M.): Original, 8.12.14; Appt. Term., 2.10.19; wounded, 14.6.15
SOLOMON, Private Roy Henry: Original, 8.12.14; wounded, 30.6.15; died of wounds at sea (off Gallipoli), 30.6.15
SOMERFIELD, Driver Henry: 15th Rfts., N.T.O.S.; 1/Fld. Sqdn., 12.10.16
SOMERS, W.O. 2 Robert: Original, 8.12.14; Discd., 29.3.19
SOMERSET, Captain Charles William H. R. (M.C., Mentioned in Despatches): Original, 8.12.14; 1st Bn., 2.3.16
SOUTHAM, Gunner Albert (M.M.): 14th Rfts., 9.3.16; 13th F.A.B., 27.3.16; killed in action, France, 18.9.18
SPEED, Private Robert (M.M.): 22nd Rfts., 14.3.17; Discd., 12.9.19
SPEERING, Private Colin Roy: 27th Rfts., 28.7.17; Discd., 19.6.19
SPEERS, Private Alfred: 11th Rfts., 23.2.16; Discd., 27.9.19
SPENCE, E.R./2/Cpl. Charles Frederick: 11th L.H.R., 29.8.15; 11th L.H.R., 22.2.16
SPENCELEY, Pte. Gordon Thomas: 4th Rfts., 22.5.15; Discd., 12.9.19; wounded, 12.9.15
SPENCER, Driver Henry Charles: 12th Rfts., 7.1.16; 13/F.A.B., 27.3.16
SPENCER, Private James: 11th Rfts., 23.2.16; Discd., 4.10.19
SPILLER, Private Joseph: 1st Rfts., 23.2.16; wounded, 16.7.18; died of wounds, Palestine, 17.7.18
SPILSBURY, Private Gordon Fulton: 10th Rfts., 23.2.16; 2/L.H.B.M.G. Sqdn., 24.7.16
SPORLE, Private Henry Neptune: Original, 8.12.14; Discd., 5.9.19; wounded, 25.11.15, and 7.11.17
SPOTSWOOD, Driver Frank Leslie Somer: 13th Rfts., 19.2.16; 14th F.A.B., 27.3.16
SPREADBOROUGH, Driver Arthur Joseph: 29th Rfts., 31.5.18; Discd., 4.9.19
STAINES, Private Leslie: 8th Rfts., 28.7.17; Discd., 1.11.19
STAINES, Private Oscar Rywong: G.S. Rfts., 13.1.19; Discd., 19.8.19
STALLARD, Gunner William John: Original, 8.12.14; 14/F.A.B., 27.3.16
STANFIELD, Captain Ernest Alfred Field: Original, 8.12.14; Appt. Term., 17.10.17 (to Indian Army)
STANFORD, A/Cpl. Albert: Original, 8.12.14; Aust., 15.11.15; 16th Rfts., N.T.O.S.; 4/D.A.C., 1.11.16

STANLEY, Lieut. Arthur: 3rd Rfts., N.T.O.S.; Aust., 14.11.15; 41st Bn., 22.10.18.
STANLEY, T/Cpl. Gerald William: 4th Rfts., 22.5.15; Discd., 8.10.19; wounded, 28.6.15.
STANLEY, Private Smith: Original, 8.12.14; Discd., 26.2.19.
STANTON, Private John: 26th Rfts., N.T.O.S.; Discd., 22.4.18.
STAPLES, Private Frank: 11th Rfts., 7.1.16; Cml. Cps., 2.11.16.
STAPLETON, Private Robert Thomas: Original, 8.12.14; Discd., 2.4.19; wounded, 9.8.16.
STAUNTON, Private Patrick Francis: Original, 8.12.14; Discd., 24.3.16
STEDDY, Gunner George Stanley: 3rd Rfts., 29.7.15; 14th F.A.B., 27.3.16.
STEELE, Driver Bertram Rudolph D.: Original, 8.12.14; 14th F.A.B., 27.3.16; died of wounds, France, 10.6.18
STEELE, Private Joseph: 11th L.H.R., 29.8.15; 11th L.H.R., 1.3.16
STEELE, Private Joseph Maitland: 6th Rfts., 25.9.15; Discd., 4.9.18; wounded, 3.5.18.
STEELE, Private William George: 9th Rfts., 18.1.16; killed in action, Dueidar, 5.8.16
STEELE, Private William James: 15th Rfts., N.T.O.S.; 12th Co. I.C.C., 15.7.16; 3rd Cml. Btn., 28.7.18; Discd., 27.9.19
STEEMSON, Private Edward Arthur: 7th Rfts., 14.11.15; Discd., 4.10.19; wounded, 21.11.15
STELEY, Private Robert Charles Abel: 3rd Div. Cav., 15.4.18; Discd., 19.9.19
STEPHAN, Private August William: G.S. Rfts., 14.10.18; Discd., 20.8.19
STEPHAN, Private Herman William Fredrick: G.S. Rfts., 9.10.18; Discd., 20.8.19
STEPHSON, Private Walter Harold: 21st Rfts., 21.4.17; Discd., 16.4.19
STEVEN, Captain James (Mentioned in Despatches): Original, 8.12.14; 1st F.S. Engrs., 9.12.16.
STEVENS, Private Cecil: 24th Rfts., N.T.O.S.; Dental Unit, 24.6.18
STEVENS, Private Harold Rowton: 11th L.H. Rgt., 2.10.15; 11th L.H. Rgt., 22.2.16; killed in action, Sinai Pen., 7.8.16
STEVENS, Private Robert William Pellow: 15th Rfts., 20.8.16; Discd., 27.9.19
STEWART, Gunner Ewen Gore: 11th Rfts., 18.1.16; 14th F.A. Bde., 27.3.16
STEWART, Private James Alexander: Original, 8.12.14; died (bronchopneumonia), Port Said, 1.2.15
STEWART, Sergeant Robert Joseph: Original, 8.12.14; Discd., 26.2.19; wounded, 2.7.15, and 9.8.16
STEWART, W.O. (1) Samuel John: 13th Rfts., 19.2.16; 4th Div. A.O.C., 18.3.16; killed in action, France, 2.5.18
STEWART, Private William: Original, 8.12.14; killed in action, Gallipoli, 13.8.15
STINSON, Private Laurence: 11th Rfts., N.T.O.S.; died (meningitis), Suez, 19.12.15
STIRLING, Private David: 11th L.H. Rgt., 29.8.15; Discd., 9.8.16
STIRLING, L/Cpl. William Lorne: 15th Rfts., 20.8.16; Discd., 21.8.19
STONE, Private Stewart: 11th L.H. Rgt., 29.8.15; 11th L.H. Rgt., 23.3.16
STOKER, Private James Thomas: 30th Rfts., 18.6.18; Discd., 8.9.19
STOKES, Driver Albert: 14th Rfts., 9.3.16; 13th F.A. Bde., 27.3.16
STOODLEY, Private Douglas Graham Norman: G.S. Rfts., 15.2.19; Discd., 19.8.19
STORER, Private Alfred Bertram: 2nd Rfts., 7.7.15; 49th Btn., 17.10.16
STOREY, Private Clarence Henry: 20th Rfts., 12.10.16; Discd., 19.9.19; wounded, 23.4.17

HISTORY OF THE 5th LIGHT HORSE REGIMENT. 223

STOREY, Private George Harry: Original, 8.12.14; Discd., 27.10.17; wounded, 28.5.15
STOREY, Lieut. George Percival (M.C.): Original, 8.12.14; 47th Btn., 2.4.16
STRAHAN, Private David: 28th Rfts., N.T.O.S.; A.A.S.C., 13.8.17
STRANG, Corporal John Thomson Fletcher: Original, 8.12.14; Aust., 5.9.15; 47th Btn., 19.4.17; killed in action, Belgium, 7.6.17
STRANGE, Private George: 3rd Rfts., 29.7.15; 14th F.A. Bde., 27.3.16
STREET, Private Joseph Dandy: 2nd Rfts., 16.5.15; wounded, 23.8.15; killed in action, Gallipoli, 5.11.15
STREETER, E.R./Cpl. Albert Henry: 15th Rfts., N.T.O.S., Discd., 16.9.19
STREMES, E.R./2/Cpl. Thomas Ernest: Original, 8.12.14; A. Prov. Cps., 1.1.17
STRIKE, Private Edward Henry: 11th L.H.R., 2.10.15; 11th L.H.R., 26.2.16
STRIKE, Driver Leslie: 1st Rfts., 16.5.15; A.S.C., 19.2.17
STRIKE, T/S.Q.M.S. William Percy: 11th L.H.R., 29.8.15; Aust., 4.11.15; 25th Rfts., N.T.O.S.; 11th L.H.R., 8.7.17
STRONG, Private Joseph Charles: Original, 8.12.14; 49th Btn., 17.10.16
STUBBS, Corporal Eric Charles: 11th Rfts., 21.2.16; 47th Bn., 3.10.16; 47th Bn., 1.8.17; Discd., 4.10.19
SULEY, Private James Ernest: Original, 8.12.14; Discd., 2.8.16; wounded, 20.9.15
SULLIVAN, Sergeant Ernest Lawrence: 11th Rfts., 23.2.16; Discd., 27.9.19
SULLIVAN, Private Henry Ernest: 10th Rfts., 28.12.15; 1/F. Sqdn., 29.6.16
SULLIVAN, Private John: 7th Rfts., 23.2.16; Discd., 20.10.19
SULLIVAN, Private James Edward: 12th Rfts., 1.2.16; Discd., 27.9.19; wounded, 9.8.16
SUMMERS, Gunner John (M.M.): 14th Rfts., N.T.O.S.; 13th F.A.B., 28.3.16
SUMMONS, Gunner Edward John: 12th Rfts., 7.1.16; 14th F.A.B., 27.3.16
SUNNER, Private Benjamin: 9th Rfts., 18.1.16; Discd., 3.5.19
SURAWSKI, Driver Martin Theodore: 16th Rfts., N.T.O.S.; 1/F.A.B., 4.6.17
SWALLING, Private William Eldridge: 21st Rfts., 11.6.17; Discd., 7.3.18
SWAYNE, Corporal John Eric: 1st Rfts., 16.5.15; Discd., 26.2.19
SWEEPER, Gunner Samuel: 16th Rfts., N.T.O.S.; 1st D.A.C., 13.3.17
SWEET, T/Sgt. James Inglis: Original, 8.12.14; Discd., 11.7.19; wounded, 19.4.18
SWINDELLS, Private Harry James: Original, 8.12.14; Discd., 25.10.16
SWORD, Lieut. Robert Stevenson: 49th Bn., 2.4.16; 3/D.A.C., 20.5.17
SYKES, Private Henry Tyldesley: Original, 8.12.14; Discd., 28.6.16; wounded, 31.5.15
SYKES, Private Thomas Alfred: 4th Rfts., 22.5.15; died at sea (off Fremantle, W.A.), phthisis, 28.12.15
TALBOT, Private Harold Benjamin: 5th Rfts., 25.9.15; 14th F.A.B., 27.3.16
TALBOT, Private James: 9th Rfts., N.T.O.S.; Discd., 1.3.15
TANNER, Sergeant James Edward: 11th Rfts., 18.1.16; 13th F.A.B., 27.3.16
TANWAN, Private Edwin: 18th Rfts., N.T.O.S.; 52nd Bn., 31.7.16
TAPPENDEN, T/Cpl. James: 14th Rfts., 9.3.16; Discd., 8.6.19
TARDENT, Lieut. Jules Louis (C. de G., French): 11th L.H.R., 29.8.15; Aust., 13.12.15; 42nd Bn., 5.6.16

HISTORY OF THE 5th LIGHT HORSE REGIMENT.

TAYLOR, Private Arthur John: 2nd L.H.R., 23.1.16; 12th M.G.C., 2.8.16
TAYLOR, Private Charles Alfred: Original, 8.12.14; wounded, 20.11.15; died of wounds, Alexandria, 1.12.15
TAYLOR, E.R./Sgt. Charles Edward: Original, 8.12.14; 2nd M.G.S., 9.4.18
TAYLOR, Lieut. Frederick Anthony James W. (Mentioned in Despatches, Order of the Nile, 4th Class): Original, 8.12.14; Aust., 3.1.16; 18th Rfts., 17.8.16; Appt. Term., 30.11.18; wounded, 8.11.15.
TAYLOR, Driver Francis George: 13th Rfts., 19.2.16; 13th F.A.B., 27.3.16
TAYLOR, Private Richard: 11th L.H.R., 29.8 15; 11th L.H.R., 22.2.16; died of wounds, Palestine, 12.11.17
TAYLOR, Private Richard: G.S. Rfts., 15.2.19; Discd., 18.8.19
TAYLOR, Sergeant William Edward: 24th Rfts., N.T.O.S.; 2nd L.H.R., 27.7.17
TEALE, Driver Harry Stanley: 12th Rfts., 23.2.16; 2nd L.H.F.A., 15.3.17; A.A.M.C. (attached), 7.11.18 to 14.1.19
TEARE, Private Frederick: 30th Rfts., 4.7.18; Discd., 28.8.19
TEGGE, Gunner George: Original, 8.12.14; 13th F.A.B., 27.3.16
TEMPLE, Private William Fairbairn: 11th L.H.R., 2.10.15; 11th L.H.R., 6.3.16; killed in action, Palestine, 30.3.18
TEMPLETON, Private Robert: 20th Rfts., N.T.O.S.; 2nd M.G.S., 6.10.16
TERRY, Private Alexander McDonald: 5th G.S. Rfts., 13.2.19; Discd., 21.9.19
TESMER, Private John Alfred: 11th Rfts., N.T.O.S.; 17th Coy I.C.C., 7.2.17
THOMAS, T/Cpl. Arthur Morris: 13th Rfts., 19.2.16; 13th F.A.B., 27.3.16
THOMAS, Driver John: 22nd Rfts., N.T.O.S.; B. Trp. Sig. Sqn., 9.3.17
THOMPSON, Private Andrew: Original, 8.12.14; A. Prov Cps., 17.12.17
THOMPSON, Gunner Albert Wallace: 14th Rfts., 9.3.16; 13th F.A.B., 27.3.16.
THOMPSON, Private Cecil Stanley Joseph: 11th Rfts., 31.12.15; 13th F.A.B., 27.3.16
THOMPSON, Driver John: 26th Rfts., N.T.O.S.; 34th Coy A.A.S.C., 31.8.17
THOMPSON, Private John Cornelius: 5th Rfts., 28.8.15; Discd., 2.11.19
THOMPSON, Corporal Robert: 11th L.H.R., 29.8.15; 4th Aust. Camel Reg., 2.11.16.
THOMPSON, Private Rowland Hamilton: 28th Rfts., 12.5.18; Discd, 14.9.19
THOMPSON, Far./Sgt. Thomas: 11th L.H.R., 29.8.15; 11th L.H.R., 6.3.16
THOMPSON, Private Thomas Edward: 11th Rfts., 31.12.15; Discd, 25.10.16
THOMSON, Corporal John Arthur: 11th L.H. Rgt., 29.8.15; 11th L.H. Rgt., 22.2.16; wounded, 8.10.15; died of wounds, Palestine, 8.11.17
THOMSON, Private Parker: 12th Rfts., 14.2.16; Discd., 11.10.16
THOMSON, Gunner Robert: 12th Rfts., 7.1.16; 13th F.A. Bde., 27.3.16
THOMSON, Private Robert: 27th Rfts., N.T.O.S.; Discd., 18.7.17
THORN, Corporal Kenneth Stanley Willis: 11th L.H. Rgt., 29.8.15; 11th L.H. Rgt., 22.2.16; killed in action, Palestine, 25.9.18
THORNE, Private Neil Ernest Albert: 15th Rfts., N.T.O.S.; 17th I.C.C., 7.2.17; died after dis., 2.7.21
THORNTON, T/Cpl. Frederick: 1st Rfts., 16.5.15; 2nd L.H.B.M.G.S., 12.9.16
TIBBEY, Private George Thomas: 2nd Rfts., 7.7.15; Aust., 29.1.16; 15th Btn., 21.10.16

HISTORY OF THE 5th LIGHT HORSE REGIMENT.   225

TIDMARSH, S.S.M. Reuben Herbert Edward: Original, 8.12.14; Discd., 24.2.19
TIERNEY, L/Cpl. Michael Joseph:, Original, 8.12.14; died (pneumonia), Heliopolis, 6.3.15
TOCHER, Private William Alexander: 11th Rfts., 23.2.16; Discd., 27.9.19
TOMLEY, Private John: 12th Rfts., 7.1.16; 2nd L.H.B.H.Q., 7.11.16; 2nd L.H.B.H.Q., 9.7.17; Discd., 21.8.19; wounded, 19.4.18
TOMPKINS, Private Levi Joseph: 15th Rfts., N.T.O.S.; 4th Cml. Rgt., 2.11.16; 3rd Cml. Bn., 28.7.18; Discd., 8.6.19
TONKS, Private Arthur James: 25th Rfts., 2.7.17; Discd., 28.7.19
TOOHEY, A/Cpl. Patrick John: 19th Rfts., N.T.O.S.; Cml. Cps., 7.9.16
TOOTH, Captain Eric Noel: Original, 8.12.14; 1st F.S.A.M.D., 27.5.16; wounded, 27.6.15, and 10.11.15
TOPP, Private Cecil Floyd: 15th Rfts., N.T.O.S.; 1st F.S. Engrs., 27.6.16
TOSI, Sergeant Percy Thomas: Original, 8.12.14; Discd., 10.12.14; 11th Rfts., N.T.O.S.; Discd., 14.2.17
TOURLE, Private John Morse: 11th L.H. Rgt., 2.10.15; 11th L.H. Rgt., 22.2.16; wounded, 8.11.15
TOWNER, Sergeant Alfred George: Original, 8.12.14; Discd., 12.4.19
TOWNLEY, Lieut. Dudley Arnold Langford: Original, 8.12.14; 1st Anz. C.L.H.R., 7.7.16
TRAIL, Gunner Albert: 9th Rfts., 18.1.16; 14th F.A. Bde., 27.3.16
TRAPP, Private Peter: 19th Rfts., N.T.O.S.; Cml. Cps., 7.9.16; 3rd Cml. Bn., 28.7.18; Discd., 19.9.19
TRAPPES, Private Joseph Byrnand: 27th Rfts., 27.11.17; Discd., 4.9.19
TREICHEL, Private George: 7th Rfts., 14.11.15; 12th Co. I.C.C., 15.7.16; 3rd Cml. Bn., 28.7.18; Discd., 4.10.19; wounded, 21.11.15
TRELOAR, L/Cpl. Alfred Vivian: 7th Rfts., 14.11.15; Discd., 19.3.18; wounded, 5.12.17
TREMBATH, Private William: Original, 8.12.14; Discd., 19.7.16; wounded, 27.6.15
TREVETHAN, Driver Stanley Fletcher: 5th Rfts., 25.9.15; 2nd Sig. Trp., 13.6.16
TROTT, Private Leslie Arthur: 24th Rfts., 6.6.19; Discd., 4.9.19
TROUT, Lieut. Leslie Gordon: 15th Rfts., N.T.O.S.; Cyc. Btn., 1.5.16
TROY, Gunner John Francis: 8th Rfts., 10.1.16; 13th F.A. Bde., 27.3.16
TUBB, Private Herbert: 27th Rfts., 12.12.17; Demob., U.K., 28.9.19
TUBMANN, Chaplain Francis de Moag: Chaplain (attached), 8.12.14 to 10.9.15
TUCKER, Driver Ewart Thomas: 22nd Rfts., N.T.O.S.; 9/Mob. Vet. Sec., 17.6.17
TURNER, S/Smth. George: 28th Rfts., 28.2.18; Discd., 4.9.19
TURNER, Private Wilfred: 28th Rfts., 28.2.18; Discd., 4.9.19
TWINE, Driver Ralph Charles: 11th Rfts., 26.1.16; Discd., 16.8.16
TWIST, Sapper William George: 10th Rfts., 23.2.16; 2/Sig. Trp., 26.11.16; died of wounds, Sinai Pen., 17.4.17
TYLER, Private William Bernard: 9th Rfts., 23.2.16; killed in action, Palestine, 10.11.17
UHLMANN, Bombdr. Thomas Percy: 11th Rfts., 9.3.16; 15th F.A.B., 25.10.16
UNDERHILL, Sergeant James Foster: 8th Rfts., 14.11.15; Discd., 4.10.19; wounded 2.5.18
UREN, Private Richard: 12th Rfts., 23.2.16; Discd., 27.9.19
UREN, Private William: 12th Rfts., 23.2.16; Discd., 18.4.17
URQUHART, Far./Cpl. Alexander John T.: Original, 8.12.14; Discd., 26.2.19

URQUHART, Private William Thomas B.: 1st Rfts., 16.5.15; Discd., 7.8.15 (granted Commission, Imperial Army)
VAUGHAN, Private Jack: 20th Rfts., N.T.O.S.; 4/Camel Rgt., 21.11.16
VENESS, E.R./Sgt. Henry Albert R.: 28th Rfts., 18.11.17; 8th L.H.R., 12.3.19
VIDLER, Private John Thomas: Original, 8.12.14; Discd., 26.2.19; wounded (acc.), 2.7.18
VINES, Private Thomas: Original, 8.12.14; Discd., 24.2.19; wounded, 27.6.15
VIZER, Private Edward Holmes: Original, 8.12.14; 12/Coy. I.C.C., 15.7.16; 12/Coy. I.C.C., 19.11.18; Discd., 15.4.19
VOWLES, Private William Robert: 6th Rfts., 14.11.15; 2/L.H.M.G.S., 1.8.16; wounded, 15.12.15
WADE, Private Edward: 22nd Rfts., N.T.O.S.; 2nd M.G. Sqdn., 21.5.17
WADE, Sergeant Walter Franklin: 10th Rfts., 23.2.16; Discd., 4.10.19; wounded, 6.12.17
WAIN, T/Sgt. Joseph Harvey: 8th Rfts., 23.2.16; Anz. Mtd. D.H.Q., 1.6.18
WAINWRIGHT, Private Norman: 1st Rfts., 16.5.15; Discd., 6.9.16; wounded, 25.11.15
WAINWRIGHT, Private Robert: 12th Rfts., 23.2.16; Discd., 11.7.19
WAITE, Captain Frederick Mitchell (M.C., Mentioned in Despatches): Original, 8.12.14; Aust., 21.5.17; 9th L.H.R., 17.1.18; Appt. Term., 18.8.19; wounded, 5.8.16, and 26.3.17
WAKE, Driver Sydney Jack: 14th Rfts., 9.3.16; 14th F.A. Bde., 27.3.16
WAKEFIELD, Corporal Philip Dunster: 9th Rfts., 28.12.15; Discd., 4.10.19
WALDECK, S.S.M. Raymond Miller: Original, 8.12.14; Discd., 28.3.17
WALDON, Private William: Original, 8.12.14; Discd., 26.2.19
WALKER, Private Clarence: 10th Rfts., 18.1.16; Discd., 4.10.19; wounded, 6.4.18
WALKER, Private Cyril Campbell: 10th Rfts., 23.2.16; Discd., 16.6.19; wounded, 9.8.16
WALKER, L/Cpl. Duncan Bettie: 1st Rfts., 16.5.15; Discd., 15.4.19; wounded, 28.6.15
WALKER, Gunner Francis Alyn: 9th Rfts., N.T.O.S.; 13th F.A. Bde., 27.3.16
WALKER, Gunner George: 13th Rfts., 19.2.16; 13th F.A. Bde., 27.3.16.
WALKER, Driver Henry Frederick: 10th Rfts., 29.12.15; 13th F.A. Bde., 27.3.16.
WALKER, Gunner Harold George: 9th Rfts., N.T.O.S.; 13th F.A. Bde., 27.3.16.
WALKER, Driver Harry James: 17th Rfts., 11.12.16; Discd., 19.9.19; wounded, 26.3.17
WALKER, Private Reginald George: 7th Rfts., 14.11.15; 1st Div. Art. H.Q., 14.11.15; 1st D.A.H.Q., 11.2.16; Discd., 6.6.18; wounded, 2.12.17
WALKER Driver Stephen Thomas: 12th Rfts., 7.1.16; 14th F.A. Bde., 27.3.16
WALKER, Private Thomas Allan: Original, 8.12.14; killed in action, Gallipoli, 11.9.15
WALKER, Private William Frederick: Imp. Cml. Cps., 28.7.18; Discd., 19.9.19
WALL, Private David Damke: 16th Rfts., 28.3.17; Discd., 30.9.19
WALLACE, Private George: 7th Rfts., 14.11.15; Discd., 4.3.18
WALLACE, E.R./2/Cpl. Stanley Carl: 5th Rfts., 2.8.15; Prov. Cps., 25.5.18
WALLACE, Private William: 23rd Rfts., 28.7.17; Discd., 19.9.19

HISTORY OF THE 5th LIGHT HORSE REGIMENT.   227

WALLACE, Driver William Alfred: 22nd Rfts., N.T.O.S.; 38th A.S.C., 6.9.17
WALLER, Gunner Charles George: 16th Rfts., N.T.O.S.; died (cerebrospinal fever), France, 13.4.17
WALLER, Private William Edward: 7th Rfts., 14.11.15; 2nd L.H. Bde., 18.4.16
WALLER, E.R./Sgt. Walter Rupert: 21st Btn., N.T.O.S.; Discd., 25.10.19
WALSH, T/Cpl. Berner Nugent Theodore: 20th Rfts., N.T.O.S.; 2nd M.G. Sqdn., 6.10.16
WALSH, Private Callaghan Baird: G.S. Rfts., 15.9.18; Discd., 8.5.19
WALSH, Private Edward Joseph: 16th Rfts., N.T.O.S.; 4th Cml. Rgt., 2.11.16
WALSH, Private Frederick William: Original, 8.12.14; Discd., 2.4.19
WALSH, Private Michael: 25th Rfts., 2.7.17; Discd., 12.9.19
WALTERS, Private Stanley Edward: 11th L.H. Rgt., 29.8.15; Discd., 13.12.16
WALTON, Private Allan Roger: 20th Rfts., 12.10.16; Discd., 3.3.18; wounded, 23.4.17
WAPPETT, Private George Andrew: Original, 8.12.14; Discd., 4.4.17
WAPPETT, Private Walter Anthony: 11th Rfts., 30.6.16; Discd., 4.8.19
WARBROOK, Private James: 6th Rfts., 14.11.15; Discd., 13.9.16
WARD, Private Arthur Ebenezer: 14th Rfts., 9.3.16; 1st B.M.G. Sqdn., 11.9.16
WARD, Private Charles Dixon: 11th Rfts., 4.6.16; 9th Btn., 27.10.17; killed in action, France, 19.9.18
WARD, Private Edward Joseph: 21st Rfts., N.T.O.S.; 2nd M.G. Sqdn., 10.7.17
WARD, Private Frederick: 16th Rfts., N.T.O.S.; Discd., 1.1.18
WARD, Private Patrick: 17th Rfts., 20.8.16; Discd., 19.9.19
WARDELL, Private William Wilkinson: 22nd Rfts., 28.7.17; Discd., 22.4.18
WARDROP, Private Sydney James: 8th Rfts., 10.1.16; Discd., 4.10.19
WARE, Driver George Henry: 6th Rfts., 25.9.15; Discd., 27.5.19; wounded, 17.9.16
WARING, B.S.M. Hubert Parker: 13th Rfts., 19.2.16; 13th F.A. Bde., 27.3.16
WARMAN, Driver Burton Thomas (M.M.): 12th Rfts, 7.1.16; 14th F.A. Bde., 27.3.16
WARNES, Sergeant Horace William Stanley: Original, 8.12.14; Discd., 24.1.19; wounded, 23.8.18
WARNEMINDE, Lieut. Claude James: 11th L.H. Rgt., 29.8.15; Aust., 29.1.16; 9th Btn., 14.2.18; died (gas poisoning), France, 13.3.18
WARREN, Private Frances Norman: 3rd Rfts., 29.7.15; Discd., 11.3.16
WARRENER, Sergeant John William: 16th Rfts., N.T.O.S.; 15th F.A. Bde., 25.10.16; died of wounds, France, 18.10.17
WASLEY, Private David Edwin: 6th Rfts., 25.9.15; Demob., U.K., 24.8.19
WATERS, S/Smith: Andrew Arthur (D.C.M.): 20th Rfts., 12.10.16; Discd., 15.10.19; wounded, 25.9.18
WATERS, Gunner George Frederick: 12th Rfts., 7.1.16; 13th F.A. Bde., 27.3.16
WATERS, Private Walter: 24th Rfts., 15.7.17; Discd., 12.9.19
WATKIN, Private William Edward: 28th Rfts., N.T.O.S.; Discd., 16.8.18
WATKINS, Private George Harry: 4th Rfts., 22.5.15; 14th F.A. Bde., 27.3.16; wounded, 27.6.15
WATSON, Private Alfred: Original, 8.12.14; 2nd L.H.F. Amb., 8.9.15; killed in action, France, 4.7.18
WATSON, Private Duncan: 17th Rfts., N.T.O.S.; 2nd L.H.B.M.G.S., 12.9.16
WATSON, Private Ebb: 25th Rfts, 2.7.17; Discd., 12.9.19

WATSON, Private Eric Stanley: 1st Rfts., 16.5.15; died of wounds, Anzac Cove, 26.5.15
WATSON, Gunner Joseph George: 12th Rfts., 7.1.16; 14th F.A. Bde., 27.3.16.
WATSON, Lieut. Richard Pilkington: 2nd L.H.F. Amb., 30.8.18; Appt. Term., 16.1.20
WATSON, Private William Walter: 11th L.H. Rgt., 29.8.15; 11th L.H. Rgt., 22.2.16
WATT, Private Herbert Crook: 14th Rfts., 9.3.16; died (broncho-pneumonia), Palestine, 28.10.18
WATT, Private James Bannerman: 11th L.H. Rgt., 29.8.15; 11th L.H. Rgt., 1.7.16
WATTERS, Private Frederick Theodore: Original, 8.12.14; wounded, 28.6.15; died of wounds at sea, 28.6.15
WATTS, Private Harry (stated to be Charles Victor Broster): 14th Rfts., 9.3.16; 14th F.A. Bde., 27.3.16
WATTS, Sergeant Sydney: 2nd Rfts., 7.7.15; 49th Btn., 17.10.16
WATTS, Private Walter Reginald: 29th Rfts., N.T.O.S.; Discd., 17.5.19
WEATHERLEY, Private Robert: 11th Rfts., 23.2.16; Discd., 21.6.19
WEBB, Driver Albert James: 12th Rfts., 11.2.16; 13th F.A. Bde., 27.3.16
WEBB, Private Raymond Francis: 15th Rfts., N.T.O S.; 12th Co. I.C.C., 15.7.16; died of wounds, Alexandria, 28.4.17
WEBB, Gunner William: 13th Rfts., 19.2.16; 13th F.A. Bde., 27.3.16
WEBB, Private William Purcell: 11th L.H. Rgt., 2.10.15; 11th L.H. Rgt., 22.2.16
WEBER, Private Bertram George: 27th Rfts., 28.7.17; Discd., 4.9.19
WEBSTER, Lieut. Tom: Original, 8.12.14; wounded, 7.11.17; died of wounds, Palestine, 8.11.17
WEDDELL, Gunner William: 7th Rfts., 14.11.15; 14th F.A. Bde., 27.3.16
WEEKS, Private Ernest William: 2nd Rfts., 29.7.15; Discd., 4.10.19
WEEKS, Gunner John: 16th Rfts., N.T.O S.; 1st D.A.C., 15.6.17
WEIR, Private William Kerr: 12th Rfts., 7.1.16; 12th Co. I.C.C. 15.7.16
WEISS, L./Sgt. Leslie Edgar: Original, 8 12.14; 2nd L.H.F. Amb., 2.12.16; A.A.M.C. (attached), 2.12.16 to 15.11.18
WELBY, Gunner Albert Joseph: 16th Rfts., N.T.O.S.; 14th F.A. Bde., 29.1.17
WELCH, T/Cpl. Wilfrid Keith: Original, 8.12 14; Discd., 27.11.19; wounded, 27.6.15, and 2.5.18
WELLS. T/Cpl. Cecil: 23rd Rfts., 1.8.17; Discd., 4.9.19
WELLS. Sergeant Eric: 11th L.H. Rgt. 2.10.15; 11th L.H. Rgt. 14.9.18
WELLS, Driver James Weston: Original, 8.12.14; Aust., 31.8.15; 5th Btn., 23.11.15
WELLS, T/Cpl. Samuel John: 11th L.H. Rgt., 2.10.15; 11th L.H. Rgt., 22.2.16
WEST, Private George: 30th Rfts., 9.7.18; Discd., 29.9.19
WEST, T/Dvr. William: 22nd Rfts., N.T.O.S.; 2nd M.G. Sqdn., 21.5.17
WESTAWAY, Private William Henry: 14th Rfts., 9.3.16; 13th L.H. Rgt., 2.6.16; 13th L.H. Rgt., 26.7.16; wounded, 30.9.17; died of wounds, Palestine, 4.12.17
WESTHOVEN, Private Frank Claude: 5th Rfts., 14.11.15; Anz. Mtd. D.H.Q, 26.3.16; Anz. Mtd. D.H.Q., 11.4.17; Discd., 18.3.19
WETHERELL, Captain Henry: Original, 8.12.14; Appt. Term., 5.10.19
WHARRAM, Private James Henry: 11th L.H. Rgt., 29.8.15; 11th L.H. Rgt., 2.2.16
WHEATLEY, A/Cpl. Thomas Pilgrim: 14th Rfts., N.T.O.S.; 9th Btn., 30.12.16
WHEELER, Private John Joseph: 12th Rfts., 7.1.16; Discd., 1.3.19; wounded, 28.3.18

WHELAN, Sapper Percy: 24th Rfts., N.T.O.S.; 1st Sig. Sqdn., 14.8.17
WHILES, T/Cpl. Sidney Herbert: 3rd Rfts., 3.8.15; Discd., 8.10.19
WHITBREAD, F/Sgt. William Salisbury: Original, 8.12.14; wounded, 8.11.17; died of wounds, Palestine, 9.11.17
WHITE, Driver Arthur Cecil Fredrick: 27th Rfts., N.T.O.S.; 32nd Co. Anz. D.T., 24.9.17
WHITE, Private George: 27th Rfts., N.T.O.S.; A.M.D.T., 13.8.17
WHITE, Private Thomas: Original, 8.12.14; Discd., 29.3.19; wounded, 9.8.16
WHITE, Private Walter Richard: 20th Rfts., 12.10.16; 2nd L.H.B.H.Q., 21.3.17
WHITEWAY, Driver Wilfred Rundle: Original, 8.12.14; Discd., 26.2.19
WHITFIELD, Private Charles: Original, 8.12.14; 68th Sqn. A.F.C., 17.11.16
WHITTON, Private Joseph Henry: 4th Rfts., 22.5.15; Discd., 23.6.19
WICKINS, Private Horace Vere: 11th Rfts., 20.8.16; A. & N.Z. Div. Trn., 13.8.17
WICKS, Gunner Bert: 12th Rfts., 7.1.16; 14th F.A. Bde., 27.3.16; killed in action, France, 4.9.17
WIELAND, Private William John: 17th Rfts., N.T.O.S.; Discd., 12.9.16
WILBY, Bombdr. Roy Hubert: 13th Rfts., 19.2.16; 13th F.A. Bde., 27.3.16
WILDHABER, L/Sgt. John George: Original, 8.12.14; 47th Btn., 3.10.16
WILKINS, Driver Victor George: 16th Rfts., N.T.O.S.; 2nd L.H.B. M.G.S., 1.8.16
WILKINS, Driver William Charles: 14th Rfts., 9.3.16; 14th F.A. Bde., 27.3.16
WILLIAMS, Driver Arthur: 13th Rfts., 19.2.16; 13th F.A. Bde., 27.3.16
WILLIAMS, Private Alan Charles: Original, 8.12.14; killed in action, Gallipoli, 28.6.15
WILLIAMS, Arm./Sgt. Albert Edward: 12th Rfts., 7.1.16; 2nd L.H.B. M.G.S., 24.7.16
WILLIAMS, Private Allan Herbert: 1st Rfts., 16.5.15; 47th Btn., 3.10.16
WILLIAMS, Private Bartholomew: 9th Rfts., 23.2.16; Discd., 4.10.19
WILLIAMS, S/Smith. Clifford Rupert: 14th Rfts., 9.3.16; 2nd M.G. Sqdn., 7.4.17
WILLIAMS,, Private Charles Gordon: Original, 8.12.14; Discd., 14.6.16
WILLIAMS, Driver Esau: 13th Rfts., 19.2.16; 13th F.A. Bde., 27.3.16
WILLIAMS, Private Edward Homer: Original, 8.12.14; killed in action, Gallipoli, 28.6.15
WILLIAMS, L/Cpl. Henry Ceaton: Original, 8.12.14; Discd., 13.9.16; wounded, 28.6.15
WILLIAMS, Private Herbert John: 4th Rfts., 22.5.15; Discd., 21.11.16; wounded, 17.8.15
WILLIAMS, T/Cpl. John: 22nd Rfts., N.T.O.S.; A.S.C. H.Q. Anz. Mtd. Div. Trn., 31.7.17
WILLIAMS, Corporal James Gordon: 25th Rfts., N.T.O.S.; 2nd L.H. Rgt., 24.5.17
WILLIAMS, Private James Victor: 24th Rfts., N.T.O.S.; A.A.S.C., 20.8.17
WILLIAMS, Private Michael: 29th Rfts., 15.4.18; Discd., 4.9.19
WILLIAMS, Private Philip Carrington: Original, 8.12.14; 6th Mob. Vet. Sec., 6.2.17; died after dis.
WILLIAMS, L/Cpl. Robert Glen: 8th Rfts., 10.1.16; killed in action, Palestine, 8.11.17
WILLIAMS, Lieut. Thomas Henry Burke: Original, 8.12.14; Appt. Term., 5.11.19
WILLIAMS, T/Cpl. Thomas John: 9th Rfts., 23.2.16; Discd., 5.8.19; wounded, 17.4.17

WILLIAMS, Driver William Patrick Joseph: 8th Rfts., 10.1.16; 14th F.A. Bde., 27.3.16
WILLIAMSON, A/Bdr. Alexander: 16th Rfts., N.T.O.S.; 3rd D.A.C., 15.9.17
WILLIAMSON, Cpl. Andrew: 16th Rfts., N.T.O.S.; 3rd D.A.C., 15.9.17; killed in action, France, 16.9.17
WILLIAMSON, Pte Eardley Pearson: Original, 8.12.14; Aust., 13.12.15; 8th L.H. Rgt., 8.3.16
WILLIAMSON, Lieut. Rennard Barre: 3rd Rfts., 7.7.15; Appt. Term., 19.6.19
WILLIS, Lieut. William Louis (M.M.): 14th Rfts., 9.3.16; 14th F.A. Bde., 27.3.16
WILSON, Sergeant Arthur (M.M.): 11th L.H. Rgt., 29.8.15; 11th L.H. Rgt., 22.2.16
WILSON, Sergeant Aubrey Victor: 11th Rfts, N.T.O.S.; 14th F.A. Bde., 27.3.16
WILSON, Private David: Original, 8.12.14; Aust, 29.8.15; 42nd Btn., 22.5.17; wounded, 28.6.15
WILSON, Bombdr. Eric Radcliffe: 3rd Rfts., 29.7.15; 14th F.A. Bde., 27.3.16; wounded, 6.9.15
WILSON, Private Frank Ness: 1st Rfts., 16.5.15; killed in action, Gallipoli, 28.6.15
WILSON, Private James: 15th Rfts., N.T.O.S.; 4th Cml. Rgt., 2.11.16
WILSON, Private James Edward: 11th L.H. Rgt., 2.10.15; Discd., 24.5.16; wounded, 4.11.15
WILSON, Corporal John Harold Theodore: 9th Rfts., 30.6.16; Discd., 4.10.19
WILSON, Brig-Gen. Lachlan Chisholm (C.B., C.M.G., D.S.O., C. de G., French, five times Mentioned in Despatches): Original, 30.9.14; Appt. Term., 17.10.19
WILSON, Sergeant Montague: Original, 8.12.14; 47th Btn., 10.4.17
WILSON, Private Raymond Bede: 16th Rfts., N T.O.S.; Aust., 10.7.16; 3rd M.G. Coy., 11.1.17
WILSON, Private Samuel: 11th Rfts., N.T.O.S.; 4th Cml. Rgt., 2.11.16
WILSON, Private William Clark: Original, 8.12.14; killed in action, Gallipoli, 28.6.15
WILSON, Driver William Joseph: 16th Rfts., N.T.O S.; 4th D.A.C., 5.8.16
WILSON, Private Walter Richmond (M.M., Mentioned in Despatches): 11th L.H. Rgt., 29.8.15; 11th L.H. Rgt., 20.3.16
WINCH, Gunner John: 16th Rfts., N.T.O.S.; 1st F.A. Bde., 26.9.17
WINTEN, Private Roy John Rowland: 11th L.H. Rgt , 12.10.16; Discd., 15.10.19
WINTERFORD, Private William Henry: 12th Rfts., 12.1.16; Discd., 30.10.19
WINTERS, Private James: 30th Rfts., N.T.O S.; 11th L.H. Rgt., 29.5.18
WINTERS, Sergeant William: Original. 8.12.14; Discd., 12.4.19; wounded, 16.11.15
WISE, Driver John Oswald: 9th Rfts., N.T.O.S.; 14th F.A. Bde , 27.3.16
WISKENS, Private George: 23rd Rfts., 27.11.17; Discd., 4.9.19
WITHERS, Private John Daniel: G.S. Rfts., 9 10.18; Discd., 20.8.19
WOOD, Private Alfred John: Original, 8.12.14; Discd , 24.5.17; wounded, 27.6.15
WOOD, Sergeant Charles: 5th Rfts., 25.9.15; Anz. Pol. Cps., 3.4.16
WOOD, Lieut. Cyril Norman: Original, 8.12.14; Appt. Term., 25.10.16; wounded, 9.8.16
WOOD, Private John Malcolm: 11th Rfts., N.T.O.S.; 13th F.A. Bde., 27.3.16
WOOD, Driver William: 16th Rfts., N.T.O.S.; 4th D.A.C., 10.9.16; died of wounds, France, 28.11.16

HISTORY OF THE 5th LIGHT HORSE REGIMENT. 231

WOODALL, Private Jack Leslie: 7th Rfts., 14.11.15; 13th F.A. Bde., 27.3.16
WOODBINE, S.S.M. Norman: 11th L.H. Rgt., 29.8.15; 11th L.H. Rgt., 22.2.16
WOODFORD, Private Harry: 11th Rfts., 29.8.15; Discd., 13.6.16
WOODGATE, Private Archibald: 26th Rfts., N.T.O.S.; A.A.S.C., 13.8.17
WOODHEAD, Private Benjamin: 19th Rfts., 12.10.16; Discd., 18.5.19
WOODROW, Private George Laurie: 13th Rfts., 19.2.16; 13th Bde. H.Q., 17.3.16
WOODS, Driver James Joseph: 11th L.H. Rgt., 29.8.15; 11th L.H. Rgt., 22.2.16; wounded, 5.11.15
WOODS, T/Dvr. John Martin: 24th Rfts., N.T.O.S.; 2nd M.G. Sqdn., 10.7.17
WOODS, Private Thomas John: 11th L.H. Rgt., 2.10.15; 11th L.H. Rgt., 22.2.16
WOOLFE, Private Harold Hilton: 1st Rfts., N.T.O.S.; Discd., 23.8.15
WOOLLEN, Private Robert: 25th Rfts., 15.4.18; Discd., 12.9.19
WOOLLEY, Private Henry: 12th Rfts., 7.1.16; 14th F.A. Bde., 27.3.16; died of wounds, France, 25.4.18
WRIGHT, T/Wh./Sgt. Albert Edward: 23rd Rfts., N.T.O.S.; Aust. Mtd. Div. Trn., 13.8.17
WRIGHT, Gunner Edward William: 1st Rfts., 16.5.15; 13th F.A. Bde., 27.3.16
WRIGHT, Private Harold: 2nd Rfts., 29.7.15; wounded, 5.9.15; prisoner of war, 17.9.18; died of wounds (prisoner of war), Palestine, 3.10.18
WRIGHT, Sergeant Harry: 12th Rfts., 7.1.16; Discd., 27.9.19
WRIGHT, Private Lionel Albert: Original, 8.12.14; Discd., 2.8.16
WRIGHT, Driver Neville Thomas: 28th Rfts., N.T.O.S.; A. Mtd. Div. Trn., 28.7.17
WRIGHT, Sapper Thomas Shields: 3rd Rfts., 29.7.15; 1st F.S. Engrs., 29.6.16; wounded, 25.8.15
WRIGHT, Major William Leckey Ferguson: Original, 28.9.14; Appt. Term., 19.9.17; wounded, 31.8.15, and 5.8.16
WUTH, Sergeant Ernest Magnus: 20th Rfts., N.T.O.S.; 2nd M.G. Sqdn., 6.10.16
WYATT, Private William Harold Leslie: 24th Rfts., 10.8.18; Discd., 4.9.19
WYLDES, T/Cpl. Cyril Robert: Original, 8.12.14; Discd., 15.4.19; wounded, 2.7.15, and 5.9.15
WYLIE, Driver William Carey: 6th Rfts., 25.9.15; 13th F.A. Bde., 27.3.16; wounded, 5.11.15; died (pneumonia), Weymouth, 2.2.19
YALDWYN, 2/Lieut. Hamilton St. Clair: 11th Rfts., N.T.O.S.; Appt. Term., 14.5.16; died after term. of appt., 17.7.16
YATES, Private Albert John: Original, 8.12.14; died (pneumonia) at sea, 16.1.15
YESBERG, Private Peter: 14th Rfts., 9.3.16; 13/F.A.B., 27.3.16
YOUNG, Private Charles Henry: 30th Rfts., N.T.O.S.; 2nd L.H.R., 26.7.18
YOUNG, Private George: 12th Rfts., 23.2.16; died (malaria, M.T. gas, gangrene and exhaustion), Gaza, Palestine, 18.10.18
YOUNG, Driver George: 13th Rfts., 19.2.16; 13/F.A.B., 27.3.16
YOUNG, Private George: 19th Rfts., 25.8.16; 2/M.G. Sqdn., 29.10.18
YOUNG, Private Henry Leslie: 23rd Rfts., 18.11.17; Discd., 12.3.19
YOUNG, Private Raymond: 29th Rfts., 23.5.18; Discd., 4.9.19
YOUNG, Lieut. Rupert George: Original, 8.12.14; 13/L.H.R., 24.8.17
YOUNG, Private Walter Alexander: Original, 8.12.14; killed in action, Anzac, 28.6.15
YOUNG, Sergeant William John: 29th Rfts., 9.10.18; Discd., 4.9.19

YOUNG, Corporal William James Gregor: Original, 8.12.14; 2nd Bn., 7.1.17
YOUNGMAN, Gunner Joseph Douglas: 11th L.H.R., 29.8.15; 3/F.A.B., 8.1.16
ZIESEMER, T/Cpl. Charles: 7th Rfts., 10.1.16; Discd., 23.6.19
ZILLMAN, Private Maurice Lang Wilson: 10th Rfts., 23.2.16; Discd., 30.10.19
ZOLLNER, Driver William Clement: 14th Rfts., 9.3.16; 13/F.A.B., 27.3.16

MAPS

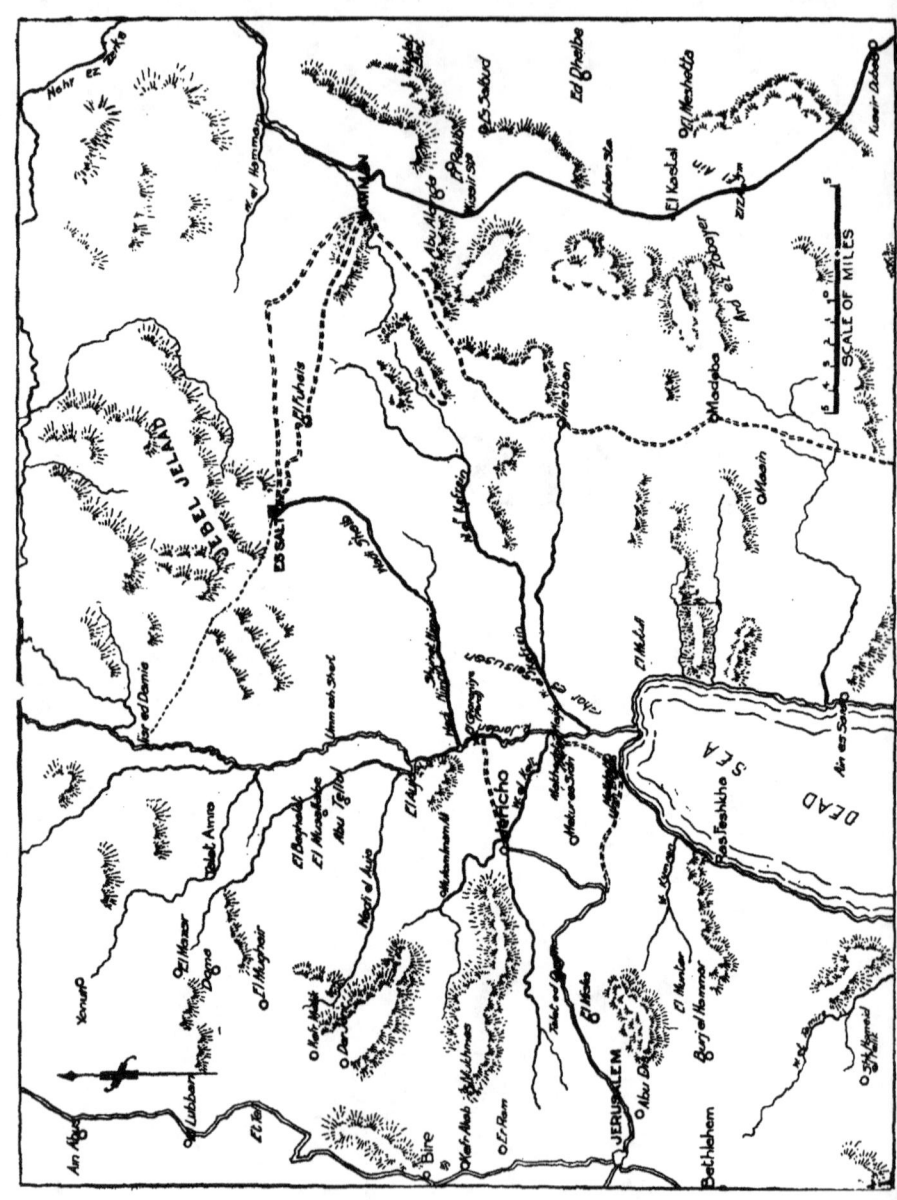

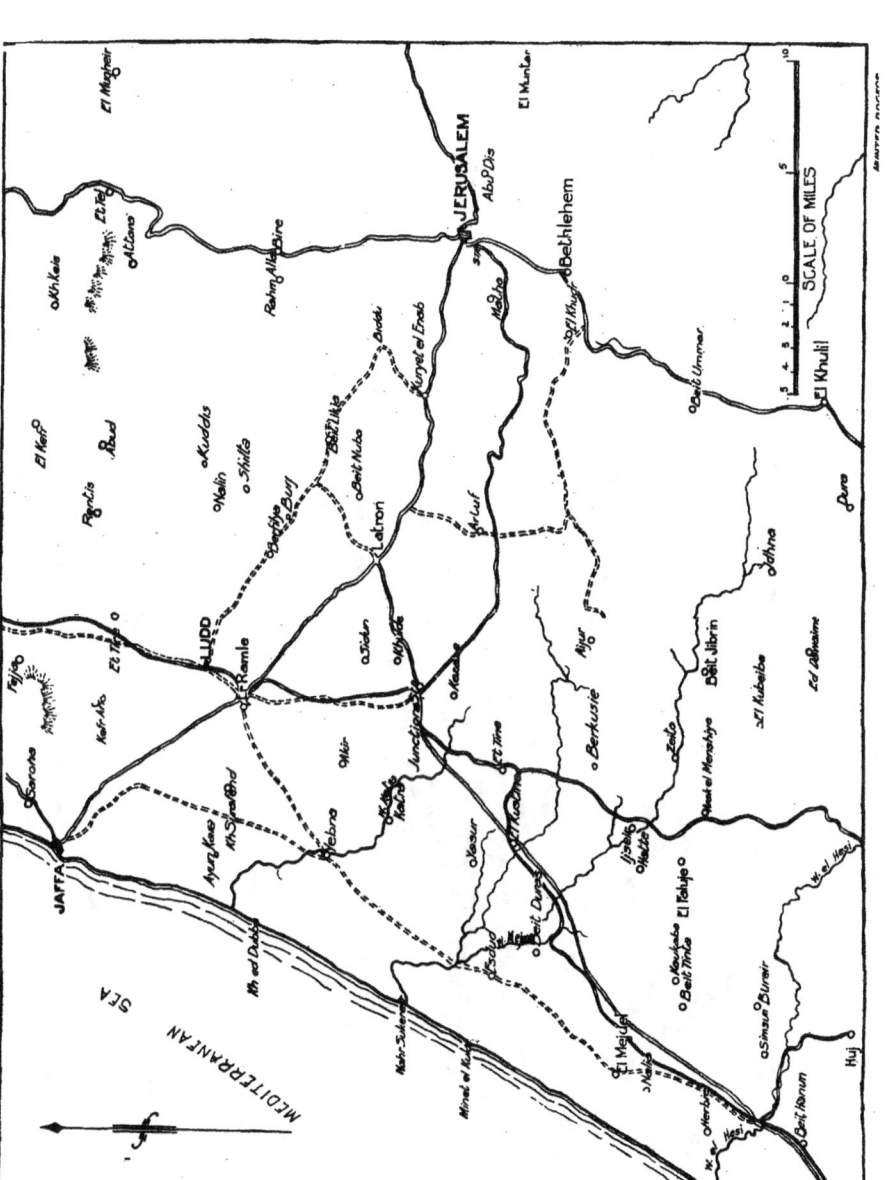

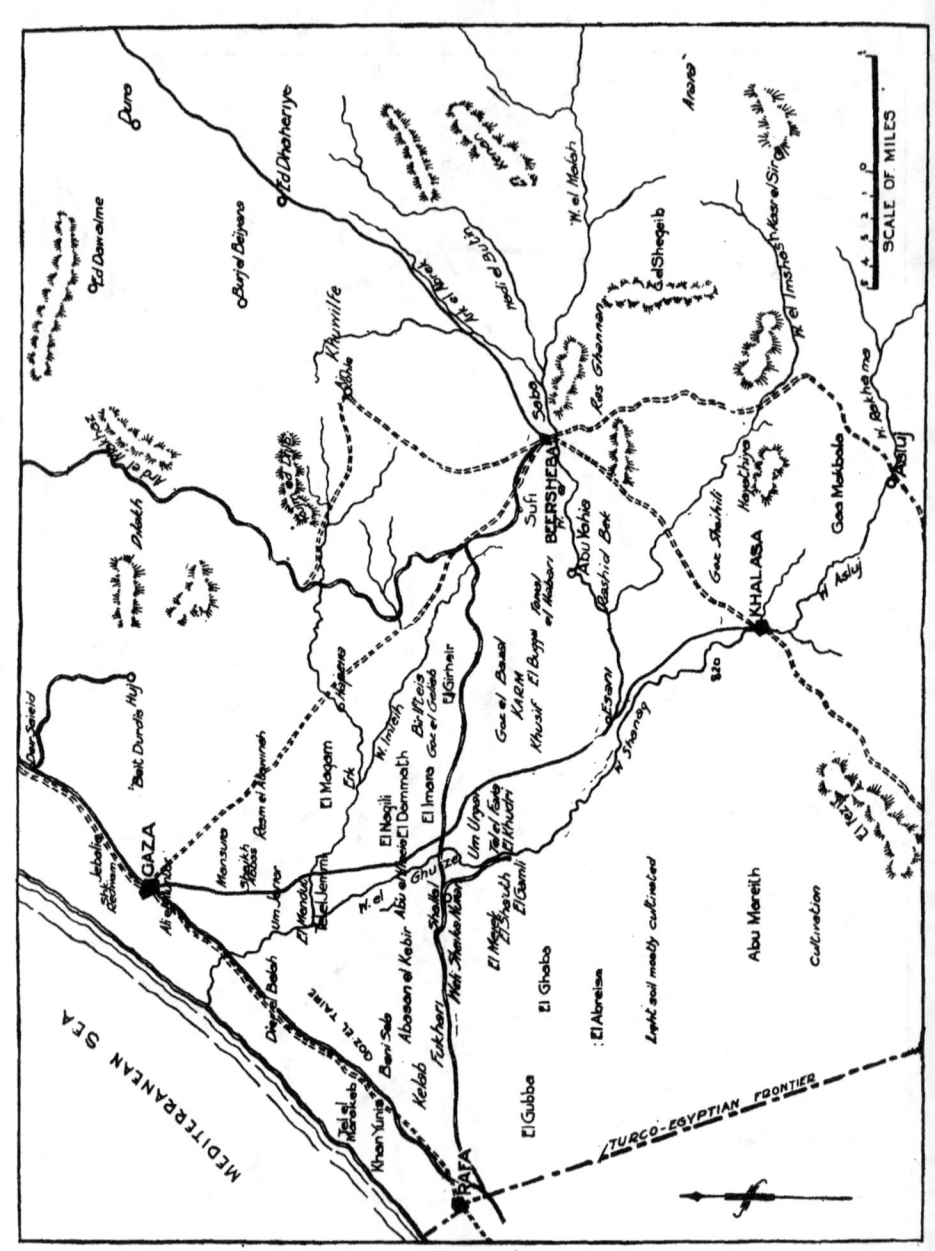

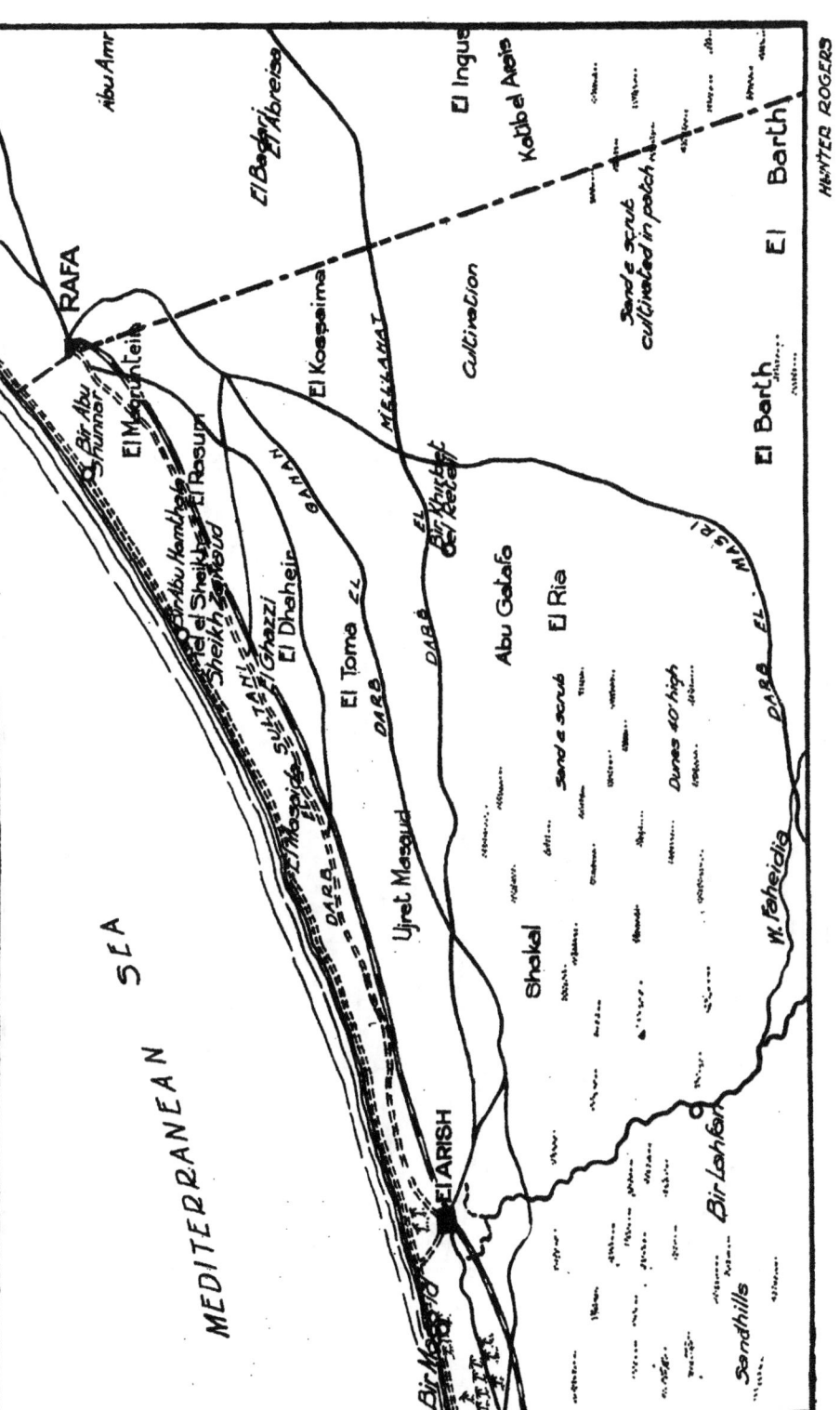

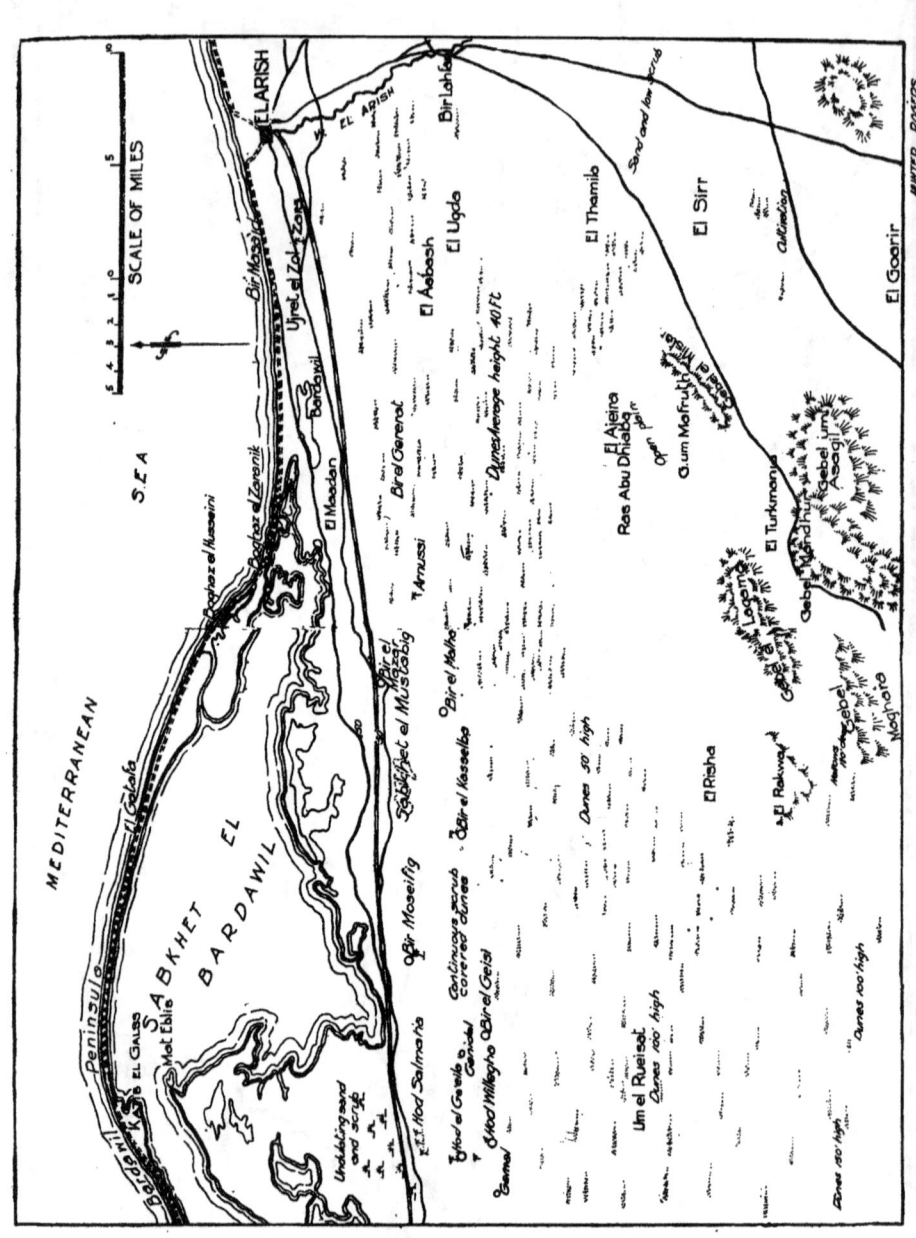

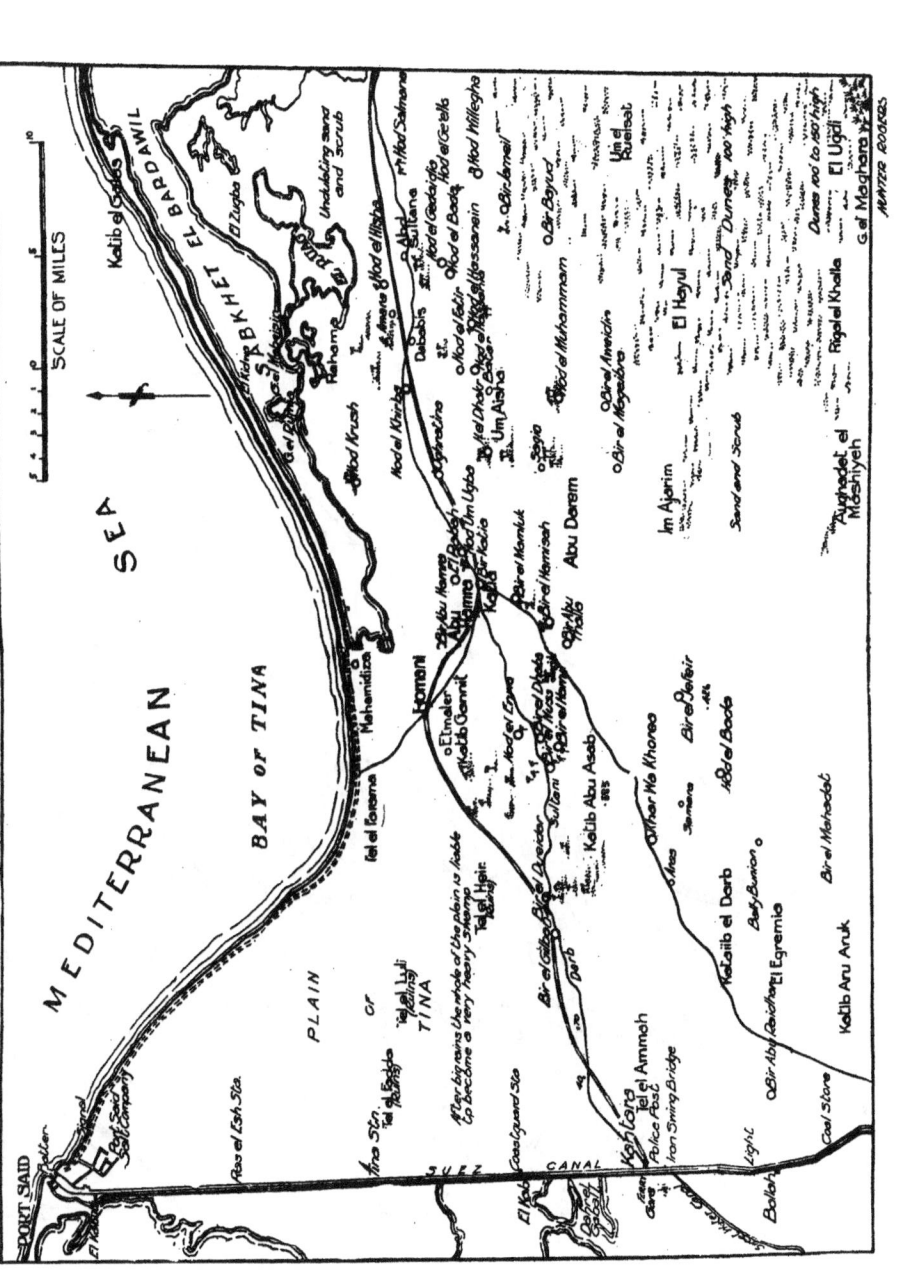

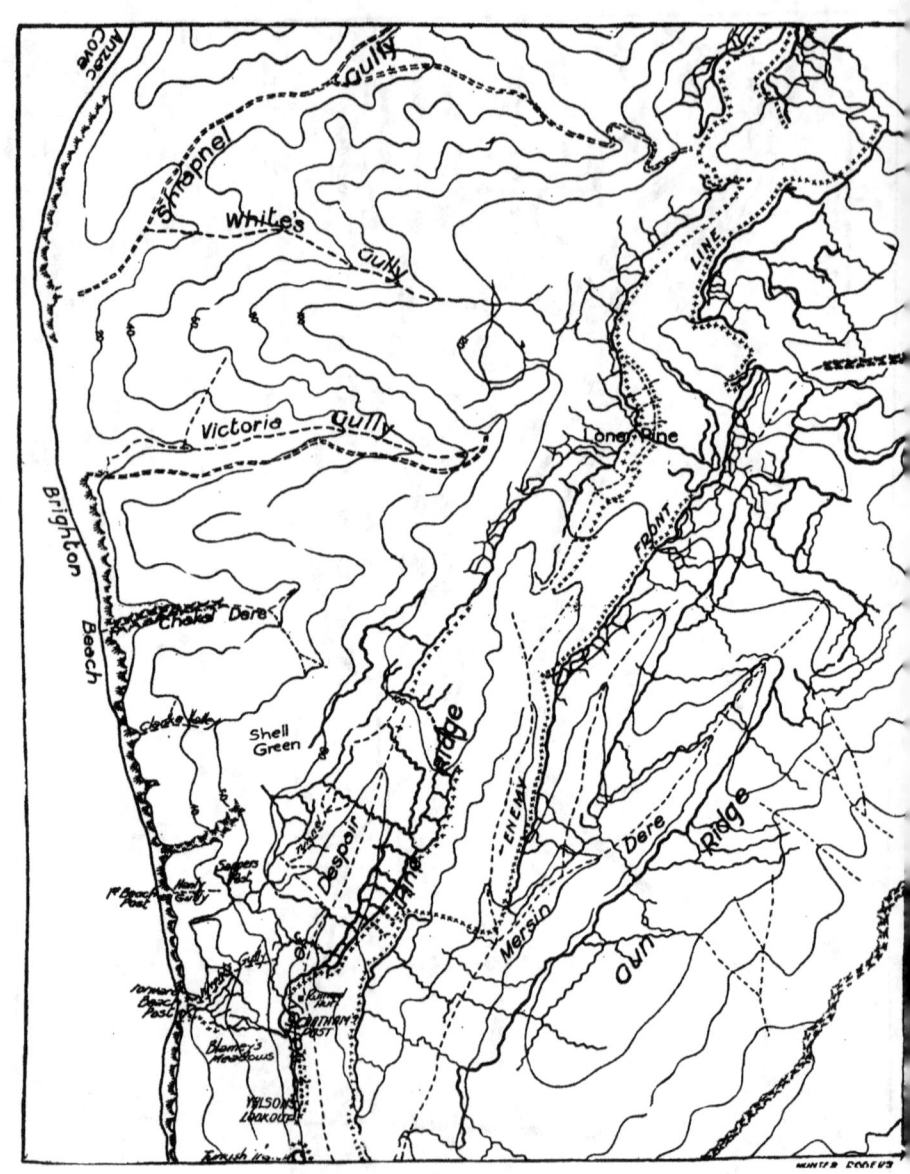

www.ingramcontent.com/pod-product-compliance
Lightning Source LLC
Chambersburg PA
CBHW052049220426
43663CB00012B/2497